EDUCATIONAL ADMINISTRATION:
The Secondary School

EDUCATIONAL ADMINISTRATION:

The Secondary School

SECOND EDITION

JOHN E. CORBALLY, JR.

Professor of Education and Vice President for Administration
The Ohio State University

T. J. JENSON

Professor of Education and Chairman of the Department
of Education
The Ohio State University

W. FREDERICK STAUB

Professor of Education
The Ohio State University

ALLYN AND BACON, INC.
Boston, 1965

FOREWORD

IN THE FOREWORD TO THE FIRST EDITION OF THIS
text, the authors expressed their conviction that if a book is to deal
effectively with any part of the profession of educational administration,
it must be developed around concepts rather than around the "how-
to-do-it" approach. The four years since the first foreword was written
have served to emphasize that basic point. Educational leadership during this period has been called upon to deal with problems that could
not have been well described a few brief years ago, much less subjected
to stereotyped or to standardized solutions.

This edition represents more than an updating of the material
found in the first edition. The text has been reorganized to reflect more
clearly than was true earlier the emphasis upon an approach to leadership through a consideration of the job, the tasks, the person, and the
profession. While the authors still must focus upon an audience composed largely of novices in administration—and, to some extent, in education also—attention has been given to providing information and,
hopefully, insights that are of value to the more experienced practitioners.

Some users of the first edition have not found the case studies
or incidents that introduce the book to be as helpful as have the majority of users. Perhaps it is worthwhile to suggest that the incidents
will be of particular value if they are used not only to introduce the
reader to the text, but also to provide material for discussion as the
reader proceeds through subsequent chapters. The incidents themselves
do not provide answers; rather, they present, within a framework of
reality, an overview of the kinds of decisions which administrators are
called upon to make.

While the authors are as usual fully prepared to accept whatever
credit or blame results from the content of this revised edition, it is
only fair to mention that credit for improvements should belong to the
many students, professors, and educational administrators who have
been kind enough to provide constructive criticism of the original text.

v

While it is perhaps trite to say so, this edition does result from extensive field testing of the first edition. This testing has resulted in many changes. The aim, however, to stress the role of and the need for high-quality leadership in secondary education remains the basic reason for this volume.

J. E. C., Jr.
T. J. J.
W. F. S.

CONTENTS

PART ONE—THE JOB

PART TWO—THE TASKS

PART THREE—THE PERSON

PART FOUR—
THE PROFESSION

I
THE JOB

PART ONE PRESENTS, IN BROAD FOCUS, THE JOB OF SEC-
ondary school administration. Chapter 1 relates incidents illustrative of
happenings in today's secondary schools. Chapter 2 discusses the historical background and growth of secondary education. Chapter 3 gives the
theme of leadership to which the authors subscribe. Its leadership concepts, in a very real sense, provide the central girding for the entire book.
Chapter 4 presents a view of the job of administration in terms of the
teamwork concept of leadership.

1

INCIDENTS IN SECONDARY SCHOOL ADMINISTRATION

WHOEVER FINDS HIMSELF AT THE POINT OF IMPACT rarely can spend time in leisurely problem-confrontation. The press of circumstances demands decisions made in the best possible organizational environment. Today's secondary schools are at this point of impact, and they will likely remain there for years to come. Burgeoning enrollments and consolidations are accounting for their increased size. The demands of a rapidly-paced society have added heretofore unknown complexity to their functions. Those who anticipate a career in secondary school administration can find few prototypes from their past experience to use as reliable guidelines, for we believe that tomorrow's junior and senior high schools will be vastly different from yesterday's. Living as we do in such a volatile world, it is difficult to predict with accuracy what they will be like. We are convinced, however, that tomorrow's principal will function increasingly as today's superintendent

3

operates. Thousands of details will continue to play against the back-drop of his largely teen-age environment, but less and less can he afford to get as personally involved in the solution of problems created by them as he did in the past. He will need to move, with keen insight, from de-tail to those broad policy areas which the specific illustrates. Increasing autonomy of operation will accompany an interlacing interdependence with elementary schools, as well as colleges, universities, and other post-secondary educational enterprises. At the same time the secondary schools will strengthen existing links and forge new ones with other facets of society-at-large.

We have written this book to help you think through the feasibility of a career in secondary school administration. Presented are the major task areas, in which most of the problems arise, and some of the ap-proaches which might be useful for the administrator as he responds to the unique challenge which each of the problems presents. If you basically like people, particularly teen-aged youngsters, and those who choose to teach them, and if you enjoy the stimulation of those prob-lems which crop out in the secondary school milieu, read on, for you have passed the first test of the would-be administrator.

We open the door to secondary school administration by presenting some slice-of-life incidents. They are open-ended because each reader is invited to provide his own solution to the problems they illustrate. No attempt is made, through these incidents, to depict "good" or "bad" administrative practices. Rather, we submit that the problems provide a glimpse of reality, and that their brief analysis by the reader can be a fruitful and stimulating leaping-off place for a more intensive analysis of secondary school administration.

SOME INCIDENTS

The follow-up study

Bob Franklin picked up his coffee cup and stared thoughtfully at the row of figures before him. For several nights now he had gone to the desk shortly after dinner. There, with some excitement, he had opened the day's mail and accumulated a mounting stack of returned questionnaires. Near the middle of his master's program in educational administration, he had chosen to make a follow-up study of graduates, during the past five years, of Reynold's Grove High School, where he was serving his third year as principal. A major section of the questionnaire had been constructed to give the respondents a chance to react to the curriculum they had followed in the light of the perspective they had gained since graduation. From the replies, Bob Franklin hoped to amass data that would give direction to further curriculum development.

Reynold's Grove, with a population of 900, was the largest of several villages that dotted the countryside beyond the rim of Graham, an industrial city of 45,000. Formerly populated predominantly by shop-keepers, retired farmers, and employees of the village's two small industries, the creamery and the foundry, Reynold's Grove suddenly began to grow. The road that threaded through the hills to Graham, nine miles away, afforded choice building sites, and houses began to sprout in profusion. Occupying them, in the main, were supervisory and middle-management personnel from the industries of Graham. Although outside the corporation limits of the village, the homes were in the Reynold's Grove School District, and each year several new pupils came from them to either the elementary or high school.

In the village itself, more and more of the city's industrial workers appeared, attracted by the availability of older but well-built houses in the lower price brackets. Two years ago, shortly after Bob Franklin had been employed as principal, the board of education requested approval of a bond issue for the building of a new high school. When the voters approved the request, Virgil Kennedy, the district's superintendent, asked Bob to begin an assessment of the current program in order to recommend changes for the program of the new school.

In breaking down his information for purposes of analysis, he had divided the respondents into college and noncollege groups. The table he was developing tonight dealt with reactions of the college respondents to the English program of the high school. He had concluded that section of the questionnaire with an open-ended item, "What suggestions do you have for the improvement of the English program?" The reactions were telling a consistent story: more work in theme writing, a better grounding in grammar, crack-down on the spelling requirements.

As he lit his pipe, Bob thought, "These will be easy enough to work into the thesis, but doing something about them will be another matter." Ethel Patton, wife of the editor of Reynold's Grove's weekly newspaper and English teacher at the high school for the past fifteen years, was the source of the ruffled thought. A long-time resident of the village, she was typical of about half of the teachers on the staff. Working primarily to bring in a comfortable second income and to combat boredom, this group did not get excited very easily about the professional problems of education. Instead, their own families, social affairs of the village, and the latest conversation piece around the school gave them more concern. Teaching in Reynold's Grove was convenient, and no serious thought was directed to the possibility of moving elsewhere. The other half of the staff was composed primarily of young teachers in their first year or two of professional experience. After gaining experience, this group usually moved out, attracted by systems with better salary schedules. Because of this mobility factor, Bob found that a major share of his time during the past two years had been spent with this inexperienced group. As a consequence of these conditions, curriculum development proceeded rather slowly.

If the recommended changes in the English program were to be effected, something would have to be done concerning Ethel Patton. Fond of literature and dramatics, she poured most of her energy into the junior and senior class plays. That grammar concerned her slightly was attested to by the malapropisms and other inaccuracies which dotted her own speech. She carried them off, however, as if they had been made respectable by long-time membership in the family. Consistently, her pupils ranked lower in grammar and spelling sections of achievement tests than they did in other sections of the examination.

"One solution to the problem would be to assign her to ninth and tenth grade English when we move into the new building next year," thought Bob, although he knew she would balk at the idea because she preferred working with the older students. Another deterring factor was that she and her husband often visited socially with Virgil Kennedy, the superintendent, and his wife. Bob Franklin had no doubt but that she had paved the way for her next year's assignment on more than one of those occasions.

"Well, there's no solving that one tonight," reflected Bob, "I'd better watch my own grammar and spelling instead." With that thought, he turned back to his thesis material.

*   *   *

How much attention, in curriculum appraisal and development, should be paid to the evaluation made of it by the students? To what extent should a course be geared to the needs of college-bound pupils if they do not exist in sufficient number to justify setting up a special class for them? What recommendation should the principal make to the superintendent regarding the work of Ethel Patton? What other sources should a principal tap in making an evaluation of the curriculum?

Frank wonders which way to turn

Frank stirred uneasily at his desk, as his mind wandered away again from the theme he was trying to write. "Somehow," he thought, "it isn't quite right that I should have to make the choice." As they had already on several occasions during the morning, the incidents that led to his dilemma paraded once more through his mind.

Last May, near the end of Frank's junior year, Mr. Farley, faculty adviser to the yearbook staff, had asked him to be editor-in-chief. When Frank had accepted the responsibility, his schedule was arranged so that the last period of the day would be available for his editorial duties. Accordingly, all others of the yearbook staff who held major assignments had a similar arrangement. Under Mr. Farley's direction, a work schedule had been blocked out, the theme had been selected, and now, in the last week in February, much needed to be done to prepare for meeting the printer's deadline. Frank's work as editor stepped up in its demands.

Each year at Fairfield High School, the senior class had a tradition of writing, directing, and presenting a variety show. Revenue from this production financed most of the senior class expenses. During the summer, Frank wrote a script. In November, when scripts were submitted to Miss Carson, the faculty adviser, he was delighted to have his chosen. Miss Carson and the senior committee that worked with her on this production offered Frank the student directorship. At that time, he was somewhat uneasy about getting himself overcommitted, particularly since he knew that he was in the running for senior scholastic honors. All through school, however, he had carried a heavy schedule reasonably comfortably, and he had found the diversity to be stimulating. Before he accepted the directorship he had discussed it with Mr. Farley, who told him that he had no objection if it did not interfere with his editorial responsibilities. When Miss Carson indicated that rehearsals would be held primarily after school and in the evenings, the conflict was seemingly resolved and Frank accepted the directorship. The early work on the variety show presented no particular problem. Casting and other organizational work consumed December and January. In early February, however, the pace accelerated. It became increasingly difficult to find sufficient rehearsal time. With production scheduled for early March, each person involved began to feel the tension of the pace. Most members of the cast were free at 2:00 P.M. as the result of a staggered schedule, which permitted seniors sufficient flexibility to leave at that time for part-time jobs, to participate in athletics on their own time, or to be available for other extracurricular activities. Finally, Miss Carson announced that rehearsals, three times a week, would start at 2:00 P.M. Frank raised an objection to this arrangement, indicating that he had editorial responsibilities with the yearbook at this time. Miss Carson said that she would speak with Mr. Farley to see if some compromise plan could be worked out.

At 2:00 P.M. the next afternoon, when Frank walked into the year-book staff meeting, Mr. Farley drew him into his office.

"Frank," he had said, "Miss Carson informed me that she needs you three times a week at 2:00 P.M. You remember I told you that I didn't have any objection to your taking the directorship if it didn't interfere with your editorial work. With our deadline to meet, things are getting to a crucial stage, and if you aren't here to do your work, we'll be in a bad way. I just don't see how I can release you. See if you can work it out with Miss Carson."

That evening, at rehearsal, Frank reported to Miss Carson what Mr. Farley had said to him. She grew visibly annoyed.

"I suggested to him that I'd cut down 2:00 P.M. rehearsals to two a week, as a way of working it out, and I don't see why that isn't all right. You know that this is supposed to be a student production, Frank, and it's too late to work anyone else into your place. If you don't do it, I'll have to. If Mr. Farley won't compromise, I'm afraid you'll just have to choose between the two."

Frank stared at the incompleted theme, and he knew that he had to make the decision, for Mr. Farley had been similarly annoyed when he related to him the details of his conversation with Miss Carson during homeroom period this morning.

"Maybe you will have to choose, Frank, if there's no other way, but you know how I feel about it."

Frank wondered why Miss Carson and Mr. Farley hadn't worked something out, but he knew, too, from his experiences with both of them, that each was determined. Picking up his pencil, again, Frank decided to see the principal, Mr. Moore, at the end of the period. From previous experience, he had found it helpful to talk things over with him.

"Come in, Frank," said Mr. Moore, looking up from his desk. He knew from the troubled look on Frank's face that something was on his mind. What it was was no mystery, either, for just the period before Ralph Farley had been in his office. "Every year," he had stormed, "she puts me in this same position, and this time I'm not going to give in to her."

*   *   *

What should Mr. Moore say to Frank? Is Frank at all right when he thought that he shouldn't have to make the choice? Should Mr. Moore enter into the problem, since both teachers apparently had issued an ultimatum? Should a point system that would limit the number of activities in which students might participate be developed?

A request for a transfer

"Mr. Harper," and Linda's voice grew more intense as she continued to speak, "I want to be a nurse, and I need to get as much as possible from this biology course. I don't see how I can, though, if Mr. Chapman won't even let us ask questions about our assignments. May I please be transferred to Miss Wright's class?"

Tom Harper, principal at Ardmore High School, felt weary as he listened to Linda, and he forced a trace of a smile to disguise the feeling. Although she continued to give reasons for making the change, there was really no need for her to supply the details. Tom could have anticipated nearly everything that she was saying. It was near the end of the first six-week period of the year, and at least five other students, all as capable and sincere as Linda, had made a similar request for transfer by relating a similar story.

Mr. Chapman prepared assignment sheets, on which the daily work was designated, a week in advance. Class time was primarily for individual preparations in the biology workbook. When questions arose about the assignments, he would say with increasing irritation, "You'll find what you need to know in the reference books. They're listed at the end of each assignment." Several students also reported that Mr. Chapman spoke very little in class; and that when he did speak he was rather difficult to understand. A further complaint centered around insufficient periods devoted to laboratory work. Several assignments required instead the reproduction of drawings from one or other of the various reference books.

Although Tom Harper was in the first year of his principalship at Ardmore, he had taught there some years before. He knew that what the students were reporting about Sam Chapman and his classes was true, and he knew why. Early the past summer, Sam had suffered a slight stroke. After several weeks of convalescence, he seemed greatly improved and informed the superintendent that he would be able to begin the year on schedule. Sam was two years away from retirement, and he had taught for 32 years at Ardmore. During this span he had been active in many phases of the school's life, although in recent years he had confined himself to teaching his biology classes. When Tom was on the teaching staff at Ardmore, he got to know Sam quite well and bowled on the same team with him one night a week. From this experience, and from eating lunch with him occasionally, Tom concluded that Sam's army experience in World War I had never quite rubbed off and that he was rather inflexible about what he expected of people and when he expected them to do it.

After the initial two requests for a transfer from Sam Chapman's class, Tom Harper, first indicating to the students that Mr. Chapman had been ill during the summer and probably needed to conserve his strength during the opening weeks of school, talked with Sam about the requests.

"They'll pull that every year, Tom," Sam had said rather brusquely. "Tell them to get to work and they'll be okay."

When Tom Harper had become principal he had determined to cut student transfers to a minimum. From his teaching experience he had remembered that the office counters were lined each period for the first three days. As a teacher it had annoyed him not to be able to stabilize his class roster until these shifts had been made. Accordingly, upon becoming principal he had established the procedure that no transfers would be made during the first three days of classes, and then they would be considered individually, with the written consent of parents and all teachers involved. This seemed to reduce the quantity of requests considerably, and the staff had indicated its approval of the plan.

Still, the requests came in persistently for transfers from Sam Chapman's classes. Three parents had felt strongly enough about the matter to discuss it with Tom Harper. Each seemed to understand why transfers presented such a problem, and each, too, grew less insistent upon learning of Sam Chapman's recent illness. Tom Harper recognized, though, that unless the situation changed, these explanations would no longer suffice. From his talk with Sam about the matter, he had little to hope for on that score. The problem was further complicated because he knew that the school system did not have a policy about physical examinations. Tom had hesitated to bring the matter to the attention of the superintendent. With Sam so close to retirement, and substitute biology teachers so hard to get, Tom felt that he could predict the response he would get.

Looking up from his desk, Tom Harper said, "Well, Linda . . ."

*   *   *

Should Tom Harper make a discrete appeal to Linda, a serious and intelligent student, to help make the most of a difficult personnel problem? Should Tom lay aside his personal feeling of regard for Sam Chapman and tell him that he must loosen up his classroom procedures? Should the superintendent be informed of the situation? If Sam persisted in his same inflexible pattern, should he be permitted to continue teaching?

The class reunion

Although no ashtrays were visible on the desk of John Warner, principal of Coolidge High School, Phil Acton and Marvin Potter lit cigarettes shortly after entering his office. "We're here, John," Phil announced, "to . . ."

John Warner's facial muscles twitched with annoyance at the flip familiarity of the pair, as he recalled them as students some ten years ago. Irascible then, they had managed to stay just enough inside the school rules to graduate. Both had indulgent parents who had bought them automobiles when they were still juniors. Too much money had contributed to their irresponsibility. During the past ten years Phil and Marvin had cut a swath in the service club and young country club sets.

". . . make arrangements with you to get the thousand dollars that our class set aside ten years ago for our reunion. Marv and I have been named cochairmen, and we're planning to have a real affair."

"Just a moment, please," John Warner answered, as he moved to one of the filing cabinets, "I'll need to get the ledger." While Phil and Marvin looked around the office searchingly and finally flicked their ashes into a wastebasket, John Warner turned to the pages containing the class financial record.

"Yes, here it is," he resumed, and he placed a finger on the figure that represented the balance of the fund.

"According to the records, though, there is a total of $731.24 in the class account."

Phil and Marvin rose to their feet swiftly. With more than a trace of anger, Marvin was the first to speak.

"But the class specifically set aside a fund of one thousand dollars to be used for its tenth reunion. It should still be there."

Irritated at the implication, John Warner took a deep breath and reviewed the picture calmly. He explained that when the class had graduated there was a balance of well over one thousand dollars. Bills for expenses of the senior prom, however, were slow in being presented. He produced the vouchers showing that the last of the bills was not paid until the August following the class's graduation.

Phil and Marvin gave the records no more than a cursory glance. Reaching for their hats, they turned to leave the office.

"This is not the first time I've heard of trouble like this," Phil remarked over his shoulder, "and I intend to find out what happened to our thousand dollars." With that they left.

John Warner sat for some time at his desk, shaken by the brief but unexpected encounter. Thinking of the trouble caused by earmarked funds and of the difficulty in getting seniors and their class sponsors to follow good business procedures in the frantic days surrounding graduation exercises, he turned, with some anxiety, to all of the class records and hoped that everything would be complete.

Two days later, when John Warner answered his phone, he heard the superintendent, Mr. Harvey, say, "John, this is Jim Harvey. Two fellows, a Phil Acton and a Marvin Potter, have just been in my office. They were mad as hops about some reunion fund of a thousand dollars that their class is supposed to have left in the senior account. I know how these things go, John, so I calmed them down some, but I promised to look into the matter and get in touch with them. Could we . . ."

*   *   *

Should the high school be the custodian of earmarked funds? What are the public relations implications of a case like this? Assuming that all the records in this case are complete and accurate, what action should be taken toward Phil Acton and Marvin Potter? What accounting and auditing procedures should pertain to high school funds?

A run of bad publicity

It seemed to begin the night of that basketball game, thought Ralph McIntosh, principal of Middlebrook High School. As he sat in his office the week before school was to resume in September, his mind kept returning to some of the events of the previous semester. Each recollection brought a shudder of disquietude. "No doubt about it," he mused, "things surely piled up after that game."

Back in February, Middlebrook was scheduled to play Barton. A rivalry of many years' standing between these teams was intensified by the fact that both of them went into the game undefeated. Anticipating a sellout crowd, Ralph had worked late in his office and had eaten a packed lunch in order to be on hand early to supervise the sale of tickets. A half hour before the doors were scheduled for opening, however, a crowd of several hundred people had gathered outside the building. Banging at the doors and elbowing for position, each person seemed to be in surly competition with the others. Ralph had gazed at the sight with dismay, deciding that no matter how bad things became it was still better to open the doors at the announced time rather than let some in early in order to reduce the tension. The next hour was a nightmare. When the doors were opened the mob surged in. Ralph's enjoiner for them to take their time was lost in the onrush. When his glasses were bent and he became ruffled and shouted that the doors would be shut, those who heard him responded with cat calls. Fifteen minutes before the game was due to begin, Red Wyatt, sports editor of the newspaper, was pushed through the door, disheveled and chewing furiously at the split remnant of a cigar. Ralph caught his disdainful scowl as he was swept into the gymnasium. Surcease did not come with the sale of the last available ticket, however. The doors were shut on three or four hundred disgruntled people, many of whom Ralph recognized as steady patrons of past games. His explanation that to sell more tickets on an emergency basis would be a violation of fire regulations, and a placing of the players in jeopardy, didn't reach the angry fans. He finally gave up trying to explain and pacify. The snatches of the game that he saw did nothing to reduce the tempo, for the score always was tied or the teams separated by no more than one or two points. Most of his time was spent in going from door to door and window to window. Refusing to accept the fact that they would not be able to see the game, many fans tried to force doors open in remote sections of the building. Two windows were broken and an attempt made to gain entrance through them.

What seemed to be the final blow occurred in the last five seconds of the game, when a Barton player deftly scooped the ball away from a confidently dribbling Middlebrook guard and drove half the length of the floor to score the winning points of the game. Every jubilant action of the Barton fans served as a barb to the shocked Middlebrook crowd, which shuffled angrily out of the school.

But the worst incident of all, Ralph McIntosh was not to learn about until even later. As the two teams were showering, one of the Barton players was struck and his nose was broken. In the ensuing investigation, reports were very confusing in reference to who struck whom first. The upshot of the incident, however, was that the Barton coach was furious. A complaint was lodged the next day with the State Commissioner of Athletics, and Middlebrook was put on a year's disciplinary probation for failure to maintain sufficient control. Specifically, the ruling called attention to the fact that no policeman had been on duty at the game, and that this, among other things, constituted negligence.

In the newspaper accounts of the game and the subsequent probationary action, Red Wyatt, the sports editor, reflected the annoyance he so obviously had felt previously. For several nights afterwards he included in his column letters criticizing the school for its "obvious mismanagement of the ticket situation."

Then came a succession of annoying events throughout the remainder of the year.

In March, a boy cut his hand in a shop accident at the school. He was taken to the emergency room of the hospital and treated. The next day, a reporter called Ralph McIntosh to inquire about it. In the conversation the reporter asked why the paper had not been called earlier. Obliquely, he suggested that the school might have been trying to "cover up" another embarrassing incident. The article, although written with a straight news coverage format, appeared conspicuously on the front page.

Later that month, several parents called Ralph McIntosh to protest the contents of a "gossip column" in the latest issue of the school newspaper. With the prom less than two months away, the student columnist had written entertainingly but vividly about the maneuvers of certain seniors to "line up dates." Parents of the girls named in the column saw the vividness but not the entertainment.

In the middle of May, when senior awards were announced, Joe Hunt received considerable publicity as the class salutatorian. Joe had majored in the vocational curriculum and had had an excellent record in school citizenship. Several disappointed parents, however, failed to take this news in a sanguine light. "Why," they had asked Ralph McIntosh, "are grades in vocational and commercial subjects counted the same as those in the tougher college preparatory courses?" They seemed less than satisfied with his explanation.

After a string of beautiful days in June, it unexpectedly rained on the afternoon of commencement. Traditionally Middlebrook had its commencement exercises out-of-doors in the stadium, where there was ample room for all who wished to attend. Although plans always were developed for the possibility of indoor exercises, practice for that contingency lagged because few believed that the optional plan ever would be needed. It was this year, though, and unfortunately the weather broke so late in the day that there was little chance to forewarn aunts, uncles, grandparents, and friends from out of town of the change. With limited space in the auditorium, only four tickets per graduate could be allocated. Not only was the commencement a lackluster ceremony by comparison, but many relatives and friends found with dismay that they had driven to Middlebrook in vain.

"What will they find next to light on?" Ralph wondered, as he turned to the plan he was developing to reduce the chances for hazing of incoming sophomores by the upperclassmen on the opening day of school.

*   *   *

Are incidents such as these indicative of serious community dissatisfaction with a school? How many of these problems were of an "act of fate" nature? Might some of them have been avoided by a planned course of action? Must a principal learn to take problems like these reasonably lightly in order to avoid becoming emotionally trapped by his position?

CHALLENGES TO ACTION

Playing with almost infinite variety around some central problem cores, incidents similar to those described occur every day in thousands of secondary schools. Each tends to arise because of the virtual impossibility of complete predictability where people and other factors are concerned. Each in a sense represents a conflict, or at least a problem, situation. No "best laid" organizational plan that will keep situations similar to these from arising has been devised. Assuredly, a school without problems would exist only hypothetically; and indeed, if it were possible for one to come into being, it would not be desirable.

This is no attempt to rationalize our inability to do away with problems by setting up the position that it would be an undesirable goal to achieve. To keep certain types of problems from existing by careful planning is obviously necessary; to encourage the development of others, such as the type of problem a youngster has in preparing for a career choice, is just as apparent.

The point, however, is that a challenge is presented to administrators when problem situations arise, be they unexpected or anticipated. Those who feel secure only when not assailed by problems, particularly the kind brought to them by others, cannot, in all probability, perform productively as administrators. Security in a problem-solving environment, however, can be acquired by most responsible people, if they are willing to accumulate the skills that make this possible.

To return to a thought expressed earlier in this chapter, one of the first steps is to develop further a genuine respect for people and a favorable attitude toward working with them, particularly as they struggle to find ways of coping with their environment. Basically, this is an assessment that must be made by each person, as he reacts introspectively to what happens to him when he works with others. There are those who ostensibly relate productively and harmoniously with others but lack any genuine personal satisfaction in the process. Indeed, it is possible to perform with apparent success in this area, experiencing at the same time discomfort with or antipathy toward people.

An additional necessary step is a building up of the skills that enable the administrator to gain control over problems in order to avoid being controlled by them. By this process, he can exercise a great deal of choice about the battleground on which he will meet the problem. As this skill becomes finely honed, he finds that he is ambushed less and less frequently. This skill-building process is a many-faceted thing, however—one that must be adapted, refined, and developed throughout an entire administrative career. There is no perfect correlation, no magic touchstone, that leads to an "if this—then this" type of control. The most important thing is the ability to recognize the types of problems that are most crucial. Control over these keeps serious trouble from arising and results in an atmosphere that permits the learning of more subtle aspects of the problem-solving process.

The incidents presented above were designed to illustrate problems that might confront secondary school administrators in some of their major task areas—instruction, pupil and staff personnel, business management, and school-community relations. No attempt was made to construct them in comprehensive fashion. Much, purposely, was left to the imagination of the reader. They all, however, have this common component: each involves both people and problems in interaction. The problems woven into them were those that might have been anticipated and those that were unexpected. The most fruitful analysis of these incidents arises when the reader makes an effort to put himself into the complex of the problems. In this way a "feel" for the situation results, and a warp and woof kind of analysis permits a situational investigation of the problems. Approaching the incidents with a detached air of objectivity might easily lead to the type of tactical error that often results when hindsight is employed. Identifying, thus, with various people in the problem situations quickly makes it obvious that solutions are rarely pat, at least the type of solution brought to the problem by only one of the persons involved directly or indirectly with it. There is a variability in perspective of the problem, in value patterns, in the number of components to be considered as evidence before solutions are determined, which shows, in bold relief, that problem-solving is rarely an easy process to be exercised unilaterally by the administrator. It is, rather, a process at which he is almost constantly working with others to effect solutions that are compatible, workable, and appropriate to the problem at hand.

CONCLUSION

For those interested in equipping themselves with the necessary skills, leavened with the right kind of temperament, administration is an exciting and rewarding business. Ever since society delegated to the schools a large measure of responsibility for the education of its young people, each point in time has had its challenges. Particularly stimulating is secondary education now, with our society confronted by so many crucial issues. More and more educators must see a promising avenue for their skills and interests in the career of a secondary school administrator. No book alone can provoke such commitment. We hope, however, that it will help to make more meaningful those experiences in secondary education through which you have already lived and better equip those of you who see the challenge of a leadership career in this administrative field.

SUGGESTED ACTIVITIES

1. From your experiences in the secondary schools, present an incident involving an administrative problem. Analyze the action taken and identify the key factors in the problem. If you believe that a different solution would have been more appropriate, present your proposed action and analyze the relative merits of the two approaches.

2. Select one of the incidents reported in this chapter and answer the following questions:
   a. What was the central problem confronting the administrator?
   b. Were sufficient facts presented to permit a solution of the problem? If not, what additional data are needed?
   c. What steps should the administrator take to effect a solution? Why do you advocate this action?

3. Read one of the cases in Sargent and Belisle, Anderson and Davies, or Campbell, Corbally, and Ramseyer (see Selected Readings). How does this case differ from those you have read in this chapter? What are the components of the case approach that you are finding most beneficial in your analysis of administrative problems?

4. Jot down your proposed solution to the basic problems which you see in each of the incidents. After reading the book, return to the incidents and repeat the process. Compare your two sets of responses.

SELECTED READINGS

Anderson, Vivienne, and Daniel R. Davies, *Patterns of Educational Leadership*. Englewood Cliffs, N.J.: Prentice-Hall, Inc., 1956. (Chapters I–VIII).

Campbell, Roald F., John E. Corbally, Jr., and John A. Ramseyer, *Introduction to Educational Administration*, 2nd ed. Boston: Allyn and Bacon, Inc., 1962. Chapter 1.

Culbertson, Jack A., Jacobson, Paul B., and Reller, Theodore L., *Administrative Relationships: A Casebook*. Englewood Cliffs, N.J.: Prentice-Hall, Inc., 1960. Chapter 1.

Sargent, Cyril G., and Eugene L. Belisle, *Educational Administration: Cases and Concepts*. Boston: Houghton Mifflin Company, 1955.

2

SECONDARY EDUCATION: ITS GROWTH AND PURPOSES

IF ONE IS TO ADMINISTER A SECONDARY SCHOOL, IT IS important that he gain understanding of the ways in which secondary education has come to be what it is today. The present-day high school or junior high school did not spring full grown from the ground. As one faces today's tasks, it is important to realize that secondary education has a long history and that this history has deep meaning for today.

In this chapter, three major aspects of the historical background of secondary education will be considered. First, a brief review of the history of secondary education will be presented; second, a statistical review of the quantitative growth of secondary education will be provided; and finally, the evolving purposes of secondary education will be reviewed. The chapter will conclude with a discussion of the ways in which these background facts and factors are related to the current scene in secondary education.

HISTORICAL DEVELOPMENT

Probably no secondary school teacher or administrator has proceeded through his undergraduate teacher education program without hearing and reading about the Latin grammar school, the academy, or the Kalamazoo case. We shall discuss these and other historical elements briefly here, pointing out those developments that seem particularly pertinent for consideration by a secondary school administrator.

The Latin grammar school

The Latin grammar school was transplanted from England to the colonies with very little change in either function or format. The first such school in America was the Boston Latin Grammar School, established in 1635. Although known as secondary schools, most colonial Latin grammar schools were parallel to existing elementary (common or dame) schools rather than upward extensions of such schools. Actually, attendance at the Latin grammar school instead of at the common school was more an indication of a student's social and economic position than of his educational attainments. Brubacher reports that a number of boys (girls were not eligible for attendance) entered the Latin school at the age of seven or eight and that it was not unusual for beginning reading to be included in the curriculum offering of these schools.[1]

The curriculum of the Latin grammar school was designed to prepare boys for college and for eventual service in church or state. Study of the classics comprised the great bulk of the curriculum. Although these schools were theoretically free, the narrowness of the curriculum and its obvious inappropriateness except for those few destined for college made the school less than popular with the great majority of the population. For example, Massachusetts towns of a certain size were required by law to maintain Latin grammar schools and many preferred to pay the fine levied for failure to establish such schools rather than to maintain them.

Requirements for graduation from the Latin school were nebulous. For the most part, a boy attended this school until he reached the age and attained the necessary proficiency in the classics to enter the college of his choice. In this sense, then, these schools were college preparatory schools with the curriculum dominated by the entrance requirements of either colonial or English colleges and universities.

[1] John S. Brubacher, A *History of the Problems of Education* (New York: McGraw-Hill, Inc., 1947), pp. 428–429.

While historically significant as the first institution for secondary education in America, the Latin grammar school did not ever prosper greatly in this country. In the New England colonies it experienced some success, but even there the success was not widespread. In the Southern colonies, the wealthier families usually sent their sons back to England for all of their formal education. It seems fair to say that this period in our history was virtually devoid of general opportunities for education beyond the common school.

The academy

By the end of the first half of the eighteenth century, social and political conditions led to increasing demands for either a changed Latin grammar school or a new institution to meet those needs that the Latin school could not meet. Because of unwillingness or of inability, or perhaps a combination of the two, the Latin grammar school did not make any major changes to satisfy new demands. Consequently, between the years 1750 and 1800 a strong new institution known as the academy gained strength rapidly.

The first and probably the best known of the early academies was that founded by Benjamin Franklin in Philadelphia in 1751. It was Franklin's hope that the classics could be abandoned in favor of English grammar and literature. He also added such subjects as accounting, astronomy, geography, history, and natural science, although he was unable to persuade his backers to make the school as "practical" as he had hoped.

The Andover Academy in Massachusetts was the primary model for academies in America.[2] This school included a wide variety of "practical" subjects in addition to Greek and Latin grammar. It is worth while to note that the academy recognized the value of certain terminal programs as well as the usual college-preparatory curriculum. Commercial and scientific fields of endeavor were assuming importance, and these fields did not necessarily require college graduation for entrance into their practice.

Another step taken during this period was the organization of academies for girls. This early development of secondary education for girls represented a growing recognition of the need for something more than elementary reading and writing instruction for the women of America.

In certain respects, the academies had the same defects as the Latin grammar schools. They generally paralleled common schools. They were,

[2] *Ibid.*, pp. 430–433.

for the most part, private tuition schools and as such served only a small and select group of students. In spite of the broader curriculum, the academies did not serve the broad needs of a wide segment of the population.

On the positive side, the academies did greatly broaden the curriculum that was considered appropriate for secondary education. Perhaps the most important fact about the academies is the large number of them established in this country. Popular sentiment for secondary education in America was reflected by the fact that the academy experienced such rapid growth during the late 1700's and the early 1800's. Although estimates vary, it would appear that there were well over 6,000 such institutions in the United States around the middle of the nineteenth century.

The high school

Two conflicting ideas present in the academy movement led to the establishment of the high school. The first idea was that secondary education should be available to all American children. This idea was reflected in the rapid growth and broadened curriculum of the academy, and in the establishment of academies for girls. Against this was the idea that secondary education was a privilege for which the students should pay—an idea reflected in the lack of free academies except in a few areas, notably New York. Also in opposition to the first concept was the carry-over to the academies of a great deal of classical curriculum material from the Latin schools. This somewhat less than utilitarian subject matter stood in opposition to the growing demands for a curriculum that would serve certain practical and terminal ends. A final important consideration was the need for a school that would follow rather than compete with the elementary or common school.

Because of factors such as these the free public high school was developed. Although Connecticut had enabling legislation for the creation of such schools as early as 1798, the first free public high school was opened in Boston in 1821. Known first as the Boston English Classical School, this school became the Boston English High School in 1824. In 1826, a similar school was organized for girls.

The important characteristics of these schools, which were the direct forerunners of today's high school, were that they were upward extensions of the elementary school (graduation from the common school was usually a prerequisite to admission to the high school), they stressed the "practical" fields and de-emphasized the classical curriculum, they provided terminal education as well as college preparatory work, and they were open to all children at public expense. The high school was an immediate success, although it was not until well after the early years of the high school that the academy rapidly declined in importance. It seems safe to say that the high school for all children grew because of the recognized strength of the academy for a few children rather than because of any inherent weaknesses of the academy. As the high school continued to grow, academies either were replaced, became colleges or normal schools, or continued as strong, private, college-preparatory institutions.

In 1827, Massachusetts passed legislation requiring all communities of certain size to maintain a public high school supported by taxation. It was not, however, until the famous Kalamazoo Case of 1874 that the legality of public tax support for secondary education was finally settled. The complainants in this case claimed that education beyond the common school was an unnecessary luxury and that those who desired such education should pay for it. Judge Cooley, in the decision of the Supreme Court of Michigan which he authored, traced the history of public education in Michigan and reported the unanimous opinion of the court that both educational history and educational law in Michigan supported the right of a school board to offer secondary education at public expense.[3] This decision became a precedent for similar cases in many other states. Cubberly cites it as a major victory in what he has called "the battles for free public schools."[4]

Following the decision in Kalamazoo, the growth of the public high school was phenomenal. The social, political, and economic conditions that first gave rise to the high school continued to support its increase. Continued industrialization, the expanding frontier, the rise of state universities with the impetus of the Morrill Act, and increased national wealth all contributed to the growth of the public high school.

Strangely enough, many of the vexing problems that face secondary school educators today faced the early high school. Terminal curriculum tracks as opposed to college preparatory tracks were discussed and debated. The place of the classics in the public school was as "hot" a subject in 1900 as it is now. As a matter of fact, some students of the

---

[3] *Stuart vs. School District No. 1 of Kalamazoo.* 30 Mich. 69 (1874). The decision in this case is cited in detail in Robert R. Hamilton and Paul R. Mort, *The Law and Public Education*, Revised Edition (Brooklyn: The Foundation Press, 1959), pp. 156–162.

[4] Ellwood P. Cubberly, *Public Education in the United States*, Revised Edition (Boston: Houghton Mifflin Company, 1934), pp. 263–64.

secondary school curriculum agree with Parker's contention that little else than more courses has been added to the high school since its early days.[5]

The first high schools recognized two objectives: that of preparing directly for adult life (terminal work) and that of preparing indirectly for adult life via college or university (college preparatory work). As the high school grew in enrollment, it became apparent that the students who saw this school as a terminal schooling experience had many and varied life objectives. The two-fold division became complicated as the noncollege-bound segment of the student body expressed desires for preparation to meet varying objectives. This led to two developments. The first was the establishment within a single high school of a number of courses of study. Students entered a course of study suited to their objectives, whether commercial, technical, or college-preparatory. The second was the development of separate high schools for students with specific objectives. Thus, commercial high schools and technical high schools were developed for those students not preparing for college.

Both of these developments created problems that still plague secondary education. The discussions in the 1960's of the place of the "comprehensive" high school, of the values of separate technical and vocational schools, and of the question of types of graduation diplomas or certificates that should be issued, all stem from problems that have been present since the first high school opened its doors.

The junior high school

The history of college-high school articulation is long and interesting, and careful scrutiny of it must await a discussion of purposes. However, it should be noted that college and university personnel played a greater role than did secondary school educators in the creation of the junior high school. The National Education Association's Committee of Ten (1893), the Committee of Fifteen (1895), the Committee on College Entrance Requirements (1895), and the Committee on Economy of Time in Education (1912) were all composed predominately of college presidents, deans, and professors; and all recommended the downward extension of secondary school education into the seventh and eighth grades to facilitate increased preparation for college.

In the early 1900's various communities began to experiment with the development of a senior and a junior high school division. Junior

[5] J. Cecil Parker, unpublished lecture notes (Berkeley: University of California), 1955.

high schools in Columbus, Ohio, and in Berkeley, California, claim to be the first in the nation. Many communities were content to departmentalize the seventh and eighth grades and retain the typical 8–4 organization, but even in these early years one could find 6–6, 6–2–4, 6–4–4, and 6–3–5 plans as well as the more typical 6–3–3 arrangement.

Although the idea of better, or at least more, preparation for college gave impetus to the junior high school movement, psychological and sociological bases soon gave added support. Psychological studies indicated that children of the age to be in the seventh, eighth, and ninth grades were undergoing great psychological changes that required special recognition. Problems faced by students in the transition from elementary to secondary schools also gave support to a transitional school.

Finally, expediency played an important role in the rapid growth of junior high schools during the 1920's and 1930's. School enrollments rapidly outgrew school facilities and many communities chose to build junior high schools rather than construct more expensive high schools. By eliminating the ninth grade from the senior high school, high school facilities were often made to meet enrollment growth without constructing new high schools. This process led to many junior high school programs that were little more than upper elementary school programs transferred to a separate building.

Growth of secondary school administration

The principalship in American secondary education is a position with a much longer history than is possessed by the position of superintendent of schools. In the early days of education in the United States, lay school committees performed those tasks now commonly performed by superintendents of schools. However, whenever a school had more than one teacher, a head teacher or principal teacher was almost always appointed by the school committee. The early academies had headmasters, and many schools use this term today to describe the position of the principal.

Early head teachers were generally given little released time for administrative duties. They were usually responsible for discipline in the school and would conduct school committee members and other visitors on inspection trips through the schools. As secondary schools became larger, principals became responsible for scheduling students and teachers and were required to submit various reports concerning attendance, courses of study, and the like.

By the last half of the nineteenth century, there was a growing tendency to recognize a profession of educational administration. Administrative duties became too burdensome for school committee members and the superintendency became recognized as the administrative arm of the committee. In many cases, high school principals were named as superintendents and the duties of the superintendency were added to those of the principalship. In other cases, the two positions were kept separate.

It is fair to say, then, that the high school principalship has existed in the United States from the time that there were high schools with more than one teacher. The concept of educational administration as a profession, however, is of more recent origin.

ENROLLMENT TRENDS

In tracing the history of the secondary school, it is important to describe certain quantitative facts about secondary education. These quantitative facts have certain qualitative implications. In considering enrollment data—or any figures relating to public education in the United States—it is well to remember that even the best sources often give little better than highly informed estimates. The transmission of figures from the teacher to the principal to the superintendent to the state department of education and, finally, to some national agency such as the United States Office of Education is a process not conducive to complete accuracy in the final report. Another problem is that of definition. What, for example, is a high school student? Is he anyone in grades 9 through 12 or is he anyone in grades 7 through 12? If a school district uses the 6-4-4 plan, how are students in grades 13 and 14 classified? Often different states will answer these questions differently, which leads again to certain distortions in national reports.[6]

In the discussions to follow, efforts are made to indicate the definitions used in arriving at the figures presented. The reader should pay attention to trends and to relative positions, however, rather than become too engrossed in particular figures.

Number of students

Table 1 provides information concerning enrollments in secondary schools in the United States since 1889. It should be noted that second-

---

[6] See United States Office of Education, *The Common Core of State Educational Information*, State Educational Records and Reports Series, Handbook 1, Bulletin No. 8 (Washington, D.C.: Government Printing Office, 1953).

ary schools are defined as grades 9 through 12, that data are for both public and private schools, and that territories of the United States (and also the states of Alaska and Hawaii) are not included in the tabulations.

The most significant column in Table 1 is probably the one relating to secondary school enrollment as a percentage of secondary-school-age youth (ages 14–17). It is not surprising that the number of children in school has increased steadily, for the total population of the United States has shown a regular increase. The great increase in the attracting and holding powers of the secondary school, however, presents problems of much greater scope than the mere provision of increased seating space for an increased audience. It is apparent from even a casual analysis that the student body of the secondary school today is of a much different make-up than was the student body in, say, 1920. It is not our purpose here to analyze the vast political, economic, and social changes that have resulted in the fact that almost all children who are of the age to be in a secondary school are, in fact, there. We would stress, however, that the facts show that they are in attendance and, furthermore, show that the

TABLE 1. ENROLLMENT DATA FOR SECONDARY SCHOOLS IN THE UNITED STATES, 1889–1963

Year	Secondary School Enrollment	Population,[1] 14–17 years of age	Secondary School Enrollment as a per cent of population aged 14–17
1889	359,949	5,354,653	6.7
1900	699,403	6,152,231	11.4
1910	1,115,398	7,220,298	15.4
1920	2,500,176	7,735,841	32.3
1930	4,812,000	9,341,221	51.4
1940	7,130,000	9,720,419	73.3
1950	6,453,000	8,443,000	76.4
1960	9,600,000	11,341,000	84.7
1963	12,100,000	13,500,000[2]	89.6

[1] Includes population in Armed Services and institutions.
[2] Estimated.

Sources: U.S. Office of Education, Biennial Survey of Education in the United States, 1952–54. Washington, D.C.: Government Printing Office, 1957, p. 26; U.S. Bureau of the Census, Statistical Abstract of the United States, 1963, pp. 113 and 116; U.S. Bureau of the Census, Historical Statistics of the United States, Colonial Times to 1957, pp. 207 and 214; Health, Education, and Welfare Indicators, December, 1963, p. v.

trend appears to be continuing toward a 100 per cent enrollment of those who, by age alone, are eligible for enrollment.

Number of graduates

It seems important to pay some attention to the number of students who are successful in their high school careers. Table 2 provides information concerning graduates from both public and private high schools. It is

TABLE 2. HIGH SCHOOL GRADUATES, 1870–1960

Year	Number of High School Graduates	Population, 17 years of age	High School Graduates as a per cent of population, aged 17
1870	16,000	815,000	2.0
1880	23,634	946,026	2.5
1890	43,731	1,259,177	3.5
1900	94,883	1,489,146	6.4
1910	156,429	1,786,240	8.8
1920	311,266	1,855,173	16.8
1930	666,904	2,295,822	29.0
1940	1,221,475	2,403,074	50.8
1950	1,199,700	2,034,450	59.0
1963	1,960,000	2,772,000	70.7

Sources: U.S. Bureau of the Census, *Historical Statistics of the United States, Colonial Times to 1957*, p. 207; U.S. Office of Education, *Digest of Educational Statistics, 1964*, p. 56.

apparent not only that an increasing percentage of the school-age population is attending school, but also that an increasing proportion of the population is graduating from high school. This fact, of course, is interpreted in different ways by different people. To some it represents the increasing challenge to the high school; to others it signifies decreasing standards for high school graduation. Regardless of interpretation, the fact is present and must be dealt with by the secondary school administrator.

Number of secondary schools

There are various estimates of the number of secondary schools in the United States. The most recent complete national survey revealed that there were 25,350 public secondary schools and 4,129 private secondary schools.[7] These figures include four-year high schools, junior high schools, senior high schools, and undivided (usually six-year) high schools.

The average high school is still a small high school. In the academic year 1963–64 there were 31,705 school districts in the United States. Only 19.9 per cent of these districts enrolled 1,200 or more students in all grades, kindergarten through the high school years. Almost 50 per cent of these districts had less than 300 pupils enrolled.[8] As unbelievable as it may seem in these days of "bigness," the fact remains that the small high school is still present in very large numbers.

In brief, an ever-increasing percentage of youth in the high school age group is in attendance in American public and private secondary schools. In addition, the number of graduates from high school is increasing. The number of secondary schools in this country has remained fairly stable for the past twenty years and the small high school is still much in evidence.

CHANGING PURPOSES

Almost every definition of administration or leadership includes some mention of the function of assisting an organization in meeting its purposes. It is necessary, then, to consider carefully the purposes of the American public secondary school as one prepares to exert a leadership function in secondary education.

Early purposes

In the days of the Latin grammar school, the question of purpose was not a difficult one. The major purpose of these schools was to prepare boys for college and for eventual service as leaders in the church or government. Enrollments were small, and secondary school education was a privilege of the few rather than a right of the many.

For the most part, this singleness of purpose was an accepted pattern. In many cases, the secondary school prepared boys for an English college or university. Thus, with no real "free" schools and with a well-accepted single purpose, there was little cause for confusion about or study of the functions of a public secondary school.

[7] United States Office of Education, *Digest of Educational Statistics, 1964 Edition* (Washington, D.C.: Government Printing Office, 1964), p. 44.
[8] *Ibid.*, p. 43.

New demands and purposes

With growing economic, political, and social demands upon American citizens, many began to challenge the value of a totally classical secondary education. Benjamin Franklin was but reflecting a general attitude when he began his efforts to create a "practical" secondary school. By "practical," Franklin and other leaders in the academy movement were referring particularly to preparation for careers in business and commerce as opposed to the early emphasis on the ministry and politics (law) alone. For example, the growing merchant fleet required navigators, accountants, and insurance underwriters—to name but a few of the "practical" occupations. These positions required more mathematics, history, and geography than were available in the Latin grammar school and there seemed little reason to avoid English in favor of Latin and Greek.

The concept of a "practical" school as represented by the academy movement was not synonymous with a concept of universal, free, public secondary education. The abilities to read, to write, and to "sum"—the abilities gained in the common school—were still seen as the maximum needs of a majority of the people. However, the problems of purpose were beginning to grow as many began to claim that the single purpose of the Latin grammar school was not enough and that certain "practical" purposes must also be served.

By the second decade of the nineteenth century, even broader purposes for secondary education than those represented by the academy movement were enunciated. In Boston, a committee indicated that a school should be established that would, at public expense, prepare young men for life as well as for college. This was not to say that college was neither life nor a preparation for life, but the committee was particularly concerned with those students who, in 1820, went directly from the common school into life. It is difficult to isolate the specific purposes that the high school was to meet, but it seems clear that by the first half of the nineteenth century people desired something beyond the common school for all of the children of this country.

Brubacher points to a number of factors that led to the growth of the high school and which are related to its purposes. Rapid industrialization made apparent the economic value to the individual of further education. Equalitarian principles, particularly on the fast-moving frontier, made the highly-selective secondary school unpopular. Increased economic strength made the support of public high schools possible. Education, open to all, became a medium for the upward social mobility of vast masses of people. And, it must be admitted, unemployment problems which were faced from time to time during the period of the high school's growth, made high school attendance "something to do" for young people who could not find jobs.[9]

Through all this period of growth, the high school continued as a necessary prerequisite for entrance into college. Thus the "split personality" of the secondary school was a continuing problem. As at least a dual-purpose organization—college preparatory and terminal—the development of a proper balance was, and is, a constant problem. This problem led to a number of formal efforts to describe or to define the purposes of the American secondary school.

The "committee approach"

By 1900, the general idea that secondary school education should be provided at public expense for all children was well accepted. We might say, then, that the purpose is to educate youth. But this statement leads to two questions—one of content and the other of method. In the early days, before the impressive contributions of psychology raised questions of teaching methods, the major concern was with content. Thus, the first major study of secondary education was essentially a study of content. This study was conducted by the Committee of Ten, a group dominated by college professors, which was appointed by the National Education Association. The report of the Committee, published in 1893, attempted to define the proper learnings in each of nine subject fields for high school students. The apparent assumption of the Committee was that the only legitimate purpose of the high school was to assist students in gaining mastery of these nine academic subjects.

By 1918, things had changed. Two committees had studied the high school between 1893 and 1918, but both had been concerned solely with college entrance requirements. These studies had led to the "unit system"—a system given new emphasis in 1906 with the definition of the "Carnegie Unit" by the report of the Carnegie Foundation for the Advancement of Teaching.

In 1918, an entirely new direction was taken by the Commission on the Reorganization of Secondary Education with the development of the so-called Cardinal Principles of Secondary Education. This group expressed objectives not in terms of subject-matter goals but in terms of what might be called "life-adjustment" goals. Briefly, the objectives of

[9] Brubacher, *op. cit.*, pp. 433–436.

the secondary school were seen to be the development in youth of health and physical fitness, command of fundamental processes, worthy home membership, vocational effectiveness, citizenship, worthy use of leisure time, and ethical character.[10]

This list led to a conflict between "content" and "adjustment" advocates that is still present. Later statements of purpose from national commissions or committees reflected the "adjustment" viewpoint, although the extent to which such national pronouncements lessened the actual influence of college entrance requirements on high school curricula is subject to question. Reports of the Committee on Social-Economic Goals of America (NEA) in 1933,[11] of the Committee on Orientation of the National Association of Secondary School Principals in 1936 and 1937,[12] and of the Educational Policies Commission in 1937 and 1944,[13] all stressed ends other than content for the public schools.

Other formulations

A complete review of all statements relating to the purposes of secondary education in America would be a several-volume collection. Only three more statements will be mentioned here. In 1955, after extensive state and local meetings, almost two thousand delegates assembled in Washington for the White House Conference on Education. This Conference was organized to provide opportunities for a thorough study of educational problems in the United States. The report of the Conference stressed three purposes: adequate training in the fundamental skills, training in citizenship, and vocational training.[14] That this is an omnibus statement is recognized when the report also cites that "during the past two generations this list of school goals has grown with increased speed

10 Commission on the Reorganization of Secondary Education, *Cardinal Principles of Secondary Education* (Washington, D.C.: Government Printing Office, 1918), p. 3.

11 Committee on Social-Economic Goals of America, *Social-Economic Goals of America* (Washington, D.C.: National Education Association, 1933).

12 National Association of Secondary School Principals, Committee on Orientation, *Issues of Secondary Education*, Bulletin No. 59 (Washington, D.C.: National Education Association, 1936); and *Functions of Secondary Education*, Bulletin No. 64 (Washington, D.C.: National Education Association, 1937).

13 Educational Policies Commission, *The Purposes of Education in American Democracy* (Washington, D.C.: National Education Association, 1937); and Educational Policies Commission, *Education for All American Youth* (Washington, D.C.: National Education Association, 1944).

14 The Committee for the White House Conference on Education, *A Report to the President* (Washington, D.C.: Government Printing Office, 1956).

. . . should this broadening of the goals be recognized as legitimate? This committee answers *Yes.*"[15]

During recent years, a national organization known as the Council for Basic Education has provided much comment on public school matters. Primarily concerned with the intellectual development of children and youth, the Council has commissioned a panel of scholars in various fields to draw up curriculum standards for secondary schools. In a statement of purpose, the Council made the following summary:

> CBE believes that the school has many subsidiary purposes but that its primary purpose is fourfold: (1) To transmit the facts about the heritage and culture of the race; (2) to teach young people to read and write and figure; (3) in the process of (1) and (2) to train the intelligence and to stimulate the pleasures of thought; and (4) to provide that atmosphere of moral affirmation without which education is merely animal training.[16]

The curriculum studies of the Council represent an attempt to specify those "facts about the heritage and culture" that should be a part of the secondary school curriculum. The Council appears to be a good representative of those groups and individuals who believe that the purposes of secondary education have been permitted to stray too far from intellectual development toward vocational and "adjustment" pursuits.

The final report to be mentioned here is the Conant report.[17] With the support of the Carnegie Foundation, Conant studied the American high school for two years. He produced a series of recommendations based on the premise that the American high school must fulfill three basic functions: provide a good general education for all youth as future citizens of a democracy, provide elective programs to assist the majority of pupils to develop useful skills, and educate adequately those with a talent for handling advanced academic subjects. This statement of function leads Conant to the support of the comprehensive high school and his recommendations are specific suggestions for reaching this comprehensive status.

As one reads any historical analysis of the changing purposes of American secondary education, two things become apparent. First, there is a cyclical trend in the ebb and flow of various concepts of the purposes. Secondly, the change in purposes is closely related to and quite likely an effect of changing enrollment characteristics. The first point is undoubt-

[15] *Ibid.*, p. 9.
[16] "What Do We Mean By 'Basic'?: Some Notes for a Definition," *CBE Bulletin*, 2:1–2, September 1957.
[17] James B. Conant, *The American High School Today* (New York: McGraw-Hill, Inc., 1959).

edly not an isolated fact—actually, the trend in statements of purpose follows closely the history of the United States. Wars bring war-related purposes to the fore; depressions bring social action purposes; prosperity and peace bring renewed demands for leisure-oriented content and the like.

Furthermore, the high school principal must recognize that national statements of purpose may or may not coincide with local aspirations. The definition of purposes for any complex organization requires careful study and thought and is a never-ending task. This is part of the challenge of educational leadership about which we shall be talking throughout this volume.

THE CURRENT SCENE

We have now explored the growth of the American secondary school and of secondary school administration, enrollment trends in the secondary school, and the changing purposes of the high school. Beginning with Chapter 5, we will discuss the tasks of the secondary school administrator under headings such as "instructional leadership" or "management." Under each of these headings there are conflicts and concerns which face the secondary school principal as we move toward the three-quarter mark of the twentieth century. Many, if not all, of these conflicts and concerns have been present since the beginning of secondary education in the United States and are unique only because of the unique demands of the present era. In concluding this chapter, some of these conflicts and concerns will be highlighted briefly.

Purposes

We have already indicated that the secondary school is conceived to have different purposes by different people. Purpose underlies curriculum and questions of purpose must be resolved before curriculum can be developed. So many catch-words and cliches are in use today to define the purpose of education that it is difficult to clarify the conflict. Such terms as "progressive," "comprehensive," "life-adjustment," "basic," and "vocational" have many meanings. The use of such terms in debating the purposes of secondary schools does more to cloud than to clarify the issues.

Essentially, the current conflict centers about the same things that were discussed in the 1780's and deals primarily with subpurposes rather than with major purposes. Democracy needs an educated citizenry and citizens in a democracy have a right to realize their full potential. These seem to be the unquestioned purposes of secondary education. But when is a citizen educated? What role should the school play in helping a citizen realize his potential? These are the questions that create conflict, and these are the matters that will concern secondary school principals as they wrestle with the problem of purposes.

Instructional leadership

With conflict in setting purposes and with a heterogeneous student body, curriculum problems in the secondary school will continue to plague the administrator. General education, vocational training, college preparatory curricula, education for safe living, these and many more represent demands to be fitted together into a four- or six-year secondary school program. Little or no progress has been made in deleting courses from high school programs, although great strides have been made in adding courses. New approaches are needed in the development of the secondary school curriculum. Leadership in discovering these approaches is expected of the secondary school administrator.

Staff personnel

As more demands are made upon the secondary school, the position of secondary school teacher becomes highly technical. As technology has grown in the United States, demands for highly-skilled technicians have grown in all fields. While we often bemoan the shortage of teachers, we must recognize a corresponding shortage of personnel in all skilled work. There will probably never be an abundance of skilled manpower in any profession. If the demands made upon secondary education are to be met, administrators will need to find new ways to utilize the talent available to them. This will require new methods of organizing the secondary schools, new arrangements of curricula, and new uses of such media as radio, television, and recordings. New ways to reduce the clerical load placed upon teachers will have to be discovered. In these, and in other endeavors related to staffing our schools, administrative leadership is necessary.

Student body

As we have seen earlier, the percentage of children of high school age who are actually attending high school is approaching the 100 per cent mark. There is no evidence that this trend will reverse itself. As a matter of fact, colleges and universities are now struggling with enrollment problems as an increasing percentage of college-age young people seek admittance. The secondary school principal will, therefore, administer an organization with a complex and heterogeneous clientele. He will have the able and the barely educable, the motivated and the unmotivated, the rich and the poor. And he will have problems. Nevertheless, it seems clear that the comprehensive high school with a comprehensive student body will be the order of the day.

Management

While this overview of secondary education has devoted little or no attention to fiscal problems, it should be obvious that the decisions required as secondary education grows in quantity and in quality each have fiscal implications. Education must compete with many other governmental services for financial support and governmental demands for funds have received increasing public resistance in recent years. The educational administrator must view his proposed actions in terms of financial resources and must be aware that educational conflicts and concerns need ultimately to be viewed in relation to financial ones. Education, not dollars, is the primary focus for decisions and for planning, but the school administrator should be aware of the school as a social institution whose financial needs will be viewed in the large context of all social institutions.

Community relations

Much of this chapter has dealt with conflicts and concerns which arise from increasing complexities in secondary education. This complexity is, unfortunately, too often little understood by the professional educator and not understood at all by the general public. Much of the growth and complexity which we have described in this chapter has developed almost in spite of, rather than because of, public awareness of the purposes and problems of secondary education.

In these times, public awareness of the framework of secondary education is essential if the schools are to realize their full potential. The school administrator cannot succeed as a complete educational leader unless he devotes careful attention to community relations. Many current conflicts and concerns arise because of lack of public understanding of the factors leading to the present status of secondary education. The educational leader needs to understand these factors and to develop techniques and skills for the creation of public understanding.

THE SCHOOL AND SOCIETY

One final aspect of the current scene must be referred to in this discussion. In a real sense, this topic is little more than one special application of the broader ideas underlying the previous parts of this portion of Chapter 2. Because of the importance of this application, however, we would be remiss to neglect it.

American society is in a period of turmoil. In a time of general plenty, there exist in our society some pockets of financial and cultural deprivation that would threaten to destroy any society which would tolerate them. While these pockets are not restricted to large cities, they are a particular problem in our urban areas. In many large cities today, the so-called "central city" has been virtually abandoned as a residential area by all those who can afford to move to suburban or "outer-city" areas. This exodus from the central city has created in many urban communities sharp—and, in some cases, violent—divisions between "haves" and "have-nots." The question of "have" or "have-not" is no longer solely one of money or material possessions, but even more fundamentally strikes at the basic concept of American democracy—equality of opportunity. In addition, the divisions between groups have assumed racial overtones which have aroused emotions to the point where many of the more basic issues are clouded by peripheral considerations.

The American public school system has long been seen as a major institutional vehicle to provide young people with the skills and competencies which will make equality of opportunity a meaningful goal. In an era in which education and training are no longer merely desirable, but essential for every member of society, the task of the public school is vital, but nowhere is it more crucial than in those pockets of cultural and material deprivation which exist throughout America today.

If it is to meet this current challenge, the American public school system must make sure that several basic concepts are not ignored. The fact that learning must proceed from and be built upon the environmental and hereditary background of the learner is a key fact which is too often ignored as we concentrate upon the "haves" and forget the "have-nots." Methodology, curricular programs, instructional materials, and all other aspects of the educational program must be based upon the realities of specific teaching-learning situations rather than only the great

American "middle class." Theologians engage in great debates over the relevance of the church in today's world; educators must be equally aware that public school systems may be in danger of losing their relevancy in precisely those portions of our society in which the role of education is most crucial.

CONCLUSION

In short, every element of the growth of secondary education in the United States points to increasing difficulties. This is not said to discourage the prospective secondary school principal, but rather to indicate that a major contribution can be made by those who choose to serve in this role. The public high school in America is only about 125 years old and it was less than a hundred years ago that the Kalamazoo case gave it firm legal sanction. No greater challenge to leadership ability exists than to work toward the continued growth of the American high school.

SUGGESTED ACTIVITIES

1. Select any current statement of the purposes of the American secondary school and describe some specific proposals that would lead to the attainment of any one of these purposes.

2. Describe several events in American history that had an influence on enrollment characteristics of the secondary school. Indicate the nature of the change caused by each event.

3. Describe some differences between the secondary school you attended and the secondary school as it now exists. How do you account for these changes?

4. Describe what seem to you to be some major events of the next twenty-five years that will tend to influence the nature of secondary education.

5. Describe briefly two problems in secondary education that seem to have been with us since colonial times. How do you account for our failure to solve these problems?

SELECTED READINGS

Brubacher, John S., A History of the Problems of Education. New York: McGraw-Hill Book Company, Inc., 1947. Chapters I, II, III, IV, XIV, and XIX.

Butts, R. Freeman, and Lawrence A. Cremin, *A History of Education in American Culture*. New York: Holt, Rinehart & Winston, Inc., 1953.

Chase, Francis S., and Harold A. Anderson, (ed.), *The High School in a New Era*. Chicago: University of Chicago Press, 1958. Pp. 3–193.

Conant, James B., *Slums and Suburbs*. New York: McGraw-Hill, Inc., 1961.

Counts, George S., *Education and American Civilization*. New York: Bureau of Publications, Teachers College, Columbia University, 1952.

Drake, William E., *The American School in Transition*. Englewood Cliffs, N.J.: Prentice-Hall, Inc., 1955.

Educational Policies Commission, *Education and the Disadvantaged American*. Washington: The National Education Association, 1962.

Edwards, Newton, and Herman G. Richey, *The School in the American Social Order*. Boston: Houghton Mifflin Company, 1947.

Myers, Alonzo F., and Clarence O. Williams, *Education in a Democracy*, Fourth Edition. Englewood Cliffs, N.J.: Prentice-Hall, Inc., 1954.

Riessman, Frank, *The Culturally Deprived Child*. New York: Harper & Row, Publishers, 1962.

Rugg, Harold, *Foundations for American Education*. New York: Harcourt, Brace & World, Inc., 1947. See particularly Part Six.

3

LEADERSHIP

IN CHAPTER 2 WE INDICATED THAT THERE IS A NEED for real leadership in meeting the problems that face secondary education today and that will face it tomorrow. The term "leadership" requires careful definition if it is to be of any practical use in a discussion. This chapter defines leadership, explores the purpose of and the necessity for leadership, and describes the process through which it is exercised.

SOME MEANINGS OF LEADERSHIP

"Leadership" is what can be called a "bushel basket" term. So many meanings can be attached to the word that it becomes almost meaningless. Actually, the word is rarely used without an adjective, and even then the intended meaning is often hidden. It seems necessary first to explore the meaning of the unaccompanied noun and then to examine the common concepts that are usually implied by the noun plus one or more adjectives.

"Leadership" without adjectives

"Leadership" in itself means the condition or skill of being a leader. A leader is, quite simply, one who leads. The verb "to lead" has a number of recognized meanings. Two of these meanings are germane to this discussion. The first is that "to lead" means "to guide in direction, course, action, and the like," or "to show the way." The second meaning of "to lead" that seems appropriate is "to command" an organization or group.

Both of these meanings imply that to lead is to take some responsibility for getting a group from one place to another, from one idea to another, from one state of being to another, or merely from one action to another. Although this may be an oversimplification, for our purposes let us accept this meaning of the verb and the corresponding meanings of the simple and of the complex noun. This means, then, that leadership will here mean skill in assuming responsibility for getting a group to take some sort of purposeful action.

Before continuing to a discussion of leadership with adjectives, we shall make clear our perceptions of the relationship between the terms "leadership" and "administration." "Leadership" is the more inclusive term. Administrators are leaders. All of the leadership in an organization, however, is not exercised by the administrator, nor is all of the leadership present in an organization exerted from within that organization. We usually say that the administrator plays a "leadership role," which means that he has certain specific responsibilities in the leadership activity within an organization. Thus, when we talk about leadership in an organization, we are talking about administrators as well as about others; when we talk about administrators, we are not talking about all of the leadership in an organization. We shall indicate shortly what we believe to be the specific purposes of and necessity for administrative leadership in a secondary school.

Extremes in leadership types

There are extremes in leadership types. Far out on one end of the continuum is the autocratic leader. On the other end is what some call the "disappearing leader." Probably no leader is a pure example of either extreme. By examining the extremes, however, we can gain insight into the more conservative positions.

The autocratic leader. The term "autocratic" is so value-loaded that it is difficult to write or hear it without inserting a loud exclamation of distaste in parentheses. Essentially, the autocratic leader is one who assumes almost all of the responsibility in deciding for what purposes a group will strive, what actions will be followed in reaching these purposes, and, specifically, what action each member of the group will contribute to the total group action. This means that the autocratic leader must assume responsibility for seeing that group members do in fact perform as he has decided they should perform. In addition, it means that the autocratic leader may assume a major portion of credit for group success and must assume a major portion of blame for group failure in actually performing the actions and reaching the goals previously set by this leader.

Although much of the literature on leadership asserts that the autocratic leader rules by fear, this is by no means always the case. If, for example, the autocrat can convince his group that he is more able than any other member of the group to make decisions and if the group experiences what it considers to be success by following his decisions, the members of the group may be perfectly happy to permit the autocrat to do their thinking for them. The key to autocratic leadership is that for one reason or another—through fear or through conviction—one person makes the decisions for a group regarding the purposes of the group and the ways in which group members will participate in attaining these purposes.

The "disappearing leader." On the other end of the leadership continuum is the "disappearing leader." This term is used to describe the leader as he has sometimes been characterized by certain advocates of group dynamics or of some other "human relations movement." In essence, the disappearing leader is one who feels that leadership should reside with the group rather than with any single member of the group. The leader's primary responsibility is to assist the group in recognizing the problems that face it and to establish situations so that the group can address itself to the solution of these problems. As Gordon describes him, the ideal group leader is one who, among other things, feels that his task is to reduce dependency of group members upon himself, believes that to be most effective a leader must lose his leadership position, hopes that the group will eventually forget that he is "the leader," and feels that he must become accepted more and more as just another group member.[1]

The autocratic leader assumes that he "knows the answers"; the disappearing leader assumes that no one member of the group knows any of the answers. The autocratic leader is identified easily as *the* leader; the disappearing leader hopes to lose his identity as a leader. According to the disappearing-leader concept, therefore, the school administrator becomes a discussion leader and an expeditor for the group.

The middle ground

Obviously, the school administrator as a leader cannot function as a pure example of either of these extreme leadership types. The nature of American society and the characteristics of secondary school teachers make it unrealistic to expect to find a pure autocratic principal. On the other hand, the nature of the principal's responsibilities to his superintendent, to his teachers, to his students, to his board of education, and to his community makes it unlikely that he can be a disappearing leader. School principals will actually exhibit leadership behavior somewhere between these two extremes. The description of various positions between the extremes leads to many other qualifications to the term "leadership."

Thus, we speak of the "effective group leader," the "managerial leader," the "strong leader," the "paternalistic leader," the "humane leader," the "authoritarian leader," the "considerate leader," and so on. In the literature of educational administration in America, however, the most overworked adjective of all is "democratic." We speak of the democratic leader, democratic principles of leadership, or democratic leadership behavior. Unfortunately, this adjective has been used to describe an infinite number of positions along the leadership continuum.

Effective leaders in a democracy will have different leadership styles, and no effort should be made to define democratic leadership so narrowly as to give guilt feelings to effective leaders who differ from the narrow definition of the "democratic" leader. If, for example, we accept re-election as one criterion of the effectiveness of political leaders in the United States (and we accept this with some qualms) it is apparent that three effective leaders—each of whom experienced re-election—Franklin

[1] Thomas Gordon, *Group-Centered Leadership* (Boston: Houghton Mifflin Company, 1955), p. 167.

Roosevelt, Harry Truman, and Dwight Eisenhower, differed greatly in their leadership behavior. Who is to say that one was more "democratic" than the others?

Our description of the democratic leader, then, must provide room in the middle ground for various leadership styles.

THE LEADER IN A DEMOCRACY

When we speak of a "democratic leader," we imply that we are talking about a leader whose leadership behavior is based upon democratic principles. Counts describes in some detail the Hebraic-Christian ethic, the humanistic spirit and its science and scientific method outgrowth, and the heritage of the rule of law, all of which he feels underlie what he calls our democratic faith.[2] In discussing this democratic faith, Counts describes seven characteristics essential to such a faith. These are an affirmation of the worth and dignity of the individual, the declaration that in a most profound sense all men are created equal, the belief that political and civil liberty are the only dependable guardians of individual worth and equality, a foundation of law and orderly process, a foundation of basic morality, a foundation of individual opportunity, and a foundation of individual responsibility.[3]

The National Conference of Professors of Educational Administration listed three ideals that they believed were fundamental to democratic educational leadership. These were the declaration of the dignity and worth of the individual, the placing of reliance upon the method of intelligence, and the placing of reliance upon the cooperative use of intelligence in the solution of problems common to the group.[4]

The democratic leader

These and other statements about democracy indicate that the democratic leader must organize his leadership behavior so as to recognize and to utilize the rights and the abilities of the individual members of

---

[2] George S. Counts, *Education and American Civilization* (New York: Bureau of Publications, Teachers College, Columbia University, 1952), pp. 220–277.

[3] *Ibid.*, pp. 281–284.

[4] *Educational Leaders—Their Function and Preparation*, A Report of the Second Work Conference of Professors of Educational Administration (Madison, Wis.: The Conference, 1948), pp. 5–6.

the group he leads. This idea can be carried to the extreme of the disappearing leader, but it is difficult to see how the pure autocrat can live
up to this requirement. Why is it, then, that we cannot recommend that
the secondary school principal become a disappearing leader? Basically, it
is because of the need to consider that most organizations do not exist
solely to serve the group that is officially a part of the organization. Thus,
the public secondary school does not exist to serve only the teachers and
other employees of the school, nor does it exist solely to serve its students,
nor does it exist solely to serve the local community. A visible and active
leader is necessary to make decisions that involve demands from or requirements of more than any single group served by the school.

In addition to serving many groups, the school is often a large and
complex organization itself. Many times it would be wasteful of the intelligence of the professional staff of the school to ask each member of
this staff to engage in careful deliberation of every decision that must be
made. Here again, a visible and active leader is necessary to ensure that
group involvement in decision-making is efficiently and intelligently used.

This means that the democratic leader should not aspire to become
either a disappearing leader or an autocratic leader. We have now seen
what the democratic leader should not be. Let us try to define what he
should be.

First, he should be a person who feels a responsibility for assisting
a group to reach goals, some of which will be defined by the group and
some of which will be defined for the group.

Second, he should be a person who recognizes that for any given
problem facing the group there will be intelligence from within and from
without the group that will lead to better solutions than he can devise
through the use of his intelligence alone.

Third, he should be a person who can delegate appropriate responsibilities to group members and who can, consequently, also openly recognize the contributions of group members to group success.

Finally, he should be a person who can utilize group intelligence
and, at the same time, accept personal responsibility for the progress of
the group toward its goals.

Although it is difficult, if not impossible, to construct a single-
sentence definition of democratic leadership, the following definition
contains most of the concepts we have been discussing:

A democratic leader accepts responsibility for playing a major role in
assisting a group or an organization to reach its goals and meets this
responsibility in such a way as to recognize and to utilize the contribu-

tions that individuals inside and outside the group or organization can make toward reaching these goals and in such a way as to secure the maximum cooperation of these individuals in making their contributions.

This definition makes clear that "one-man rule" is not democratic leadership. On the other hand, it indicates the need for a nondisappearing leader to play a major role in the group or organization. At the same time, the definition is not so restrictive that it calls for any single style of leadership. As we have seen in the incidents presented in Chapter 1 and as we will see throughout this text, different groups and different situations call for different leadership styles. Because of this, it is probably more accurate to speak of "a leader in a democracy" than it is to speak of "a democratic leader."

Leadership behavior studies

A variety of studies have been made of leadership behavior and many terms have evolved to describe the concepts which are included in the definition given above. While it is not our purpose here to provide a comprehensive review of such studies, it is important that the administrator have some understanding of the terminology used to describe leadership behavior.

In general, these studies show that leadership involves at least two major dimensions. Shartle speaks of the "human relations" and the "get out the work" dimensions;[5] Halpin (and others) refer to the "consideration" and "initiating structure" dimensions;[6] while Getzels, in a somewhat broader sense, speaks of the ideographic or personal and the nomothetic or institutional dimensions of activity in a social system.[7]

Each of these studies concludes that the leader must be effective both in terms of criteria related to the individuals within an organization and in terms of criteria related to the organization itself. The delicate balance required to permit progress in meeting institutional goals without sacrificing individual rights and satisfactions is one which an

[5] Carroll L. Shartle, *Executive Performance and Leadership* (Englewood Cliffs, N.J.: Prentice-Hall, Inc., 1956), p. 120.

[6] Andrew W. Halpin, "The Leader Behavior and Leadership Ideology of Educational Administrators and Aircraft Commanders," *Harvard Educational Review*, 1955, 25, pp. 18–32.

[7] Jacob W. Getzels, "Administration as a Social Process," in A. W. Halpin (ed.), *Administrative Theory in Education* (Chicago: Midwest Administration Center, University of Chicago, 1958), pp. 150–165.

effective leader must establish and maintain. He cannot settle for the "happy ship" which is going nowhere, nor can he strive for "full speed ahead" with a sullen or mutinous "crew."

Authority and leadership

Educational administrators in a democracy are often troubled by the concept of authority. In spite of the facts that policemen patrol our democratic streets, that tax collectors invade our democratic wallets, and that signs tell our democratic bus passengers to refrain from smoking, we somehow feel that authority in a school principal is undemocratic.

In discussing this problem, Gregg makes the following statement:

> Authority and its judicious exercise are not inconsistent with democratic principles. Democratic society has found it necessary to allocate authority to numerous offices and positions which it has created in order that the freedom and opportunities of individuals and groups may be guaranteed. It is necessary that the school administrator have appropriate authority in order that the school system may have the necessary freedom of action. Without such authority the school administrator would be handicapped in providing the creative leadership expected of a person in his position. If he had no authority, he would be unable to be of most help to members of the staff in solving their problems. The administrator must, however, use his authority in such a way as to guard the rights of staff members as well as his own.[8]

Authority and autocracy are not synonymous. Every principal has authority, given to him by his board of education and his superintendent in terms of legal powers granted by the state. This possession and subsequent use of authority cannot be escaped. It is in the use of authority that one is faithful or unfaithful to democratic principles.

In addition, principals must have what is often called the authority of ideas. Members of a group should be willing to take direction from a principal because they recognize that he has the knowledge and the wisdom to provide good direction. In a democracy, this is probably the ultimate authority, because without it the authority granted by law becomes ineffectual. In spite of this, the educational administrator needs to be aware of the fact that he has both the responsibility and the authority of his position and that neither attribute is "undemocratic."

[8] Russell T. Gregg, "The Administrative Process," *Administrative Behavior in Education*, edited by Roald F. Campbell and Russell T. Gregg (New York: Harper & Row, Publishers, 1957), pp. 303–304.

Status and actual leadership

One final word should be said about the leader in a democracy. We have been talking specifically about leaders, not about secondary school principals. It is of course our hope that the two are the same, but appointing a man a principal does not automatically make him a leader. An actual leader is one who exhibits leadership behavior; a status leader is one who holds a position requiring leadership. The fact that one is a status leader —that is, that he has been appointed to a position which requires that he exert leadership if he is to fulfill the requirements of the position— does not guarantee that he will be an actual leader, that he will or can exhibit leadership behavior.

We are all familiar, unfortunately, with secondary schools in which the actual leadership is not exerted by the principal. Perhaps the superintendent is the actual leader, or perhaps it is a teacher with long tenure in the school. There may be a number of reasons for this situation, but regardless of the reasons, it is always possible that the principal of a school is a status leader only.

THEORY IN ADMINISTRATION

A major undertaking in recent years has been a search for a theory (or theories) of educational administration. This search has been complicated by discussions of the meaning of the term "theory," by debate over whether a theory as opposed to theories of administration is the object of the search, and by discussions of the place of values—concepts of right and wrong—in theory development. The purpose of theory is to provide a basic conceptual framework which can be used to develop hypotheses for testing. If a theoretical framework provides hypotheses which are consistently proven valid, the framework moves toward classification as a "law."

Theory building in educational administration is still in its infancy. While some theories have been proposed, perhaps the major contribution of the movement toward theory building has been the stress upon the systematic analysis of administration which is necessary if theories are to be proposed. The educational administrator has not been particularly noted for viewing administration as a discipline. The search for theories brings with it the necessity of systematic analysis of administration as a discipline. This by-product may prove, in the long run, to be the major contribution of the theory movement in educational administration.

PURPOSE OF LEADERSHIP IN SECONDARY EDUCATION

The general role of leaders has been considered, but what are the purposes to be met by secondary school administrators? It is probably little better than a truism that the basic purpose of any educational administration position is to facilitate the teaching-learning process. The important consideration for us is to discover the specific purposes of educational administration.

The school community

A community is difficult to define. There are at least eighty definitions that are used to describe the concept of "community." It is not our purpose here to develop a sociological treatise on this concept; it is merely to point out that the secondary school exists in a community and that secondary school administration is carried out against a community background.

For the most part, the immediate community of the secondary school can be defined as its attendance area, that is, the geographical area from which it draws its students. This community is a part of larger communities, of a city, a county, a state, a region, a nation, and, indeed, of the world. Each of these larger communities plays a role in shaping the characteristics of the school attendance area, but in the final analysis the day-to-day operations of the secondary school take place in the attendance area. The hopes and aspirations of the people in this area, its socio-economic characteristics, and the over-all climate of the area shape the development and operation of the school and influence the school administrator.

The secondary school principal, then, needs to be a student of his attendance area. The extent to which he understands and is understood by his community plays a major role in determining his effectiveness. The principal cannot be content to be an "office manager" or even to devote the great bulk of his time to staff personnel and curriculum development problems. It is inherent in his leadership position that he take advantage of existing opportunities and create new opportunities to know his community in much more than a superficial manner.

SECONDARY SCHOOL ADMINISTRATION:

OCCURS IN

CONSISTS OF

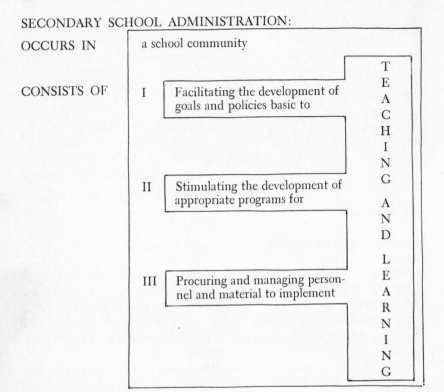

Goals and policies

The first area of administrative leadership is in facilitating the development of goals and policies. "Facilitating" is probably an overworked word in educational literature, but its meaning is important as a basic part of the administrator's concept of his role. The school principal does not develop goals and policies, but he must set the stage so that goals and policies are developed. It is this "setting of the stage" to which the word "facilitating" refers.

In Chapter 2 we discussed at length the problems related to the development of the purposes of the American secondary school. We saw that a statement of purposes is basic for the development of programs and for the selection of staff. The first responsibility of the secondary school principal is to be sure that his school has an understandable and useful statement of goals. The superintendent of schools in a district will be responsible for facilitating the development of goals for the district. The principal will need to work within this framework and see to it that the goals developed for his school are appropriately related to district goals, to the needs of his attendance area, and to the particular grade levels encompassed by his school.

In this process of goal development, the principal will need to involve lay citizens as well as professional staff members. One of the basic tenets of the American public school system is that the people have the right and the obligation to determine the purposes of their schools. The "people" does not mean only the PTA or the local service club. The principal should make every effort to involve broad segments of his school community in the development of goal statements.

Occasionally, a school administrator excuses a lagging school system by explaining that it represents "all that the people want." Lay responsibility for stating purposes is not an excuse, it is a challenge. The school principal as a leader needs to play more than a passive role in this undertaking; he needs to raise the sights of his community, to gather facts for the people to consider, and to motivate their thoughtful consideration. A lagging or lackluster school is very likely in the image of a lagging or lackluster administrator. Facilitating the development of goals basic to teaching and learning is a key purpose and a demanding one for the school principal.

Policy development

Policies usually establish certain guidelines that indicate ways in which goals shall be met. We commonly associate policy development with the board of education in the school enterprise. However, the principal has two tasks in meeting the purpose of policy development. First, he and his staff need to assist the superintendent of schools in developing policy recommendations for the board. Second, he needs to facilitate the development of specific policies within the district-wide policy framework for his school. Here again, the need to involve the intelligence and experience of many in developing policy is evident. It is an old axiom of administration that those who are to be affected by a policy should have a voice in the development of the policy. This means that lay citizens, teachers, secretaries, students, custodians, and others need to be involved appropriately by the administrator in the development of policy. As we discuss the task areas of school-community relations, of staff personnel administration, and of pupil personnel administration, much more is said about specific ways in which the purpose of facilitating the development of policies basic to teaching and learning is met.

Program development

Again, the principal is to stimulate the development of programs for teaching and learning rather than to develop such programs. This purpose of administration represents the heart of the professional-education job of the administrator. The lay citizenry, the board of education, or the students may play major roles in developing goals and policies, but the development of programs for teaching and learning is essentially a professional matter.

Chapter 6 is devoted to a discussion of the instructional leadership or program development role of the principal. It is important to note here the inter-relationships of goals, policy, and program. We should not ask the principal to be a leader in program development unless we ask him and give him time to be a leader in goal and policy development. Most principals accept a role as a stimulator of program development, but many seem to be unaware of the important factors that underlie program development.

Procurement of personnel and material

Once goals and policies have led to development of the program, the purpose of educational administration is to secure resources—human and material—to make the program of teaching and learning work. What kinds of teachers and other professional personnel does the program require? What physical facilities are needed to house the program? What supplies and equipment do teachers and pupils need to make the program of teaching and learning succeed? What nonteaching personnel are needed, and what supplies and equipment will they need to support the program?

These questions—and many others—are faced by the principal. After they are answered, the principal is responsible for creating a situation wherein personnel and material are coordinated, balanced, and related to produce a coherent program of teaching and learning rather than a hodgepodge of isolated activities.

Teaching and learning

Finally, we return to the basic purposes of the school—teaching and learning. The secondary school principal is not administering a factory nor an advertising agency—he is administering a school. All his efforts must somehow be related to the basic purpose of the school—teaching and learning. The school he administers is not the only educating agency in his community, but it is a unique agency charged by the people with particular teaching-learning responsibilities. It is to the meeting of these responsibilities, to leading the school to the meeting of these responsibilities, that the educational administrator devotes his professional life.

THE ADMINISTRATIVE PROCESS Read - Next 10 pages

We have examined the meanings of leadership in general and in a democracy and the purposes of secondary school administration. In meeting these purposes, the principal will need to perform many tasks. The task areas are discussed in detail in Part Two of this volume and include such things as instructional leadership, staff personnel administration, and the like. In performing in any or in all of these task areas, the administrator will need to follow the steps of the administrative process. This process is essentially the same whether the administrator is attacking a problem in the area of school-community relations or a problem in the area of school business management. It is, in short, the way in which the administrator goes about the business of administering.

Descriptions of the administrative process have been in existence for many years. The first important modern description of process is that developed by Fayol in 1916 and described in his *Administration Industrielle et Generale*.[9] Other well-known statements of the administrative process include those developed by Gulick and Urwick,[10] Sears,[11] and Gregg.[12] For our purposes, we shall use the description of the administrative process developed in an earlier volume in this series. Here the steps in the administrative process are listed as follows:

1. Decision-making
2. Programming
3. Stimulating
4. Coordinating
5. Appraising[13]

[9] See translation of Constance Starrs, *General and Industrial Management* (London: Sir Isaac Pitman and Sons, Ltd., 1949).

[10] Luther Gulick and L. Urwick (eds.), *Papers on the Science of Administration* (New York: Institute of Public Administration, 1937).

[11] Jesse B. Sears, *The Nature of the Administrative Process* (New York: McGraw-Hill, Inc., 1950).

[12] Gregg, *op. cit.*, Chapter 8.

[13] Campbell, Corbally, and Ramseyer, *Introduction to Educational Administration*, Second Edition (Boston: Allyn and Bacon, Inc., 1962), p. 138.

In the sections to follow, each of these steps will be discussed briefly. Before proceeding with this analysis, however, it is important to recognize the difficulties inherent in any attempt to analyze the components of a behavioral process. The administrative process is not something that can be observed in each of its parts; it is, rather, a series of behaviors from which process can be implied. What we are describing, then, is a concept rather than a concrete object. The concept is both important and useful, but an observer cannot expect to study an administrator in action and say, "Oh, now he is programming!" With this warning in mind, let us consider the steps in the administrative process.

Decision-making

For the administrator, decision-making is deciding upon a course of action. A problem arises and something needs to be done. The administrator needs to clarify the problem and gather information about it, to envision the various alternatives that may lead to a solution to the problem, and, finally, to choose from among these alternatives one to pursue. This is decision-making.

Some students of administration define the entire field as a job of decision-making. It is true that each of the steps in the administrative process requires that certain alternatives be considered and that certain choices be made. It is possible, then, to define the total process as one of decision-making. We have rejected this usage, however, because we feel that it leads to a lack of clarity in describing the process. Perhaps the best way to illustrate our thinking would be to speak of "capital D" decision-making and "small d" decision-making. As a step in the administrative process, we are thinking of "capital D" decision-making—that decision-making that involves a choice of alternatives for the solution of an institutional (in our case, a school) problem. Once this "capital D" decision has been made, the other steps of the process come into play. In these steps, decision-making is necessary, but it is subsidiary to the steps of the process rather than being the major step in these processes. This decision-making is of the "small d" variety.

Decision-making is a step in the administrative process, but it is not something that the administrator should do in isolation. The problem must be clarified, information gathered about it, and the alternatives defined. Each of these phases of decision-making should involve people other than the administrator. Suppose, for example, that the problem centers about high school–college articulation. The principal believes that the high school which he administers is not articulated well with certain colleges and universities. In clarifying this problem and in defining alternative courses of action to remedy the situation, the principal will need information and advice from teachers, graduates, college personnel, to name just a few. The final choice among alternatives may be made by the principal, but in the process many people have been involved and the decision will probably be a school decision rather than only the principal's decision.

Programming

Once a course of action has been chosen, something must be done about it. The course of action decided upon will no doubt require the participation of certain people, the use of certain supplies and equipment, the use of some space, and—without fail—budgetary provisions. The availability of these items will have entered into the thinking of the administrator during the decision-making step, but once the decision is made, specific program arrangements must be made.

Using the example of high school–college articulation, it may be that a decision is made to offer several special courses for college-bound students. Teachers for these courses must be chosen and assigned; arrangements for selecting students, perhaps on the basis of some tests, must be made; the daily schedule must make it possible for students to enroll in these classes; special teaching materials must be selected; cost items must be budgeted; and other arrangements may need to be made. The extent to which programming is carefully done will play a major role in the success of the venture.

Here again, the principal will involve others as he engages in this step of the administrative process. Teachers, guidance personnel, curriculum consultants, central administrative personnel—all these and others will assist in the programming process. Although responsibility for programming resides with the principal, the principal relies upon the advice and help of many others.

Stimulating

A decision has been made and the machinery has been selected to pursue the course of action called for by the decision. To this point in the administrative process, nothing has been done that represents concrete action toward the specific problem under attack. The machinery must be put into motion. This is what we have called the stimulating phase of the administrative process.

One obvious way to stimulate action on the part of the members of an organization is to use the "action or else!" approach. Although this approach may be used from time to time, stimulation assumes a more intelligent methodology. By arousing the interest of his staff in the solution of problems, by recognizing success in overt ways, by establishing an institutional loyalty and an *esprit de corps*, in these and other ways the effective principal stimulates his staff to work for the solution of problems in the ways decided upon earlier. It is apparent that procedures used in the decision-making and programming phases of the administrative process will play a major role in determining the extent to which the principal can stimulate the action necessary to carry out the planned program. Unless teachers are aware of the reasons underlying the actions they are asked to take, the degree of enthusiasm with which they act will be considerably less than ideal.

It may be necessary for the administrator to exert certain pressures to achieve some results with some people, but if pressure becomes his only means of stimulation, it will, in the long run, be hampered. Stimulation is essentially a matter of building attitudes. Although pressure may get one job done, it may also build attitudes that will make future stimulation extremely difficult.

Coordinating

As any high school principal will gladly testify, any single action in a high school is related to a whole series of other events. Although this fact is considered and, hopefully, taken care of in the programming phase of the administrative process, the principal must constantly be aware of the need for coordinating actions once they are begun. In our example of the problem of high school–college articulation, it was apparent that more than one person would be involved in the actions proposed to help solve the problem. The principal needs to assure himself that these people are working together, that supplies and equipment are arriving as planned, that other parts of the school program are not being handicapped by actions taken to solve this one problem, and that, in general, the new activities are blending into the total program of the school.

One of the most difficult tasks of any administrator, and particularly of the high school principal, is to "keep in harness" a team of professional staff members, each of whom is legitimately striving to further a special field of interest and each of whom is likely to feel that his field of interest is more important than any others in reaching the goals. The better the staff, the more difficult this coordination process becomes.

Many times a teacher will become so engrossed in a new venture that even though this venture represents but a portion of that teacher's assignment, it is given an undue amount of time and effort by the teacher. The principal, as he fulfills the requirements of the coordinating phase of the administrative process, is the person who must keep an eye on the total school operation as it relates to the complex of goals. He needs to strive for balance, without unduly hampering the enthusiasm of a good teaching staff.

It is also necessary for the principal to keep abreast of activities outside of the school that may need to be coordinated with in-school programs. It may be, for example, that a group of colleges might start new freshmen programs in an effort to improve high school–college articulation. How do these relate to the new high school programs? Are the gaps being narrowed or widened? Is unnecessary duplication introduced? Coordination is more than an intramural affair. The principal will find this phase of the administrative process a challenging and demanding part of his work.

Appraising

The final step in the administrative process, and a step that completes a circular rather than a straight-line process, is appraising. It is here that the administrator must ask himself some crucial questions; and it is here that invariably new problems will be identified, which lead in turn to another round through the administrative process. A decision has been made, a program established, and action stimulated and coordinated. All of this was done for a purpose. The appraising phase represents an effort to determine the extent to which all of this has actually met the purpose.

Appraising is perhaps the least well done phase of the administrative process in the schools. This is true not because educational administrators do not believe in appraising school activities, but primarily because the need for appraising is recognized too late to build a framework for appraisal into activities. Appraising must be done in terms of some predetermined criteria—some yardsticks to measure change. Although the term "criteria" may seem quite "textbookish," the concept it connotes is a most practical one.

Take our earlier example. The principal wanted to do something to improve high school–college articulation. If he is to be able to appraise the effectiveness of the actions he takes or others take to improve this articulation, he must have a measuring device for this appraisal. Before the new efforts are started, he will need to know the state of articulation between his high school and the colleges concerned. This state of articulation will need to be expressed in terms of some observable factors, for example, how do the graduates of his high school succeed, in terms of grade point averages, in their freshman year at college? Or, what percentage of the graduates from his high school who enter college continue on to earn a bachelor's degree? Or again, how do the graduates of his high school succeed in terms of grade averages in various subject-matter fields in college? These are not presented as ideal measures of high school–college articulation, but are merely examples of the kinds of data that are necessary to provide a base line for appraisal.

The program designed to improve articulation should be designed to bring about some specific changes from the base line. In other words, today our situation in terms of these factors is "thus and so"; after a few months or years of the new program, we want our situation in terms of these factors to be "this." Appraising, then, becomes a matter of determining the extent to which actual progress from the base line is equivalent to desired progress. The factors used to define the baseline plus some quantitative and qualitative statements of desired progress are the criteria that underlie the appraising phase of the administrative process.

It is important to recognize some measure of institutional stability. Suppose, for example, that real progress is achieved in improving the college records of the graduates from a high school, but that the teachers of courses not considered to be "college preparatory" feel that they are being ignored, that they are not receiving their share of the budget, and that guidance counselors are ignoring the noncollegebound student. These latter judgments may be of much greater long-range importance than is the fact of the improved college records.

Appraising, then, involves a consideration of both long- and short-range goals. It should also involve a consideration of the process used in developing the program being appraised. The program may appear to be successful, but was it established with a minimum of wasted effort or of "spinning of wheels"? Were the right people involved at the right time in establishing the program? Were details involving the requisition of supplies or the procurement of equipment handled with dispatch? These and other questions need to be asked as the administrative process itself is appraised.

In brief, the appraising phase of the administrative process involves an appraisal of the effectiveness of a specific course of action in meeting a specific problem, an appraisal of the degree to which a specific course of action has influenced the way in which a school proceeds toward long-range goals, and an appraisal of the way in which the administrative process functioned during the development and implementation of the specific course of action. This is not a job to be handled single-handedly by the administrator. Here, again, many people will need to be involved.

One final word about appraising needs to be said. Too often we neglect to appraise school activities on the grounds that it is not possible to be objective enough. All appraising has subjective features. The very definition of what we will consider to be improvement (in other words, our choice of criteria) is a judgmental process based on certain professional beliefs, understandings, and aspirations. Appraising will never be wholly objective. Relative values must be assigned certain findings, and progress must be judged in terms of other related factors. The aim is to have an appraisal plan, to make this plan as sound as is possible, and to use the appraisal plan to lead into new action programs. School activities need to be purposeful and, in the long run, purposeful activities need to be based on careful appraisals of previous activities and their results.

The total process

We have now examined each of the steps in the administrative process. Before going on to new considerations, it is important to look at the total process once again. It is apparent that the process is cyclical. A problem is recognized and then the process, from decision-making through appraisal, is brought to bear on the problem. The appraisal step will identify new needs, which call for new decisions, and the cycle begins again.

It is also necessary to note that the administrative process is used in meeting all the problems that face the principal as he performs his administrative tasks. At any given point in time, the principal will be following different steps in the process as he deals with different problems. He may be considering alternative proposals for action to deal with a curriculum problem (decision-making) and in the next hour be considering the success of a new internal accounting plan (appraising). He may follow this with the development of assignments to implement a new plan for supervising after-school activities (programming) and then spend some time writing some letters to thank a group of parents for assisting in the early stages of a school recreation program (stimulating). During all of this, the principal may very well have been considering in his mind the relative time that staff members are devoting to each of these various activities (coordinating). Certainly, as he goes from job to job, the principal will not be saying to himself, "Now I'll coordinate and next I'll decision-make!" But whether he knows it or not, the successful principal will, as he goes from job to job and task area to task area, be following the steps of the administrative process.

CONCLUSION

This chapter has dealt primarily with abstractions and with concepts. Subsequent chapters will deal much more consistently than has this one with the ways in which these concepts are put into action by the principal in the schools. It is our conviction, however, that the principal in action needs to be a man who understands the conceptual framework that underlies and guides his administrative behavior.

The principal is faced daily with the tasks of administration. Only rarely is he asked in his daily work to explain his concept of leadership, to explain the purposes of and necessity for leadership, or to describe the administrative process he uses as he attacks the administrative tasks. Because of this, the principal sometimes confuses the frequency of occurrence of something with the measurement of its importance. Because he is often faced with the necessity of planning faculty meetings, for example, the principal, in many cases, feels that it is more important that someone tell him exactly how to plan such a meeting than it is that someone discuss with him the concepts that underlie his role as he plans faculty meetings. It is our contention that the latter kind of explanation should, in the long run, lead to better faculty meetings than will the former.

Hunt and Pierce support this idea in the following statement:

> Administrators too frequently depend upon experience, descriptions of practices, or the following of particular patterns for solving problems that develop suddenly or difficulties that they encounter in the course of their work. They should strive to sense problems in advance and *through the use of principles* develop and carry through appropriate procedures for their solution . . . New problems will occur that have no counterpart in previous experiences; whether they will be met with guesses or intuition, or *with procedures indicated by principles*, is a mark of the professional training and effectiveness of the school administrator [italics ours].[14]

This chapter has dealt with concepts and with principles. As we move ahead to consider the task areas of administration, it is important

[14] Herold C. Hunt and Paul R. Pierce, *The Practice of School Administration* (Boston: Houghton Mifflin Company, 1958), p. 15.

to remember that this volume is not a "how-to" manual for secondary school principals. The suggestions made here will need to be modified— or discarded—in terms of the situation in which the principal finds himself and in terms of his understandings of the nature, purpose, and process of educational administration.

SUGGESTED ACTIVITIES

1. Describe a situation that you have observed in which the status leader was not the actual leader. Indicate who assumed actual leadership. Explain why you think this happened.

2. Describe the various sources of authority of a secondary school principal.

3. Some teachers express themselves as being in favor of a principal who is an "enlightened dictator." How would you account for this preference? Do you feel that some principals need to fit this description? Why or why not?

4. Describe some methods that you feel would be effective in stimulating teachers to participate in community affairs in a medium-sized or small city or town.

5. Briefly outline an administrative problem and indicate the ways in which the steps of the administrative process would be followed in working with this problem and the proposed solution.

SELECTED READINGS

Barnard, Chester I., *Functions of the Executive*. Cambridge: Harvard University Press, 1938.

Gibb, Cecil A., "Leadership," *Handbook of Social Psychology*, Volume II, edited by Gardner Lindzey. Reading, Mass.: Addison-Wesley Publishing Company, Inc., 1954. Pp. 877–920.

Gregg, Russell T., "The Administrative Process," *Administrative Behavior in Education*, edited by Roald F. Campbell and Russell T. Gregg. New York: Harper & Row, Publishers, 1957. Chapter 8.

Gulick, Luther, and L. Urwick, *Papers on the Science of Administration*. New York: Institute of Public Administration, 1937. Chapter 1.

Hemphill, John K., et al., *Administrative Performance and Personality*. New York: Bureau of Publications, Teachers College, Columbia University, 1962.

Hunt, Herold C., and Paul R. Pierce, *The Practice of School Administration*. Boston: Houghton Mifflin Company, 1958. Chapters I, II, and X.

Jenson, T. J., and D. L. Clark, *Educational Administration*. New York: Center for Applied Research in Education, Inc., 1964. Chapters 3, 4, and 5.

Miller, Van, *The Public Administration of American School Systems*. New York: The Macmillan Co., 1965. Chapter 19.

Newman, William H., *Administrative Action*. Englewood Cliffs, N.J.: Prentice-Hall, Inc., 1951.

Sears, Jesse B., *The Nature of the Administrative Process*. New York: McGraw-Hill, Inc., 1950.

Simon, Herbert A., *Administrative Behavior*. New York: The Macmillan Company, 1950. Chapter I.

Tead, Ordway, *The Art of Administration*. New York: McGraw-Hill Book Co., 1951.

Weber, C. A., and Mary E. Weber, *Fundamentals of Educational Leadership*. New York: McGraw-Hill, Inc., 1955.

4

ADMINISTRATIVE
TEAMWORK

PART ONE OF THIS VOLUME IS CONCERNED WITH THE
perceptions of the *job* of secondary school administration, the position,
the office, and the over-all responsibility involved in the profession of
the principalship. Incidents, descriptions of the spatial environment and
the discussion on leadership provide beginning bases for a more accurate
perception of the job. But, as experienced administrators know and
neophytes soon learn, a true perception of the responsibilities of the
principal is most illusive and dependent upon many variables.

A number of principals, teachers, students and parents were polled
recently to obtain perceptions of the image of the high school principal.
The responses were both amazing and interesting. Try it sometime. Some
of the more common reactions indicated the following: (1) the job and
responsibilities of the principal are perceived as specific performances

and behaviors; (2) perceptions vary widely among the groups polled; (3) the principal's perceptions of their jobs varied markedly; and (4) the commonalities among the perceptions included concepts of "leadership," "head of the school," "manager," "in charge of," "responsible for," and "authority over."

As a further dimension of the position of the principalship, this chapter suggests that the job of administering a modern high school is a *shared obligation*—a team effort. Responsibility finds expression through behaviors, tasks, duty assignments, performances and functions. These are alluded to here as means of implementation, but in succeeding chapters they are discussed in the frame of reference of task areas.

A rationale is presented here for the shared or teamwork concept of administration. Some commonly accepted ideas about administration are discussed and related to the administration of secondary education. Problems of administrative teamwork are discussed, including some pitfalls. Finally, we stress the point that the job and responsibilities of the principal cannot be so completely proliferated, shared and democratized that his leadership becomes a limbo.

Teamwork is imperative in the modern administrative organization. Size, complexity, functional expectancies, distribution of responsibilities, specialization of function, operational patterns, and concerns over efficiency and organizational structuring of enterprises, all have brought on a proliferation of administrative positions, titles, assignments, and responsibilities. The one-man show in administration is as outdated as the Model T Ford. Even if we were to ignore size and modern organization and construct for ourselves an administrative job that could conceivably pass as a one-man operation, we would be obliged to take into account the findings of research in the administrative and behavioral sciences, which indicate several advantages of shared responsibility and involvement of others in the administrative processes. Can you imagine a situation, involving several people, where one man can effectively do all the decision-making, the programing, the stimulating, the coordinating, and the appraising? Note we have used the word "effectively." Yet you will probably say, "Yes, I know of a situation in a high school just exactly as described like that, where the principal does the thinking for everybody." So do we. Let us look at one.

This particular situation involves a small high school where the principal, a benevolent dictator, ran a fair high school until two or three years ago, when he retired. The staff had learned to love the old man. Nothing was done without his specific approval. He delegated no authority. He saw no need for study committees, or any other kinds of committees. When he had to be out of town, no one was in charge, except perhaps his secretary, who second-guessed for him part of the time. He did not want an assistant principal and saw no need for department heads or any other administrative assistance. Under his philosophy of leadership and administration the administrative processes were his responsibility and his alone. He had no concern about teamwork, administrative or otherwise.

Three years ago this principal was succeeded by a young man with limited administrative experience but with many theories of staff involvement in administration and a somewhat naive belief in the group process. His theory was to relegate completely the administrative process to committee action, to what he called shared responsibility and involvement in administration. But he had inherited a staff with a minimum of experience in sharing in decision-making, planning, coordinating, and appraising.

His first act was to create a series of committees and committee chairmen with delegated responsibilities and authorities. Staff members, accustomed to the old procedures, began taking their problems to the new principal only to be told that the problem would have to be brought before a certain committee for action. Committees began making decisions that created new problems, for which more committees were established. In some instances, one committee countermanded the decisions of another committee. The entire process became so involved that one teacher was heard to say that to get permission to put a thumbtack in the bulletin board called for a committee meeting. On the side the staff members began calling the new principal "Committeeitus Jones." After two years in the position Jones saw fit to move on, we hope a wiser man for the experiences he had encountered.

The situation described here was extreme in that it involved two distinctly opposite points of view on teamwork and staff involvement in administration and secondly that an experienced staff was called upon to make a radical shift in operation. Any observer could detect the factors in the situation described that eventually lead to a failure of what might normally be considered good administrative practice. The most obvious thing, of course, is that teamwork is rarely the result of accident; it must be anticipated, planned for, and constantly nurtured. The new principal plummeted his staff into a theoretical framework of operation far beyond their experience and without proper readiness, planning, programing, and coordination. Given another year or two, things might have worked out for him, but in the meantime he lost the staff's respect as an administrator and leader.

IDEAS ON ADMINISTRATION

Although this book is directed toward school administration and particularly toward secondary school administration, the students should see this special field in relation to the work of administrators generally. Obviously, whenever men engage in purposeful activity of any sort they organize it, sometimes to lighten the work involved, sometimes to improve or increase achievement and productivity. Men organize even their simplest tasks.

Take a simple job, such as sorting apples, involving only one person, apples, and containers. The job is relatively simple: put the red apples in one box, the green ones in another, and the culls in a third. Yet a man learns that through simple analysis and experience he can make the work easier by rearranging the containers with reference to himself and the pile of apples. So he organizes his work.

If organization works for one man and his job, organization works for a team of workers. With several workers on the job there can be a division of labor, which provides opportunities for each person to perform the tasks most commensurate with his particular skills. The size and complexity of the operation magnify the place and importance of organization and administration. The assembly line requires planning, coordination, timing, and attention to details; that is, it requires organization. Hence, it is clear that the processes of organization and administration are closely interrelated, and the larger the enterprise, the greater the need for organization and administration.

The factor of bigness

Competition, costs, efficiency standards, population trends, urbanization, and other socioeconomic factors appear to be pushing us relentlessly toward "bigness." We are moving from small, inefficient administrative units to larger administrative units, larger factories, mergers and combines that make ever greater demands on organization and administration. It is certain that some school organizations are too small to provide economical optimum educational opportunities and services. The authors believe a good secondary school requires an enrollment of at least 500 students. With a smaller enrollment, a quality program becomes exorbitantly expensive. There is little evidence that indicates optimum relationships of size to effectiveness, but there is evidence that indicates that the problems of organization, management, and administration definitely increase with the size and complexity of an enterprise.

The administrative function

Organization and administration are interrelated and interdependent. Organization can be defined as a phase of the process of effectively accomplishing purposes whose achievement requires the continuous physical and mental output that we call work. The other phase of this process is administration. The organizational phase deals with making arrangements that permit the beginning of purpose realization. Sometimes organization is, in effect, reorganization. Sometimes it is coordination. "The major purpose of organization is coordination," says Luther Gulick.[1]

The administrative phase of the process of purpose achievement is concerned with the conduct, operation, control, and management of the enterprise as organized so that the purposes continue to be satisfied. Thus, the two phases complement each other. In reality, the organization phase logically precedes the administrative phase. The school administrator is accountable for both phases; and in practice he combines the two concepts into "administration."

Major general tasks *(Read)*

So far we have explored some general aspects of administration and organization, which are applicable to both educational and noneducational enterprises. The administrative process as applied to educational administration was explored in detail in Chapter 3. Chapter 8 will focus on administrative tasks of the secondary school principal. Broadly conceived, the task areas in educational administration are (1) school-community relationships, (2) curriculum development, (3) pupil personnel, (4) staff personnel, (5) physical facilities, (6) finance and business management, and (7) organization and structure.[2] These are broad areas in which the principal will find many specific tasks to perform. Obviously he cannot and will not perform all of these tasks himself. Here is where organization enters the picture. There must be a division of

[1] Luther Gulick and Lyndall Urwick (eds.), *Papers on the Science of Administration* (New York: Institute of Public Administration, Columbia University, 1937), p. 33.

[2] Roald F. Campbell, John E. Corbally, Jr., and John A. Ramseyer, *Introduction to Educational Administration* (Boston: Allyn and Bacon, Inc., 1958), p. 85.

labor. The administrator may have an assistant principal, who will have charge of pupil personnel and other assignments. There will probably be heads of departments. There will be assistance from the central office on matters of curriculum. A staff member may be assigned part-time to some aspects of school-community relations and so on. What really exists in such a situation is a team of workers, each with specific tasks to perform, all directed toward achieving the over-all purposes of the school.

It is this team approach that we wish to discuss in the pages to follow. The principal is the key man in the team. The qualities, expectancies, and traits of a good leader have been discussed in detail in previous chapters. Our attention here will be focused on the concept of administrative teamwork, components of the team, teamwork techniques, pitfalls in administrative teamwork, and administrative responsibilities in the team approach to administration.

CONCEPT OF ADMINISTRATIVE TEAMWORK

Teamwork is not a new concept; it requires no elaborate definition. Experience in teamwork constantly teaches us new things about the dynamics of corporate effort. One coach described his football team recently in these words, "We have a lot of good talent out there and the boys are willing and work hard but they just have not 'jelled' as a team yet." What did he mean—"jelled"? Not being coaches, we can only imagine that he meant that the boys needed experience in learning their individual assignments, coordinating their assignments with each other, learning what to expect of each other player, and timing the operation to execute the play with smoothness and finesse. There are many good administrative teams that are in much the same situation as was the football team just described—good talent, able, willing, but not "jelled" as yet.

Identification of the total objective

In football, the ultimate objective is scoring. This is true in spite of what we sometimes hear about the character-building objectives of the sport. In educational administration the total objective is more involved and complicated, for it is the sum of a number of subobjectives. Sometimes the subobjective overshadows the larger objective or gets lost in the day-to-day operations. For instance, economy is sometimes placed ahead of what might be best for boys and girls, or, on the other hand, ignored. Often this is a matter of attitude or the lack of a proper attitude. The principal, the department head, or any other member of the administrative team feels burdened with his responsibilities and opines, "I have enough worries running my own show and I cannot be bothered with the broader aspects of administration in this school system." This is obviously a limited view of the total objective, which definitely hampers the individual's effectiveness as a member of the administrative team. It is the specific duty of the administrator, then, to help each team member gain a clear understanding of the total objectives and those attitudes that will make him an effective contributor to the group effort.

Total objective as a discipline

Crash programs and tremendous team efforts have wrought miraculous developments in this age of atomic energy and man-made satellites orbiting about in the universe. In these efforts the total objective was very clear to every man involved. Many talents were brought together, briefed thoroughly on the main objective, briefed on the subobjectives of each member of the team, and then directed to come through with results that made sense. Although the process was undoubtedly much more complicated than this brief analysis would indicate, it has implications for educational administrative teamwork.

After a certain accomplishment in one of these programs, one of the team workers was asked what it was that kept the team working and trying, failing and trying again, until ultimate success. His answer is worthy of note; he said it was the discipline of the ultimate objective. Every man knew that everything depended on his small part of the project working and functioning perfectly, and that failure anywhere was failure for the entire objective. Thus, the ultimate objective was the driving discipline that motivated every member of the team to do his utmost and best.

Providing quality education may not be as glamorous as producing a space station, but it is an objective capable of taxing, challenging, and disciplining the best minds and talents available for its realization.

Delegation implications

Every man on the team must have a specifically delegated assignment, a clear understanding of his role, an understanding of the roles of the other players. Everyone must operate within the limits of his prescribed responsibility. Normally, in the school situation, titles reflect the duties, roles, and responsibilities of various administrative personnel; but this cannot be taken for granted. At this very moment, many assistant principals in secondary schools throughout the country are just not sure of where their authority and responsibilities begin or end. No clear-cut job analysis has been made, and the delegation of responsibilities to them has been left pretty much to chance. There are some definite things for which the assistant principal is responsible—attendance, substitute teachers, records, and the like, but there are many areas in which the assistant's role may not be clear. These areas are the sources of trouble and frustration. A person can hardly be an effective member of the team when he is unsure of his role, when he hesitates or feels that he has to clear with the man above before he acts.

The successful administrator delegates. He makes sure that the person to whom responsibility and authority are delegated understands. He also insists that the delegation is respected by himself and others, that is, that the areas of delegated responsibility are not invaded by others or by himself.

Communication concerns

Few things are more disastrous to team effort than to have communications break down. Communication must be multi-dimensional. That is, the flow must be to and from communicants and shared with others as the situation requires. It is the responsibility of the administrator to see that channels of communication are established and that they are used effectively and efficiently. Knower and Wagner, in studying communications in educational administration, found that administrators checked the following communications problems more frequently than teachers:

Know that he may be a poor judge of his own communication.
Understand that failure to respond to a communication may arise from differences in interpretation as well as from its opposition.
Provide opportunities for regular communication among subordinates.
Blame others for his own failures in communication.
Make use of his position to seek out and provide sources of information about communication and its nature which helps his people improve.
Clearly show the reasons for his decisions and policies.
Talk in a manner that clearly fits the purpose of his communication.
Select a time and place for the communication carefully because of the meaning they add to the message.
Talk or write about a problem which he can correct by more satisfactory direct action.
Show that he realizes that subordinates are especially alert to all physical cues and nonverbal signals.
Use communication to prevent as well as solve conflicts.
Know that in communication success depends on whether others accept him.

Make use of visual aids, charts, diagrams, and sketches.

Keep a record of all communication and decisions of policy.

See to it that official papers and reports concerning the school are carefully edited.

Use many methods of communication because no one method meets all needs.

Fix responsibility for special types of communication and/or delegate them to persons most able to carry them out.

Give new direction and motivation for a program which has bogged down.

Show appreciation for cooperation of fellow workers.[3]

The implications of these responses appear to indicate that (1) administrators are more apt to see the items above as concerns about communication, than are other professional workers; and (2) administrators, in general, are sensitive to the needs for good communication, and the problems of maintaining effective communications in administrative relationships. The relationship of communication to shared obligations of administration is patently obvious.

Characteristics of teamwork

Volumes have been written on teamwork and its various facets, and it is somewhat presumptuous on our part to summarize all the good ideas here in a paragraph or two. However, a brief recapitulation of some of the important characteristics follows:

1. Teamwork should demonstrate effective leadership.

2. Team members should have a predisposition to work as a team.

3. A democratic atmosphere should prevail.

4. A high level of cooperation should be maintained.

5. Full and effective communications should prevail.

6. There should be mutual acceptance of the goals of the team.

7. There should be high morale.

8. Team members should have faith in each other.

9. Mutual respect for members of the team should exist.

10. A high degree of dedication to goals and purposes should exist.

[3] Franklin H. Knower and Paul H. Wagner, *Communication In Educational Administration* (Columbus, Ohio: Center for Educational Administration, The Ohio State University, 1959), p. 157.

11. There should be acceptance of individual responsibilities for furthering team objectives.

12. Clear definitions of roles and assignments of team members should exist.

13. The team members should be able to adjust to the new and unexpected.

14. Team members should continually evaluate and assess team effort.

15. There should be signs of high motivation.

16. Team members should demonstrate good coordination.

17. The team should achieve respect and backing by earning it.

18. The team should rise above unfavorable circumstances.

19. The team should demonstrate ability for decisive action.

20. The team should make use of experience to improve and refine practices.

An administrative team that scores high on these characteristics is well on its way to success.

THE TEAM

A team, by common definition, is a group of people organized to work cooperatively to accomplish a purpose or objective. This presumes a division of labor; a one-horse team cannot exist. There are always two or more people involved in any team effort, with all of the psychological and sociological implications of a group—social interaction, shared responsibility, give and take, leadership transfer, dependence, to mention just a few. The team imposes its own social controls upon itself and responds as well to exterior social controls. Team members have expectancies of other members of the group; at the same time, others outside of the team have expectancies of the team as a unit. Also, there may be other teams that have expectancies of a team or group.

All this takes on meaning as we relate it to the over-all administrative team operation in the school system, which includes central administration, the high schools, junior high schools, elementary schools, and any other of the subdivisions; the administrative team of the secondary school or any other individual unit; and the relations and interactions of these several administrative teams in the system with each other and the over-all administrative team. It sounds complicated and it is. Although our primary concern is with the administrative team of the secondary school, we must see it in relation to the whole social system in which it functions.

The central administrative team

The over-all administrative team for the school system, often referred to as the superintendent's cabinet, usually includes the top administrative heads—assistant superintendents, supervisors, principals, directors, and the like. In a very real sense, the superintendent's team has the administrative responsibilities for the complete educational enterprise in the community.

As a major unit in the school system, the secondary school is represented on the superintendent's administrative team through the secondary school principal. Although the concerns of this group generally are those of the entire system, many decisions are made that affect the secondary school. Issues involving coordination, general policy-making and interpretation, articulation, supervision, curriculum development, public relations, finance, organization, and other over-all phases of operation and control make up the bulk of agenda items for the central administration team.

The secondary school principal has a dual team role to play here. In one instance, he has the responsibility for representing the secondary school on the central administrative team. On the other hand, he must identify himself with the unit or school administrative team as a member and leader. He must maintain loyalties to both of his team activities. This is not always an easy task.

The principal is expected to represent his school in his role on the central administrative team. However, he must be conscious of other divisions and units in the organization and of the over-all purposes and concerns of the system. This does not mean that the principal should be a complete neutral, but it does suggest that being a good member of the central team poses problems and situational difficulties that must be appreciated and understood by the principal, the central administrative team, the secondary school staff, and the community.

The secondary school administrative team

The autocratic type of secondary school administration is *passé*. In its place is democratic leadership, with wide involvement in decision-making, policy formulation, and administration. Naturally, the first essential to the democratic process in any situation is a predisposition of all, and especially of the status leader, to operate and function under principles and policies conducive to democracy. Occasionally, some staff members, tired with committee meetings and group decision-making, question wide staff involvement in administration. Fortunately, the majority of staff members want the opportunity to share in matters concerning them.

Who should be on the secondary school administrative team? In the very small school, this is not a major problem. Everyone on the staff has a face-to-face relationship with the principal and practically every teacher can be included in a team approach.

The large secondary school, with many staff members, presents a more difficult situation with regard to involvement in administration. Without necessarily being designated as such, the nucleus of the administrative team in the large school consists of the titled administrative staff—assistant principals, deans, directors, and the like.

Many principals desire more involvement in the administrative team and have worked out a variety of measures to bring more staff members in on decision-making affecting the school and faculty. We shall examine two such plans, among many, that appear to have proven satisfactory.

House plan in a high school. Brookline, Massachusetts, has a secondary school with an enrollment of about 2200 students. As the principal explored ideas for staff involvement and representation on the administrative team, he borrowed an idea from Harvard College—the House Plan.[4] The school was divided into four subadministrative units, one for each grade level. The "housemasters" are chosen from the school faculty; each has an assistant of the opposite sex, chosen from the faculty of each house. In the Brookline version of this plan, housemasters teach part time and are given some extra compensation for the extra duty involved in their administrative roles. This plan places eight additional members on the principal's administrative team, along with regularly titled administrative personnel. The plan clearly extends the involvement of staff on the administrative team and provides an orderly way of determining team membership.

Imaginative principals will find many ways of implementing the above idea. Grade levels are only one of several more or less natural classifications that might be considered in a large school. One secondary school has worked out a similar scheme based on a functional division—academic, vocational, and general courses offered by the large comprehensive school. In this instance, the directors of divisions are elected by staff and hold status equal to that of the assistant principal. These direc-

---

[4] Ernest R. Caverly, "House Plan in a High School," _School Executive,_ November 1959, p. 54.

tors teach part time and receive extra remuneration for extra duty as members of the administrative team.

Principal's administrative advisory council. Both large and small secondary schools have successfully used some form of a principal's advisory council to extend the team concept of administration and provide wider involvement in the process. In one school, with an enrollment of 1400 students and a staff of 65 teachers, an advisory council of ten is elected by staff to serve on the administrative team.[5] Elections are for two years, with five new members elected each year, thus providing continuity in the group. The council meets regularly with the administrative personnel of the school. Their function is advisory rather than legislative. Administrative concerns and problems are placed before them for review and consultation. Likewise, members of the council bring up matters that have come to their attention. Minutes are kept of all proceedings. Ultimate responsibilities and decisions, however, are assumed by the principal, according to his legal responsibility as head of the school, but with the aid of a representative team of advisors closely allied to operations.

Occasionally, where it seems advisable, officers of the student government association are asked to sit in with the council to present student points of view. For instance, when the traditional "Hobo Day," (a surprise day, which usually coincided with other evidences of spring fever, when students would come to school dressed as hobos) seemed to be going to extremes, the advisory council and the student council worked out a "Dress-up Day," which proved to be much more satisfactory to all.

In the same situation, the principal involved parents on the administrative team through the development of a Parents' Advisory Council. Through homeroom meetings eight parents from each grade level were elected to serve on the Council. This group meets with the principal on call or at stipulated meetings quarterly throughout the school year. Here, again, the group is advisory rather than legislative, but it often assumes the role of an action group in marshaling parent assistance for school functions and affairs.

On some major administrative concerns, such as planning a new building, the annual prom, student driving and safety, the principal calls into action parent, student, and staff advisory groups to work as a team in assisting in decision-making and policy formulation.

The secondary school administrative team, as envisioned here, may assume a variety of forms. These are the mechanics of implementing the idea. The alert principal will give leadership in providing ways to extend

[5] Shorewood High School, Shorewood, Wisconsin.

involvement in administrative functions and processes. There is great need for experimentation and refinement of techniques for involving people in team efforts to improve constantly the effectiveness of administration in secondary education.

PITFALLS

A number of what appeared to be good examples of administrative teamwork have run into difficulties because certain precautions were not observed. There are many situations, circumstances, acts of commission and omission that spell trouble for team activity. Many of these obstacles are obvious; others are more deepseated and subtle. Many times they take the form of a creeping paralysis that gains momentum and accomplishes much harm before it is discovered.

Size

The number involved in the team activity has a direct relation to the potential for difficulties in the team operation. In a simple matter, such as scheduling meetings, it is much harder for a large group than for a small group to find a time when all can get together. If meetings are held with several absences, communication breaks down, the team is deprived of the contributions of the absentees, absentees have to be briefed on what took place at the last meeting, and so on. Thus, although wide involvement in the team effort is a desirable goal, of itself it poses possible difficulties in scheduling, communication, and coordination. Group productivity and possibilities for effective interaction break down in large groups unless extreme care is exercised.

How differently would you handle the matter of shared administrative obligations in North Central Senior High School with 135 teachers and Poloma Union High with 21 teachers? Is the town meeting technique, involving the entire faculty, appropriate on some matters in either or both schools? At what point in size of operation does one need to consider the viability of representative committees? Group dynamists have several answers and suggestions that should be thoroughly explored.

Although there are certain obstacles to effective teamwork in the large group, confining administrative teamwork to a small group also has its distinct disadvantages. Disenfranchisement cuts deeply. Even though advantages of representation, once provided, are not exercised as well as might be desired, it is better to have provided the opportunity. For example, a likely trap for the principal to fall into is to select a few of the experienced members of the staff to confide in and use as an inner cabinet. When the newer teachers find they are being left out on decision-making, a staff rift is in the making. In such a situation, not only the size of the group but also its exclusiveness was a factor. Clearly, then, size and representativeness are factors to be carefully considered.

Faulty communication

Effective communication has been mentioned as a necessary ingredient to effective teamwork. Faulty communication is devastating to teamwork. Two aspects of communication that are subject to shortcomings are communication within the group and communication between the group and the larger community it serves. Unless high level communication is maintained between members of the group, effective teamwork cannot be sustained; faulty communication between the administrative team and those it serves tends to nullify much of the team effort.

Losing sight of major purposes

Major purposes have a way of getting lost in everyday operations. One of the responsibilities of the principal is to assist the administrative team to keep purposes and major objectives clearly in focus, to recognize attainment of goals, and to establish new targets. Occasionally it is an individual on the team who needs assistance in keeping the goal in sight.

Conflicts in job analysis

Careful attention to job analysis and the resolution of conflicts arising from misunderstandings about responsibilities may be necessary now and then in order to maintain effective administrative teamwork. Here is one scheme that has worked for some. A member of the team, faced with the possibility of conflict as to tasks and responsibility does three things: (1) lists in writing the things for which he feels he is responsible and for which he feels he is in full authority to make decisions; (2) lists in writing the things for which he feels responsibility and about which he makes decisions, but for which he feels the necessity for reporting his actions to his superior; and (3) lists in writing the responsibilities and actions that he feels are his, but for which he must seek clearance before taking the action. These are then discussed with his superior, conflicts resolved, and agreements reached.

Whether the conflict is between the team and a member or between an individual and his superior, a review of the lists described above may clear up many misunderstandings, which, if unresolved, have adverse effects.

Indefinite delegation

Delegation of responsibilities is sometimes tenuous and indefinite. The earliest signs of difficulty in this regard should be dealt with promptly if a deteriorating effect on teamwork is to be avoided. There should be complete understanding with regard to whom responsibilities are assigned.

A wise administrator avoids putting his team to maximum tests until it is seasoned. Experience helps the team to see its potentials, its weaknesses and mistakes, and its most effective operational patterns. Smooth, well-coordinated administrative teamwork requires continuous attention and maintenance.

The team or group is a living social organization, subject to the many psychological and sociological phenomena. The principal, as leader of the team, must be a student of the group process, skilled in the dynamics of group leadership, and constantly reappraising his role and efforts to use the team approach in administration of the school.

INTEGRITY OF LEADERSHIP

What of all this democracy and teamwork in administration? Are we envisioning the principal as merely a glorified chairman? Must everything be decided by committee, by teams? Where is the integrity of leadership? How does it function in the administrative team concept?

These are reasonable questions. The value and effectiveness of administrative teamwork is largely dependent on how the administrator conceives his leadership role with the group, the quality of leadership given the administrative team, and the integrity of the leader. There is a great deal of difference between the administrator with an idea who "hands it down for approval," and the one who "passes it on for study and development." Certainly there must be found a way for the leader to infuse good ideas into the teamwork process.

Unloading

Integrity of leadership is not maintained where the leader chooses to unload responsibility and blame on the administrative team. This is likewise true of all members of the team. Instances have been known where the principal, after being a party to making a decision, when faced with enforcing and implementing it, comes up with this explanation, "This is not necessarily my idea; in fact, I am in complete sympathy with your point of view, but it is policy and all I can do is be guided by it." This is not integrity. Once a decision was made and he was a party to it on the administrative team, he is obligated to support it. He might have said, "We realized that there are several points of view on this matter. These were discussed and weighed but the decision is this, and we will be guided by the decision."

The administrator who hides behind the group process in decision-making is a weakling. He runs grave risks of losing any respect he may have as a status leader, to say nothing of the respect held for him as a functional leader. The same is true for any member of the administrative team.

Extending administrative service

Administration has a service function to perform in any organization. Unless the administrative team extends and augments this service function it has missed the goal. The principal should not look upon his administrative team as a "buck passing" mechanism to assume his role and function. Rather, it should be an assist, an aid, an extension to provide better the services intended and expected. It is not an administration by committee, but an administration by a principal aided by a representative committee in arriving at decisions affecting the entire group.

In spite of all the assistance he can muster from wide and devious sources, ultimate decisions are the prerogative and responsibility of the principal. He must have the integrity to assume his role to the best of his ability.

CONCLUSION

Shared responsibility for administration has become an imperative in modern administrative organization. The demands and dimensions of administrative services require the team approach.

Both in business and education, shared responsibility for administrative services will grow and increase with the ever-mounting complexity of organizations. Much more needs to be learned about administrative team operation. Effective involvement of persons for any function is a complex task. There are tremendous opportunities for secondary school principals to exercise imagination and experimentation leading to new knowledge, improved techniques, and more efficiency in the practical operation of administrative teamwork as related to the secondary school.

SUGGESTED ACTIVITIES

1. What factors should be taken into consideration in selecting individuals to serve on an administrative team?

2. To what extent and under what circumstances is every staff person a part of the administrative team?

3. What would you suggest to improve the situation in the secondary school discussed earlier in the chapter, where Mr. Jones has assumed the principalship?

4. What pitfalls to administrative teamwork, other than those discussed in this chapter, do you see?

5. Why is maintenance such a vital factor in the smooth operation of the administrative team?

6. What are some of the ways in which an administrative team can be truly an extension of administrative service?

7. Explore the possibilities of shared obligation for administration beyond the immediate school or unit.

SELECTED READINGS

Austin, David B., Will French, and Dan J. Hull, *American High School Administration.* New York: Holt, Rinehart & Winston, Inc., 1962.

Campbell, Roald F., John E. Corbally, Jr., and John A. Ramseyer, *Introduction to Educational Administration,* Second Edition. Boston: Allyn and Bacon, Inc., 1962.

Caverly, Ernest R., "House Plan in a High School," *School Executive,* November, 1959, p. 54.

Education Administration in a Changing Community. Washington, D.C.: National Education Association, 1959.

Gulick, Luther, and Lyndall Urwick (eds.), *Papers on the Science of Administration.* New York: Institute of Public Administration, Columbia University, 1937.

Hare, Paul, Edgar F. Borgatta, and Robert F. Bales, *Small Groups.* New York: Alfred A. Knopf, Inc., 1955.

Knower, Franklin H., and Paul H. Wagner, *Communication in Educational Administration*. Columbus, Ohio: Center for Educational Administration, The Ohio State University, 1959.

Leu, Donald J., and Herbert C. Rudman (eds.), *Preparation of School Administrators*. East Lansing: Michigan State University Press, 1963.

Mackenzie, Gordon N., and Stephen M. Corey, *Instructional Leadership*. New York: Bureau of Publications, Teachers College, Columbia University, 1954.

Ross, Murray G., and Charles E. Hendry, *New Understanding of Leadership*. New York: Association Press, 1957.

The Superintendent as Instructional Leader. Washington, D.C.: National Education Association, 1957, Chapter 10.

II
THE TASKS

PART TWO EMPHASIZES THE BASIC TASK AREAS IN which the secondary school administrator works. Chapter 5 provides an overview of the task areas which are to be discussed in detail in the chapters to follow. Chapter 6 discusses instructional leadership, the central responsibility of the administrator. Chapter 7 analyzes the staff personnel area. Chapter 8 presents pupil personnel administration, and Chapter 9 focuses on the financial and business management aspects of secondary school administration. The administrator's role in school-community relations is discussed in Chapter 10.

5

COMPONENTS OF SECONDARY SCHOOL ADMINISTRATION

THERE ARE GENERALIZED ADMINISTRATIVE PROCESSES common to the major fields of government, business, the military, and education. Perceptive skill in planning, coordinating, and appraising enables an individual to shift with reasonable success from field to field. Each major organization in our society, however, has its unique purposes. As a result, specific areas of operation are designed to facilitate achievement of the organization's objectives. Each administrator, in every enterprise, therefore, must have competence in those "bread and butter" task areas that are central to the organization. How much and what kind of competence is needed, and in how many of the areas, are dependent upon many factors. Basically, this question is resolved by determining whether the administrator is to work as a generalist or as a specialist. This in turn is often determined by the organizational structure. In the secondary school, for example, much depends on whether or not a principal is directly responsible for leadership in all of the task areas, and whether he alone holds this responsibility. In this case, of course, he functions as a generalist. In a more structured school, one or more assistant or vice principals might be assigned to specific areas of responsibility. In addition, deans or counselors or both might be available. Supervisors or directors in such areas as curriculum might also exist as staff or line personnel in the superintendent's office, who likewise would have responsibilities in specified areas. In the organizational activities, where these conditions existed, the specialities of the administrative staff would probably be used in determining functional working areas. Therefore the principal would still, in all likelihood, have overall administrative responsibilities of coordination in the specific task areas, but his personal leadership role might be directed to a constricted range of them. In this case, he becomes more of a specialist.

The vast majority of secondary school principals function as generalists. Their direct leadership is needed in each of the task areas. For that reason, half of this book is devoted to a comprehensive analysis of each of those task areas. To most readers, who probably will become generalists or who already are acting as such, the entire book will be appropriate. Task areas are discussed in depth, however, with the hope that the specialist can read selectively as his needs direct him.

In Chapter 3 we differentiated between administrative processes and administrative tasks. Processes are skills that are generally applicable to all administrators. Since the processes in a sense are action processes, however, it is obvious that they must have a specific area of application. The area of application relates them purposefully to the achievement of specific organizational objectives. The first purpose of this chapter, then, is to provide an over-all view of those working areas that are particularly relevant to the secondary school administrator: instructional leadership, staff personnel, pupil personnel, financial and facilities management, and school-community relationships. It is important that the administrator have competence in each of these fields and understand the direct relationship between activities in them and the accomplishment of secondary school objectives.

Anyone sensitive to the educational scene knows at a glance that these tasks areas are not the unique province of the secondary school administrator. They could be listed just as validly as task areas for elementary principals and superintendents. Specific skills representing areas of emphasis, however, are more obvious as the objectives become manifest for each level of operation and are related to the unique characteristics of pupils, attendance areas, and many other factors.

TASK AREAS IN BROAD FOCUS

Discussion of the task areas, then, will be geared to their broad aspects in this chapter, leaving their complexities and many of their specifics to later analysis. It is important for the potential administrator to gain an over-all view of those areas in which he is apt to spend major amounts of time. At the same time, it is obvious that each task area is of sufficient scope to require a chapter for its presentation.

There are values to be gained, we think, in presenting an overview to the task areas in a separate chapter at this point in the book. As has probably become obvious to you already, rarely is an administrative problem "pure" in the sense that it deals exclusively with curriculum or finance, for example. Rather, most problems have a central core in one of the task areas, but there are also ramifications from the other task areas. This chapter should help you to confront each of the subsequent ones which deal, in depth, with the task areas more perceptively than otherwise could be expected.

As we direct attention to the specific ways in which the secondary school administrator relates himself to the task areas, a few things can be highlighted at the outset. As he works in each area, it is necessary for him to know, for example, the policy boundaries within which he is operating. Not being the executive officer of the board of education, which sets the broad policy framework for the system, he must become knowledgeable about the implications of the policy for the work he does in the task areas. Within the existing school district structure, the sensitive and alert secondary school administrator will know those areas in which he has virtually autonomous operation, or at least responsibility for operation. Also, he will know the degree to which this exists for others, administrative, teaching, and service personnel within the system. In addition, he will be alert to the way in which this responsibility is exercised. Only by knowing these things will he be able to discharge his responsibilities by planning, in a coordinated fashion, the activities in which he and others engage.

To operate successfully in the task areas, the secondary school administrator must have a flair for dealing with the specifics that abound in them day by day. One need but turn to a few of the research studies done on this question to see their multifarious character.[1] They illustrate

---

[1] For example, see Dean O. Clark, "Critical Areas in the Administrative Behavior of High School Principals" (Columbus, Ohio: The Ohio State University, unpublished doctoral dissertation, 1956).

dramatically how the successful administrator must bring into play an adept facility with the administrative processes, particularly decision-making, coordinating, and appraising. Without these skills, secondary school administrators either flounder in the swamp of countless problems, unable to pull away from them, or they become addicted to what has been called the "administrator's malady," an inordinate fondness for the minutiae. Either can cause the administrator to operate far short of the leadership performance required.

What is needed, then, is an administrator who feels the challenge of the specific problem, who knows how to assess its relative importance in the total scheme of things, and who can bring about its solution by an effective use of the skills of those who should be involved in working it through. Quite often, he is not a direct participant in the process, so his satisfactions in those instances must come in helping to set the conditions in which others can work effectively. By operating this way, the administrator does not use each moment as an assault upon a wave of day-by-day problems. Rather, time becomes available for long-range planning, which is essential for maximum goal achievement.

Because the administrative processes must be related to the task areas, the second major focus of this chapter will be on an element common to all of them—organization. Organizational skill is a key that unlocks many doors for meaningful, effective administrative action. Organizational skill not only will be discussed broadly, but also many specific illustrations will be given to demonstrate its applicability.

THE ADMINISTRATIVE TASKS

Instructional leadership

The primary purpose of leadership is to facilitate teaching and learning in the secondary schools. To perform effective instructional leadership, the secondary school administrator must be able to trace a direct relationship between the acts in which he engages and the improvement of teaching and learning conditions. At times this line may be nearly indistinguishable, but the administrator should be able to see the relationship and help others to see it. This is not to imply that his leadership function becomes a vehicle by which to put his own personal views about the curriculum into operation. His views and professional commitments are important, and he need not feel a reluctance to express them; but others on the staff, in the student body, in the community, and in the profession of education also have contributions to make. His challenge, primarily, becomes that of creating conditions under which the contributors can work productively, of helping to assess the conditions under which curriculum development can take place, of marshalling evidence that becomes part of the working material of curriculum development.

As a facilitator of curriculum development, the administrator is responsible for recognizing the potentials of those individuals involved in the teaching-learning process and for providing the conditions in which sustained creative effort can take place. In leading, he must understand that curriculum development is a continuous process, when the end and the beginning become relatively unimportant. Herein lies one of his greatest challenges, because people strive to find a sense of security in constants. A curriculum committee, for example, may take for its working period a given point in time. The type of program that it may develop, then, sometimes can become a reflection of those things most obvious— a guideline established by a state department of education, a program laid out clearly in scope and sequence by a series of textbooks, a quintessence of time-honored learning experiences that have shown their value by persistence. These may or may not represent a curriculum geared to the needs of the students or the community served by the school. It is virtually certain, however, that the needs will not be served if the curriculum becomes fixed in time. Only as it becomes a fluid, on-going experience can it be vital and meaningful and perform the function for which it is intended. Even those learning experiences, sensed as timeless in their importance, come through the stream of history to take on new meanings when viewed in the perspective of each succeeding age. But security in change requires a type of maturity toward which we all must strive. It is far easier to strike off a section of experience that has become meaningful and act as if it never will, or never should, change.

How is instructional leadership performed when beset by admittedly formidable obstacles? Obviously, the secondary school administrator cannot hope to know, in depth, the content of each of the teaching areas in the school. This is not the avenue through which effective instructional leadership very often passes. As a matter of fact, it is even conceivable that the administrator might be a respected and skilled historian and yet give poor leadership to the development of a social studies program in the secondary schools. What is needed for competent instructional leadership is a person who understands the learning processes of adolescent youngsters and who is a sensitive interpreter of the community, the state, the nation, and the world. Equipped with this kind of understanding and working sensitively with people, the administrator can make meaningful contributions to the development of a dynamic curriculum program.

The administrator must not become dismayed at what appears to be a cyclical process. Curriculum development, in this dynamic sense, is going from objectives to program to evaluation to revision and so on, through the whole process again. This is not to imply that the process takes on herculean proportions, or that neat starting points are always obvious or the same. The entire curriculum is in broad focus very infrequently. Operationally, a staff or individual members of it will be working on different phases of this process at different times. The administrator, then, needs to shuttle along this moving scene, able to discern problems and to facilitate solutions to them.

Unique personnel situations, which must be recognized and dealt with carefully if his leadership efforts are to be productive, confront the administrator. He cannot engender confidence in his leadership if staff members feel that he is questioning their competence by continuing to press curriculum development. Teachers, by and large, are sensitive, intelligent people, who feel that their professional preparation and experience have equipped them to do a job skillfully. The real skill of leadership is that of working with basically competent people in such a way as to take the threat out of the process of looking for the better approach. The leader can do this by encouraging those with whom he works to use their intelligence in handling problems—to find solutions that make sense to them—rather than by touching off defensively-based reactions.

The administrator's role, then, is that of keeping central questions to the fore. These questions relate to purposes and objectives more frequently than they do to methods, at least at the beginning. When people see a problem in its relationship to an objective, they become far more receptive to experimenting to find the best way through which to solve it.

This, then, becomes the challenge of instructional leadership in secondary school administration—to work in such a way as to provide optimum conditions for effective teaching and learning.

Staff personnel

Most principals come to their administrative positions after some years of classroom teaching. In most instances, they have been capable teachers, who experienced both success and satisfaction in working with pupils. One of the most apparent transitions involved in going from teaching to administering is that of shifting working relationships from youngsters to professional peers. Many a secondary school administrator works at reduced effectiveness because of his inability to make this transformation. Either because he feels that it is still his responsibility to work directly with pupils—albeit concentrating probably on disciplinary cases—or because this is the way in which he derives his major professional satisfaction, the shift often is not made. A principal's major responsibility is to work with adults. He becomes a facilitator rather than a practitioner, helping to develop conditions under which pupils can learn effectively and function most productively as persons and as citizens of the school.

Many studies have indicated that a staff is concerned with having professional leadership that will help them find a release, a freeing of their creative, productive efforts for the task of purposeful teaching.[2] It is obvious, therefore, that the most important function of the secondary school administrator is his responsibility toward the staff with which he works. The manifestations of this responsibility are diverse in nature. In this chapter, we wish to highlight only a few of them.

Selection, orientation, and induction.   One of the most productive ways in which the administrator can meet this responsibility is by assuming a role in the selection, orientation, and induction of new staff members for his school. The superintendent of schools, or someone appointed by him, will often enlist the assistance of the principal in whose building the prospective employee is to serve. This is a desirable state of affairs. When this situation does not exist, the resourceful principal often can help to create it. Quite frequently, once this procedure has been established, the principal will do his most productive work in two ways. Knowing the nature of the vacancy that the prospective employee is to fill, he is in a key position to assess the kind of person who best can do the job. From the insights he gains from preliminary data, such as placement folders and letters of recommendation, and from the interview, he can make an appraisal that can be communicated to the superintendent of schools. The principal is also in the best position to determine what is needed, in the new personnel, to complement the existing staff. Thus, in establishing criteria for the new position and in the interviewing process, the principal can play a direct part in developing the strongest staff possible. In many instances, he enlists the assistance of the resident staff, directly or indirectly, in these two activities. Where this is done, staff members

---

[2] See, for example, Francis S. Chase, "Professional Leadership and Teacher Morale," *Administrator's Notebook,* 1:1–4, March 1953

know that they have some measure of control over the selection of those
with whom they will work.

A vital period for the new employee and for the school is the first
few weeks of his service, and also over that period of time when a judgment is made in reference to continuing contracts. Usually this will
extend to three or five years of service. Again, the administrator has an
important function during this period. The common mistake is to plan
a flurry of activities around the first week of school, when the obvious
orientation matters are paraded in a sometimes bewildering procession.
After a new teacher has been exposed to "the ropes," it is often assumed
that orientation is over.

A greater challenge, however, lies in planning and conducting over
time a series of experiences designed to build up competence and strong
professional relationships in the new staff person. Here, again, a competent administrator often exercises leadership by enlisting the assistance
of the staff. These activities, often mutually planned, are carried out
within the limits of agreements previously established. Thus, there is
purposeful movement toward the goal of helping the newcomer to adjust as soon as possible and to increase his professional productivity while
experiencing personal satisfaction at the same time.

Responsibility for professional growth.   The principal's responsibility
does not end, of course, with the new staff member. Of even more importance is the role he plays in facilitating the continued professional
growth of the more experienced colleagues with whom he serves. In
most school systems, the principal has a direct and specified responsibility in the area of staff evaluation. Quite frequently, though, reports
are sought only for those who are not as yet on tenure. Where this is
the case, the principal, because of other pressures, is often tempted to let
his responsibility to the rest of the staff go by default. Where this has
been true for some time, there can be genuine resistance to a plan for
instituting a general evaluation program. Staff members, particularly
those on tenure, often enjoy "not being bothered" and frequently can
make quite a vocal rationalization about their "diplomatic immunity."
This is an unfortunate situation. Almost sole authority, or at least control over the learning situation, and the resultant pleasure from having
arrived at this state, can blunt anyone's effectiveness who upon occasion
is not helped systematically to evaluate the job to be done and how he is
doing it.

When a program of evaluation for continued professional growth
exists, it can work in an ideal direction only if mutual respect exists be-

tween the teacher and the administrator. Without this, the program becomes a perfunctory pass at effectiveness. Real leadership is required to engender the confidence that must underlie such a program. Mutual agreement must exist about purposes and methods of a program of professional growth and evaluation.

Where such a program is not in operation, an administrator can pave the way for its development by demonstrating his own willingness to grow. There are many ways in which this can be done, but one of the most demonstrable and meaningful of them is to solicit the help of the staff on matters that are of concern to them. This must result in action, where staff members have played a part in determining its course, else they soon will feel that conferences and meetings are just window-dressing and that the principal "will go ahead and do what he wishes anyway." A quality of human relationships develops in this process that soon promotes the kind of candor that people of good will must bring to the solution of those mutual problems confronting them.

Supervision. It would be of little value to add but one more exhortation about the vital importance of the secondary school administrator's responsibility to supervise instruction. This in itself might compound already apparent feelings of guilt held by those of this profession. Illustrative of this situation is the often-heard statement that principals feel that supervision is their most important single function, but because of the pressure of other duties it is the very one to which they devote the least amount of time. Since this problem will be dealt with extensively in Chapter 6, very little elaboration of it is appropriate here. Suffice it for the moment to say that if this responsibility is to be met, the principal must first utilize his organizational skills effectively to make available the time required by this activity. It is important at this point to stress, though, that if the administrator is to supervise instruction effectively, he must work with a guide of mutually recognized and developed objectives. When a professional staff has threshed out some purposes of education in the secondary schools to which they as members can subscribe, points of destination become evident and progress toward reaching them can be measured more easily.

It is important for the administrator to recognize that there must be flexibility in the teaching-learning process. This is not a Procrustean task, lopping off or stretching out, as he makes his supervisory rounds, those who fail to fit into the mold that he feels is most desirable. Within any secondary school there is room for diversity in teaching-learning methods and even for modifications in the philosophy to which the staff may subscribe in broad outline. Some members of the staff, for instance, may have developed an ability to relate themselves most effectively to larger groups of students primarily through the use of a well-developed lecture style. If this is their most efficient method, the administrator should, in his role as a supervisor of instruction, help provide the circumstances in which this particular teaching talent can best operate. This assistance could appear in many forms. One of the most obvious would be in scheduling. There are optimum times of the day when pupils are more receptive to the lecture method, and the sensitive principal can do his best to set up a schedule that permits such a teacher to receive youngsters then.

The job of the principal, as a supervisor of instruction, is to use his knowledge of learning patterns and of psychological growth of secondary school students to the best possible advantage as he assesses the personalities and abilities of members of the instructional staff. As he consults with the staff, he should focus attention on the particular learning problem that groups or individual students are experiencing, not the inability of the teacher to solve (or be willing to try to solve) problems x or y. To dwell on this latter theme is to inject a threat to all but those with sufficient maturity. The principal must work with members of the staff so that they will become working partners in setting sensible ground rules for the learning process and in experimenting with flexible ways of solving problems. Also, the principal and the staff members must agree on the type of evidence that will be recognized as admissible that some progress is being made. Every supervisor needs to be on his guard against teachers shifting over to him those pupils who represent particularly knotty learning problems. Teachers, with the many problems confronting them, are apt to do this, particularly if it is the principal who is playing the supervisor's role.

Effective supervision by the principal, then, depends upon his using his organizational skills to provide the time for accomplishing the task, working with the staff to develop agreements about the jobs to be done, developing some measuring sticks that will provide evidence that a problem exists and that some progress is being made toward its solution, and upon working with staff and pupils in such a way that both become psychologically ready for assuming the responsibility that both must bring to the particular teaching-learning job to be done.

Importance of policy development.   Even in education, where professionally trained people take a large measure of individual responsibility for determining key teaching-learning variables in the classroom, it is still necessary to have rules by which to live. Although most policies affecting personnel throughout an entire school system are not developed at any one building level, there is usually some involvement by the staff of a building or by selected representatives of the staff. A principal can often help in this process by facilitating such things as opinion-sampling of the entire group and by participating in forums where ideas are being sought or tentative recommendations considered. In addition, each building needs a policy that is tailored to the particular conditions that exist there. Development of this kind of policy affords a much more direct leadership challenge to the principal. Such policies range from a philosophy for the school to such things as determining procedures to follow in taking disciplinary action against some recalcitrant pupil.

Often a principal can make the mistake of feeling that structure is antithetical to democratic administration, especially where capable professional people are concerned. Often too, he learns that this assumption breaks down. To hammer out sensible policy by which capable, intelligent people agree to live, is a difficult process, particularly when a considerable divergence of opinion exists, but the gains far outweigh the effort expended. Not only is more efficient operation possible, but learning opportunities are enhanced, too, because responsibilities are clarified, channels of communication are clear, and these same intelligent people are freed from the necessity of using their time and energy to clear away or to work around the underbrush of confusion.

Pupil personnel

In some ways, the work the secondary school administrator does in the pupil personnel area is the most critical aspect of his varied responsibilities. We can almost say that the *sole* purpose of the secondary school is to educate teen-age pupils. The administrator's central concern, therefore, is to provide an organization that promotes optimum learning experiences for these youth. Chapter 2 stressed how our society has taken the position that its young people should have more and more education. This has been reflected in our compulsory attendance laws, which now almost universally require all educable youth to attend school until they are sixteen years of age. As every teacher knows, however, it takes far more to accomplish a creditable job of education than mere physical presence. Providing the "far more" is a responsibility that must be shared by many, but it is a particularly acute one for the secondary school administrator.

Often the principal can gain the support of some staff members and that of those in the broader community who have their particular interpretation of the pristine values prized by our society, if he takes the stand that the school's primary responsibility is to provide the opportunity for youngsters who value that opportunity to receive a good basic education. It is our job to go this far, bringing to bear the most productive effort we can, becomes the position of those who react this way, and it is the responsibility of the student to travel the remaining mile. This position should not necessarily be disparaged. It is an attractive position, which too many may be tempted to take too hastily. A careful appraisal of the true cost of this position must be made, however, because to take it should be the result of a calculated assessment of the risk involved.

Developing understanding of purposes. The fundamental job of the school is to work productively with the student so that he is increasingly able to see the "whys" of learning. As students of human behavior, we all know that man is not always disposed to do something simply because someone in authority tells him it is for his own welfare. Teenagers in particular are not authority-prone. The positions they take must be of their own choosing before they are willing to unleash the astounding sources of energy that they seem at times to possess. Teaching, then, often has as its major task that of helping these young people to unlock motivational doors. A sensitive balance of external and internal pressures is needed to jar these doors loose.

Lest this position be construed as too visionary or rebellious, it is important to stress here the point about externals. These often are the easiest to cope with, because they are so apparent. It often is very surprising, however, how they are neglected. Because they are neglected, the total atmosphere for effective learning is sometimes seriously impaired. An efficient plan for pupil accounting is of utmost importance. Having pupils where they are supposed to be, day-by-day and class-by-class, on time, is excellent for the morale of both teachers and students. Developing such a plan requires careful attention to detail and organization, but the time spent by the administrator, working with those to be affected by the plan, is most productive.

In this same category is the plan for scheduling. Many principals feel that the development of a master plan for scheduling and a working of it through to a schedule for each teacher and pupil in the building is the most demanding task that confronts them year in and year out. For the beginning administrator this is often an awesome responsibility. Another problem is that of making enrollment projections. Frequently, the principal works with others—the superintendent of schools, members of the central administrative staff, or with elementary principals—to accomplish this task. In some aspects of the problem, however, he plays the crucial role. For instance, in secondary schools of all sizes, but particularly in the larger ones, it is very important to keep an accurate count of dropout figures and to assess as early as possible what retention figures will exist by classes and by subject-matter areas. This is especially important if the subject is one that the pupil is required to pass for graduation. Such information is vital to the accurate projection of how many teachers will be needed in what areas, how individual pupil-projected curriculum plans will be affected, and how much space and what quantity of specific materials will be required. Scrupulous attention to these details pays off in morale and efficiency. These, in turn, can affect the "tone for learning," which is so important.

Pupil personnel policies. Another pupil personnel area where the administrator's leadership skills are needed lies in the development of policy that becomes the guide for pupil behavior. From his knowledge of people, again, he realizes that these guides will be more useful if those who will be affected by them have some voice in determining what they are. Depending upon staff skills, the needs of the situation, and other factors, the principal's role in this process may be direct, indirect, or more likely a combination of the two. To have these guides, preferably in written form, is important, though, and the administrator has an obligation to see that they are developed. Structure is necessary, and it is often sought by teen-age youngsters, but it works best if they feel it is fair and appropriate.

Guidance. Just as a plan needs to be developed for the regulation of group behavior according to sensible patterns, it is exceedingly important for the individual pupil to work out an educational program for himself. This raises the problem of guidance, which can be approached in many ways. Choosing the most appropriate one requires an assessment of many conditions, which will be discussed later in greater detail. For the moment, however, it is important to see the problem broadly. Rarely does the individual pupil know himself in relation to his long-range needs well enough to do this planning alone. The school, therefore, has a responsibility to assist him with this problem, and the administrator has an obligation to see that the best possible effort is made.

Some kinds of problems, such as those regarding individual adjustment and making the best use of personal potential, obviously can be grouped. Were this not so, the schools would have an almost insurmountable task. Even those pupils who by some measurement can be classified as atypical have enough common characteristics to permit the group approach. Often the job of the principal is that of gathering evidence that these youngsters are not able to make progress in the usual learning experiences and of seeing if there are enough pupils to justify the establishment of different organizational plans geared to the unique problems of the atypical. The result of this kind of effort is often the establishment of special classes for the mentally accelerated or retarded and for those who have physical or emotional impairments. In this way, the structure of the secondary school becomes a flexible instrument that can be molded to provide the best possible setting for productive learning.

Briefly, too, it should be mentioned that the school needs to keep a discerning eye on the types of experiences that the students will have upon terminating, either by dropping out of school or by completing their prescribed program of study. Watchful of those forces, the school often can gear its program in a more meaningful manner. Thousands of youngsters of high school age continue to terminate their formal programs of education short of completion. Until society wills otherwise, most schools still have the obligation to retain the educable until age sixteen and in many states until age eighteen. Work needs to be done here, and the administrator has a challenge he cannot slough off. For many students, too, skills must be acquired that will permit them to profit from college and university experiences. Many other students plan to go directly into business and industrial life. The demands presented by each of these possibilities require, in many ways, preparatory kinds of activities that become, at least in part, the working province of the secondary school. For many, too, additional educational experiences are sought after high school that seem not to be available in other institutions. Increasingly, then, the lights of secondary schools are burning as adult education classes are conducted in response to community needs.

The challenge of the secondary school administrator, then, lies in his recognition of the fact that the school exists for the learner, and that it is his task to see that the best possible learning experiences are available.

Finance and facilities management

With the increased ground swell of post World War II youngsters currently flooding the secondary schools, serious problems in the finance and facilities areas demand consideration. Because of the direct relationship between program and money, the fiscal planning and management functions of the secondary school administrator are always significant. Basic to efficient operation in these areas is the understanding that exists between the principal and the central administration about financial responsibilities and procedures. This understanding is often the starting point of a new administrator as he seeks to develop competence in this area of his operations.

Budget-making.   In most school systems the principal is given responsibilities in annual budget-making. Some kinds of data, necessary for the development of the annual budget, can be obtained most easily from him. This is especially true in reference to the instructional materials needed at the secondary level. To discharge this responsibility, the principal can avoid the frenzy of meeting deadlines by last moment scurrying if he has a well-planned inventory system that will reveal the amount and condition of instructional materials on hand. It is most advisable, in addition, to enlist the staff's assistance in the preparation of requests for instructional materials. To do this efficiently, it is helpful to work from a budget that designates the amounts available to individual staff members or, more likely, to various instructional areas. Working with individual teachers or committees the administrator can help to get these requests into workable form. It is well to work from the latest catalogues available, so that price estimates are accurate as possible. If, as is likely, the material will be up for bidding, it helps, too, to have specifications developed and an indication of the purposes to be served by the material. This can be of considerable assistance to the superintendent of schools or school business official, who may be involved in the mechanics of purchasing, often during the summer months when the instructional staff is not available to provide the necessary information. Then, too, not all budgetary requests can be authorized, because of the gap that often exists between the asking and the granted budgets and because of contingencies that could not have been foreseen or forestalled. To ensure that those items ordered are those that are most needed, a priority list of requests should be available. The principal, again, needs to develop this with the staff.

Responsibility for internal accounts.   Other financial areas become sizeable responsibilities for the secondary school administrator. Most high schools, for example, have substantial internal accounts. These include athletic funds, student activity money, cafeteria operation, supply store accounts, and often many others. One of the wisest things a new administrator can do is to make sure that an audit of these accounts has been made shortly before he assumes his position. A clear understanding of his accountability in the financial area is one of the first things the principal should work out with the superintendent. Very often, in all but larger secondary schools, the principal has direct financial responsibilities. This means that he should operate under a fidelity bond. Periodic financial reports need to be prepared and transmitted to the superintendent, and often to others, such as an athletic board. In addition, an annual, outside audit is essential.

Because many of the funds with which the principal deals are earmarked, careful controls have to be developed. Many problems occur because of the absence of a systematized plan and because much of the business comes at a time when students, often, and teachers, sometimes, are not psychologically geared to careful operation. One of the most obvious cases is the senior class account. Anyone who has worked with this class knows the activity surrounding the senior prom, baccalaureate, and commencement. Unless a warrant and voucher plan has been carefully developed, and unless those having responsibilities are particularly vigilant, loose practices during this period can confuse the accounting.

Planning use of facilities. In the physical facilities area, increased problems emerge at times of booming enrollments. During a period of total pupil increases, the impact is felt first at the elementary level. Many communities have found it necessary to expand their facilities first in this direction. As a consequence, they have moved close to their bonding limits for capital outlay and have not had sufficient time to recover, through normal amortization, to turn their attention to added facilities at the secondary level. With heightened demands on the secondary schools, maintenance factors and the most efficient use of existing facilities have taken on added importance. A particular challenge confronts the secondary school administrator during these times, because he must be especially alert to maximum usage of space, on the one hand, and mindful that the purpose of facilities lies in the contribution they make to the learning program, on the other hand. Adaptability is a central concern as he analyzes existing space and conjectures about the purposes that might be served. Value questions come to the fore, and decisions often have to be made in terms of those values; else expediency rules and the price is frequently a heavy one. Should a study hall overflow be moved to the library or not is a question that illustrates this kind of problem. Expediency requires a realistic appraisal, but the administrator must weigh in his decision the requirements posed by the over-all learning program.

Working with the central administration, the administrator of the secondary school also helps to define how the school facilities are to be used. In many communities, the secondary school is the most frequently sought location for meetings. Although use of the school as a community center has many desirable features to commend it, there are potential problems that should not be ignored. In conflict situations, for instance, do school or school-related activities take precedence over those activities that are not school-related? Unless a policy has been clarified, situations detrimental to good public relations can easily arise.

Policies, too, are most applicable for staff and student use of facilities. Mobile facilities, such as projectors, need a plan for usage and care. Student use of the facilities requires coordinated action, too, for bothersome flurries often occur when two groups inadvertently get scheduled into one place at one time.

Protective maintenance is extremely important, especially when the existing facilities are approaching maximum usage. Whether the custodian is responsible directly to the principal or to someone on the central staff level, such as a school business official, there must be close operating lines between the principal and the custodian. For morale and productivity reasons, the principal must develop some standard procedures regarding work orders. In many schools there seems to be a belief that the custodian is "fair game in season," subject to the beck and call of teachers and pupils alike. A room that is too warm for one teacher becomes too cool for the next to occupy it, so it is obviously important for common working agreements, based on good sense and a respect for the rights of the custodian as a person. Policy is also necessary to provide guides by which students must live in reference to their responsibilities to the physical facilities of the school. Schools in which pupils have some role in determining the rules defining their responsibilities seem to have the most success in this area.

Careful attention to maintenance details pays good dividends for the secondary school administrator. Not only are activities coordinated by the development of a good plan, but the effort results in increased teacher and student morale. It is a common dictum that when many live under the same roof, a respect for the rights of others is a must to forestall confusion and petty bickering. In the broad sense, the high school in most communities is regarded somewhat as a symbol, and excellent public relations often exist when the symbol is well-groomed, an object of pride.

School-community relationships

Because the secondary school is a status symbol in most communities, problems of the nature that status symbols fall heir to often accrue. Some of these problems are those over which the administrator often has very little control, but even these pose a responsibility for him. An example of this would be a community that tends to take an inordinate interest in its athletic teams. The school's fortunes, in the community's eyes, tend to rise or fall with the success or failure of these teams. Although this is a difficult kind of problem, the resourceful principal, who realizes that people who are capable of taking intense pride in one thing can have enough of that characteristic to let it spill over to other things if they are approached in the right manner, can make some headway. For example, we've seen that booster clubs formed to support an athletic program can become interested in promoting speech programs, scholastic recognition banquets, and other affairs of this nature.

In a real sense, the secondary school reflects the needs of a community. Often it is capable of giving expression to its sometimes inarticulate aspirations. The secondary school administrator needs to understand these diverse needs, if they are to become articulate enough and sufficiently recognized to find their way into meaningful programs. No community is too small, for example, to be devoid of organizations and agencies. These may be structured to promote social, service, or welfare functions. These organizations are usually eager to find ways by which they can cooperate with the local school. Through them can indigent children receive care, students be given new outlets for searching out vocational opportunities, classes be given access to field trips that relate meaningfully to that which they are studying. In this age, when a hue and cry is often raised over the issue, "should the schools be all things to all people," here are concrete ways in which the school and community can develop a shared responsibility for the task in which they have a common interest.

ORGANIZATION—A VITAL ADMINISTRATIVE SKILL

Rarely does a single factor account for an individual's success or failure in the performance of his job. Despite the implied complexity of the issue, though, key skills can be isolated. To highlight our discussion of the basic task areas in secondary school administration, we have chosen to deal rather extensively with organizational skill, for it seems to be central to success or failure. Although, to be sure, there are some occasional cases to the contrary, an analysis of the careers of people who have been outstanding administrators reveals a common thread linking them together—an ability to get important things done well, on time. Further analysis shows that this is no intangible, esoteric trait, the prized possession of the insightful few. It starts with a disposition for action. The skill develops as one learns to recognize increasingly what should be done, what are the conditions, and who can and should do the job. The emphasis here is on organizational skill as applied to the job.

Previously we have stated that the task areas of secondary school administration are not solely the province of this particular educational level. It would be simpler if this were true, for then responsibilities would be easier to fix. Because instructional leadership, for example, is needed throughout the entire educational system, it is obvious that if the job is to be done purposefully and systematically some commitments must exist. These can be established easily in those systems that take the time to determine objectives and general agreements about how to go about meeting them. Often these objectives and agreements need to be hammered out building by building because of the diversities in the school-community environment. In a predominantly rural high school, for instance, the instructional leadership demanded of the principal might differ markedly from that exercised by the principal of a suburban school.

Aspects of organizational skill

Developing organizational skill has a logical starting point. It begins at the level of the jobs to be done. The prior experience of the new principal, whether it has been administrative in nature or not, tells him that some of these jobs are relatively constant from year to year and from school to school. For instance, each state has minimum requirements for graduation. Organization to accomplish this objective is a relatively simple matter of scheduling the required courses at times when they are available to those who need them and of having them taught by teachers certified to do so.

Quantitative aspects of organization pose relatively few problems in comparison to those that arise from qualitative considerations, for it is in this area that value judgments are more prevalent. Being able to define with clarity the jobs to be done has the essential complement of identifying and assigning to them the individuals who are best able to accomplish them. Here is where qualitative judgments enter the picture, for it is a common temptation in the secondary school, with its more characteristic pattern of inflexibility, to have personnel continue to serve in roles to which they have been assigned previously. Teachers easily can become identified with a specific subject-matter field, often at a particular level, or with such activities as sponsoring a class, directing plays, or advising the student council. Either a person becomes so entrenched in one of these positions that it becomes a delicate administrative problem even to raise the question of whether continued assignment is in the best interests of all concerned, or the situation lingers on by default, and certain staff members remain saddled with particular jobs for which they no longer have the interest or skill or both to do justice to them.

Matching people and jobs. The administrative skill needed is that of matching the right person to the right job. Accept for the moment that a general agreement about those objectives with which the secondary school should be concerned and the jobs needed to facilitate their realization has been reached. The key to success, as anyone close to education knows, in the final analysis is the teacher. Therefore, an assessment of how existing staff members can be involved most productively in the jobs of the school is vital. Sometimes these jobs require a specialized skill and more often a multiplicity of skills. Sometimes the jobs require considerable ingenuity and a real capacity to sense the obligations and subtleties of discharging responsibility.

Common sense should guide the administrator in this matching of the person to the job. In the day-by-day interaction of any school, clues about people, their insights, their capacity to take responsible independent action, their ability to work with others, their sense of humor, their leadership potential, their flexibility, their tolerance for handling concurrent assignments with skill and obvious enjoyment, exist in abundance. These are the factors that should be weighed in making decisions about assignments. The clues, however, will not necessarily parade past the principal's desk. He must gather them as he sees people at work, as he talks with them about their concerns, as he observes them under many different circumstances.

The skill of matching people and jobs is fed from the wellspring of observed behavior. This is not to imply that the process is entirely a random one. Systematic ways exist by which people can display what they can do. The principal can develop a system whereby the opportunities for diverse action are expanded. For instance, a teacher should not stay at one level of operation too long. If a general policy of rotation is accepted and developed, a teacher of English might not always be responsible for this subject at the sophomore level. In many high schools a teacher can move into different areas of his major teaching field or into minor fields as well. This is often a refreshing professional experience for the teacher and affords an opportunity for the administrator to see how easily and responsibly the new challenges are met. This same policy can exist relative to committee assignments and cocurriculum responsibilities. It is particularly important to test the flexibility and ingenuity of the new staff person prior to any decision about his tenure contract.

When this atmosphere of testing, observing, and evaluating exists, benefits accrue to the staff member, who has more opportunities to assess his own interests and abilities, and to the administrator, who has the final responsibility for determining assignments. The knowledge that results permits the establishment of a program with a good chance of success, because it is linked to those skills that the staff has. Also, the administrator is able to secure new staff members with abilities that fill the gaps in existing staff skills.

When testing the potential of a staff person for the acceptance of responsibility, it is advisable to choose wisely in terms of the importance of the job to be done and what already is known about the person's ability. Another rule of thumb is to have the task of reasonably short time span when uncertainty exists. Thus, checks can be established that will answer the questions at issue and that ensure that the activity does not stray out of bounds too far. For instance, it would be very unwise for a principal to assign a new staff member the responsibility of advising a senior class and to cut him adrift, so to speak, without guiding policy and without systematic checking to see how the responsibility was being met. It would be far better to observe how a short-term assignment, such as chaperoning a dance or planning a specific activity with a group of students, is met.

Establishing right conditions. It would be naive of the administrator to assume that this phase of the job ends when the right person is linked with the right assignment. The establishment of optimum conditions can weigh heavily in determining whether or not the job is accomplished; and this is where the principal can play an important role. These conditions are of at least two kinds. The first, and perhaps most important of these, refers to sanctions and other controls needed by those assigned to a job. It is frustrating to even the most capable individual to have responsibility for accomplishing an assignment and not to know what authority he can bring to bear. Administrative skill in organization is defeated if no action can be taken without a decision at every turn by the principal. Thus, working agreements or policy understandings need to be established between the principal and the staff member who undertakes a responsibility. When these are clearly developed and understood, the limits become clear and the staff person has some guideposts for decision-making. Another condition is the physical factors conducive to the successful handling of responsibility. To give a committee responsibility to do a job and not to be concerned with where or when they meet or how they get secretarial assistance when needed is to handicap its operation. Therefore, the administrator needs to direct his organizational thinking to creating optimum conditions under which people have the best opportunity to show what they can do.

Planning office routines.   A cluster of organizational skills exists in the area of the principal's day-by-day office routines. Whether they are managed simply and efficiently is often the difference between an administrator who is a leader of his staff and one who is handicapped because he is chained to his desk. Efficiency can be brought to bear irrespective of the size of the school or of the secretarial staff, or even if the principal has no secretary and must handle the office by himself.

A starting point in this kind of organization is to know what reports are due when, what they will entail, what the district's calendar will be, and other matters of this nature. These, then, can be entered on the school calendar prior to the opening of school. Predated reminders can be inserted on the calendar, and often, depending on the nature of the activity, responsibilities can be assigned. Frequently, in such things as statistical reports involving attendance, for instance, the help of such a group as a mathematics class can be enlisted. This provides a real problem for them, and it sometimes puts the computation in the hands of those who may have more skill in the operation than the principal himself. Developing a clear set of instructions to the staff about the nature of their involvement on reports often saves much time otherwise spent in face-to-face explanations.

Procedures, too, can be developed for the most efficient method of handling correspondence, telephone calls, and conferences. An administrator, for instance, should not be sought out whenever a call comes for him. Often what he is doing is of considerably greater importance. The person who takes the call can develop discrete, polite procedures for determining if the matter is sufficiently urgent for the principal to be called to the phone. What is primarily needed is for the administrator to indicate how he wishes this to be handled, and a line of direction will be provided for the secretary.

Prescheduling is another important organizational device. It is desirable that certain times, agreed on by the staff, be reserved for general staff meetings. These should be set well in advance, with respect for the rights of the individual. The better developed this calendaring of events is, the less friction is apt to result. Regarding his own activities, the principal, for example, should schedule himself out of the office for the job of supervision in the building. Thus, the most important things are provided for, and sufficient time will later be found for other jobs.

Lest the student think that all problems can be solved through systematic calendaring, reporting, and the like, it is necessary to point out that from such effort a bureaucratic maze that impedes rather than facilitates can easily result. Thus, it is important for the administrator to assess carefully what purpose is served by the activity. He should be mindful that teachers dislike reports and red tape, particularly if they do not see a relationship between what they are doing and that which they feel is most important—their teaching. Consequently, simplicity and efficiency should be the concern of the principal. If a reporting form can be eliminated, it should be dispatched at once. If two can be combined into one, so much the better. If recording can be done in the office by secretarial help with efficiency and purpose, then it should be done this way.

Planning for emergency situations is extremely important. A policy should be made about what should be done in case of accidents. A first-aid station can be established. Often people on the staff have skills in this area. The physical education staff, for instance, by training and by the nature of their jobs, can frequently serve here. Pupil file cards that indicate family physicians and emergency numbers to be called can be established. Plans for evacuations of the building in case of fire, for safety activity when tornado warnings go out, and for other such emergencies, can be developed, communicated, and practiced.

Role of policy. Formulation and communication of policy is perhaps one of the most vital of the organizational skills to be developed by the administrator. Information about policy and regulations can be broad in nature, pertaining to the entire staff or student body, or specific, relating perhaps to those who come into the building as substitute teachers. These statements should be developed clearly and concisely and should be available in printed form. They may be communicated through assembly programs, staff meetings, the student newspaper, student councils, homeroom or class periods. Good policy, like a good garden, must be reworked. Two-way communication, therefore, is vital, for policy often looks different to those who view it from the underside. This structure can assume different forms, depending on the size and nature of the school. At times it can be the staff as a whole, or an administrative advisory committee selected from or appointed by the staff, or a student council, or a homeroom. From these internal sources, the principal can ascertain the degree to which policies and regulations are clear, accepted, and appropriate to the purposes for which they were established. In these forums, too, modifications and new ideas develop.

This working with others, though, is a process that must have flexibility and imagination. Organizing is a give-and-take proposition. No matter how systematically a secondary school is organized, the principal must sense the impact of the problem at hand on the person involved. Even though a carefully developed plan may exist for the eventual solution of the problem, it may be preferable to have the matter handled with dispatch by the principal. This sense of assessment and timing is a very important one for an administrator. Without it, a basically skilled administrator, through miscalculation of staff, pupil, or community concerns, can frequently get into serious difficulty.

Schedule-making

The single outstanding nemesis confronting new secondary school administrators is the development of the master schedule. Viewing it from the incompleted side, it appears to be at times a hopeless maze involving hundreds and sometimes thousands of detailed operations.

This task should be undertaken while the school year is still in progress, leaving as little as possible to the summer months.

If a curriculum guide has not been developed, it is well to start at this point early in the school year. Some of the preliminary work is easily accomplished by checking the requirements of the state department of education and the accrediting association to which the school may belong or wish to belong. These outline required or recommended courses of study. These courses can become the skeleton of the guide. At this same step, the principal can check what has been offered in the school, and whether or not the staff is working in major or minor certified areas. This information is available from existing personnel records, often at the central office, and it offers clues about what courses might be offered.

At this point it is advisable to involve the entire staff, or at least a representative committee of the staff, in the project. If consultative help is available from the central office in independent school districts or from the county office in local school districts, such help should be solicited. A curriculum guide is much more than a listing of required or offered courses, by years or by patterns. Since, in most high schools, options exist for the student, either in choosing a major area for concentrated study or in selecting elective subjects, the curriculum guide and those activities planned for its use must be as clear, explicit, and helpful as possible. It should state what the subject deals with and indicate concisely what major objectives are associated with the subject. Quite likely, the subject may not have been considered in that light for some time if the staff responsible for its teaching has not been asked to verbalize the content and objectives.

In addition to developing this information, the staff can provide other data. For instance, in schedule-making, policies should exist about the number of courses available to each student, at what level courses can be taken, who should be involved in working out a projected schedule for each student, what criteria should determine whether a course should be offered or not, what size classes should be, and other similar questions. The more of these matters that can be threshed out by a principal working with the staff, the easier will be the process of schedule-making. Understanding lends form and order to the job.

Student course selection. Once these decisions have been made, the next step is to have students indicate their subject selections. Guidance at this point is extremely important, for without it selections are often haphazard and lack a real relationship to the student's needs, abilities, and interests. In most secondary schools, the classroom teacher plays an important role in this guidance process. If a homeroom plan is in operation, the process is of sufficient importance to warrant spending several homeroom periods in its accomplishment. We favor a plan that permits students in the eighth grade to project a program for the next four years. Guidelines for this can easily be established. The first of these are the state department of education requirements for graduation. Normally these include specifications for units in English, social studies, mathematics, science, and physical education. These, then, become the skeleton of each student's program. Variations are available as recommended course patterns for college preparatory, commercial, vocational, and general emphases. This type of information clearly can be established as part of the curriculum guide or as a separate course of study bulletin. In written form, it affords a roadmap for choice.

Counseling data often vary from school to school. If testing information has been kept and analyzed, normative guides may be available that help to determine who should consider courses in, for instance, advanced mathematics. If a count has been kept of the colleges and universities attended by graduates of the school, entrance requirements can be abstracted and used as guidance information. This list, of course, can be elaborately extended.

Parents, too, should be brought into the guidance process. In many schools, a night is set aside for a counseling session with students and their parents. At any rate, pertinent information should be available to them, and they should sign their approval of the courses selected.

A form can be designed on which the student can write each course he selects for the upcoming year. These individual cards are very useful for making up specific classes. In addition, the form can have a place for all courses to be written in. Sometimes this is set up in triplicate, and a copy is then available for the student, the homeroom teacher, and the office.

The master schedule. As a step in making the master schedule, the administrator should have a summary sheet for each homeroom, with all available courses printed on it. Tally marks can then be made by the teacher, or quite likely by responsible students, that show at a glance total registration by room in each of the various subjects. This information can be assembled on one master chart. From his knowledge of capacity, and following policy agreements concerning class size, the principal can determine how many sections of each subject will be needed.

At this point, organizational skill and planning are very important, because miscalculations can easily result unless these are exercised. Correction factors have to be produced, based on rates of failure, dropouts, and in-migration. Keeping these figures year by year and subject by subject, particularly in those areas required for graduation, will provide a percentage that can be used in determining the likely required number of sections. Whether or not the school has a summer program will also affect the planning picture. If such a scheme for making these calculations has not been established, it is recommended that it be begun by the administrator. In the meantime, he can get an indication from the teachers as to which students might fail which subjects. These schedule cards then can be coded for special attention and revised once this information becomes certain.

From the master tally sheet and calculations concerning class size, the number of class sections is easily determined. At this point, it is necessary to make provision for any special classes. It may be for instance, that 25 seniors need to be scheduled into English during the last period of the day, where they will work on the school newspaper. Classes that must come at a specified time and contain certain students should be blocked first into the master schedule. The schedule cards of those students should be coded and pulled for special handling. Those classes that have other special characteristics, such as double-period requirements, as a laboratory course might have, should also be put into the master schedule at this time.

Use of a conflict chart. Developing nonconflicting blocks is the next step. In a four-year high school, these would be established for each of the classes. Essentially, the plan sets up classes in such a way that incompatible choices of subjects are reduced to a minimum. Cards with the columns representing periods in the school day and the rows classes available to each of the four classes can be used. Reference to the tally sheet will show how many sections of a particular subject can be offered and where the optimum periods are in which the conflicts disappear or are held to a minimum. Several authors have written helpfully about the mechanics involved in the step, and the reader with a particular interest in how conflict sheets are developed is directed to those sources.[3]

After subjects have been put into their most appropriate periods, the next steps follow quite rapidly and systematically. Sections can be assigned to rooms and the students comprising each section can be determined. If the individual course cards have been used, they then become available to the teachers as their records of those who comprise each section.

As events occur that affect the process to this point, careful records should be kept so that the schedule can be as accurate as possible by the first day of school. Such records would include year-end failures, dropouts, in-and-out migration during the summer, and those who wish to change their schedules for some valid and acceptable reason.

During the summer months, secretarial help can be applied to the job of preparing individual schedules for each student and member of the staff. The office file cards can be alphabetized and filed. Packets can be assembled for homeroom teachers, who can distribute the new schedules to students on the first day of school. With the plan organized to this degree, the new school year can be started with a minimum of lost time. This is excellent for the morale of both teachers and students.

The discussion of schedule-making, as a concrete illustration of the secondary school administrator's use of his organizational skill, has been pegged thus far to the relatively small school or to the larger one with rather conventional scheduling problems. Increasingly, though, with larger sized operational units and added scheduling complexity, secondary schools are turning to machine processing in the student accounting area, of which scheduling is a major component. However, only the naive administrator feels that the involvement of machine processing will be a panacea to his scheduling problems. If anything, he finds that organizational details need to be thought through more specifically than

[3] For example, see Will French, Dan Hull, and B. L. Dodds, *American High School Administration Policy and Practices* (New York: Holt, Rinehart & Winston, Inc., 1957), pp. 279–289; and D. H. Eikenberry, *Building the High School Schedule of Recitations* (Columbus, Ohio: The Ohio State University, Department of Education, 1954), pp. 7–8.

ever before. Components of the schedule must be communicated clearly to those who program the machines and advise about how cards must be punched, because, in general, the machines will only do what they are "told" to do in advance.

Fortunately, the companies which supply machine processing equipment have consultants who have by now accumulated some significant experience in handling those scheduling problems which are unique to educational enterprises. Thus, the administrator who wishes to check the feasibility of converting to machine processing has an ample opportunity to get consultative assistance. Then, too, it is quite common to have short-term workshops and convention sessions on machine processing available to administrators.

The situation is somewhat analogous to the construction of a new building. Just as the administrator needs to communicate to the architect, in advance, about the program which is to be housed, so also must he spell out what the schedule should accomplish, what its limitations need to be, and what flexibility can exist in what areas, before the machine processers can work effectively. A good beginning point is the reading of James W. Whitlock's *Automatic Data Processing in Education.*[4]

CONCLUSION

The skilled organizer is he who has the disposition to see the essential details involved in any job and the knack of using his own ability and the abilities of others to work through those details. It also is he who can see the most efficient way to accomplish a job. Often he recognizes that this requires the coordinated skills and effort of others. Many administrators fail to accomplish important jobs on time because of the misguided notion that they personally must be involved in each step. With the complexity of today's secondary schools this degree of detailed personal involvement on the part of the principal is a one-way ticket to frustration. His hope lies in thoughtful planning, organizational skill, and coordinated effort.

SUGGESTED ACTIVITIES

1. Take one of the task areas discussed in this chapter and isolate the principles that it illustrates. In terms of your personal experience, what additions or modifications would you suggest?

[4] New York: The Macmillan Co., 1964.

2. The task areas in this chapter have been discussed primarily from an administrative point of view. Analyze the areas from the standpoint of a teacher, a student, or a member of the community. Are any divergences apparent?

3. Select an activity in any of the task areas. Consider the organizational problems involved, and indicate what persons should take what actions to accomplish the anticipated jobs.

4. On the basis of your experience, what problem areas in education are most difficult to resolve? Why do they seem to defy solution? Would any of them be more manageable if better organization skills were developed and applied?

SELECTED READINGS

Austin, David B., Will French, and Dan J. Hull, *American High School Administration: Policy and Practice,* Third Edition. New York: Holt, Rinehart & Winston, Inc., 1962.

Chase, Francis S., "Professional Leadership and Teacher Morale," *Administrator's Notebook,* 1:1–4, March 1953.

Clark, Dean O., "Critical Areas in the Administrative Behavior of High School Principals." Columbus, Ohio: The Ohio State University, unpublished doctoral dissertation, 1956.

Douglass, Harl R., *Modern Administration of Secondary Schools,* Second Edition. Boston: Ginn & Company, 1963.

Edmonson, J. B., Joseph Roemer, and Francis L. Bacon, *The Administration of the Modern Secondary School,* Fourth Edition. New York: The Macmillan Co., 1953.

Eikenberry, D. H., "Building the High School Schedule of Recitations." Columbus, Ohio: The Ohio State University, Department of Education, 1954. Mimeographed.

Faunce, Roland C., *Secondary School Administration.* New York: Harper & Row, Publishers, 1955.

Jacobson, Paul B., William C. Reavis, and James D. Logsdon, *The Effective School Principal in Elementary and Secondary Schools.* Englewood Cliffs, N.J.: Prentice-Hall, Inc., 1954.

6
INSTRUCTIONAL LEADERSHIP

6, 7, 8,

EDUCATION IS THE PROCESS OF ACQUIRING THE KNOWL-
edges, skills, appreciations, and standards of a culture, and of learning to
contribute to that culture. It is the means of continuing the heritage of
a society and of providing opportunities for the present generation to
make its contribution. Good education is that which does most to enable
students to develop their abilities and serve their society. Therefore,
education must be geared both to the needs of each individual and to
the needs of a relentlessly changing society. To accomplish this, it must
be both dynamic and diverse. It must be sensitive to the past, present,
and future, and educational leaders must strive for an efficacious balance
between time-tested educational precepts, on the one hand, and the
never-ending adaptations, innovations, and improvements that accompany progress, on the other. Similarly, it must be clear that not all change

represents progress, and that innovations in and of themselves do not assure improvement.

In the previous chapters we have explored some of the major concerns of the secondary school administrator. There is constant reference to the end product of operating the school—instruction. Invariably, when school principals are asked to cite what they believe to be their most important function, the answers indicate high priority for instructional leadership. Hence, this chapter is devoted to the problems, concerns, goals, techniques, and principles relating to the functions of the principal in the process of improving instruction. Elements of theory and philosophy, although tangentially treated and involved, are very much in evidence.

EMPHASIS ON THE INDIVIDUAL

Respect for the individual is a central theme in our culture. From this value spring two fundamental characteristics of American education—universality and diversity. Universality has been interpreted in this country as classroom education extending through the secondary school for all individuals, wherever practical. Our commitment to a high school education for all places a heavy responsibility upon the quality and character of instructional leadership.

Education, to be truly universal, must be diversified. This diversity stems both from the varying needs of individuals and the multiple needs of society. As communities differ, so must the educational facilities serving them differ, while still maintaining certain essential commonalities. The secondary school must serve all—urban, rural, suburban, poor, rich, talented, slow, adept, clumsy, frail, strong. All have definite educational needs and potentials for which the school must provide. Recent emphases on education for the culturally deprived, for technical skills development, and for retraining of the skilled whose skills are no longer needed are clearly related to the above views and concerns for individuals.

PRIMACY OF INSTRUCTIONAL LEADERSHIP

Instructional leadership is only one—albeit a very important one—task area in which the high school principal must demonstrate competence. Both the school and the community have positive expectations regarding the role to be played by the leader. The office of the principal carries with it a certain prestige and status in the school community. The role of principal also has many commitments to action. There are discipline policies, athletics, cocurriculum activities of many kinds, conferences, role of substitute teachers, scheduling, office business routines, and a host of other duties and responsibilities within the school for which the principal is expected to provide leadership.

There are also demands upon the principal's time and energy from the community. He is expected to be a community leader and to participate in and give leadership to worthwhile community efforts. Service clubs, veterans groups, youth agencies, churches, and other civic and social organizations welcome the participation and leadership services of the "head man at the high school." The truth is that many principals are so bogged down with demands from within and without the school that little time remains for the important task of instructional leadership.

It is unrealistic to say that the many calls upon the principal's time and energy are "unimportant," "unnecessary," or "unproductive." He has many task areas of real importance. Importance is, however, a matter of degree. Where should the principal invest his time and energy? When he is overloaded with demands on his services, what systems of priorities shall he use? How important is instructional leadership compared with his other duties? These are questions of deep concern to many principals, and ready solutions are not easily obtained. It can be unhesitatingly conjectured, however, that the role of instructional leadership is one that cannot be slighted nor treated lightly.

Criticisms of instruction

A clue to the importance of instruction in the secondary schools may be gleaned from the quality of criticism leveled at education in general. Honest, constructive criticism serves as a basis for progress and improvement. Further, when critics are silenced, a vital feature of democracy ceases. Nevertheless, educators must be selective in addressing their energies to criticism that appears to be honest and responsibly interested in what may be best for youth and our country.

Much of the negative criticism about education comes from self-styled experts from within and without the teaching profession. Some critics seemingly derive expertise based upon playing the role of the critic. The nature of criticism regarding education is common knowledge and includes a broad spectrum of involvement. However, regardless of the fairness or validity of criticism, there is common agreement that education is not perfect, that it probably never will be perfect, and that continuous effort should be made to improve it.

It is interesting to note that much of this criticism is focused on instruction—what is taught, how it is taught, and to whom it is taught. Our patent need to improve instruction is a product of the times. Every age makes new demands on education, and the future holds infinitely more demands for good instruction in a world of ever increasing complexities. Education, by its very nature, makes continued improvement essential. Such educational goals as trained, amused, exercised, accommodated, or adjusted children, worthy and important as these may be, will not suffice unless the intellectual powers of youth are correspondingly developed. Sheer competition for survival, now, as in the past, leaves us no other choice. Education for life has taken on a new and significant meaning. It will come about only through improvement of instruction through competent leadership and teaching.

Point to a community that prizes intellectual achievement highly and you will find a heavy emphasis on such achievement reflected in the instructional program of its schools. Schools are to a great extent a mirror of the hopes, aspirations, and beliefs of the people who support them. In other words, the quality of education is directly related to the value system of the citizens in the community. Some communities want good education, and they get it. Many studies have pointed to the direct relation of school support to quality of the educational program.[1] Consequently, it would seem appropriate for the principal to give careful thought and consideration to the climate of opinion, as related to quality of education, in the community. Perhaps, as an educational leader, he has a responsibility for upgrading the climate of opinion toward education in his area.

The challenge is to apply much more widely and with increased vigor the know-how demonstrated by our better schools. Our better schools are the least complacent about the quality of instruction. Staff members constantly seek new and better ways of doing their work, for such schools are most alert to new needs and conditions and are most likely to succeed in tailoring the instructional program to the varied needs of youth. Principals in our better schools are invariably strong in instructional leadership.

The principal knows that his most important task is that of improving instruction. This is not to say that all present instruction is not up to par, but that the principal, as other professionals, is presumed to

[1] Studies by Dr. Paul Mort and others have shown a relationship among quality of schools and the factors of esteem and support for education in communities. See Paul R. Mort, Walter C. Reusser, and John W. Polley, *Public School Finance* (New York: McGraw-Hill, Inc., 1960), pp. 77–86.

be dynamic and interested in continually increasing his store of knowledge and improving and refining his techniques. Instruction is placed first in many ways. Nearly every action the principal takes has some bearing on instruction, and some of the tasks that appear as trivia often have direct bearing on some aspect of the instructional program. The plea here is that the focus on good teaching and learning be remembered in the myriad of administrative duties and responsibilities. Occasionally, every administrator must back off from his job to look at himself and his job objectively. It is in these moments of reflection that he may see the relatedness of his work to the central purposes of operating the school.

Demands for quality in education

"Quality" is an overused word, but judging from its use in manufacturing, advertising, education, and elsewhere, it appears to communicate a concept of worth. Industry speaks of "quality control" wherein checks are made to determine if desirable standards are being maintained in manufacturing processes. What is meant by quality in education? Is there a simple test of quality in education? Many feel that there is no single criterion by which the quality of an educational program may be measured. What is seen as top quality for one student in a given situation may be viewed quite differently when applied to another student. Yet both programs may be excellent for those involved.

Excellence, then, may be the key to quality—excellence as against superficiality, tawdriness, and compromise, regardless of the particulars involved in any situation. This means not settling for the second best, but insisting everywhere on high-grade performance and the best in the way of curriculum, teaching, guidance, and educational opportunities. A statement from the Educational Policies Commission on the matter of quality in education says, in effect, that "a high-quality school program is characterized by a curriculum which makes possible, and teaching and guidance which make real, the promise of educational opportunity for each pupil."[2] A fundamental commitment of education in a free society is to assist individuals in the pursuit of excellence.

In education, as in other commodities, there are few short cuts to quality. The "get-by" attitude on the part of students cannot be tolerated in a program geared to excellence. Only that which challenges the best

[2] Educational Policies Commission, National Education Association, *An Essay on Quality in Public Education* (Washington, D.C.: The Association, 1959), p. 7.

in students at all levels of ability is worthy of inclusion in an educational program that seeks to maintain high standards. Excellence begets excellence. Any compromise is a sure road to mediocrity.

Competing demands

What shall be taught? To whom? When? How? This is the problem faced by the instructional leader. Let us look for a moment at the competitive aspects of what shall be included in the curriculum offerings. How do subjects find their way into the curriculum? What is the rationale behind offering driver training, first aid, modern dance, and flycasting, or teaching French, history, and solid geometry? The conventional high school offers three general categories of subject matter: regular academic subjects, special subjects, and electives. The academic subjects are more or less constant and comprise the main diet of classroom experiences for students. Special subjects are course offerings to meet particular needs of students. Electives may be either academic or special subjects and are made available to students to round out their programs and to complete the necessary units for graduation.

Competition for inclusion in the curriculum experiences of youth is not restricted to the multiplicity of subject offerings. It is also a function of time—the periods in the school day, the days in the week, and the weeks in the school year. One of the major problems in the modern high school is obtaining time to do all that is expected and desirable. The time factor has given rise to possibilities of extending the school time schedule. Many schools have extended activities to include a portion of Saturday. Nine-and-a-half- and ten-month school terms are becoming more common. The summer term for special and remedial purposes is being used by a number of school systems. A few systems have experimented with the four-quarter system, but so far the year-round school has not convincingly demonstrated its worth.

There is good evidence that the high school of the future will take a sharp look at the time factor for instruction. Intelligent decisions will have to be made with regard to what shall be included and what shall be excluded in the secondary school program. It is entirely possible that some of the experiences now being offered in high school could be offered earlier, particularly for the more talented students.[3] In addition, better and more efficient methods of teaching must be explored along with improved utilization of instructional materials and media.

[3] Languages, science courses, and other high school experiences are being offered in seventh and eighth grades.

Current assessment of instruction

Assessment of the secondary school instructional program at present appears to indicate the following:

1. Ever-increasing demands are being made upon the high school instructional program.

2. Mass education has influenced the instructional program markedly to meet the needs of the average.

3. Provisions for the talented and the slow learners need careful re-examination.

4. Better teaching by more qualified master teachers is needed.

5. Educational guidance needs improvement.

6. Careful re-examination of the curriculum is necessary.

7. Enrollments in high schools are establishing new records and will continue to do so.

8. Many high schools are too small to meet current and future expectancies for materials, equipment, and programs.

9. The values of a high school education in our culture need reappraisal.

10. The over-all investment of time and money in secondary education must be re-evaluated.

These are but a few highlights of the projects and problems, all of which have a direct bearing on the quality of instruction, facing the instructional leader. Along with these, the leader is challenged to provide intelligent direction to a high school program in a culture dedicated to equality of opportunity in education, diversity of curriculum offerings, and quality instruction.

COMMONALITIES IN SECONDARY EDUCATION

The most common element among high schools is teen-age youth—youth in a unique community, the main function of which is to provide educational experiences. Evolving in much the same way as other social organisms, the high school has adjusted itself to furnishing educationally related experiences as demanded by a critical and vigilant society. Recreational activities, club activities, athletics, and similar program features have become as commonly identified with high school as English, science, and mathematics. In fact, educators and others have often expressed con-

cern lest the nonacademic features of high schools transcend in importance the basic common purposes. Indeed, it may be said that one of
the commonalities among high schools is the studied effort to strike a
proper balance of program features.

It cannot be denied that society has wished upon the high schools
a certain degree of custodial function unique to the American culture
and quite foreign to original intents and purposes. In the not too distant
past the high school was said to be "the poor man's college." In many
respects the high schools have imitated the colleges and universities, even
to having social fraternities and sororities. Today, the high school is still
the terminal formal educational experience for a high percentage of
youth.

Accreditation

Accrediting agencies and state departments of public instruction enforce
certain commonalities among secondary schools. Sixteen units, courses
pursued for one year (four each year for four years) is probably the most
common requirement for graduation. Table 3 indicates that English and
the social sciences run strongest as required subjects, with mathematics
and science trailing. The allowed number of electives ranges from four
to sixteen. A typical state requirement for graduation from high school
includes three years of English, two years of social science, including
United States history, one year of mathematics, one year of science, and
electives to complete the typical Carnegie Unit of sixteen credits. It
should be noted that these are minimal requirements and that most
students in secondary schools exceed these minimums in specific subject
areas.

Earlier criticisms that high schools offered too much and required
too little and that students were launched from soft pedagogy, fads,
frills and fine feathers into a world of reality, work or college are not
substantiated by modern high school programs. That the average student
may skirt along the fringe of the curriculum, always taking the snap
courses through electives, is no longer substantiated by the facts.

Alike, yet different

With all the similar aspects of secondary schools, there are equally obvious differences. The small rural high school has very little in common
with the large urban high school except some of the basic commonalities
mentioned previously. All three are preparing students for college and
other post high school activities, but with distinct individuality. While

TABLE 3. STATE HIGH SCHOOL GRADUATION REQUIREMENTS, IN UNITS OF CREDIT, EFFECTIVE FOR 1960–61 GRADUATES

			Social studies										Science							
State	Total number of units	English	Unspecified	9th grade social studies	American history	American government or civics	American history and government combined	State history	World history or world cultures	Problems of democracy	Economics	Mathematics	Unspecified	General	Laboratory science	Biology	Fine arts	Practical arts	Health as a separate subject	Physical education or health and physical education combined
1	2	3	4	5	6	7	8	9	10	11	12	13	14	15	16	17	18	19	20	21
Alabama	16	4		½	1			½		½	½	1		1	1					1–2 (4 yrs.).
Alaska	16	3	½		1	½						1		1						½ (1 yr.).
Arizona	16	3				½	1		1											
Arkansas	16	4	1				1½						1		1					1 (1 or 2 yrs.).
California	19–24	(1)	2				1½													4 (4 yrs.).
Colorado	16					[1]														
Connecticut	16	4			1	½	1					1	3			1				[1]
Delaware	20	3	1				1	[1]			½	1	3			1				2.
Florida	18	3	2									1	1					2 1	4 1	0 (4 yrs.).
Georgia																				
Hawaii	18	4			1	½						2	2						½	2.
Idaho	17	3										2	2							½.
Illinois	16	3	½				1					1								1.
Indiana	16		½		1	½						1			1				½	½ (1 yr.).
Iowa																				0 (4 yrs.).
Kansas	17	4	½		1	½		[1]				1	1							1 (1 or 2 yrs.).
Kentucky	16	3	1		1							1	2							1.
Louisiana	17	3			1							2	2							
Maine	16	4			1		1						2							1 (4 yrs.).
Maryland	16	4	2			1				1		1	2							
Massachusetts	15																			
Michigan	12[6]	4		1	1	½												1		
Minnesota	16	4		1	1							1	1	1			1	1		0 (2 yrs.).
Mississippi	17	3					1	½	1											1 (4 yrs.).

State	Units required										
Montana	16	4		1		½	1	2 1			1 (3 yrs.).
Nebraska	16	3		1			1	1			
Nevada	16	4	1	2		1	1	1 1			⅘ (4 yrs.).
New Hampshire	15½	4		1		1		1 1			
New Jersey											0 (4 yrs.).
New Mexico	16	3	1	1 or 2		1		1			1 (1 yr.).
New York	7 16 or 18	4		1				1			1.
North Carolina	16			1				1	8 2		1.
North Dakota	16	3½	1	1			1	1			
Ohio	16	3					1	1			
Oklahoma	16	4	1					1			2.
Oregon	19	3				1		1			1 (4 yrs.).
Pennsylvania	6 13	4	½	(1)			1	2			
Rhode Island					½			1			
South Carolina	16	4	1					1			
South Dakota	16	3	½	½		½	1	1			
Tennessee	16	4						2			
Texas	16	3		1				1 1			1.
Utah	6 10 15	4	½	1 1			1 1	4 1		(12)	(¹)
Vermont	16	4						1	1		1½ (3 yrs.).
Virginia	16	4				1		1			0 (2 yrs.).
Washington	16	3		1		½		1		2 1	0 (2 yrs.).
West Virginia	16	4	2					1			1 (4 yrs.).
Wisconsin	16	•									
Wyoming	16			1				1			0 (4 yrs.).

1 Instruction is required of all pupils but credit or years is not specified.
2 Homemaking for girls.
3 A second year of mathematics may be substituted for this course.
4 Unless taken in the 8th grade.
5 One unit may be waived under certain circumstances.
6 Only the units earned in grades 10 through 12 are counted toward graduation. For comparative purposes, 9th grade subject requirements are included in this tabulation.
7 Sixteen units for a "local" high school diploma; 18 for a Regents (State) high school diploma effective June 1961.

8 Two units of homemaking or vocational agriculture may be substituted for 1 unit of science.
9 All pupils must enroll in English each year. A pupil failing in 1 year of English or graduating in 3 years may graduate with only 3 units in English.
10 Any pupil on a personal guidance basis may be exempted from meeting any one of these requirements provided the number so exempted does not exceed 5 percent of the class enrollment; any student may be exempted from meeting two of the units provided the number so exempted does not exceed 2 percent of the class enrollment.
11 Algebra taken in the 9th grade will not meet this requirement.
12 One unit is required in grades 7, 8, or 9.

Source: Grace S. Wright, "Requirements for High School Graduation in States and Larger Cities," Bulletin No. 12 (Washington: U.S. Dept. of Health, Welfare and Education, 1961), pp. 6-7.

one school may offer several years of training in a wide choice of languages, another may offer none. A typical rural agricultural community is served by a high school offering vocational agriculture, while an urban community is served by a high school with no such area in its curriculum.

The impact of widespread adoption of the new mathematics, physics, biology and other new curricula along with new testing programs is seen by many as the beginning of a trend toward more standardization—precursors of a national high school curriculum.

Many things can be said about the American high school with a large degree of certainty: (1) There is no such thing as a typical American high school. (2) Most high schools are too small to provide an adequate program economically and efficiently. (3) High schools are serving an increasingly higher percentage of high school age youth; that is, more youth of high school age everywhere are going to secondary schools. (4) The high school program has been predominantly college preparatory. (5) An increasing proportion of high school graduates are going to college. (6) Standards are generally weighted in favor of the average student. (7) Effective guidance and individualization of instruction are among the goals commonly listed by educators and patrons as problems seriously in need of attention.

GOALS OF EDUCATION IN OUR SOCIETY

The process of education is a continuing one. From conception to death the human organism participates in experiences that modify later behavior. This is learning. The moment a spark of life is generated needs arise that must be satisfied if the organism is to live. Learning experiences that modify subsequent behavior multiply in frequency and complexity until that spark of life is extinguished by death, and the needs of life are terminated. During the first few years, the education of a child is centered mainly around the informal life of the home. In later childhood and adolescence, society provides formalized experiences through a sequential program of schooling. Adults have many and varied opportunities for learning—formal and informal, organized and unorganized, structured and unstructured.

Inter-relatedness

We are concerned here with secondary education, one segment of the continuum, with the full realization that all education is inter-related. For convenience and emphasis, we have come to designate various periods of education as preschool, kindergarten, primary school, elementary school, junior high school, high school, and college or higher education. All are important. Occasionally these stages are referred to as "steps" in the educational process. When considered from the point of view of inter-relatedness, it might be better to consider the periods as part of a ramp. This concept provides us with an opportunity to consider the comprehensive program of education for youth in local schools from start to finish.

Complex societies alone require formal and organized school experiences. Primitive societies get along quite well with informal, incidental learnings passed on by the parents and sages in the group. In these societies the goals of education are minimal. Incidental and accidental learning suffice. Eventually the necessary skills for survival are learned and the young take on their responsibilities of adulthood. In more advanced societies, elders assume the teacher function to assure the passing-on of the heritage in a quasi-formal manner. With each level of complexity, the increased body of knowledge to be learned makes formalization of the learning experiences more necessary.

Interestingly enough, the less complex societies do not envision education for the masses. Their technology demands very few specialists requiring extensive training, and only a chosen few are trained for ceremonial and leadership roles. This selective process has some vestiges in modern societies, where the intellectual elite are given advanced training and the rest minimum educational advantages.

Evolvement

In our consideration of secondary education as an organized part of the educational experience, we are not unmindful of the impact of home, church, various social agencies, play, work, and other contributors to the general educative process and the changes it brings. Change is inevitable —it is society's only constant. The role of organized education on the high school level is different today from what it was a quarter of a century ago, and it will be different a quarter of a century hence.

Much of the confusion about curriculum stems from controversies rooted in change. There are always those who feel that the program is too antiquated and static or too forward-looking and radical; too rigid or too flexible, too academic or not academic enough, or too practical or not practical enough. The optimum program would be so arranged as to be in complete synchronization with changing society, the individual needs of each student, and the informal community influences that effect the total education of youth. The achievement of such a program is most unlikely.

Changes in behavior

Every society tends to measure the end product of its educational system by the behavioral changes affected. Likewise, according to Allport, "maintaining, actualizing, and enhancing of the capacities of the individual organism" is the basic motive of life in the individual.[4] Thus, behavioral changes resulting from formal educative experiences as well as those derived from the informal experiences of life and maturation substantiate the fact that the ascribed goal has both social and individual pertinence. It has been said that human nature seeks to *become* and is not satisfied merely to *be*. We live in a dynamic social situation, calling for continued effort to utilize and develop the capacities we possess that we may better satisfy this need to *become*.

What should the students be able and willing to do, in an observable way, as a result of this high school education? How may we expect the high school graduate to think and feel and act? Valid and authentic answers to these questions are constantly being sought by leaders of instruction, curriculum planners, test-makers, teachers, and interested citizens. Again, the effectiveness of the high school education is measured in terms of behavioral changes. It is not surprising, then, that every effort to postulate statements of purpose or objectives for secondary education is based on behavioral anticipations.

Purposes and objectives

The year 1918 marked two important contributions to the literature on purposes and objectives of secondary education. Alexander Inglis wrote *Principals of Secondary Education*, in which the secondary school was recognized as a part of our "common schools" to be available and experienced by all youth;[5] and *The Cardinal Principles of Secondary Education* was published.[6] Previous commissions and committees dealing with the objectives and purposes of secondary education had centered mainly on the degree of mastery of certain subject matter to be required of students.

[4] Gordon W. Allport, *Becoming: Basic Considerations for a Psychology of Personality* (New Haven: Yale University Press, 1955), pp. 16–17.

[5] Boston: Houghton Mifflin Company, 1918.

[6] Commission on the Reorganization of Secondary Education, Bureau of Education, *The Cardinal Principles of Secondary Education* (Washington, D.C.: Government Printing Office, 1918).

Proficiency in subject matter is important to the high school instructional leader, but the publications mentioned above marked the advent of a new approach, which measured results by the effect upon behavior.

Numerous statements and reports, such as *The Imperative Needs of Youth*,[7] *The Unique Function of Education in American Democracy*,[8] *The Purpose of Education in American Democracy*,[9] *Education for All American Children*,[10] *The Education of Free Men in American Democracy*,[11] and other efforts to express education ideology appeared. These contributions were not directed solely toward secondary schools but had wide implications for all levels of education. They attempted to put into words the evolving concepts of purposes and objectives of American education.

More recently, the Russell Sage Foundation, under the leadership of Kearney and French has published two significant reports on the objectives of elementary and secondary education.[12] The report of the objectives of secondary education took a sharp look at the behavioral goals of general education in the high school. The movement in education toward a program that attempts to assist youth to meet life's needs has come to be known as the "general education" movement. In 1893, the Committee of Ten first used the term "general education" and defined it as the four major subjects: language, science, history, and mathematics. Much has been written about general education, but for our purposes general education refers to those nonspecialized, nonvocational aspects of education that should be the common possession, the common denominator, so to speak, of educated persons in a free society.

General education has two purposes. One is concerned with the development of a person as an individual; the other is concerned with the development of a person as a member of society. It is easily seen that

[7] Educational Policies Commission, National Education Association, "Imperative Needs of Youth," *Education For All American Youth* (Washington, D.C.: The Association, 1944).

[8] Educational Policies Commission, National Education Association, *The Unique Function of Education in American Democracy* (Washington, D.C.: The Association, 1937).

[9] Educational Policies Commission, National Education Association, *The Purpose of Education in American Democracy* (Washington, D.C.: The Association, 1938).

[10] Educational Policies Commission, National Education Association, *Education for All American Children* (Washington, D.C.: The Association, 1948).

[11] Educational Policies Commission, National Education Association, *The Education of Free Men in American Democracy* (Washington, D.C.: The Association, 1941).

[12] Nolan C. Kearney, *Elementary School Objectives* (New York: Russell Sage Foundation, 1953); and Will French, *Behavioral Goals of General Education in High School* (New York: Russell Sage Foundation, 1957).

knowledge alone is not the complete answer to self-realization and effective citizenship. Performance is the ultimate criterion by which general education is to be judged rather than the more narrowly defined terms of factual competence and knowledge.

A half-century of conceptualizing what secondary education should be and do has produced a number of excellent statements and ideas. There is substantial evidence that there is considerable agreement on purposes and goals with rather wide general understandings as to implications. The difficulty arises in implementation, in translating the objectives and purposes into program features, courses, instruction, and high school experiences. This is indeed the crux of the responsibility of the instructional leader.

Phenomenal development

The development and expansion of organized education has been accomplished by a long, unremitting process, paralleling man's mastery over his natural and physical environment. It has constantly quickened until the major concern has become the adaptation and broadening of education to meet the needs of a dynamic society. The development of American secondary education is the result of neither mere chance nor theoretical premise or belief, but rather of the efforts of many to find means of understanding, transmitting, perpetuating, and further developing an enormously complex culture. Urbanization, economic interdependence, industrial development, international position, communication, mobility, and other sociological factors have caused the informal and unorganized means of education to become increasingly inadequate, while at the same time placing a greater responsibility upon organized formal education.

Accompanying the growth and change in society's expectations for the secondary school have come ever-increasing numbers to be educated. In the period from 1949 to 1959 public secondary school enrollments increased by almost four million students, and projections into the future show continual increases.[13] Any fair assessment of the secondary school and its program must consider the phenomenal growth factors both as to scope of activities and numbers being served.

Some of the nonacademic responsibilities assumed by the schools have been questioned by many educators and lay citizens. Vocational

[13] National Education Association, *Research Bulletin*, Vol. 37, No. 3 (Washington, D.C.: The Association, 1959), pp. 75–77; also, Vol. 42, No. 1, 1964.

education, recreational activities, cocurriculum programs, and health education are frequently regarded by some as being outside the province of the secondary school. In fact, many on professional staffs would be happy if the schools could shed some of these responsibilities. The truth is that these services have found their way into the school program because no other social agencies were available to provide youth with the necessary skills, understandings, attitudes, and appreciations necessary for today's growing youngsters. Questioning the school's effectiveness in discharging these new responsibilities is always pertinent. Further exploration of this problem may unearth other agencies and devices for meeting some of these needs of youth effectively.

OTHER PROBLEMS OF IMPROVING INSTRUCTION

Completion of the high school experience stands today where the requirements for completing the first eight grades stood a half-century ago. A new minimal standard for general formal educational requirements that includes secondary school training has been accepted. Employers in almost every field show distinct preferences for hiring high school graduates. Our potential capacity to provide time and resources for education was never more promising. Only blindness to the realities of world conditions and the role that must be played by citizens of free nations in domestic and international affairs would allow us to settle for less than optimal quality in education. Regardless of temporary set-backs, trends and the ultimate goals toward which society is moving indicate extension and expansion of educational opportunities. Ever greater numbers of students will be continuing education in some form beyond high school.

Parallel with these developments and as added dimensions to the problems of improving instruction, new knowledge to be learned is multiplying at a prodigious rate. Some old knowledge has turned out to be false or incomplete. The relevance of knowledge and skill to the present and future is being conditioned by a rapidly changing society. New tools for teaching and learning are being developed calling for new methods, skills and approaches.

Our value system and education

Many parents have said, "I want to give my children the benefit of an educational opportunity that is better than I had." Another expression

often heard is, "I want my child to have an education that will open opportunities to him that have been closed to me because of my lack of
training." These and similar statements are the echoes of fundamental
feelings of value that people attribute to education. People are becoming
aware of the educational opportunities available here as contrasted with
other parts of the world. In Europe, for instance, three-quarters or more
of the youth begin work at fourteen or fifteen years of age. At the turn
of the century in this country, approximately half of the boys and girls
fifteen years of age were not attending school. Many of these were at
work. Sixty years later approximately 85 per cent of the boys and girls
age fifteen are in school.[14] The period from 1910 to 1920 saw vigorous
campaigning against child labor and the subsequent introduction of
regulatory legislation. One effective argument employed in this movement was the negative effect of early employment on opportunities for
education and values obtained therefrom. Hence, as a result of laws
affecting employment, as well as the attitude of management and labor,
it is difficult for youth even at the age of seventeen to obtain many kinds
of jobs.

The problem, as seen by many, is that our highly materialistic, push-
button, entertainment-seeking, complacent culture is losing sight of
basic values in education and becoming satisfied with lip service to the
ideal. When a society pays many workers more than its teachers and
spends several times as much on the luxuries of comfortable living than
on education, the sincerity with which values of education are held can
be questioned. A socioeconomic climate in which competent people are
lured away from teaching allows but one conclusion to be drawn concerning its effect on the quality of instructional staffs in our schools:
downgrading will occur.

Yet the fact that these factors are deplored in many quarters and
that whole communities are taking steps to remedy the situation gives
credence to the idea that basically the worth of education maintains a
relatively high priority in our value system. Organizations such as the
National Citizens' Council for Better Schools, The National Education
Association and its divisions, and the National Congress of Parents and
Teachers have done yeoman service to education through their efforts
to alert the public to the value of education and the need to improve it.
The evidence is convincing. Homes and communities everywhere are
the ultimate determiners of the quality of education.

[14] James B. Conant, *The American High School Today* (New York: McGraw-
Hill, Inc., 1959), p. 7.

Contrast between American and foreign education

Historically, and with greater pertinence recently, European models of secondary education have been contrasted and compared with those on this side of the Atlantic. The instructional leader is discomforted when the purported excellence of continental education is played up as something to be emulated in this country. It is both interesting and amusing that continental education is faced with the problem of emulating aspects of purported excellence in American education. Many first-hand observers, studying both systems, feel that although elements of both systems could be shared for mutual profit, accurate comparison between them is unrealistic. The organization for education is entirely different in America from that on the continent. Secondary schools in Europe perform secondary school and general college functions, since the university system does not fully encompass general education or the liberal arts. Finally, with rare exception, the continental preuniversity school consists of eight or nine years of rigorous training in languages, mathematics, science, history, and literature administered to the select fifteen to twenty per cent of the youth, chosen at approximately age ten to twelve. It would be much as if we were to adopt a system of selecting the top fifteen per cent of fourth graders to go on to secondary school.

Woodring, in his *Fourth of a Nation*, makes in essence a compromise suggestion that the specially gifted fourth of the youth receive intensive training, similar to the European pattern, with modifications for the less talented groups.[15] Conant and others have recommended the comprehensive high school with "multiple track" experiences based upon abilities and interests.[16]

Educators here and in foreign countries feel that substantial intellectual resources in Europe might be salvaged through the adoption of some of our practices, particularly with regard to extending the time in school before making final decisions regarding specialization.

Secondary education for the masses

Not the least among the problems of improving instruction is that of providing quality education effectively for the wide range of students enrolled in our secondary schools. This is not a dream or an impractica-

[15] Paul Woodring, A *Fourth of a Nation* (New York: McGraw-Hill, Inc., 1957).
[16] Conant, *op. cit.*, p. 96.

bility. Many communities do quite well toward accomplishing the ideal; in other communities, the implications of universal secondary education have not been fully realized by the profession or the general public. Actually, too many communities provide selective educational programs and provide for universal secondary education with only the superficial motions of espousing an educational program with diversity and flexibility.

Profound differences among individuals have been scientifically charted, and realistic educational programs must reflect variations to meet individual needs. No uniform program or single technique will suffice. Effective provisions for individual differences require multiple program implementations and a variety of techniques carefully selected and planned to be commensurate with the needs of youth to be served. In practice, this means that in a heterogeneous student body, standards of achievement, based upon the individual student's capabilities, must be established and recognized. Reports of the student's achievement should communicate a description of the particular work and success of the individual in relation to established standards in a differentiated program. Under this policy a standard high school diploma would be inappropriate, since it could not attest to the satisfactory completion of a uniform experience. In fact, granting identical diplomas to high school graduates is even now viewed by some employers and colleges as merely certification of attendance. A record of the individual's achievement is necessary in appraisal and selective processes. The granting of the differentiated diploma and the course description diploma by many schools approaches much more nearly the realities of recognizing program completions truly geared to individual needs and achievement.

Problems of instruction improvement, stemming from educating all youth, may be summarized as follows:

1. Reaffirming the ideal that all youth should be educated to the fullest potential of their abilities, needs, and capacities, by the general public, the instructional staffs, and the students.

2. Translating this ideal into practical program offerings and practices in the high school.

3. Establishing minimum standards of acceptable achievement in the differentiated programs in the school.

4. Providing quality instruction in the differentiated programs.

5. Fusing content mindedness and student-centered mindedness on the part of staff and the general public to support and implement a program truly dedicated to meeting the individual differences in a heterogeneous grouping.

6. Providing means and techniques for effectively determining individual differences, capacities, and interests.

7. Establishing means for guidance and appraisal appropriate to a differentiated program.

Major functions of secondary education

Any concern about improvement of instruction must eventually take into account the major functions of education. Education has a number of important and valuable functions, but these are seldom clearly defined either in terms of educational practices or of what lay people think the high school accomplishes. In the decade between 1930 and 1940, the National Association of Secondary School Principals published committee reports on issues and functions of secondary education. In 1955, the White House Conference on Education addressed itself to this task. In 1957, the National Conference on Secondary Education, held at The University of Chicago, and a subsequent conference at Teachers College, Columbia University, again explored the functions of the high school. A review of the findings reveals many commonalities. French and his associates have synthesized the findings of these statements into four general functions: the integrating function, the development function, the exploratory and guidance function, and the differentiating function.[17]

The integrating function. The function of integration assumes that education should contribute to the cultural integration of students. This is predicated upon the full development of individuality in the person while relating him to the common understandings, attitudes, beliefs, knowledges, skills, and purposes necessary for effective actions in society. No man lives entirely unto himself, and this fact becomes more and more meaningful in an increasingly complex and interdependent society.

Special problems arise in this area, due to the fact that the school is only one of several social agencies and institutions having impact on the social integration of the individual. Under a philosophy of selective and uniform education for all, the school's contribution to social integration is made much simpler than under a philosophy of universal education with differentiated programs. It appears clear that the comprehensive high school has a greater multiplicity of problems with regard to the social integration function and, at the same time, the greatest opportunity to execute the desirable function once the problems are seen and met.

[17] Will French, J. Dan Hull, and B. L. Dodds, *American High School Administration—Policy and Practice* (New York: Holt, Rinehart & Winston, Inc., 1957), pp. 71–78.

The developmental function. The developmental function envelops the full growth and attainment of all apparent and latent potentials in the individual. This function is subject to controversy. Some hold that the school's responsibility should be largely limited to academic considerations. At the same time, it must be conceded that every individual has an existence apart from the group life and the vocational pursuits for which the school has a responsibility. Therefore, a program of differentiated activities designed to ensure maximal maturation of individuality must be provided to enlarge and develop the student's interests and talents. The more highly organized and complex society becomes, the greater the need for the development and the maintaining of individuality.

Youth organizations, the home, the church, and other social institutions, all provide vital assistance in the developmental function. This suggests the need for close cooperation between the school and other community agencies in this and other functions of education. Communities such as Shorewood, Wisconsin, have found a Community Parent and School Council an effective organizational pattern for cooperative efforts in the developmental function. The mere fact that other community agencies perform this function to some extent does not justify the school's abdication. The school, as a representative and dynamic community agency, should assume leadership in a cooperative effort to make the best possible use of all potential sources for the development of youth.

The guidance function. This function is taking on a new and more significant meaning in the modern high school. It is during the high school years that students face problems of determining and crystallizing their own particular interests and purposes. The seriousness with which secondary education is attempting to provide diversified programs to meet the varying needs of youth compels us to take a careful look at the guidance function, for the effectiveness of a differentiated program rests squarely on the foundation of intelligent and efficient guidance procedures.

Guidance has long been one of the chief concerns of the high school principal. It has long been an integral part of his job. Disciplining, programming, advising, counseling, all were among the major responsibilities of the principal. This concept was entirely in keeping with the earlier concepts of guidance, which was an admixture of teaching and authority administered to students to assist them in making the proper choices and adjustment to life situations.

With the advent of specialized training in guidance procedures and techniques, and with the evolvement of the concept of the guidance function, staff members began to share these responsibilities. Specialists were hired to assist staff members in their guidance activities. Counseling began to be synonymous with guidance, and in some situations replaced the term in keeping with the thought that students should be provided with wide experiences and information with which they should be encouraged to arrive at proper decisions on their own.

In the modern developmental concept of the guidance function we see a synthesis of counseling (nondirective as contrasted with the more authoritarian directive approach) coupled with curriculum experiences designed to provide the student with a proper basis for making efficacious, critical decisions concerning life problems, courses, vocational pursuits, and other personal adjustment problems on his own.[18] Guidance, in this concept, becomes one of the functions of the high school as a social institution. The whole secondary school experience is seen in terms of its guidance values and of its impact upon individual students and the student body collectively.

As we see it, the major problem of the principal, as he endeavors to improve instruction and the quality of education through a differentiated program, is to (1) establish a proper climate among the community, staff, and students for the implementation of the guidance function; (2) provide exploratory, self-assessment, informational, and other experiences commensurate with the needs of students in making choices and decisions; (3) provide channels, resources, personnel, instructional materials, and opportunities for continued growth and development based upon decisions and choices arrived at by students; and (4) from time to time appraise the effectiveness and efficiency of the guidance function in his school.

The differentiating function. This function, closely related to the developmental function, embodies the tremendous task of providing the appropriate differentiated curriculum experiences required by a heterogeneous student body. In addition to providing a sound general education, differentiation encompasses program developments for those for whom the secondary school is terminal, those preparing for college, those preparing for vocational pursuits directly after finishing high school and those with no special plans for the future.

[18] G. F. Farwell and H. J. Peters, *Guidance: A Developmental Approach* (Chicago: Rand MacNally & Co., 1958).

Some of the problems here are the following:

1. To provide for compatibility in the integrating and differentiating functions of a high school.

2. To provide for minimum general education for all.

3. To keep the program in balance so that it does not become all general or all special.

4. To determine the degree to which special programs should be structured or left open for election on the part of students.

5. To decide how to guide and program students into the differentiated curricula.

6. To determine how to finance and staff the differentiated program.

7. To determine cutting points, inclusions, and exclusions in providing for differentiation, particularly in the small high schools.

Differentiation, in this context, means running two or more shows in the same tent. The allusion to a circus tent is not entirely facetious; the three-ring circus is a fairly good example of differentiation for the entertainment interests of a heterogeneous group.

RELATED ISSUES AND CONCERNS

The problems of improving instruction are legion, and only problems that may have application in many situations are included here. For the most part, the principal will find it much easier to discover problems than to find their solution. It is in the latter aspect of the job that the men are separated from the boys, and that leadership shines through. The following are problems practicing principals will readily recognize and the neophyte very soon discover.

Staff attitude

Staff attitude and inclination to want to do something about improving the instructional program can be a most vexing problem. Attitude and climate of opinion on a staff are not matters of accident. Good teachers with high morale and willingness to cope with problems of instruction are usually the product of quality leadership operating according to design to bring together the best people possible into a team relationship. Good teachers tend to gravitate to the better situations and to avoid the less desirable positions, where staff attitude is uninviting.

Abilities among teachers vary. The wise administrator will assess the strengths and weaknesses of his staff and move in the direction of making the best possible use of the talents available. Recognition, evaluation, encouragement, praise, undertaking, and growth are key concepts in building staff attitudes and morale. This should not be overlooked as one of the more common problems with relation to the program of improving instruction.

Schedule-making

Scheduling is another problem of increasing dimension in the improvement in the quality of instruction and learning. Methods and techniques for scheduling are discussed in Chapter 5. It is our purpose here merely to highlight scheduling as it is related to differentiation in the high school program. In some schools, where transportation is a factor, it is almost a matter of adjusting the daily schedule to the bus trip in the morning and the return trip in midafternoon. With ever-increasing consolidations and longer transportation routes, this factor has become very significant. Many schools have experimented with longer class periods, but they have encountered difficulties in finding enough periods in the day to do what seemed necessary. Yet when the periods are cut short, teachers often complain that there is not enough time to do what is necessary. Schools operating a selective program, that is, strictly vocational or general education, have the least difficulty. The comprehensive high schools, operating a differentiated program to meet varied student interests and needs, are bound to have a greater problem with scheduling.

Instructional needs are not the only factors that impinge upon scheduling. Most high schools have substantial programs of cocurriculum activities—clubs, athletics, music, forensics, dramatics, and so forth. Either the academic program must be interrupted to provide for these activities, or they must be scheduled before or after school hours. However provided for, these experiences take time out of the day.

Another factor in many schools is overcrowded buildings, which result in double shifts. This is even more constraining in providing time for a differentiated program that permits wide choices in student participation.

Transiency

Mobility of students appears to be an increasingly difficult problem. Seasonal employment, industrial expansion, personnel development programs, and new opportunities for parental employment make it necessary for students to change residence from one high school district to another. Arrangements must be made for such students to continue the kind of training and the courses pursued in the previous high school. Evaluations of credits, substitutions, and adjustments often make it difficult for the student to maintain his original course plans and still be provided with what may be considered best in the way of a quality experience on the secondary level.

Size factors

School size and enrollment is another factor to be considered in providing for improvement of instruction. Many schools are faced with economic and personnel problems in meeting the wide range of needs. Can a class be operated for two or three students? What is the cutting point for a class to "make"? What is the relation of class size to the nature of subject matter taught?

Some schools have solved these problems rather ingeniously by combining two small groups in advanced mathematics and individualizing the instruction. Others have supervised and paid for correspondence courses. In still other instances, special classes have been scheduled outside of the regular class periods.

At the other end of the scale, where enrollments exceed the operating facilities, communities have resorted to double-shift programs. This arrangement is makeshift at best, but is sometimes the only solution until more building facilities can be provided. Mounting enrollments and costs have made optimum use of facilities and the avoidance, whenever possible, of duplication of facilities for the same program uses of utmost importance.

Other problems of improving instruction include ways of gaining community support, policy, the use of consultants, staff time for the study of instructional improvement, and many other details. All of them must be considered in any effort to build quality into the instructional program.

KEY ROLE OF THE PRINCIPAL

"Principalship" and "leadership" are synonymous in education. The principal is in a position to affect attitude, social climate, morale, progress, cooperation, and direction of effort in the secondary school. He is the key person, charged with the responsibilities of improving instruction. Despite the frustrations of administration and demands on his time, the effective principal realizes that the improvement of instruction is his most important responsibility. No one expects him to be an expert in all instructional areas, but he is expected to be an expert in coordinating, organizing, stimulating, activating, encouraging, arranging, planning, and evaluating techniques directed toward improvement of instruction in all areas and on all levels.

Studies of role expectancies of the high school principal invariably point to leadership as the number-one expectation, partly because of the position's status factors, but more because the principal is expected to exhibit leadership with his personal and professional competencies. Surely a certain amount of prestige accompanies the office, but it hardly follows that an individual is a leader merely because he holds a status position. Nor does it follow that a person is a leader because he exercises authority. Leadership studies in the armed forces revealed many factors other than authority as vital to good leading.[19]

Concept of the job

Role expectancies have much to do with the principal's concept of his job. Many of the disappointments that come to principals, particularly to the neophyte, are directly traceable to unrealistic and deficient concepts of the position. Teaching was so different! Some assume the responsibilities of principalship with inadequate preparation. Others, because of personal and professional limitations for dealing with frustrations and responsibilities, might better have remained in the classroom as good teachers. Actually, every teacher is an administrator in his classroom and shares many of the concerns and responsibilities of the principal. It is the dimensions of the job that make the difference.

The principal comes to his tasks with a certain self-expectancy based on what he, himself, conceives to be his job, his duties, and his responsibilities. But this is only one aspect of the concept of the principalship. The community has a concept of what it thinks the principalship should be; teachers have their views; the superintendent, the board of education, and even the students have their concepts of the principal-

[19] Carroll L. Shartle, "Studies in Naval Leadership," *Groups, Leadership and Men*, edited by Harold Guetzkow (Columbus, Ohio: The Ohio State University Research Foundation, 1952).

ship. It is readily seen, then, that the concept of the principalship, as it exists in reality, is a composite of several points of view and several sets of expectancies. Unless conflicts between the principal's concept of his job and those held by others are resolved and understood, the effectiveness of the principal as a leader is bound to suffer. Essentially his job is not so much knowing all the answers as it is knowing how to work with and through people to obtain answers and solutions to problems.

Position of influence

The principal is in a unique position of influence in education. He stands, as no other person does, in a pivotal relationship between the people and the school. His office is a medium for two-way communication, reporting and interpreting school activities to the community, and assessing and implementing the community's educational objectives in his school.

Who is in a better position to help citizens, teachers, and others in the community to define their educational goals than the principal? Who is in a better position to help in the assessment of educational values? Who assumes the leadership for facilitating the teaching-learning process to develop greater effectiveness in teaching? Who builds the organizational structure that develops the leadership qualities of staff members at all levels, and promotes group solidarity and group productivity? One man—in a unique position of influence resident in the principalship of a secondary school.

Not unlike the 500-mile auto racing classic, where a "pacer" leads out to unleash the skills of highly selected participants in order to produce a spectacle in speed, the high school principal sets the pace for his staff and his community. He is a catalyst that initiates a process, sets it off and gets it going. He puts leadership into practice by creating the proper atmosphere for cooperative teamwork and production in order that fruitful interchange of ideas and sharing of knowledge may be established and maintained.

The effective principal perceives the right moment to initiate action, to lend encouragement, to inject new zest, to give recognition, to evaluate, and to culminate activities. Many leaders are good "starters." The true test of leadership comes in carrying through to the finish. It is what happens between the start and the finish of a project that establishes the value of the leader as a pace-setter. Starting an activity and carrying it through to a conclusion is a phenomenon of group dynamics that cannot be left to chance. The principal is responsible for this nurturing process.

Conditions and processes

The principal is the key person in the cooperative problem-solving process. As such, he is concerned with conditions and processes—the conditions under which problems are to be solved and improvements made, and the processes necessary to achieve the intended goals. For example, the time at which a staff committee meeting is scheduled to work on a problem is a condition that may make or break the effectiveness of the participation. Conditions for work that are undesirable and unwelcome are decided roadblocks to successful activity.

The leader is likewise concerned with process: the sharing, studying, evaluating, data-gathering, hypothesizing, testing, and concluding activities of the group. He can do much to initiate, encourage, stimulate, organize, and nurture a healthy group effort in the solution of a problem or, through his own conduct, he can discourage all productive effort. Conditions and processes go hand in hand, one dependent upon the other. The able leader not only recognizes this, but becomes adept at handling and manipulating these two factors so as to provide the best possible circumstances for productive group effort.

Successful instructional leaders are becoming more convinced that instructional improvement is a matter of change in people—change in their behavior and attitudes. According to Sharp, the improvements a community brings about in its instructional program are due largely to changes in the professional behavior of its school personnel,[20] and to make these changes effectively requires an understanding of the process.

Any conscious change in teaching or in the selection or use of instructional materials is initiated by a feeling of dissatisfaction with existing methods. When we are dissatisfied, we begin to explore, searching for improvements. We select possibilities that look promising, design a way of implementing them, and "try them on for size." The key concepts are appraisal, dissatisfaction, search, selection, design, trial, and evaluation. This is the intelligent process of change—the process, nurtured under favorable conditions, with the greatest possibility of consistent success.

Leadership competencies

Let us again examine the role expectancy of the instructional leader before we look at specific competencies. In the cooperative approach to

[20] George Sharp, *Curriculum Development as Re-education of the Teacher* (New York: Bureau of Publications, Teachers College, Columbia University, 1951).

instructional improvement the responsibility of the leader is two-fold. First, he is a provider of the necessary resources for members of his staff. Second, he is a teacher of skills in the cooperative problem-solving process. This concept of role differs somewhat from those conventionally practiced, although it is hardly foreign to our better instructional leaders. The role of instructional leader envisioned here is not so much concerned with what he is, what he is like, or his status, but is concerned with what he does, how he behaves, and how he works with and through people.

By conventional standards, this description of an instructional leader's role may sound strange, largely because the popular concept of the successful leader is someone who can, single-handed, quickly assess situations—in a kind of a one-man show—and then get others to do what *he* thinks needs to be done. The sad fact is that most men now in positions of leadership in our schools run one-man shows because they have not been trained in the cooperative team approach to problem solving. Some attempt it by appointing committees and imagining this act alone to be the essence of cooperative group effort. Under these circumstances it is quite impossible for them to serve as resources to help staff members learn processes that they themselves have not sufficiently experienced.

What competencies, then, should a provider of resources and a trainer in the group process possess in addition to those required to meet the manifold expectations required of his office? Since leadership behavior is our point of reference, let us take for granted that the individual possesses all the personal traits and professional virtues generally accredited to a principal, and go directly to an examination of leading as a process.

A competency is a factor that contributes to or is an integral part of effective leader behavior. Research studies on effective leader behavior patterns are far fewer in number than those exploring leadership traits, yet evidence of a high positive relationship between good character traits and effective leader behavior is indisputable. Some of the personal character traits of the effective leader, as noted in Chapter 3, may be summarized in these words: capacity, achievement, responsibility, status, and empathy. The instructional leader works with people in many and varying situations, much the same as a coach works with members of a team. He works with individuals, pairs, groups, and the team as a whole. Although there can be no doubt about the positive values of good leadership traits as desirable assets to any leader of people, however, the mere possession of desirable traits in an individual is of itself no guarantee of associated behavioral competencies requisite to effective group leadership.

Competencies for providing resources. What are some of the special-ized competencies for providing resources? First, the principal must possess the ability to perceive and recognize various resources that will aid the process of improving instruction. Many resources in the school situation are ignored and wasted simply because no one recognizes them. Some of these hidden resources are in the staff, in the community, and in professional groups. Teachers and community members often have valu-able contributions and encouragement to offer. Nearby colleges and uni-versities may have resources and resource persons available. Frequently other school systems are interested in similar problems and cooperate willingly in programs of instructional improvement. The perceptive leader will not allow these resources to go unnoticed and unused.

Resources of many kinds—material, personal, spiritual, time—all are needed in the process of instructional improvement. All need to be weighed and evaluated in terms of appropriateness, availability, perti-nence, and plausibility. Funds, equipment, and supplies required for any effort to study and improve instruction must be anticipated. Teachers, consultants, resource persons, and community members are needed in any program of dealing with instructional problems. *Esprit de corps* is essential. Time must be arranged for meetings and deliberations. Cleri-cal assistance must be provided for reporting results.

Second, the leader must possess an ability to procure resources. This encompasses more than the ability to process requisitions. It in-volves planning, budgeting, organizing, scheduling, and justifying acqui-sition.

Let us consider the following illustration of poorly executed pro-curement. The experimental engineering division of a large manufac-turing company needed some specialized equipment for a very im-portant project. A team of engineers appeared at a meeting of the board of directors, which, incidentally, was composed largely of business men with nonengineering backgrounds, to request the purchase of $250,000 worth of special equipment. The request was couched in such technical language that only a few board members understood the request. The only action taken at that meeting was to table the request until the board could gain a better understanding of what was wanted.

Third, the principal must have an ability to make effective use of resources. Regardless of the nature of the resource, ineffectual use of it is hardly excusable. Additional staff personnel brought on to assist in a program of improving instruction will be of little value if they are as-signed chores easily handled by high school students. Likewise, equip-ment and materials that are allowed to remain in storage have little value.

Perceiving, procuring, and using wisely are the hallmarks of the leader's competence in providing resources. Naturally, the use of these skills varies with situations and circumstances, just as the resource requirements vary with the nature of the problem to be solved or the project to be undertaken. Whatever the needs, the leader must see it as his responsibility to provide unfailingly the optimal resources commensurate with the task at hand.

Competencies for training in the group process. The role of the principal in training for group and cooperative approaches to problem-solving is in many ways similar to that of the conductor of a symphony orchestra. A musical organization is the combination of many individuals, groups, talents, temperaments, and skills. Each section in the orchestra makes its distinct contribution, and when all are organized into a harmonious interpretive effort the results are pleasing. Let the same musicians gather to make random sounds on their instruments, however, and, regardless of their skills and talents, the result is noisy confusion.

How does one train people for group thinking, for teamwork, and for cooperative effort? How does one help people learn to work together? More especially, how does one help people to think together in a problem-solving situation? The answers to these questions form the substance of the leadership competencies necessary in training people to work productively as group members and to realize definite personal satisfactions and growth in the process. Working together should be in an atmosphere in which opportunities and encouragement for experimenting with new ideas exist; where there is recognition of, respect for, and utilization of participants' opinions and ideas in determining action that will affect them; and where experiences build confidence and skill in cooperative problem-solving.

Five contributions. First, the instructional leader is expected to bring to the problem-solving situation a demonstrable competence in and understanding of the group process. No one can lead or assist others to better understandings of processes he, himself, does not thoroughly understand. The successful teacher of group dynamics is a student of group interaction. He knows how to involve people, how to arrange conditions and initiate processes that will bring out the best in each participant. He knows the relation of organization, communication, scheduling, timing, fact-gathering, deliberation, evaluation, and summarization to the cooperative problem-solving experiences.

Second, he will have skill in establishing rapport among the members of a group. He will be sure that teachers come to know and understand each other. This is fairly easy with a relatively small faculty where everyone is more or less acquainted, but where several school faculties are involved and there is widespread representation on committees, getting acquainted and developing understandings becomes more important and involved. Sometimes a cup of coffee preceding a work session is just the thing needed to set the stage and establish a climate for subsequent group effort. A few minutes of socialization prior to the work session often do wonders.

Third, the leader will know how to define the problem and relate it to the participants in the group. He will encourage participants, explore and redefine the problem and the subproblems.

Fourth, he will recognize individual contributions—advice, ability, and ideas preferred by group members. He will encourage the group to share in this recognition and give credit where due. A word of praise is often worth a dozen admonishments, especially since group members need to feel secure before they will speak their minds about issues. To be summarily "ruled out" or "laughed at" for expressing an idea undermines the confidence necessary in the team approach to problem-solving.

A fifth competence of the leader in the group process is a demonstrated integrity of leadership. Every leader is called upon to accede to a great variety of demands, pressures, and urges from within and without. He has his own status to think about, yet he desires to be popular, to please. Other members of the group have aspirations and ambitions. In working with problems of instructional improvement there are often pressure groups with selfish motives, or well-meaning but uninformed parents. Hence, every person responsible for group activity must steer a course between initiating and directing, on the one hand, and showing consideration for himself and for others, on the other. The maintenance of a proper balance between the two forces may be called the integrity of leadership. One author has referred to it as a leader inner-directedness, a certain integrity for seeing that things move in a positive direction regardless of distractions and inhibiting factors.[21]

These five general competencies of the leader in group process are not only positive values for the instructional leader but also potentials to be cultivated and shared by emerging leaders within the group. Every participant should grow through sharing in the group activity and assuming, from time to time, the leadership role. Instructional improvement

[21] T. J. Jenson, *Some Important Considerations For Leadership* (Columbus, Ohio: The Ohio Trade and Industrial Education Service, The Ohio State University, 1958), p. 8.

does not take place in a vacuum; it occurs in the minds and attitudes of people—teachers, administrators, citizens, students, and all others connected in any way with the school program. As people grow in ability to pool energy, ideas, imaginations, experiments, evaluations, and inspirations in a cooperative effort to improve instruction, the possibility of satisfactory change is proportionately enhanced.

This more or less abstract discussion of the role of the instructional leaders is in no way intended as a dodge to the realities of the principal's job. Obviously, he has problems of curriculum, special services, cocurriculum activities, scheduling, staffing, extended school day, inservice education, educational camping, adult education, parent education, vocational education, public relations, and many other concerns. In solving problems of any kind, however, *he works with people.* He probably should involve people more than he does. Success—his own and that of his school—will ultimately be measured by the degree to which he has helped others to grow and cooperate in solving the many problems related to modern secondary education.

There are no pat answers to all problems of secondary education that have universal application in all situations and all communities. The small school has its peculiar problems, as does the large school, and a satisfactory solution in one situation might be quite out of order in another. Therefore, it is clear that good leadership, with wide involvement of people in the problem-solving process, is the most logical and potentially successful technique for obtaining solutions, while at the same time assuring growth of the participants in the process.

Good instruction

Good instruction is very complicated. Basically, it is a matter of providing the right experiences. All experiences in the classroom, in the gymnasium, on the athletic field, and elsewhere in the school lead to learning. Learning occurs at home, on the street corners, and with "the gang." Although the principal's responsibility for instruction lies normally with arranging for the experiences in school, he cannot ignore the learning that occurs elsewhere.

There are many criticisms of the curriculum. Not enough students are enrolled in advanced science courses. Too many students are electing the "soft" courses. Graduates do not know enough mathematics. The pressure is on the principal to give an account of his stewardship. In the next instant some one approaches the principal with the request that a new course be added to the curriculum. In such conditions, what is good instruction?

Curriculum (experiences and content of instruction) is not to be confused with instruction (teaching and providing learning experiences). Our concern here is with the latter, especially with the relation of the principal to the improvement of teaching and the instructional program.

Good instruction is characterized by: (a) providing the basic and general learning experiences commensurate with the cultural, vocational, civic, and moral requirements of the affected society; (b) ensuring that the abilities and talents of students, individually and in groups, are challenged in the process to a degree that will assure effectiveness and efficiency; (c) securing measurable growth, achievement, comprehension, and mastery of skills, consistent with the level of instruction; (d) achieving the desired goals through leading and guiding students in the spirit of enthusiastic cooperation shared by students, parents, school staff members, and citizens.

Again, each principal and his staff define good instruction for themselves, in terms of their own peculiar situation. Two fundamental concepts seem to us to be very important in the principal's approach to what constitutes good instruction: (a) the instruction must meet the varied needs of youth in the community, and (b) there must be demonstrated growth on the part of the students.

THE CASE OF MR. JONES

Thus far we have discussed the problems, theory, philosophy, and other related aspects of instructional leadership in secondary education. Now let us look at a theoretical situation in which a principal attempts to give leadership to the improvement of instruction.

Madison High School is located in a small town serving an urban and a large rural area. There are thirty-eight teachers on the high school staff. The system has a minimum central office staff. Consequently, the leadership for improving instruction is left to the superintendent and the principals. Mr. Jones is relatively new in office of principal, but he has been there long enough to have observed that not all is well with the science instruction in the school. The physics teacher serves as the head of the science department, and after thirty years on the job he has begun to coast toward retirement. Madison High School is much better known for its winning football teams than for its instructional prowess, and the staff has been too busy to address itself to curriculum concerns.

Nearly one-third of the graduates go on to college. A number of these seem to be having more than usual trouble in college science courses. Science courses are the least popular among the courses at Madison. In addition, only one unit—general science in the ninth grade—is required for graduation.

Jones begins

Mr. Jones begins his first step in his leadership role by making a personal assessment of the situation. He does this quietly, gathering various kinds of evidence and carefully evaluating it. Mr. Jones wants to be reasonably certain about the situation before he makes any moves, because there are the usual touchy personality and human relations factors involved. He is, however, convinced that the community wants good instruction.

Checking his judgment.   Having satisfied himself that there is a problem, Mr. Jones seeks to check his judgment with the superintendent in a conference meeting. He brings his evidence to the superintendent as a check on his own thinking and to obtain support and sanction for moving ahead with trying to solve the problems and bring about improvements. He knows that his role in providing resources and perhaps a consultant has budget implications. The superintendent sees the problem quickly and encourages Mr. Jones to try to improve science instruction. Mr. Jones was fairly sure of this encouragement, but he is one who "plays it safe." Besides, he wants the superintendent to know that he is on his toes with respect to giving leadership to improvement of instruction.

Checking with staff.   Mr. Jones contacts Mr. Smith, the head of the science department, and arranges an interview with him about his concerns regarding science instruction. To Mr. Smith, this is somewhat routine, since Mr. Jones and he have held appraisal conferences periodically. During the interview, the principal alerts Mr. Smith to some of his observations and concerns about the situation in science education in the school and suggests that some of the staff be involved in looking into the situation. He will arrange time, a meeting place, and perhaps a cup of coffee. Then they discuss which staff members should be involved in this initial review of the science problems. They agree that all the high school science teachers be brought together and that Mr. Jones will issue the invitation through Mr. Smith.

The meeting is held in Mr. Jones' office directly after the last period on a Tuesday afternoon. The cup of coffee is a good ice-breaker as well as lift at the close of the teaching day. Mr. Jones opens the meeting by suggesting that he and Mr. Smith have talked about this problem of science instruction and desire to get the science teachers' ideas on the matter. Mr. Jones presents only a few of the observations that he had discussed with Mr. Smith and the superintendent, so as not to over-structure the meeting or give the notion that the problems were already solved. He does point out the new need for science in our technologically oriented society, some of the enrollment figures on students taking advanced courses in science, and some of the literature on the need for strength in science education for our times. Then, as a leader, he points up some things to do—gather the facts, organize the information, interpret the information, hypothesize changes, test the changes, make further changes, continue to evaluate, and, eventually, arrive at some satisfactory solutions.

Members of the group make a number of good suggestions. One teacher is assigned to explore student attitudes toward science instruction. One challenges some of the figures published on the per cent of students taking science today as compared to yesteryear and volunteers to check these in the local school. Another teacher raises the issue of the adequacy of instructional materials in the school and agrees to look into it. It is agreed that these things be done and that the group meet again to look at the facts.

Science curriculum study group formed

The next meeting, held two weeks after the first, brings out some interesting information. The problem is larger than originally anticipated and it is agreed that more study should ensue. It is suggested, for instance, that it might be well to know what science teaching was going on in the elementary schools, that it might be well to know what other high schools were doing in similar circumstances, that some technical assistance and consultative services might be helpful, and that perhaps some elementary teacher might be involved for further exploration of the science instruction. An agreement is reached to meet regularly as a study group, and Mr. Jones promises to contact Mr. Pella from the university to act as a consultant to the group.

As the group continues to meet, Mr. Jones continues to expedite, coordinate, provide resources, arrange communication, get reports typed, establish the right conditions for group activity, stimulate effort, see that the group sets up target dates for the accomplishment of portions of the work, and give recognition for progress and accomplishments.

Some results

Although this case is mythical as far as school and names are concerned, it is an actual situation now in progress. The study group has made its first report to the staff and the board of education after a year's study. All teachers in that system now know about the scope and sequence of science instruction from grades one through twelve. The budget for the coming year includes funds for much new equipment in the laboratories, new text materials, and instructional aids. The group has sensed accomplishment and has been recognized for it. The study is continuing next year with several innovations to be tried out in science instruction, after which an evaluation will again be made.

This case is just one example of how a principal goes about initiating improvement of instruction through people on his staff. Although the details of the operations are too much to include here, it is clear how Mr. Jones operated as a leader, how he took responsibility for initiating the activity, marshalled resources, set up conditions, involved people, looked for group activity and individual growth, encouraged and kept things going, gave recognition, insisted on target dates for accomplishments, cleared the road for the implementation of new ideas and innovations to be tried, and encouraged evaluation and experimentation.

Other examples

We have intimated throughout this chapter that leadership concerns itself with a wide variety of staff activities related to instruction. The perceptive leader will select and employ approaches appropriate to the situation and task as in the case cited above. For example, if a new building is being planned the architect should first be furnished specifications for the building that describe the instructional needs to be met by the structure. The administrator should provide leadership to a staff of teachers that help formulate the educational specifications for the building, and he should work with the architect in translating these specifications into the technical, working drawings.

The curriculum council, the committee on textbook selection, staff study groups, action research activities, evaluation and appraisal activities, inservice growth and development projects, student affairs, guidance, school community relations, college relations, team teaching efforts, grouping, and discipline are among the many other areas where leadership of staff and community groups relates to instruction. Each activity is different, yet the same principles of leadership apply.

CONCLUSION

The quality of secondary education is a function of instructional leadership. A positive and direct relationship exists between the two. Quality in education is an elusive concept, particularly in a culture dedicated to maximum development of the potentials of all youth. It is, however, the objective in any appraisal or assessment of an educational program and is, therefore, a factor to be thoroughly understood by anyone who would assume the role of a leader of instruction.

The discussion of instructional leadership earlier in this volume, dealing with the task areas of the secondary school principal, is not by accident. Instruction comes first. The primacy of instructional leadership is indisputable, particularly in situations where there are competing demands on the principal's time and the content to be included in the secondary curriculum, and emerging concepts of the purposes and objectives of education.

The principal is the key person in instructional leadership. He needs a thorough understanding and appreciation of his job, so that he can use his unique opportunity to effect growth and improvement.

The relationship of instructional leadership to the other task areas, such as staff personnel, pupil personnel, management, and public relations, is easy to see. The principal's tasks, in all areas, should be directed toward good instruction. The final definition and implementation of quality educational provisions rests with the local communities under the leadership of competent instructional leaders.

SUGGESTED ACTIVITIES

1. Discuss the reasons for instructional leadership receiving a priority rating in the high school principal's allotment of his time and energy.

2. Describe the implications to American secondary educational administration of the concept of education for all. Why has a high school education come to be accepted as the common school education desirable for all youth?

3. Who should determine the goals and objectives of secondary education?

4. List and discuss some major administrative problems in a program of improvement of instruction in secondary education.

5. Show how the leadership role described here differs from that of the authoritarian leader. Is there a place in secondary educational administration for the authoritarian leader?

6. Discuss the premise that good leadership is concerned with the involvement and growth of individuals connected with the enterprise.

7. Suggest the kind of training you believe necessary to provide the kind of leadership envisioned in this chapter.

SELECTED READINGS

American Association of School Administrators, *Educational Administration in a Changing Community*, Thirty-Seventh Yearbook. Washington, D.C.: The Association, 1959.

————, *The Superintendent as Instructional Leader*, Thirty-Fifth Yearbook. Washington, D.C.: The Association, 1957.

Anderson, Vivienne, and Daniel R. Davies, *Patterns of Educational Leadership*. Englewood Cliffs, N.J.: Prentice-Hall, Inc., 1956.

Association for Supervision and Curriculum Development, *Leadership for Improving Instruction*, Yearbook. Washington, D.C.: The Association, 1960.

Bair, Medill, and Richard G. Woodward, *Team Teaching in Action*. Boston: Houghton Mifflin Company, 1964.

Bruner, Jerome S., *The Process of Education*. Cambridge: Harvard University Press, 1961.

Conant, James B., *The American High School Today*. New York: McGraw-Hill, Inc., 1959.

Cyphert, Frederick R., Earl W. Harmer, Jr., and Anthony C. Riccio (eds.), *Teaching in the American Secondary School*. New York: McGraw-Hill, Inc., 1964.

Educational Policies Commission, National Education Association, *An Essay on Quality in Public Education*. Washington, D.C.: The Association, 1959.

French, Will, J. Dan Hull, and B. L. Dodds, *Behavioral Goals of General Education in High School*. New York: Russell Sage Foundation, 1957.

Fry, Edward B., *Teaching Machines and Programmed Instruction*. New York: McGraw-Hill, Inc., 1963.

Jacobson, Paul B., William C. Reavis, and James D. Logsdon, *The Effective School Principal*. Englewood Cliffs, N.J.: Prentice-Hall, Inc., 1963, Chapter 5.

————, *Organizing for Improved Instruction*. Washington, D.C.: AASA-ASCD, NEA, 1963.

7

STAFF
PERSONNEL

PERSONNEL ADMINISTRATION IS ONE OF THE MOST IM-portant administrative task areas for which the secondary school princi-pal is responsible. Administration, as commonly understood, means management. It may include management of either material, time, or personnel resources, or all three. The inter-relatedness of management problems is both obvious and inevitable. The focus here, however, is on staff personnel. The problems of student personnel administration are dealt with in Chapter 8. Any discussion of secondary school staff per-sonnel must include consideration of the principal and the administra-tive staff, the teaching and instructional personnel, the service and non-certified personnel, and special service workers. The range and scope of staff personnel is apparent from the titles employed, such as principal, vice principal, dean, director, coordinator, supervisor, teacher, psycholo-gist, case worker, clerk, secretary, nurse, custodian, engineer and many others. All are members of the team employed to man the varied and complex operations of the modern secondary school.

This chapter deals with concepts of personnel management, the principalship, the principal's hierarchical relationships, peer relationships, staff relationships, effective working relationships, staffing considerations, and other personnel concerns.

STAFF PERSONNEL ADMINISTRATION

This volume emphasizes the team approach. Every employee is a member of a team dedicated to running the best school possible. Every position is important both in itself and as it contributes to the corporate effort. In the final analysis, citizens, administrators, teachers, pupils, custodians and all others connected with the school must exhibit a high level of cooperation and teamwork if the secondary school is to rise above mediocrity to a high-quality educational institution. Bricks and mortar, fine buildings, may do much to enhance education, but the quality of the staff is the truly significant factor in the effectiveness of the school.

Staff personnel management defined

The management of staff personnel is concerned with recruiting, assigning, and supervising people in all positions in the organization. It involves the general components of administration mentioned in Chapter 3—planning, directing, coordinating, controlling, and appraising. For our purposes, staff personnel management is that aspect of general administration that is concerned with the operation of all employed persons assigned to positions in the organization, who have a vested interest in the accomplishments and objectives of the organization. Although this definition is applicable to personnel management for all kinds of businesses, the educational enterprise is somewhat unusual in that management of personnel—students, professional workers and others—is a major administrative concern. Of the conventional managerial concerns —material, personnel, and operations—the chief concerns of the school administration are with personnel and operations.

Personnel policies needed

Staff personnel administration should operate from some well-understood and recognizable frame of reference. Such a reference may roughly be defined as a policy, that is, a plan of action sufficiently specific to provide a definite guide to action and flexible enough to allow for intelligent utilization and practical application. The development of sound, co-operatively formulated personnel policies is very important. The experiences of the National Education Association Committee on Tenure and Academic Freedom in the area of personnel practices unquestioningly point up the need for better personnel policies.[1]

Personnel policies are not a "cure-all" for all staff personnel management problems. However, many pitfalls of staffing, staff inter-relationships, staff relations with the administration, and job relationships can be avoided by the existence and use of written policies.

THE PRINCIPAL

Since about 1820, with the beginning of the development of the public secondary school, the concept of the Principal has been evolving continuously. This evolution closely parallels the growth of secondary education. The academy and the independent secondary school required several teachers, one of whom became the "headmaster." Hence, in both public and semipublic secondary schools there arose a need for a principal teacher or a head of the school. In most instances, at least in the beginning and in the smaller schools, these principals taught a full schedule of classes in addition to their other duties of keeping records, caring for the school plant, and disciplining the students.

Expanding dimensions

As school enrollments grew, the students attending became less highly selected. It became necessary to free the principal from his teaching, at least part of the time, so that he could work with students and visit and assist teachers. Scheduling, supervising instruction, and tending to public relations became part of his duties. Then, as cities grew and the burdens of the school committees became ever greater, the need for a superintendent of all the schools arose. Thus, by 1835, the hierarchy of administration, as we know it today, had developed.

Each decade was marked by increasing populations, more schools, and greater enrollments. School problems increased correspondingly.

[1] Committee on Tenure and Academic Freedom, National Education Association, *Developing Personnel Policies* (Washington, D.C.: The Association, 1958).

Heterogeneous student bodies, attendance laws, health and safety factors, use of leisure time and citizenship, all these became problems for the schools. Population mobility, immigration, and urbanization contributed to educational problems. The principal was looked to as a leader and a coordinator to assist in the solution of all these problems. Specialization and professionalization of the principal's job became a necessity.

Larger schools required larger staffs. Many inexperienced teachers required the assistance of the principal, so he became a trainer of teachers. Teachers looked to the experienced head for counsel and advice, for leadership. Even the more experienced teachers, facing new problems, looked to the principal for assistance in the solutions. Thus, in the past half-century there has been a steady growth in the authority and responsibility of the principalship. In the smaller schools, the principal continues to do some teaching along with his other duties, but in the larger schools the position has become a full-time professional job.

Perceptions of the principal's role

The administrative task areas of the principal have been described in Chapter 5. However, from the point of view of staff personnel, there are good indications that the job of the principal is not as well understood by the staff as it should be. Gauerke hints that there is confusion not equaled elsewhere in the public school system about the duties of the secondary school principal.[2] Teachers see his job as a number of routine duties, clerical work, and mechanics; and they fail to see his responsibility as the professional head of the school and the relation of this responsibility to the instructional program.

The foregoing observation suggests that an important part of the principal's job is to work closely with his teachers so that they may see his role in its true light. If a teacher fails, the principal fails, and vice versa. If the team concept is fostered and developed, more chances for successful operations and fewer chances for misunderstandings accrue. The principal is responsible for developing the team approach and the desirable attitudes that go with it. Eikenberry views the principal as one who in a measure has the responsibilities of all the members of his staff and, in addition, the responsibilities for leading the entire staff in developing the objectives of the school, for coordinating all those activities

---

[2] Warren E. Gauerke, *Legal and Ethical Responsibilities of School Personnel* (Englewood Cliffs, N.J.: Prentice-Hall, Inc., 1959).

that grow out of a dynamic program of secondary education, and for making decisions.[3]

A review of a number of studies of job expectancies of the high school principal reveals top priority for leadership in the professional improvement of staff. In studying the attitudes toward the practices of principals, Austin and Collins found a strong emphasis on the leadership role. Eleven inter-related areas of job performance were classified as follows:

1. Organizing, managing, and coordinating components of the school.

2. Improving curriculum and teaching.

3. Gaining confidence and support of staff members.

4. Winning respect and approval of students.

5. Enlisting support and cooperation in the community.

6. Delegating authority and responsibility.

7. Increasing his own professional competence.

8. Participating in community affairs.

9. Making policies and decisions.

10. Working with higher administration.

11. Executing policies and decisions.[4]

Competencies in these areas, along with related qualifications, provide a basis for recruiting and selecting a secondary school principal.

Selection of the principal

The selection of the right man to head the school is of utmost importance. Two important aspects of the process are examined here: the mechanics of recruitment and selection and the specifications and qualifications for the position. Too many principals have been selected by questionable methods and upon extraneous qualifications. Popularity in the community, a good coaching record, a Beau Brummel personality, and a good

[3] Dan Harrison Eikenberry, *Training and Experience Standards for Principals of Secondary Schools*, Bulletin No. 181 (Washington, D.C.: National Association of Secondary School Principals, 1951).

[4] David B. Austin and James S. Collins, A *Study of Attitudes Toward the High School Principalship*, Bulletin No. 215 (Washington, D.C.: National Association of Secondary School Principals, 1956).

record as a teacher may or may not qualify the person to be a principal. The administration of secondary education involves tasks and competencies of a highly specialized nature. High priority must be given to the qualifications that will ensure success in the leadership and administrative role. This requires a careful assessment of the local needs and requirements along with a careful analysis of the situation in which the person is expected to function.

Recruitment and selection. The procedure for recruitment and selection begins with an official announcement of a vacancy. It is important to alert staff members and others that a new principal is being sought, for no one should apply for a position until it is officially declared vacant. The next important task is to assess the local situation with a view toward developing a statement of the specifications and qualifications desired in the candidate. This stock-taking is a most helpful means of determining the kind of leadership desired in candidates for the position.

Various techniques are used by superintendents and boards of education in announcing vacancies and inviting candidates to apply. In addition to making local announcements, teacher placement offices of colleges and universities are sent statements of the qualifications and specifications desired in the candidates, and requested to nominate a given number of persons. In some instances, the placement officers are directed to send names, alert potential candidates, and invite them to make application in writing. In other instances, the placement officials are requested only to send credentials, with the assumption that the local school officials will contact the candidates selected or screened to make formal application. The trend appears to be in the direction of the latter method, thus obviating the deluge of applications from many aspirants who fall far short of meeting the established qualifications and specifications.

Final screening of candidates. Processing and screening qualified candidates becomes the next task in the selection of a principal. Among the more elaborate selection procedures employed is the plan used in Covina, California, schools.[5] Here openings are announced, specifications formulated, placement officers notified, applications invited and applicants notified of the final screening, and detailed testing and rating procedures employed by the system in determining a final group of eligible

[5] Paul Salmon, "How to Select a Principal," *School Management*, May, 1959, p. 47.

candidates. The applications and credentials are reviewed and rated by a committee of five—two principals, two representatives from the superintendent's office, and the director of curriculum. Local candidates receive a bonus of five points on the factors of training and experience. All candidates are then required to take an examination prepared by the Educational Testing Service. The results of the rating on credentials and the test scores form the bases for the first eliminations.

The top twelve are called back for further examinations and interviews. Another committee of five, this time including one teacher, is established. The twelve candidates are divided into two groups and each group goes with the committee to visit local school situations. Candidates are asked to make careful observations and later to suggest how these situations might be improved. Each group is also asked to discuss what has been observed, in order to provide the committee with information as to the candidates' articulateness and behavior in a group situation. Finally, a thirty-minute personal interview with the committee is provided for each candidate. Upon a review and evaluation of all the evidence the committee selects three or four candidates, from which group the superintendent and the board select a principal.

Throughout the process every effort is made to keep the screening procedure objective. For instance, the results of the first committee's ratings and the test scores are tallied and computed by someone in the personnel department. Numbers are used for identification on papers, and raters are not identified by name. Every precaution is taken to assure fairness to all candidates.

A general procedure suggested by this sample would involve: (1) announcing the vacancy, (2) preparing an analysis of the job, (3) formulating requirements for the candidates, (4) alerting placement agencies of the need for candidates' providing them with full information, (5) receiving applications, (6) conducting preliminary screening to include only those who meet general requirements, (7) obtaining enriched credentials through testing, interviewing, and other techniques to select a small number of highly qualified candidates, (8) establishing a rank order list of two or more finalists from which a selection is made.

Evaluation of candidates. The importance of finding the right person to fit the position cannot be overemphasized. More and more school systems are employing the best professional and psychological counsel available for assistance in an orderly, objective, and businesslike procedure for screening and selecting personnel. Among the several services and procedures widely used is that developed by William Flesher and Marie

Flesher.[6] This procedure has three distinct advantages: (1) Evaluative evidence is secured from a variety of sources and by more than one means. (2) A number of different people assist in the appraisal. (3) An important part of the evaluative data is secured by an impartial professional agency *outside* the school district.

The procedure consists of an essay examination, an objective test, an interview or oral examination, and appraisal of credentials, and a "field rating." Both aspects of the written testing are supervised by an agency outside the school district, although the tests themselves are usually administered in the school district. Consultative assistance for other parts of the procedure is provided by the educational testing consultants, utilizing forms that have been developed to serve as guides to boards of education and school administrators in securing and recording evidence. These procedures and tests have been undergoing constant evaluation and refinement since 1948 and have been employed in a large number of personnel selections throughout the country.

Here, as in other personnel selection assistance plans, the consultants work closely with the local school authorities in the development of job specifications and appraisal of local needs. Ultimately a select, ranked list of candidates, from which a selection may be made, is made available to the school authorities.

Relation of the principal to those above him   ✓ ʙʏ. 167

The secondary school principal is usually one of several principals in an educational system. His operations are influenced by those in authority above him—the superintendent, central office, board of education, the state department of education, accrediting agencies, and the like, his fellow principals in the system, and his staff. In practice, the relation of the principal to the superintendent and the central office may vary greatly, depending mainly upon the general philosophy of administration in the system. The policies, regulations, and rules prescribed by the board and central administration differ from system to system. Some school boards have elaborate and definite policies and regulations affecting the operation of the secondary school. In other situations, many of the operations of the high school are left to the judgment of the principal and his staff. The more able principal welcomes the opportunity to use his own ingenuity in a situation that allows wide latitude in terms of local au-

---

[6] William R. Flesher and Marie A. Flesher, A *Procedure for Evaluating Prospective Administrative Personnel for Schools* (Columbus, Ohio: Bureau of Educational Research, The Ohio State University, 1958), p. 7., mimeographed.

tonomy while being scrupulously careful to respect this freedom in operation. In either case, he must maintain good communication with the superintendent and sense items that require clearance before being acted upon.

Successful principals make good use of administrative staff meetings with the superintendent and central office personnel. Many potential difficulties can be circumvented by understandings developed through discussions at such meetings or through personal conferences. Smooth operation requires that the principal have an appreciation of the elastic limits of autonomy and is perceptive of the expectations of those above him. Some principles that the authors have developed and found to be helpful in these circumstances are the following:

1. The principal's role in the administrative organization should be carefully defined and understood by all concerned.

2. Policies, regulations, and rules should be periodically reviewed and interpreted for the purposes of maintaining thorough understandings.

3. A proper basis for two-way communication should be established and maintained.

4. The delegation of authority and responsibility should be thoroughly understood and respected by the principal and those above him.

5. Ingenuity and personal resourcefulness on the part of the principal in his operations and functions should be expected and respected.

6. The legal responsibilities vested in the several administrative positions in the school system should be intelligently respected.

In practice, the trend appears to be in the direction of granting greater autonomy to the principal in the operation of his school. Correspondingly, the principal seems to be becoming increasingly involved in cooperative general school administration teamwork, and more is being expected of him in this regard.

The principal and other principals

Most local schools are administered by principals who are regarded as responsible heads acting under the directions of the superintendent and the official regulations of the board of education. In a vast majority of the school systems throughout the country, which have one high school serving the community, the secondary school principal occupies a unique position. There may be several elementary principals in the organization, but he alone represents secondary education. Our culture, perhaps for good reasons, leans toward setting the status position of the secondary school principal just a little higher than that for the elementary principal. Not that his work is any more important educationally, but the secondary school head does have an over-all relationship to the community not shared by the principals of elementary schools. His interscholastic relationships with other schools, his added responsibilities for cocurriculum activities, his relations with accrediting bodies and colleges, and his association with the terminal common school educational offerings in the community, all add to his status.

The effective secondary school principal should accept leadership in working cooperatively with other principals. He must give consideration to this responsibility both within his school system and in his relations with other secondary schools and other school systems. The increasing mobility of students, the need for curriculum articulation from kindergarten through secondary school, and the opportunities for educational guidance and coordination, all make it mandatory for principals on all levels to establish and maintain harmonious relationships.

Likewise, the principal has an obligation to his profession. He should become identified with his local and national professional organizations. Participation in studies, conferences, and projects, together with contributions—articles, papers, ideas—are some of the means by which contact with a professional organization takes on real meaning and value. The need for sharing experiences should not be overlooked. Others are probably groping through the same problem areas, which are apt to be found in any local situation. The effective principal is constantly alert to new ideas and opportunities to improve himself in service.

Since communities vary greatly as to size, complexity, philosophy, and organization, it is difficult to describe accurately in detail the relations of the secondary school principal to those above him and to his professional peers. Jacobson and others point out seven generalizations that seem to be warranted:

1. The principal is directly responsible to the superintendent and under usual organization patterns does not have direct administrative relations with the board of education.

2. The principal is responsible for carrying out the administrative policies of the school system and is the superintendent's chief representative in the local school in his charge.

3. The principal's relations with intermediary administrative officers—supervisors and service personnel in the central office—are determined by the superintendent and, we would hope, the cooperatively agreed upon functional policies in the administrative organization.

4. In large city systems the principal's direct contact with the superintendent's office may be mainly through a deputy, assistant superintendent, area superintendent, or similar intermediary officer, but access to the superintendent should always be possible.

5. Assistant principals should be directly responsible to the principal rather than to the central office much in the same manner as the principal is related to the central office.

6. Definite channels and policies should be established and respected with regard to the principal's relationships with noncertified personnel in the central office—business managers, clerks and others.

7. The status of the principal is largely determined by the policies and philosophy of the central office—he is either the intellectual and professional leader of his school, a glorified office boy, or something in between.[7]

The principal's part in and obligation for helping to determine his own position should not be underestimated. More and more principals are being called upon by the central administration to assist in policy determinations and to contribute as a member of the administrative team. The principal should accept these opportunities whenever presented and feel a responsibility for making worthwhile contributions, both in his own interest and in the over-all values to be gained for the prestige and professionalization of the principalship.

The principal and his staff

Someone recently posed the question, "What is an assistant principal?" He might well have asked the same question about a dean of girls, the attendance clerk, a teacher, or the custodian. The person asking the question was inferring that from the point of view of staff relations the assistant principal may be one thing in a given situation and quite another in a different situation. In one school he is a positive integer in the administrative staff, with specific delegated authority and responsibilities. In another school, he is just a leg boy for the principal. The dilemma of the assistant principal and others on the administrative staff is often more pronounced because, unlike the teacher, the custodian, and some others on the staff, their time and scheduled duties are not fixed.

The question about the assistant principal is not nearly as facetious as it might appear. Too often the assistant principal is the forgotten man in the secondary school administrative force. This is symptomatic of a

[7] Paul B. Jacobson, William C. Reavis, and James D. Logsdon, *The Effective School Principal* (Englewood Cliffs, N.J.: Prentice-Hall, Inc., 1963), pp. 27–33.

real need to explore staff relationships between the principal and those who serve under him. The principal's office is a social institution, respected as something apart in the school by staff and students. It is a place where you "go to" and "come from" for a variety of reasons, some good, some not so good. Feelings toward the principal's office vary greatly. In some schools it is a pleasant place where people enjoy stepping in, in other situations it is a bastion of authority, a place to avoid as much as possible.

The key to feelings about the principal's office rests with the principal's attitude toward and philosophy of staff relations. There can be no question about the principal's office being the nerve center of a secondary school operation. But how it functions as this center of activity is directly related to the attitude and feelings of staff and students toward it.

With respect to staff personnel relations, principals' offices can be categorized roughly as follows:

1. The big "I," the typical autocratic situation where the principal feels that he must make all decisions and where there is a minimum of delegation of authority.

2. The benevolent father approach, kindly and understanding, but still a one-man show.

3. The laissez-faire approach, noninterference with little or no direction or service.

4. The ultra-democratic plan, everything decided by committee.

5. The ideal principal's office, friendly, democratic, efficient, effective, and characterized by delegated and understood assignments and responsibilities and with wide staff involvement in matters affecting personnel.

Some principals have found a staff advisory council helpful in establishing and maintaining good staff relations. The advisory council, discussed in some detail in Chapter 4, is a small group elected by the staff, either by departments or at large, with whom the principal meets regularly to discuss issues and problems. The council seems to work most effectively where the group does not have legislative power but remains strictly advisory. The advisory council is not a counterpart to the teacher's association. Its only relationship with the latter organization lies in the fact that members of the council are elected by it. The advisory council is an excellent medium for two-way communication between the principal and his staff. He can sample staff opinion and, in turn, the members can relay the view of the administration to the staff in general.

Importance of communication

Ramseyer and his associates define communication as the "ebb and flow of feelings and ideas between people."[8] The arts of communication are involved in the dynamics of human relations as related to staff personnel management. Often the root of personnel difficulties can be traced to faulty communication or to a total lack of communication. In a study of teacher attitudes toward the efforts of the secondary school principal, Blackman found that schools with "high communication" indicated a much more favorable teacher attitude than in schools of "low communication."[9]

Ebb and flow indicates at least a two-way communication and assumes that proper channels are available for the process. It is the responsibility of the principal to establish and keep open these channels. This is an aspect of administration that requires constant appraisal.

WORKING EFFECTIVELY

Staff personnel relations have their basis in any school situation where professional workers carry out their responsibilities to the best of their abilities, whether working as individuals or in groups. Much of the staff member's contribution must of necessity be of an individual nature, but there are many instances where the group approach to an activity has special merit. Under all circumstances it is the sum of individual contributions, each in a sense helping the other, that makes up the total impact of a staff effort. Cooperation is the key concept. This is a major concern of the principal. He must be skillful in assisting staff members to improve their competence in making their individual contributions as well as to gain competence in working together with others on specific assignments.

Wynn's studies of interpersonal relations in educational administration have indicated that the school leader must plan on spending about ninety per cent of his time working with people.[10] There seems to

[8] John A. Ramseyer, Lewis E. Harris, Millard S. Pond, and Howard Wakefield, *Factors Affecting Educational Administration: Guideposts for Research and Action,* School Community Development Study Series, No. 2 (Columbus, Ohio: College of Education, The Ohio State University, 1955), p. 51.

[9] Charles A. Blackman and David H. Jenkins, *Antecedents and Effects of Administrator Behavior,* SCDS Series, No. 3 (Columbus, Ohio: College of Education, The Ohio State University, 1956), pp. 52–55.

[10] Richard Wynn, "The Climate of Good School Staff," *Educational Outlook,* 27:63–69, January 1953.

be little doubt that the teacher spends a similar proportion of his time working with people. So it would appear to be important that both principal and teacher know how to work with others effectively.

Working with individuals

Much of the principal's contact with staff is on an individual basis. He is constantly conferring with individual teachers about assignments, loads, schedules, students, instruction, and many other concerns. Sometimes it may be a matter of a grievance or an evaluation of the teacher's performance as discussed elsewhere in this chapter. It is through this person-to-person relationship that he executes much of his professional leadership.

One of the more successful principals we know says he never approaches a personal contact with a staff member without first keeping three things in mind: his own preparation, attitude, and readiness to discuss an issue with the person; a thorough speculation on how the other person feels and his readiness to discuss the matter; and the possible positive outcomes of the conference or contact in light of the probabilities involved in the situation. In other words, he does not go into a situation before he has had time to think it through. Postponing a contact on these grounds sometimes pays big dividends.

The principal has an obligation to set a good example in personnel matters. Prestwood says that the principal should do the following:

Show respect for each individual in his face-to-face relations.
Be courteous at all times, even when the individual with whom he is speaking has shown in the past that he does not merit such consideration.
Reveal in whatever he does or says that he is a person of integrity.
Understand the individual with whom he is conferring, know something about his background and his abilities and about his needs and emotional adjustment.
Practice an open-door policy and be available for individual conferences.
Be warm, friendly, and considerate of the feelings and welfare of the other person.
Never criticize anyone before others or discuss in any way before others matters which pertain to the personal.
Always speak clearly.[11]

Conferences have many important applications in the modern secondary school as an administrative, instructional, and public relations

[11] Elwood L. Prestwood, *The High School Principal and Staff Work Together* (New York: Bureau of Publications, Teachers College, Columbia University, 1957), p. 52.

aid. Every staff member should become competent in conference procedures and techniques. Some of the hallmarks of good conference procedures are privacy and freedom from interruptions, informality—putting the conferee at ease and gaining rapport, maintenance of composure, time for listening, intelligent use of questions, judicious use of nondirective and directive techniques, fairness and justice, arrival at firm decisions and definite results, summarization and recapitulation of common understandings growing out of the meeting, and evaluation of the conference as a growth experience.

Working with groups

Much attention is given in this volume and elsewhere in the literature to the group process, the committee approach, the team, the workshop, and the conference. We hear about "brainstorming" and the collective approach to problem-solving. All of these have merit, but no group method is a substitute for individual effort and achievement. It is rather an extension of individual involvement by the pooling of individual resources and sharing of broad responsibilities. It provides a means by which the leader influence for growth of the participant can be extended beyond any possibilities under methods of individual contact. Hence, both group and individual contact methods tend to serve the same general purposes—the provision of better education for youth and the growth of individuals in the process. Group meetings have the added advantages of extending economical communication, stimulating individuals through group interaction, building morale, developing leadership, and providing media for better acquaintanceship.

Care should be taken to differentiate between group and mass meetings. Certainly there are times when the entire faculty must be brought together in a mass meeting for given purposes. A group meeting is a small number of individuals, say, approximately six to a dozen persons, assembled for a specific purpose.

There are many ways in which a mass can be divided into groups. This is sometimes accomplished with the larger group by one of several mechanisms, such as the "6-6" method, where the large group is divided into groups of six and allowed six minutes to discuss a phase of a problem, with a reporter bringing the ideas back to the main group. Another technique is the "buzz" session, where small groups meet separately to discuss a matter and bring back the ideas in a report to the larger assembled group. Still another method is the committee technique, where members of a larger group join or elect to work on committees established to accomplish certain purposes. This method is often used in workshop conferences where the general meeting is used to delineate a problem and the discussion sessions are provided to assure close interaction and participation of the members.

Group leader roles. The obvious importance of the leadership function in a group meeting is well understood. Whether it is the principal or a staff member in the leadership role, he must check the physical setting for the meeting—room, furniture, supplies, light, ventilation. Participants must come to know each other and know who is speaking. The agenda, goals, purposes and the direction of the session must be preplanned. The discussion must be initiated and maintained. Without apparent domination the leader must keep the meeting moving toward desired goals. Opinions and points of view must be anticipated so that they may be tested and appraised. Each proposal and idea presented must receive proper consideration. Occasionally, nonparticipators must be encouraged to comment and the overtalkative dissuaded. The leader must maintain good communication while the group is in session and between sessions, both with regard to participants and to others concerned with the work of the group. Timing is very important. Meetings should start and stop on time. Few things are more exasperating than meetings that do not respect the schedules of participants.

Roles of the group. Group participants have roles, too. Many individuals are likely to assume more than one role during the group experience. Benne and Muntyan identify the following three possible roles that staff members assume as they work together:

1. Group task roles through which the members push group effort to accomplish certain goals.
2. Group building and maintaining roles through which the group sustains itself.
3. Individual roles through which participants satisfy their own needs as aside from the group.[12]

The first two roles clearly have a positive effect on the group activity; the third a possible negative effect. In other words, if the group functions mainly to satisfy the quirks and needs of each participant there is little likelihood that the desired group achievement will be accomplished.

Group members usually play various roles during the course of the meeting or series of meetings. The leader joins in playing these roles.

[12] Kenneth D. Benne and Bozidar Muntyan, *Human Relations in Curriculum Change* (New York: Dryden Press, 1951), p. 98.

These roles are sometimes identified as: (1) initiators—those who bring up new ideas, suggest ways, and propose solutions; (2) information seekers—those who ask questions and seek clarifications; (3) information givers—those who supply information, data, experience, and examples; (4) opinion givers—those who state beliefs and orient values; (5) opinion seekers—those who want to know what others think; (6) elaborators —those who amplify suggestions already made; (7) coordinators—those who synthesize material; (8) orienters—those who keep action moving in the right direction; (9) evaluators—those who question appropriateness and relevancy; (10) energizers—those who provide zip and inspire others to action; (11) procedural technicians—those who check on points of order, distribute materials, collect and arrange materials; and (12) recorders—those who keep the record for the group. All these are known as group task roles.

Similarly, group maintenance roles are played by members in the assemblage. Maintenance roles, as identified by Benne and Sheats, are: (1) encouragers—those who praise others and their contributions; (2) compromisers—those who eliminate conflicts and deadlocks through suggestions of alternatives; (3) harmonizers—those who reconcile differences and relieve tensions; (4) expediters—those who set limits to discussion and clear the road for action; (5) standard setters—those who suggest criteria and set standards; (6) followers—those who accept whatever comes; (7) group observers—those who collect information on the progress and achievement of the group; and (8) resource providers— those who not only supply data and experience but who are able to share other group experiences, sources of information, and helpful hints to maintain the effectiveness of the group process.[13]

Individual roles, in contrast to those that expedite and foster good group activity, tend to stifle effective group consideration of a task. These fall into the following categories: (1) aggressors—those who criticize, degrade, belittle, and disapprove; (2) blockers—those who reject and resist new ideas; (3) recognition-seekers—those who boast and exaggerate; (4) self-confessors—those who vent personal feelings and seek opinions on matters unrelated to the group activity; (5) playboys— those who clown and joke and otherwise disrupt proceedings; (6) competitors—those who assert superior status or play roles; (7) sympathy-seekers—those who deplore their own position; and the (8) special pleaders—those who seek support for their own ideas.

[13] *Ibid.*, p. 100. See also, Kenneth D. Benne and Paul Sheats, "Functional Roles of Group Members," *Journal of Social Issues*, 4:2:42–47, Spring, 1948.

In staff relations, whether in individual or group contacts, the principal as well as other staff leaders must recognize and deal with the wide variety of individuals found on any staff and in any group. He must be conscious of the roles being played at various times and places. However, the mechanics of contacts and inter-relationships, no matter how interesting and intriguing, are but means to ends in staff relationships. Achievement and production through contacts of all kinds in solving problems and effecting growth in participants is the ultimate goal.

Staff meetings

Staff meetings, one of the common means of working with staff groups, serve a wide variety of purposes; e.g. instructing, communicating, interacting, decision making, socializing, inservice training, stimulating, articulating, coordinating, programing, planning and inspiring. But why are many of them considered to be so "deadly"? Why should there be such general apathy and dissatisfaction with them?

Among the more common criticisms of staff meetings reported by staff members are:

1. Meetings lack planning and definitive purpose.

2. Meetings come at a time in the day when everyone is tired and nearly worn out.

3. There is too much pontificating.

4. There is not enough involvement of the staff.

5. The programs are uninteresting.

6. Too much is expected of the staff meeting.

7. Some of the discussions are pointless, too involved, or serve only to provide a captive audience for certain staff members seeking ego satisfaction.

8. Staff meetings often are regarded too lightly by many members of the staff.

9. Too many are excused from regular staff meetings and for questionable reasons.

10. The entire staff is expected to do what might better have been a committee assignment to be reported back to the staff for action.

11. Speakers are ineffective and uninteresting.

12. Meetings fail to start and close on time.

In view of the fact that meetings appear to be a necessary mechanism for group communication and interaction, the principal is obligated to provide the leadership necessary for effective and satisfying experiences. He would do well to work with a staff committee in making an assessment of the staff meeting situation. The common criticisms should be recognized and corrected. Plans should be made cooperatively with the staff to improve staff meeting experiences.

A variety of aids are now available that have proven helpful in planning staff meetings. Among the better sources are the publications of the several divisions of the National Education Association, commercial companies publishing teaching materials, the publications of the National Association of Secondary Principals, and similar resources. The important thing is that careful planning and preparation be done and not left to chance or impromptu status. In spite of the principal's busy schedule, he can ill afford to find himself in a situation at noon on Monday, realizing that the regular monthly staff meeting is scheduled for 4 P.M. and that only some general staff announcements have been planned for the program.

Orientation of new staff members

Do you recall any of your orientation experiences as you began a new job? If it consisted of more than a guided tour down the corridors, a small package of handouts to read, an introduction at a staff luncheon and a little assistance from immediate friends on the staff, you are among the fortunate. While not desiring to be unreasonably negative about the matter, far too little attention has been given in most situations to the important matter of orientation of the new staff person to his job and environment. On the other hand, in many situations where attention is given to orientation, it is often composed of a lengthy session or two so packed with important substance to be assimilated that the participants are not able to fully benefit from the experience.

Beginnings are important—especially for the new staff person, whether he is a teacher, custodian or clerk. Early experiences on the job often condition the employee's effectiveness throughout his tenure.

The orientation program for new personnel should be planned as something more than a minimal affair a day or two before beginning work or the first day on the job. Many schools have put aside archaic concepts of orientation for new staff members and instituted well planned programs consisting of a series of experiences covering several weeks.

At Shaker Heights, Ohio, a new orientation program has been instituted covering a period of eight weeks. It is a cooperatively planned staff venture. The program consists of pre-school meetings at buildings, general meetings, four late afternoon and evening sessions (with a PTA dinner), a tour of the community, greetings from civic leaders, and other innovations. This is typical of what can and should be done in orientation efforts.

In another school system it has become standard practice for the staff orientation committee to be selected from the new staff members of last year. These people are keenly aware of the new problems to be faced by persons in the system, and, working with the principal, they can plan and execute very effective orientation experiences.

TEACHER SUPPLY, RECRUITMENT, AND SELECTION

According to Trump, the instructional staff of the school of the future may include the following kinds of personnel:

Professional teachers (teacher specialists, general teachers)
Instructional assistants
Clerks
General aides
Community consultants
Staff specialists[14]

Teacher specialists will include experienced teachers, with career interests and abilities, highly trained to teach and supervise instruction in a given subject area. General teachers, who may not look forward to teaching as a lifelong career, will be qualified persons with less experience. These teachers will assume the roles of consultants and observers for discussion and study groups. The instructional assistants will be technicians selected and trained for specific parts of the teaching job. General aides will act as supervisors of students in noninstructional situations such as the playgrounds, auditorium, cafeteria, and corridors. Community consultants will be community resource people used in specific assignments and situations in which they are better qualified than any teacher on the staff. The staff specialists will include workers in such areas as guidance, research, health, visiting teacher, and similar areas connected with the instructional program.

[14] J. Lloyd Trump, *Images of the Future* (Urbana, Ill.: Commission on Experimental Study of the Utilization of Staff in the Secondary School, 1959), p. 15.

It may be some time before we will staff our secondary schools completely along the lines described above, but there are good indications that the challenges of quality and quantity in education will direct our course in some such direction. In fact, a number of vanguard secondary schools are already being staffed along such lines. Secondary schools would profit by reviewing this plan when recruiting and selecting staff personnel. Schools must learn more and more to maintain flexibility in instructional activities if they are to deal competently with the problems of individuation, selective and general instruction, and meeting the needs of all students.

Imagination in utilization of staff

Several factors point to the need for much more imagination, inventiveness, and flexibility in the utilization of staff than now exists. To begin with, there is a problem of teacher supply to meet the needs of ever-expanding enrollments. The problem is not only obtaining an adequate supply of trained teachers but using more effectively the supply available. Secondly, the master teacher is deserving of the recognition in pay and professional status to which he aspires. He is tired of seeing the journeyman teacher and the beginning teacher as dominant elements in salary schedule and professional status considerations. He is an important and often forgotten minority in the profession. This poses a problem of evaluation, appraisal of effectiveness, and perhaps classification in the professional ranks. Nevertheless, at a time in the history of the teaching profession that calls for specialists, aides, generalists, and instructor assistants in staff personnel, we must face the realities of the situation.

A third factor in utilization of staff is the recognition that it is a waste of professional talent and money to use all staff members, regardless of training, in more or less the same capacities, particularly in such routine tasks as collecting funds, setting up machines, and monitoring study halls. These duties could be equally well handled by lower salaried personnel with less training.

A fourth factor is our imagination and inventiveness in effectively applying modern teaching aids, such as machines, films, radio, television, recordings, and tapes. What considerations for staffing does the use of these devices raise? How can the master teacher extend his influence and effectiveness through the use of modern teaching tools?

A fifth factor is the use of staff time and personnel in a program geared to large group, individual, and small group instruction consistent with the needs of students on a quantity and quality basis. Many secondary schools are experimenting with blocks of time, laboratory instruction, buzz sessions, discussion groups, library study sessions, individual conferences, and large group presentations of materials. Any effort in this direction requires careful consideration of staffing, scheduling, and effective use of professional staff time.

The questions raised here concerning the use of staff time are not new. Our objective is to spotlight the need for more consideration to the whole problem of effective utilization of staff personnel. Desirable staff relations will not be served by ineffective and inappropriate use of people in professional positions.

The older concepts of teacher-pupil ratios must be re-evaluated when we envision various group sizes in instructional activities and the implementation of study-resource spaces where students may accomplish much learning on their own. When students are reading, listening to tapes, observing films and slides, working on self-teaching and self-appraisal machines, doing research with laboratory equipment, thinking, writing, and participating in more or less individual study activities, the old ideas about teacher-pupil ratios are hardly applicable. It might be more appropriate to consider the number of master teachers needed, along with the number of general teachers, instructors, and aides, for the secondary school of any given size. In any discussion of ratios, the avenues to learning, the learning activities required and the appropriate professional personnel must replace the old head-count basis for determining staff requirements.

Recruitment and selection

Short supply of good teachers is a continuing problem. Economic trends and competition for human resources and manpower often affect teacher supply more critically than other occupations. Although salary factors are comparatively stable in the teaching profession, change comes more slowly. There can be little doubt about the fact that many potentially good teachers leave the profession for more attractive salaries outside the field. Salary considerations, however, are only part of the problem. Working conditions, fringe benefits, prestige, time for preparation, and other socioeconomic factors also play an important part in teacher supply.

Recruitment problems are also related to subject-matter areas. There is often a time-lag between the introduction of or emphasis on certain subject areas and the supply of trained personnel to man the new positions. We have faced this in vocational home economics, in commercial subjects, and more recently in the fields of mathematics and science.

In addition to competition from other occupations, salary considerations, socioeconomic factors, and critical area shortages, the supply of teachers is directly related to increasing enrollments. An ever-growing population requires more schools and more teachers. Although the figures for any one year may not be typical, the production of secondary school teachers in colleges and universities for 1963 provides some indications as to the fields of interest selected by trainees, as shown in Table 4.

Social science continued to produce the largest numbers of new teachers despite the general shortage. The increase of 14.3 per cent pointed to a new supply of 16,823, up 2,099 from the 14,724 produced in 1962.

Men's physical education again was the field of most definite oversupply; the production was 7,518, up only 7.4 per cent from last year, but still far in excess of the likelihood of employment in this field. And the evidence is lacking that many of these men have substantial preparation in any other field as a second major, or even a strong minor.

Table 4 shows the 1963 group of new prospective teachers, separately by sex and by high school teaching field. For elementary school service the women outnumber the men about 8 to 1; for all high school fields combined, women are in a slight majority, 50,036 to 46,342. Women candidates are more numerous in art, commerce, English, foreign languages, music, and speech; men lead in mathematics, the sciences, and the social sciences. (In interpreting the science figures it should be noted that many graduates listed in general science may also have a full major in one of the specific sciences.)

The time was when the board of education selected all staff personnel, and in some places this system is still in vogue. It has been well established, however, that the selection of teachers is a professional task, and a very important one. It is largely true that the school is no better than its staff. A staff of high quality is a good indication of an effective school program.

The secondary school principal should have a significant role in the selection and hiring of teachers for his school. He is in the best position to know his personnel needs, and no one is better able to provide an analysis of the responsibilities to be taken over by the new person. He knows the other staff members and associates and is able to involve them in establishing specifications for the new staff person desired. The princi-

TABLE 4. NEW SUPPLY OF TEACHERS COMING FROM UNIVERSITIES AND COLLEGES IN 1963

Type of preparation	Men	Women	Total	Per cent increase over 1962
Elementary school teaching	6,942	55,037	61,979	7.1%
High school teaching:				
Agriculture	1,084		1,084	5.0%
Art	1,086	2,489	3,575	17.9
Commerce	2,483	4,722	7,205	6.7
English	3,491	10,718	14,209	19.5
Foreign languages	1,126	3,146	4,272	32.4
French	312	1,388	1,700	26.1
German	171	290	461	28.1
Latin	150	198	348	4.8
Russian	39	56	95	63.8
Spanish	411	1,098	1,509	44.0
Other	43	116	159	96.3
Home economics		5,141	5,141	7.4
Industrial arts	3,487	31	3,518	5.8
Journalism	46	51	97	27.6
Library science	62	489	551	27.0
Mathematics	4,891	3,232	8,123	18.8
Music	2,663	3,115	5,778	9.0
Physical education (men)	7,518		7,518	7.4
Physical education (women)		3,856	3,856	12.9
Science	6,205	3,139	9,344	19.7
General science	2,511	1,120	3,631	20.5
Biology	2,363	1,572	3,935	17.0
Chemistry	896	387	1,283	27.7
Physics	435	60	495	16.2
Social science	10,427	6,396	16,823	14.3
Speech	810	1,887	2,687	12.7
Other	963	1,624	2,587	5.1
High school total	46,342	50,036	96,378	14.1%
Grand total	53,284	105,073	158,357	11.3%

Source: National Education Association, Research Bulletin Vol. 41, No. 3 (Washington, D.C.: The Association, 1963), p. 71. This report is based on reports from all institutions in all fifty states, Puerto Rico, and the District of Columbia.

pal is the person most directly connected with future orientation, supervision, and inservice training of the new person, and in participating in the selection he automatically assumes some of the responsibility for assuring the success of the teacher.

There are many factors to be taken into consideration in the principal's participation in teacher selection and hiring. In the medium-size, one-secondary-school community, principals appear to be taking the most active part in staff procurement. It is not unusual to find the principal and a staff member visiting the prospective candidate in his present teaching position to gain better insights into his suitability for a vacancy. In the large multiple-high-school community, this is an impossibility. The personnel department has a tremendous job recruiting and establishing eligibility lists for various positions. In these cases and in situations where transfer lists affect selection procedures, the principal works largely from a list or lists of names made available to him. In some instances he merely accepts the person assigned to his school. Principals in some of the larger school complexes have less to do with teacher selection than their counterparts in the smaller communities. It is likewise true that in some of the larger cities—through high requirements, required teacher examinations, and careful screening by divisions of personnel—the caliber of teachers on eligibility lists is often excellent.

The participation of principals in selecting and hiring teachers and the procedures utilized in recruitment and selection should be recognized for their significance. French and his associates comment that the principal and his staff have no greater professional responsibility than that of selecting new members for the school staff.[15] If this one task is done well enough the success of the school is assured. This suggests that when a vacancy occurs, or is reliably predicted, the administration should begin the search for a replacement aggressively. On each occasion an appraisal of the entire staff composition as well as an appraisal of immediate and future staff needs should be made. What extra assistance in cocurriculum activities is needed or anticipated? Are there staff members who will be wanting to give up certain functions in the next year or two? What about staff balance? Does the situation call for more maturity? What about program changes, immediate or anticipated? These, and related questions, should be borne in mind by the principal as he goes about the business of hiring. He will do well to involve his staff as much as possible in these assessments and in establishing and checking the potentials desired in the new staff person.

15 Will French, J. Dan Hull, and B. L. Dodds, *Behavioral Goals of General Education in High School* (New York: Russell Sage Foundation, 1957), p. 155.

We assume that candidates are legally qualified, that is, that they have the proper certification and license to teach, but this must be substantiated in view of changing certification laws, variations among states as to requirements, and the standards required by accrediting bodies. Secondly, the person must fit the job requirements and the staff of which he is to become a part. He should have the requisite personal qualities as well as the professional. The usual sources for this information are references, credentials, interviews, and visitation to observe the candidate in action. When possible, it is well to have the candidate visit the school so that the staff may have at least a small part in appraising his possibilities. A visit and interviews on the local scene are likewise helpful to the candidate, who may ultimately have to decide whether or not he or she wants to invest a portion of a professional career in a particular school system.

It is quite apparent at this point that the several aspects of hiring teachers and phases of teacher employment are inter-related in many respects. Chandler and Petty sum it up in spotlighting two significant problems of teacher employment: (1) academic and personal freedom of teachers and (2) integration of the teaching staff in the school system.[16] Without further elaboration, it appears to us that successful recruitment must take into account the point of view of the candidate and his needs and desires as well as those of the system and staff organization of which he is to become an integral part.

Retention of good teachers

Many individuals have looked upon the job of secondary school teaching as a short duration proposition, an interim occupation between college and something else. Fortunately, more and more people are going into teaching as a career. Teacher turnover is expensive. It is expensive in terms of the time needed to select, orient, and supervise the beginning teacher. It is expensive in terms of the impact of turnover on the educational program in the school. Thus, it is imperative that principals give attention to retaining staff members and securing the longest possible tenure on the part of teachers.

Better salaries will help to hold teachers, but pay is just one of the factors that keep the staff member happy. Working conditions, status and prestige in the community, protection against unwarranted demands in school and in the community, personnel policies, and professional

---

[16] B. J. Chandler and Paul V. Petty, *Personnel Management in School Administration* (New York: Harcourt, Brace & World, Inc., 1955), p. 385.

satisfactions are equally important factors in keeping a staff together. The administrator has a responsibility to upgrade all factors that assist in the retention of staff. The dividends for his effort are better staff morale, longer tenure, professional growth and development, and, consequently, an improved program of education.

OTHER STAFF PERSONNEL CONCERNS

Considerable attention has been given in this chapter to staffing the modern secondary school, to creating a working staff team, and to the role of the principal in connection with those two important aspects of administration. Good leadership, good staff, and effective working relationships are the keys to successful secondary school operation. Although space does not permit full treatment, mention should be made of other staff personnel concerns related to personnel management in relation to the responsibilities of the principal.

Implementing personnel policies

It is the responsibility of the principal and the administration to take the initiative with respect to policy formulation, interpretation, and implementation. The system-wide personnel policies, which relate to all staff members in the system, should be written in some convenient format that makes them readily available to all persons. Such policies might include salary provisions, tenure, transfer practices, sick leave, assignment, orientation, inservice education, evaluation and promotion, demotion, discharge, benefits and services, health and safety services, staff participation in management, decisions about teaching controversial subjects and issues, academic freedom, schedule of hours, utilization of substitute teachers, and special provisions for instruction.

The principal should be conversant with all general policies of the system, both those that concern personnel directly and those that may be indirectly related to personnel. For instance, there may be policies on the use of buildings, safety procedures, fire drills, field trips, transportation of students, and the like that have a direct relationship to the staff's operation. These clearly should be made known to the staff.

In addition to the system-wide policies, the secondary school is apt to need policies and regulations for its particular operation. Matters such as interruptions of classes, use of a public address system, mechanics of attendance checks, parking, cocurriculum activity participation, record-keeping, and the like are concerns of the individual school. Wherever possible, the administration should involve the staff in the formulation and periodic review of these policies and regulations.

The implementation of policies is usually accomplished through the medium of rules and regulations. Surveys indicate that most secondary schools now have some form of printed handbook for teachers in which policies, rules, and regulations are carefully spelled out. Part of the orientation of new teachers is an acquaintance with the teachers' handbook, with the principal prepared to interpret the policies, rules, and regulations as they apply in general and in specific situations.

Every profession has a body of ethics that it honors over and above prescribed policies, rules, and regulations. The secondary school administrator is a guardian of professional ethics. He is ethical in his own practices and is a leader in influencing ethical practices among the members of his staff. The profession, through the National Education Association, has adopted a code of ethics, policies for professional performance, that is generally recognized and accepted.[17] The Committee on Professional Ethics has rendered opinions on a number of ethical problems.[18] In addition to the national code of ethics, a statement of ethics is usually adopted by the state education association and, in some instances, by local teacher organizations.

Enforcement of codes of ethics is generally left to the self-discipline of members of the profession. Programs are under way at the national, state, and local levels to encourage observance of codes of ethics, but there has been no concerted effort toward enforcement through disciplinary action. In view of this, it would appear that the principal has a professional responsibility as a leader to make sure that the codes of ethics are made available to and understood by staff personnel.

Inservice education

Continued inservice growth is the hallmark of every profession. The need for this continued growth is increasingly apparent in an era of progress and change, particularly in education, for few fields of knowledge have remained static. An effective teacher must keep abreast of the times. Research has discovered much that needs to be translated into the content and practices of education. Again, it is the responsibility of the

---

[17] Committee on Professional Ethics, National Education Association (Washington, D.C.: The Association, 1955), p. 57.
[18] *Ibid.*

principal to encourage and assist in planning inservice education experiences. These experiences may include summer school, travel, research, or graduate study, but many are to be found within the school itself. Through proper leadership and organization, some of the instructional problems of evaluation, contacts with citizen groups, and public relations activities can be made the basis of very worthwhile inservice education experiences.

It is generally recognized among secondary school administrators that one of their most difficult problems of staff or personnel management is that of dealing with teachers who have ceased to grow professionally. Inservice growth experiences should be and are required of staff members in many school systems. The principal should be able and willing to counsel with his staff on matters of inservice training. Moreover, he should work for proper incentives for inservice training through recognition on the salary schedule, through promotions, assignments, and delegated responsibilities.

Teacher welfare

Teacher welfare is concerned with the personal and professional elements of the environment that have a direct relationship to the morale, efficiency and well-being of staff members. The impact of human relations on personnel management and employee-employer relationships is a growing phenomenon. Efforts to maintain and improve the morale of the working force are investments in staff production and better employee efficiency. Welfare factors have become a part of the bargaining for new employees and the holding of older employees. Indeed, the teaching profession is in serious competition with other occupations on the matter of welfare provisions for employees.

The principal must be aware of teacher welfare within the framework of a tax-supported organization. There are definite legal limits to the insurance, hospitalization plans, retirement pensions, released time arrangements, paid vacations, and the like in publicly supported enterprises. On the other hand, there are many possibilities for individual and group benefits that can be legally arranged.

Welfare, in addition to the technical and major aspects, consists of many little things. An adequate teachers' lounge, adequate restrooms, a place to eat away from the student group, released time for school committee work, assistance for chore and clerical work, recognition for services well done—these are some of the basic elements upon which morale is built. It is doubtful that teaching, from the point of view of fringe benefits, can ever fully compete with private business. However, there are many professional satisfactions that should not be overlooked. The principal must develop keen insights into the value systems of a skilled, specialized group of workers. With such knowledge as a foundation, he can do much to improve teacher welfare.

Clerks, custodians, bus drivers, and specialists

There was a time when schools required little more in the way of salaried staff than teachers. Much of the chore work was done by teachers, with the help of students. Mothers came in to help with the lunch program. The office was manned with a part-time student gaining some practical experience before graduation. Except in rare instances, those days are gone forever. Today's school operation requires a large number of non-teaching personnel. Among the noncertified personnel there are some who must meet exacting qualifications—plumbers, engineers, bus operators, psychometrists, clinical technicians, nurses and others. Since staff personnel positions in the school system are of three general categories—instructional, administrative, and service—the principal must maintain a direct relationship with the service and administrative employees as well as with his chief concern, the instructional staff. Among the service personnel, the principal is most likely to have contacts with the following:

Superintendent of buildings and grounds	Accountant
Supervisor of maintenance	Clerks
Carpenters	Secretaries
Electricians	Cafeteria manager
Plumbers	Cooks
Custodians	Food handlers
Maids	Director of transportation
Business manager	Bus drivers
Bookkeepers	Mechanics
	Attendance officers

All workers identify themselves in one manner or other with the place they work. They are often in a position to meet the public and make contacts with the students, to provide information, directions, and assistance. When they feel that they are a part of the organization, their loyalty and spirit is reflected in work output, in cooperation with other staff personnel, and in the general morale about the school. They come to their positions with needs similar to those on the instructional staff—orientation, supervision, inservice training and improvement. It is the task of the principal to work with the administration in acquiring and retaining a good staff of service personnel.

Recognition of noncertified personnel

Noncertified and service personnel should be fully informed about many of the general activities in the school program. General notices should reach service personnel as well as the instructional group. Words of appreciation are most welcome, and a commendation now and then from the principal will do much to bolster morale. Recognition for years of service, recognition at the time of retirement, or a word of congratulation upon promotion are time-tested techniques by which the administrator enhances the status and the effectiveness of these employees.

The administrator can often be of major assistance to noncertified personnel in helping them analyze and evaluate their work and contributions to the school. He is in the position to indicate the significance of the worker's efforts in relation to discipline, public relations, school morale, and the teamwork of all school employees.

Every worker is important, first as a person and secondly as a contributing member of the staff of the school. It is sometimes necessary for the principal to help instructional staff members to a more complete realization of the fact that noncertified personnel play a significant role in the day-to-day operation of the school enterprise. Understanding between the certified and the noncertified employees is most desirable. Such a situation is brought about only through careful nurturing and perceptive handling by a leader who has a proper over-all view and appreciation of staff personnel relations.

CONCLUSION

Personnel administration is one of the most important responsibilities of the secondary school administrator. The principal is the key person in a good staff relations program, initiator of personnel policies, and the coordinator of administrative, instructional, and noninstructional personnel.

The principal assumes a working relationship with those above him, those on his administrative staff, those on the instructional staff, and those on the noninstructional staff. He is responsible for seeing that his educational unit works in harmony with the over-all educational organization in the community. A significant aspect of this responsibility lies in the personnel management of all workers connected with the secondary school.

The attitudes and competencies of the principal are of utmost importance in problems concerning staff personnel. He must be capable in recruitment, selection, orientation, inservice training, evaluation, policy initiation, policy implementation, communication, and working with individuals and groups. He is charged with the over-all coordination of all employees and, as such, should be a student of group dynamics, social interaction, morale factors, sound employment practices, and personnel management techniques. In the discharge of his responsibilities he must be constantly mindful of the ethics of his profession and the over-all relationship of staff to the purposes and goals of secondary education.

SUGGESTED ACTIVITIES

1. Select a high school of your acquaintance and list the titles of all employees under the following categories:
   a. Administrative
   b. Instructional—"certified"
   c. Noninstructional—"noncertified"
   d. Special service

2. Discuss the ratio of noninstructional to instructional employees in the modern high school. What is the trend? Why?

3. Describe the selection procedures for the principalship of a high school with which you are familiar.

4. List the theories and techniques of group leadership and discuss their values and relationships to the high school principal.

5. Develop a personnel policy related to some personnel practice. How does a staff rule differ from a policy?

6. Analyze a teachers' handbook for staff personnel implications.

7. Discuss the implications of the instructional staff classification described in *Images of the Future*.

8. How can inservice staff training be improved? Suggest a program for the beginning, the journeyman, and the veteran staff member.

9. Discuss the implications for utilization of staff brought on by educational TV, cooperative or team teaching, teaching machines, and similar instructional innovations.

SELECTED READINGS

Austin, David B., and James S. Collins, A *Study of Attitudes Toward the High School Principalship*, Bulletin, Vol. XL, No. 215. Washington, D.C.: National Association of Secondary School Principals, 1956.

Blackman, Charles A., and David H. Jenkins, *et al.*, *Antecedents and Effects of Administrator Behavior*. Columbus, Ohio: College of Education, The Ohio State University, School Community Development Studies Series, No. 3, 1956.

Castetter, William B., *Administering the School Personnel Program*. New York: The Macmillan Co., 1962.

Eikenberry, Dan Harrison, *Training and Experience Standards for Principals of Secondary Schools*, Bulletin, Vol. XXXV, No. 181. Washington, D.C.: National Association of Secondary School Principals, 1951.

Gauerke, Warren E., *Legal and Ethical Responsibilities of School Personnel*. Englewood Cliffs, N.J.: Prentice-Hall, Inc., 1959.

Inlow, Gail M., *Maturity in High School Teaching*. Englewood Cliffs, N.J.: Prentice-Hall, Inc., 1963.

Jacobson, Paul B., William C. Reavis, and James D. Logsdon, *The Effective School Principal*. Englewood Cliffs, N.J.: Prentice-Hall, Inc., 1963.

Kemp, C. Gratton, *Perspectives on the Group Process*. Boston: Houghton Mifflin Company, 1964.

National Education Association, *Developing Personnel Policies*. Washington, D.C.: The Association, 1958.

———, *Opinions of the Committee on Professional Ethics*. Washington, D.C.: The Association, 1955.

———, *Research Bulletin*, Vol. 37, No. 2. Washington, D.C.: The Association, 1959.

Prestwood, Elwood L., *The High School Principal and Staff Work Together*. New York: Bureau of Publications, Teachers College, Columbia University, 1957.

Ramseyer, John A., Lewis E. Harris, Millard S. Pond, and Howard Wakefield, *Factors Affecting Educational Administration*, "Guideposts for Research and Action." Columbus, Ohio: College of Education, The Ohio State University, SCDS Series, No. 2, 1955.

Redfern, George B., *How to Appraise Teaching Performance*. Columbus, Ohio: School Management Institute, Inc., 1963.

Salmon, Paul, "How to Select a Principal," *School Management*, May 1959.

Trump, J. Lloyd, *Images of the Future*. Urbana, Ill.: Commission on Experimental Study of the Utilization of Staff in the Secondary School, 1959.

Williams, Stanley W., *Educational Administration in Secondary Schools*. New York: Holt, Rinehart & Winston, Inc., 1964. Chapter 6.

8

PUPIL
PERSONNEL

THE CHANGES WHICH ARE OCCURRING RELATIVE TO
the role of secondary school administrator certainly cannot be ascribed
to a single set of circumstances. Oversimplified, the world of the learner
and the teacher is an infinitely more complex one than it was in times
past; and as usually is the case, when much more becomes known, new
problems, calling for new solutions, are created. That area referred to
as pupil personnel services provides a telling illustration. Until fairly
recently, pupil personnel services undertaken by many secondary schools
tended to be those mandated by state law, department of education
regulations, or regional accrediting agency standards. Somewhat per-
functorily performed, they tended to be such services as pupil accounting, routine health checks, and vocational guidance. Although they often
demanded a considerable portion of the principal's or his designate's
time, the relationship between the performance of the service and the

enhancement of an individual's opportunity to learn was rarely spelled out in detail. That the pupil needed to be in school to learn, and that to learn one needed to meet some health standards, were too obvious to be worthy of much more analysis in depth.

During those years, however, when minimal pupil personnel services characterized the secondary schools, much was happening which laid the groundwork for today's broad spectrum in the field. Researchers from many disciplines—medicine, psychology, sociology, and education, to name but a few—were isolating problems of the learner, as an individual and as a member of a group with distinguishing characteristics. As a result, we accumulated a significant body of knowledge about the common and unique learning problems associated with such groups as the following: blind, partially sighted, deaf, hard of hearing, speech impaired, crippled, those with special health problems, socially and emotionally maladjusted, gifted, and the mentally retarded. The previous practice of institutionalizing those who were grossly afflicted slackened off somewhat as we gained in knowledge and understanding. Instead, these pupils began to appear in our secondary schools in ever-increasing numbers, as our understanding developed about what could be done for them in that setting. At the same time, our increasing national affluence made it possible for more and more to consider secondary school education as a realistic goal. Legislation, largely permissive in nature, made it possible to expend money for the establishment of special classes for the atypical and many state foundation programs provided funds for those school districts which did so.

Special education, however, accounted only partially for the increased complexity of the secondary school's offerings. Relatively new fields, such as guidance and school psychology, made significant developments within recent years and specialists from these fields began to appear in secondary schools in larger numbers. The National Defense Act of 1958 provided particular impetus to the guidance area, as our nation became sensitive to manpower needs and recognized the tremendous losses which were attributable to school drop-outs.

As these developments were occurring in special education, guidance, and school psychology, to mention only a few, our secondary school enrollments have expanded and schools to house them have tended to grow larger and to take on comprehensive functions. Increased size and complexity, then, have added new dimensions to the responsibilities of those who administer our secondary schools. If it had been size alone, with only an expansion of our traditional program and working relationships, most administrators would have been able to cope rather easily with the problem. It was the specialist in education, especially he who did not devote his time to the traditional act of teaching, who provided the particular challenge. The team in secondary school education was suddenly a larger, more complex one, and how to direct its functioning toward the better solution of increasingly complex problems became a challenge which has baffled many administrators.

MAJOR PUPIL PERSONNEL SERVICES

In order to delineate the nature of this challenge, as a backdrop for some proposed solutions, the major component areas of pupil personnel will now be presented, with special emphasis on those elements which account for the uniqueness of the challenge.

Student accounting

As indicated previously, this has been one of the traditional pupil personnel services. Long tied up, either on an average daily attendance or average daily membership basis, to school foundation allocations or disbursements for special programs, accounting systems have been developed and operated with meticulous care. It is still a relatively rare phenomenon to find anyone associated with secondary school operation who is not active, at some level, in this function. Almost every secondary school maintains an attendance office to which at least one professional employee, aided by full-time secretarial and part-time student assistants, gives a major share of his time. Keeping careful records of membership and attendance, however, is only one part of the ever-increasing accounting function. Secondary schools are called upon, often hundreds of times every year, to provide information to governmental agencies, employers, and colleges and universities. These responsibilities make necessary the development of comprehensive systems of records, ready access to them, and efficient duplication of that part of them which is requested at any given time. With the increased mobility of secondary school pupils, it is also necessary to transmit, from school to school, often across state and national boundaries, an accurate descriptive record of a pupil's progress to date.

A further factor which adds complexity to the accounting process is the expansion and diversification of the curriculum, and a departure from traditional forty-five or fifty-five minute blocks of time. Developing the master schedule, and then individual schedules for each pupil, requires increasing amounts of ingenuity, even with the aid of machine processing of data which has become accessible to more and more secondary schools. Obviously, machines can be programmed only as decisions are made by those responsible for the operation of the second-ary schools. Naively we sometimes assume that automation can enable us to abdicate our decision-making roles.

Of considerable importance in explaining why the accounting func-tion has become so increasingly complex, is the change in the traditional position of immunity which the schools heretofore have held. Court deci-sions and changes in legislation have chipped away at this position, until those who operate the schools are held increasingly accountable to per-form their functions as reasonable men when confronted by any con-tingency. It has been found that more records are necessary to serve as guidelines. For example, most schools maintain a record card for each student on which such information as the following is noted: name or names of physicians, home and business phone of parents, guardians, and others who might need to be contacted in an emergency, special health information which might be needed, and the like.

Because of the quickened, increasingly complex character of living today, the information on these records changes rapidly. An over-all sys-tem, well-conceived and faithfully executed, then, is a necessity for the well-ordered secondary school. No longer is it sufficient to have the traditional "records day" at the end of each school year, when the cumulative folder and other forms could be completed and then "put to bed," so to speak, for several months.

Health services

In the past, the secondary school administrator has needed to devote very little time to pupil health services. The traditional childhood dis-eases had usually run their course during those years students were in elementary schools, and the likelihood of something of epidemic pro-portions was slim indeed. High school athletes needed physical exami-nations, but these were either made a matter of individual responsibility or coaches made arrangements directly with local physicians for the service. Consequently, it was a relatively rare sight to see a school nurse on the premises of the secondary school.

This picture, too, has been changing. Much more is now known con-cerning the relationship between health and learning. Although speech and hearing therapists are still relatively uncommon, at least on a full-time basis in any one school, the services of these specialists are becoming available to more and more schools. Screening tests usually have been conducted during the pupils' elementary years, but therapists continue to work with them as they progress through the secondary schools.

Health education has been expanding, too, in recent years. Although the systematic programs in this area are conducted primarily by health and physical education personnel, there is a trend to involve other professionals in the process. Physicians, including those with a specialty in psychiatry, and public health personnel are increasingly appearing in the secondary schools. In some instances, although at present the incidence is very small, they are full- or part-time members of public school staffs.

The big breakthrough, however, has been in the field of mental health. School psychologists, counselors, and psychometrists, have appeared by the thousands, largely in recent years, and mainly in the secondary schools. Specialists in human behavior, they have added significantly to our understanding of the learning process. In particular, they use their skills to discover causes which may impede the individual pupil's ability to learn, to suggest changes in the learning environment, and to develop better skills in problem confrontation. This area represents such a significant development that it is singled out for further analysis later in this chapter.

Testing

Another important phase in pupil personnel services has been the tremendous expansion in the field of testing. Testing, *per se*, is no new phenomenon, of course. The extent to which secondary schools have become involved in external testing has added to the complexity. Commercial testing firms have increased their output tremendously; so also have the non-profit organizations concerned with research and evaluation.

Significant pressures have developed within recent years which have put every secondary school administrator squarely into the testing operation. As the impact of the population explosion hit the secondary schools, and shortly thereafter, the colleges and universities, an increased dependence upon test results occurred. Accompanying this was a spiral in costs which made the colleges and universities want to work with as high a degree of probability as possible. Consequently, tests which predicted academic readiness for higher education appeared with dramatic suddenness. As admissions standards were revised, secondary schools naturally felt the impact. To provide data for counseling and for curriculum revision, tests have been given by the millions in secondary schools during the past few years. This has resulted in increased expenditures of time and money on the part of schools and students alike.

Scholarship programs, national in scope, as well as those which have increased concurrently at state and local levels, have accounted for an expanded use of test results. This dependence upon test results has, in part, been built into scholarship programs which are highly competitive in nature. It is felt, further, that this reliance on test results has developed because people are thereby spared the necessity and responsibility of exercising meaningful, mature judgment. Superficially, there is something "fair" and "objective" about using test results. Human error, favoritism, and other reprehensible frailties can be "avoided." It is part of the same phenomenon that crops up elsewhere in our increasingly automated world. Fortunately, this position has been recently subjected to analysis, and the net result has been a more careful development of tests, a more pinpointed use of them, and a re-examination of the part evidence, other than that provided by external test data, should play in making critical decisions about pupils.

In the foreseeable future, though, both internal and external testing will play a prominent part in the program of the secondary schools. If test results are to be used wisely, personnel with knowledge about tests, *per se,* and creative insight as to how their results should be used must be in decision-influencing positions in our secondary schools.

Special classes

Special education has had a long history in this country, but classes for the atypical have been relatively rare in the secondary schools. In the past, pupils with severe limitations have either received homebound instruction or they have tended to terminate their formal education at the upper elementary level. Several factors accounted for this. Foremost, probably, subsidies for many types of special classes at the elementary level were available through state foundation programs. In most cases, however, the allocation was not sufficient to defray all of their operating costs. Consequently, school systems tended to put their scarce resources into the elementary program, about which more was known and which was more apt to be subsidized. Then, too, our thinking tended to be categorical, and it was assumed that there were fixed limits to the ability of many of the atypical to learn. Research findings and other kinds of valuable, insightful experience revealed, however, that such was not the case. The atypical demonstrated his ability to continue learning, and many, previously thought to be dependent on others, proved that they could be economically self-sufficient and practice responsible citizenship.

This development, however, has presented additional problems for the secondary school administrator to consider. In partially or totally funded programs, selection criteria both for students and instructors needed to be applied and met. Classrooms, equipment, and program had to meet specifications which were less flexible operationally than they had been in the past. When secondary level classes for the mentally retarded were established, for example, the question arose about the eligibility of such students for high school diplomas. If not diplomas, then should certificates be issued? If so, what rationale should exist to explain the difference? Should pupils be kept in special classes on a homogeneous basis throughout the entire day, or should they be interspersed in other classes?

Even though different problems need to be confronted by the secondary school administrator when he deals with special education classes which are regulated by standards that differ somewhat from those which apply to the more conventional classes, those problems can often be confronted more easily than the ones he faces when planning for and administering some of the newer ones which have been appearing under the general rubric of special education. Illustrative of these are special classes for the culturally disadvantaged or the emotionally disturbed. In these areas, guidelines have not yet been developed as universally as in classes for the mentally retarded, for example. Even classes for the gifted present special problems, although work in this field has been done for many years. With this group so much seems to be possible that curriculum and procedures have not been amenable to a single reduced formula. In addition, value questions arise in isolating these students, and these tend to retard the process. As is often true with questions of this nature, determining right and wrong answers is a difficult thing to do. Whatever is done, however, must be defended rationally by the secondary school administrator.

Psychological services

Very few secondary schools have, as yet, the full-time services of a school psychologist. It is quite unlikely that they ever will, unless unique factors of size or function pertain. Increasingly, though, these schools are having psychological services made available to them on a part-time or on-call basis. Many of the dilemmas which characterize the entire pupil personnel field are well illustrated by our experiences with psychological services. For example, if school psychologists listed those functions which they performed and then listed those which they thought they should perform, it is quite likely that there would be considerable difference between the two. This would be especially true if a percentage of time devoted to the function were added to the list. Part of the explanation lies in the fact that there are not others available who are qualified to perform functions which the psychologist can. Perhaps the best concrete example of this is the fact that most psychologists spend much time functioning as psychometrists. Many individual tests require significant blocks of time to administer. A professionally prepared psychometrist can pass along test results in such a form that they can be analyzed quite comprehensively by a school psychologist, in a fraction of the time which would be required were he to administer the test and then make an analysis from the results. Since psychologists and psychometrists are often difficult to differentiate, by functions, it is relevant to state those areas in which the psychologist can work most productively.

Primarily, the psychologist is a specialist in learning. He knows, in depth, how people learn, and what effect environmental differences have on the learning process. These individual differences may stem from a number of conditions. In many instances he is called upon to see through manifestations of behavior which are symptomatic rather than causal, and in these cases he must weave through a subtly constructed maze. In addition to diagnosis, he is expert in determining those environmental changes which are necessary if productive behavior is to occur. At times, this may require face-to-face therapy sessions in which he plays a central role. More frequently, however, his involvement may be more tangential. Because of his preparation, he, more often than not, knows more about research than any other professional in the school system. Because of these skills, then, it is most productive to utilize the school psychologist as a consultant, a teacher of teachers, as a researcher, and as a diagnostician.

Guidance and counseling services

The area of guidance and counseling was placed in this position deliberately, the last of those to be overviewed, because it offers the best illustration from the entire range of pupil personnel services of the types of problems which need to be confronted by the secondary school administrator. Then, too, guidance specialists are more frequently members of secondary school staffs than are other specialists in the pupil personnel field. The problem begins with terms. As noted, the section heading which was used was "Guidance and Counseling Services." We shall use the term "guidance" somewhat generically throughout the remainder of this chapter, knowing as we do so that some practitioners in the field shrink from the term because of its connotation.

As is true in most professions early in their development (and guidance is a relatively young fifty years old), there are current, raging battles within the field as to appropriate roles and functions. Is it necessary for the specialist in guidance to teach prior to or concurrently with his responsibilities in his new field? Should he be involved in such activities as attendance and pupil discipline? Should the guidance specialist be involved in group or individual testing? Can guidance effectively be practiced in group situations or is it only possible on a one-to-one basis? Does the specialist solve problems for his clients or does he help the client to solve the problem for himself? What kinds of information must be kept confidential by the counselor in order to maintain the proper relationship with the client? Is vocational guidance an appropriate function for the counselor to perform?

These are but a few of the questions which are discussed in the literature and at professional meetings of guidance personnel. Signs of increasing professional maturity are appearing, fortunately. Guidance realizes, as other, older fields have, too, that it is unwise to take categorical positions too rapidly about role and function questions. Instead, it appears that guidance personnel are realizing that there may be many appropriate roles and functions which can be legitimately performed.

Guidance, as has been the case with other professions, has the traditional problems of the nouveau riche. Concerned with security questions, the nation saw an outpouring of information about manpower shortages, about the waste involved in high school drop-outs, about the lamentably small percentage of able students who continued and completed education beyond high school. When the National Defense Act of 1958 was passed, resources became available for establishing and conducting institutes for the preparation and upgrading of guidance personnel. States reflected concern by including provisions in department of education standards for guidance personnel in the secondary schools. Guidance units were written into state foundation programs, and school districts which offered guidance programs were reimbursed. Emergency certification patterns were developed, and classroom teachers could take two or three courses in guidance and then function in the area for a percentage of the school day.

Since guidance was in the national spotlight, and federal and state resources were available for the preparation and reimbursement of specialists in the field, secondary schools tended to clamor toward achieving the "new respectability." Swiftly-prepared guidance personnel, naturally uncertain about their appropriate roles and functions, were employed by secondary schools, whose administrators usually knew even less than the guidance personnel about how they should be utilized most effectively. A period of trial and error ensued, which was natural to expect under the circumstances. What to do about the situation became a matter of concern to guidance specialists and administrators alike.

STAFF OPERATION—A SUGGESTED APPROACH

From the previous discussion in this chapter, in which the component areas of pupil personnel were highlighted and some indications given about current problems which confront them, it is perhaps obvious that resultant staffing problems exist which are different from the traditional ones. Basically, what has occurred is the influx of professionals whose functions do not fit within the usual classroom teaching matrix. What each one does, however, has a relationship to the teaching-learning process, although this relationship may, at times, not be clearly perceived by those involved in the process.

Since most of us in secondary education are subject-matter oriented, because of our preparation and experience, communication, at best, has been difficult. It has become increasingly complex with the addition of each new specialist whose orientation differs from our own. How does the school psychologist communicate effectively with the classroom teacher whose procedures are inhibiting, rather than facilitating, the learning of one of his clients? How does the counselor convince the principal that a disciplinary action toward a student will further complicate a problem which seems well on its way toward solution?

The new "team," therefore, may not be sure which game it is supposed to play, and certainly is unsure about which rules should pertain. In the absence of common understanding, it is often extremely difficult to determine if the team is winning or losing. In the midst of such a situation, only one person is in the strategic position to bring about mutual understanding, and with it a sense of order. That person is the secondary school principal. The solution begins with a sensitivity to the problem and a disposition to see the dimensions of it, their interrelationships, and an ability to relate the problem to the objectives of the school. Once seeing the problem clearly and in perspective, the next step is to develop an organizational pattern which, if followed, will enable the staff to work together effectively toward a better fulfillment of the school's objectives. Without a plan, and more importantly a disposition to make it work, the problem usually remains unsolved and working relationships either worsen or become stalemated. As a result the staff is unable to release its creative potential and direct, in cooperative fashion, its professional effort toward problem confrontation, analysis, and solution.

The administrator must be secure enough to create an environment in which professionals can be flexible, can continue to learn, and can honestly confront problems without becoming fruitlessly ensnarled in a web of interpersonal conflict or trapped by pseudo-professional rigidity. If the administrator demonstrates that he can continue to learn, to adapt to new circumstances, to alter his previous decisions in the light of new conditions, and to involve others in the decision-making process, others on the staff will likely manifest the same behavior. If he is to act this way, he must have good two-way communication, since his sensitivity will exist primarily because he listens to others.

An organizational pattern is facilitated if each staff member has a reasonably clear notion of what role he is to play, the functions he is expected to perform directly, and those to which he may contribute indirectly. Most of us in education are conscious of this, to a degree, although it is often difficult to see just how our efforts mesh in with the work of others toward the accomplishment of the over-all school objectives. This sort of thing is never fixed, of course, because objectives change, or at least priorities attached to them change, and personnel keep changing. All of this adds variability to the process, and this needs to be assessed constantly. In this way the nature of our interrelationships becomes clearer to us, and because of this we can usually work more productively.

Ideally this communication takes place as each new person joins the staff of the secondary school. It is vital when the person is to fulfill a non-teaching role, at least in the traditional sense of the word. When this is the case, he should be joining the staff to fill a need which is specifically known, especially to the principal. Others on the staff should be aware of it, too. How such a staff person should work, in order to facilitate the accomplishment of this objective, may not be clear. In all probability, this cannot be completely ascertained in advance. There should be agreement in broad outline, however, on the part of the principal, the new staff person, and others on the staff, particularly those with whom he will be working directly. This rarely can be developed, *a priori*, by the principal through the device of a written job description. Such an approach, though, can be an excellent starting point.

As the prospective staff member discusses the proposed position with the principal, and with any others who may be involved, he should have an opportunity to make evident his own concept of the appropriate role which he should play, those functions in which he should be involved, and the type of interrelationships which would permit him to make his best professional contribution. In all probability, rather than having one person, either the principal or the prospective employee, "dictate" the role and determine the functions, it is more likely that these will be established by mutual agreement.

It is obvious that such a procedure is not always possible to follow. Many principals will assume their responsibilities and come in anew to an already existing staff situation. Concepts of role and function already exist and working relationships have been determined, whether or not anything is written down about these matters. If such is the case, he must determine what these are as soon as possible. In most instances it is better to observe this without much fanfare and to resist the temptation to move ahead with a "grand plan" for reorganization. In other cases, the principal may not be involved in the selection of the staff assigned to him. This often is the situation when the person will be working in his building only on a part-time basis and is perhaps responsible directly to someone in the central office hierarchy. Frequently this occurs with the school psychologist or speech therapist. When such is the case, though, the principal confronts the situation at the first practical opportunity. In this way misunderstandings can be averted, and those problems which compound because no one ever faces them squarely, never have a chance to become serious.

In some secondary schools, particularly the smaller ones, where there exists an atmosphere like that which has been described, not much formal structure is needed to facilitate communication and to develop policies and operating procedures. In such places, face-to-face interaction is a daily occurrence and people keep in touch. In other places, particularly the larger ones, a more formal type of organization may be necessary, particularly if the program is comprehensive and the staff is quite diversified. In such buildings, an organizational arrangement such as the following may be appropriate.

An advisory committee on pupil personnel services can be organized. This should be representative of the staff and contain both classroom teachers and those specialists who perform pupil personnel functions. The responsibilities of the committee can be varied, but its primary purpose should be to act as a clearinghouse for problems which exist in the operational areas of pupil personnel.

A specific example might be, "Should an external test which will be taken by 60 per cent of the seniors be administered during a regular school day, with necessary modifications made in the schedule, or should it be scheduled for a Saturday morning?" Such a problem, once considered, might lead to a policy about related items so that a testing calendar for the entire year could be projected, approved, and made available to those affected by it.

At other times such a group could function in a way analogous to the operation of a hospital staff. Usually a pupil who is experiencing a problem which involves the efforts of a pupil personnel specialist, be he counselor, psychologist, or special education teacher, has concurrent problems which are known about by other members of the staff. In most cases, there is a relatedness to these problems. A pooling of information, and then judgment, often facilitates the work of all those who are dealing directly with the student. This reduces the danger of working at cross purposes.

Usually, too, such a problem is illustrative of a fairly common one encountered by many pupils in the school. From an intensive consideration of this one problem may come policy, procedures, and fruitful avenues toward solution which may help to solve it for many. At times, staffing a problem case may not involve the entire committee. When the circumstances indicate that it does not, it is sensible to explore it in depth with only those who are directly concerned. This saves the valuable time and effort of the entire committee, which can continue to work productively only if such respect is shown.

DEVELOPING A PROGRAM OF PUPIL PERSONNEL SERVICES

In a previous section of this chapter, the major pupil personnel services were overviewed. This does not imply that they exist in every secondary school, because obviously they do not. The extent to which they operate is largely a matter for local school district determination. This is not literally true, of course, because some pupil personnel services are mandated by law, such as pupil accounting. In the school codes of most states, there are forthright provisions about attendance, truancy, and other component areas of student accounting. In those cases where the law does not contain specific prescriptions for action, the provisions of state departments of education, implementing arms of the legislature, indicate directly what the schools shall or may do.

Each secondary school, thus, has a system of pupil accounting. The variety, then, is to be found in the efficiency and comprehensiveness with which it is conducted, the personnel who are involved in the process, the policy which serves as a guideline to how it is operated, the extent to which there is clear communication and understanding about the system and its underlying philosophy, and the degree to which the data collected, recorded, and reported are used creatively in the operation of the best possible program for the individual school.

It is with these latter aspects that the administrator should be mainly concerned, because the actual collecting and recording of data can be made an efficient operation with the application of good judgment, and, when needed, some consultative help, available often from state departments of education, colleges, and commercial firms which deal with forms and equipment. In secondary schools of over 500 pupil population, or in smaller ones which have unique scheduling and recording situations, it is often advisable to seek such consultative assistance to determine the advisability of utilizing the machine processing of data, since the processes have been developed quite extensively for coping with record-keeping problems in education and the necessary equipment is now available at rates well within the grasp of many school systems. Several smaller school systems have developed cooperative plans for the mutual use of such equipment, thus reducing the costs further. In addition, many secondary schools use some of the equipment as part of their commercial programs, and thus accomplish some instructional goals as well.

For a quick overview of the machine processing of data, it is recommended that administrators read James W. Whitlock's *Automatic Data Processing in Education*.[1]

In those services which are mandated, the procedure for their establishment and maintenance is usually straightforward. Many of the comments made about pupil accounting would likewise be applicable to such areas as health services. Nothing that the secondary school does concerning pupils is entirely value-free, because appropriateness is a constant dimension when children are involved. This aspect rarely can be ignored by the administrator, because if he does ignore it the conse-

[1] The Macmillan Co., 1964.

quences can be nettlesome at best, and disastrous at worst. Even in truancy cases, where the law might be quite prescriptive, to the extent of indicating those penalties which can be applied to him if he does not perform his responsibilities, community attitudes about missing school may be such as to warrant his acting very sensitively.

Some communities, or school attendance areas, may need, want, and support fairly extensive health services supplied by the schools. In other areas, there might be widespread opposition because of a prevailing attitude that these are responsibilities of the family. In developing a program of pupil personnel services, though, it is sometimes necessary for the administrator to do some probing into those areas where there may be community sensitivity, because the implications of some needs may not be clearly understood by others.

For example, a review of those disciplinary cases with which the principal had been dealing, reports of classroom teachers about learning problems which puzzled them, and manifestations of pupil behavior in the school environment might lead the administrator to ponder the advisability of recommending the employment of a school psychologist. He knows, though, that there are some parents who would resent the implication that their children needed psychological services. If such were the case, it would be wise for him to emphasize, in his exploration of the possibility, the specific ways in which a psychologist could use his skill to make even better learning opportunities available, and not to stress such things as emotional disturbances and juvenile delinquency.

In those services which are not required by law, regulation, or standards, and especially in those areas which are not reimbursable, totally or in part, from state or federal resources, it is important for the administrator to have a priority list for the establishment of new services, based on need, resources required, and other relevant data. There are several reasons for this, but the primary one is the fact that the secondary school administrator rarely, if ever, has direct control over the resources necessary to provide the proposed service. It must be "sold" by him, often directly to the superintendent or some other administrative officer. Since financial resources are usually scarce, if money is made available for the proposed service, then something else, also needed, cannot be provided. Therefore, the proposed service must offer the promise of meeting some well-documented needs.

As this approach is used, though, it is wise not to be too global in one's outlook. The field of guidance, for example, has been handicapped because of a naive assumption on the part of some teachers and administrators that once guidance personnel were available at the secondary school level, all problems would disappear, or if not, that problem cases would become the concern of guidance personnel almost exclusively. To avoid this problem, it is far better to be selective and to isolate the most important functions to be performed. For example, in some secondary schools, because of the circumstances, vocational guidance might be a vitally needed service. In others, college counseling would receive top priority. In those cases guidance resources could be directed toward accomplishing mainly those functions which had been classified as most important. Their effectiveness could be evaluated on the basis of defined objectives, and there would be less likelihood that guidance personnel would be misused or criticized for failure to accomplish more global objectives.

ADMINISTRATION OF PUPIL PERSONNEL SERVICES

Throughout this chapter, the secondary school principal has obviously played a key role in the administration of pupil personnel services. This has been so because we feel that there should be as much autonomy as possible in the operation of a comprehensive secondary school and that those who are employed to serve in that school should be responsible directly to the principal. Each school has its unique problems, and it is believed that these can best be confronted through cooperative efforts of a unified staff. In some types of school districts, usually the very large or quite small ones, there likely will be a more centralized type of administrative control. In large cities, various areas of pupil personnel are organized by divisions, each administered by a director, and the overall administration is provided by an assistant superintendent. In county organizations, a modified, but somewhat similar pattern may exist.

In these cases it is strongly urged that several conditions hold. First, the services should be administered by those who by preparation and temperament are administrators. Mistakes are often made in assuming that pupil personnel services must be administered by a pupil personnel specialist. Because he usually has had to obtain considerable preparation to function as a specialist, it frequently leads to role conflict to take him away from that specialty, as a practitioner, and expect that he will be able to function competently as an administrator. Most pupil personnel specialists, it is believed, want their services administered by someone who is skilled in the administrative processes, who is sensitive to their needs and concerns, and who can work effectively to create and maintain an environment in which they can practice their specialties productively.

In these centralized operations, some guiding principles are worthy of consideration. Those who administer at this level should be in close liaison with principals to effect coordination, communication, and guideline policy which is sensitive enough to meet the needs of individual schools. Personnel from certain divisions, such as a Division of Guidance, who are on a full-time basis in a particular secondary school, should be administratively responsible to the principal of that school. Guidance involvement can offer them professional stimulation and inservice growth opportunities, but their primary allegiance should be to the school in which they serve.

SOME CHALLENGES IN THE FIELD OF PUPIL PERSONNEL

Pupil personnel services frequently are expensive to establish and maintain, and for this reason they often do not exist, beyond the minimum level, in many secondary schools. Too rarely do we consider the question, "Are we paying an even higher price by not having them?" Many administrators contend that they cannot afford to extend certain services to the elementary schools which have become fairly common at the secondary level. This is particularly true of guidance. Secondary school administrators have a significant leadership role to play in helping to resolve this problem. The case can be documented vividly by them that many of the severe problem cases which appear in the secondary schools are so acute that they require vast amounts of resources and that, in all honesty, the positive return for the investment is pitifully small.

Entrenched behavior at the secondary school level is not easily modified. To lament this fact is not our intention. Rather, secondary school administrators should direct some concerted effort toward the sharing of resources with the elementary schools and should exert effort to secure the enactment of legislation which will provide resources that can be used at the elementary level. At the same time they can work cooperatively, and not *ex cathedra*, with elementary school principals, to strengthen lines of articulation, to study, longitudinally, problem behavior and learning difficulties, and to develop, as creatively as they can, the most wholesome learning environment possible under present circumstances. This, once accomplished, can do much to eliminate many of the problems which otherwise would grow so serious as to require the services of a pupil personnel specialist.

CONCLUSION

Because a pupil personnel program requires the services of those whose orientation is often different from that of the classroom teacher in secondary schools, it is vital to have clear understandings about how each component of the program helps to fulfill the schools' objectives. Establishing each aspect of the program with careful preparation, maintaining a smooth-functioning organizational climate, and communicating clearly about the interrelationships between classroom teachers and pupil personnel specialists, are key responsibilities of the secondary school administrator.

SUGGESTED ACTIVITIES

1. List the major behavioral problems in the school where you currently are employed.

   a. From your knowledge of motivation, what are the needs, apparently not being fulfilled through socially acceptable channels, that account for these problems?

   b. How could the number and complexity of these problems be reduced?

2. Consult a source, such as that developed by the sociologist, Robert P. Bullock, in the school-community attitude analysis field.

   a. What components of the scales suggested in the document seem particularly appropriate to the community in which you work?

   b. What other information, not contained in the scales, would be needed for pupil personnel purposes? Why?

   c. How would you, as a secondary school administrator, analyze and use data from these attitude scales?

3. From your experience with testing, discuss the uses of standardized tests.

   a. How should students be motivated to do their best when taking standardized tests?

   b. What are the advantages and disadvantages of using standardized tests?

4. If you are a classroom teacher or administrator, list the kinds of problems you have with various facets of the pupil personnel program. Then consult a pupil personnel specialist, from guidance or school psychology, for example, and discuss these problems with him.

SELECTED READINGS

Bullock, Robert P., *School-Community Attitude Analysis for Educational Administrators*. School-Community Development Study Monograph Series No. 7. Columbus, Ohio: The Ohio State University Press, 1959.

French, Will, and Associates, *Behavioral Goals of General Education in High School*. New York: Russell Sage Foundation, 1957.

Lew, Donald J., and Herbert C. Rudman (eds.), *Preparation Programs for School Administrators: Common and Specialized Learnings*. East Lansing, Mich.: Office of Research and Publications, College of Education, Michigan State University, 1963. Chapter XI.

Peters, Herman J., and Gail F. Farwell, *Guidance: A Developmental Approach*. Chicago: Rand McNally & Company, 1959.

Peters, Herman J., Anthony C. Riccio, and Joseph J. Quaranta (eds.), *Guidance in the Elementary School*. New York: The Macmillan Co., 1963. Pp. 287–293.

Roeber, Edward C., Glenn E. Smith, and Clifford A. Erickson, *Organization and Administration of Guidance Services*, Second Edition. New York: McGraw-Hill Book Company, Inc., 1955.

Yeager, William A., *Administration and the Pupil*. New York: Harper & Brothers, 1949.

Zeran, Franklin R., and Anthony C. Riccio, *Organization and Administration of Guidance Services*. Chicago: Rand-McNally & Co., 1962.

9

MANAGEMENT

THE MANAGEMENT OF THE SCHOOL IS A TASK IN WHICH many principals are extremely competent and about which many principals develop deep-seated guilt complexes. For rather apparent reasons, a principal can feel "professional" when he discusses curriculum or student personnel services, but he feels "commercial" when he talks about the proper maintenance of the gymnasium floor. Another factor that may lead to professional guilt feelings is that superintendents are often considered to be overly concerned with bonds, buses, and budget, and so principals feel called upon to underplay the "three B's" and stress the C's of curriculum, classes, and certified personnel. Unfortunately, a total underplay is not possible and the principal finds himself guilty of the same sins as those charged to the superintendent. Finally, textbooks and professional journals constantly stress the fact that the principal is an instructional leader. "Is it proper," the principal asks himself, "for a real instructional leader to spend time in supply management?" And the answer to this question is a loud, "No!"

Nevertheless, school management is a legitimate task area assigned to the principal, and proper school management is a necessary part of the development of a good instructional program. The principal should be able to view his management task in proper perspective and not feel guilty as he devotes time to this important part of his job as an educational administrator.

AN OVER-ALL VIEW OF THE TASK AREA

The task area of management in secondary school administration includes school plant management, school business management, school office management, and the principal's problems with respect to the school transportation program and the school cafeteria. Each of these phases of the management task area has instructional implications. Several involve either the direct or indirect control of fairly large sums of money. Each phase requires a systematic approach, geared to the size and complexity of the particular school.

The management task area is probably the task area most conducive to the development of routine approaches. Routine, however, should be subject to periodic appraisal and overhaul. The suggestions presented here provide a starting point for the principal as he meets management problems in his own situation. It is his job to adapt, to adjust, to modify these suggestions and to check their effectiveness as he attacks the task area of management in his secondary school.

SCHOOL PLANT MANAGEMENT

The school plant is defined as the buildings, grounds, and equipment of a school. Although estimates vary, in 1964 more than 30 billion dollars was invested in school plants for public elementary and secondary schools in the United States. The secondary school principal often administers the most imposing structure in his town or city. He has important responsibilities in planning plant facilities, in managing the utilization of these facilities, in equipping the facilities, and in administering the maintenance and operation of these facilities. Each of these areas of responsibility will be considered in the sections to follow.

Planning new facilities

The construction of a new secondary school is a major undertaking that will influence the secondary school program in a community for many years to come. Although plans for a school building should plainly grow from plans for a school program, this is often not the case. If the school plant is to be developed in terms of a school program, it is clear that the principal and his staff must understand what the school program is now and is to be in the predictable future.

Elements of planning. The specific elements that must be considered in planning a new secondary school include subject-matter courses to be taught, organization of these courses for teaching (i.e., the development of core programs or the integration of certain subject-matter areas into single courses), teaching methodology, including a consideration of supplies and equipment and their storage, and class size in various subject-matter areas. In addition to these elements, which are closely related to curriculum, school planning requires a consideration of such factors as population projections, including both numbers and location, and site selection, including such things as amount of space, location with relation to industry and highways, and room for future growth.

In most school systems, the secondary school principal is less directly involved in population and site studies than he is in the consideration of the school program phase of planning. Certainly the enrollment data for which he is responsible will be considered in developing population projections and his judgment concerning certain site possibilities will be sought, but his key role is in educational planning.

Educational specifications. Educational planning for a new secondary school results in what are known as educational specifications. These educational specifications become the basis for developing architectural plans and specifications for the building. Architects often complain that school people do not provide them with well-prepared educational specifications, which make possible sound school design based on sound educational planning. In all fairness, it should be reported that educators complain that architects do not want and do not know how to use educational specifications. Be that as it may, the development of educational specifications through educational planning is an essential activity in planning new school facilities and one in which principals should be involved.

In an excellent discussion of educational planning for school facilities, Herrick and others describe the essential characteristics of good planning.[1] Among other things, these authors stress certain features that characterize good quality educational planning. Included among these are requirements that all activities to be housed in the building be considered, that economy in terms of educational efficiency be promoted, that the plans be written in such a way as to be most helpful to the architect, that educational planning be distinguished clearly from architectural planning, that it be based on sound procedures, and that it promote proper use of the new building.[2]

Educational specifications need to include both quantitative and qualitative aspects. It is necessary to determine the number of students who will need to use various kinds of space (teaching stations, cafeteria, library, and so forth) and the number of periods each day that various kinds of spaces will be in use. In addition to these quantitative aspects, various qualitative matters, such as special requirements for lighting, work space, display space, heating and ventilating, and grouping of facilities in a single part of the building, need to be considered.

Quantitative requirements. A formula is helpful in dealing with quantitative requirements. The basic formula for calculating the required number of teaching stations of any one kind in a secondary school is as follows:

$$\text{Number of teaching stations} = \frac{\text{Number enrolled in subject} \times \text{Number of periods per week in subject}}{\text{Desired average class size in subject} \times \text{Number of periods per week that each teaching station can be used}^3}$$

Unless separate subjects can use the same kind of teaching station, separate calculations are necessary for each subject. Class enrollments should be based on projections so that the new building can accommodate reasonable increases in enrollment if such increases are expected.

To illustrate the use of this formula, let us assume that the planners expect to have 500 freshmen in a school and that all freshmen will enroll for English I. Classes in English I meet five days per week and the desired class size is 30 students. The school will operate on a six-period

[1] John H. Herrick, et al., *From School Program to School Plant* (New York: Holt, Rinehart & Winston, Inc., 1956), pp. 104–132.
[2] *Ibid.*, pp. 106–110.
[3] *Ibid.*, p. 115.

day, but each teacher will teach five periods per day and have the use of his room for his nonteaching period. Inserting these facts into formula we find:

$$\text{Number of teaching stations} = \frac{500 \text{ (students)} \times 5 \text{ (periods per week)}}{30 \text{ (class size)} \times 25 \text{ (room available for teaching 5 periods per day for 5 days per week)}}$$

$$\text{Number of teaching stations} = \frac{2500}{750} = 3.3$$

We find that we will need 3.3 teaching stations for English I. Recognizing the difficulty of building three-tenths of a classroom, we will indicate the need for four such teaching stations in our plans. Inasmuch as 100 per cent utilization of teaching stations in a high school is not realistic, the additional seven-tenths of a classroom provides some margin for less than full utilization. This type of calculation would be continued for all subject areas until a complete list of teaching stations needed was developed.

It is apparent that this formula is of little value until a number of program decisions have been made. Thus, the instructional leadership role of the principal in working with his staff to develop educational program plans needs to be exercised as an integral part of planning new school facilities.

In addition to determining the need for teaching stations, quantitative requirements for nonclassroom facilities for pupils, administrative spaces, staff spaces, custodial and service facilities, and spaces for public use need to be developed. Here, again, the number and size of such spaces will depend upon a careful description of the activities that will go on in these spaces. Such matters as the activity program, the guidance program, and the community-use program will be basic to quantitative decisions about space requirements.

An example. An excellent example of educational specifications for school buildings is a set developed by the Parma, Ohio, schools.[4] The plan begins with an introductory statement setting forth some of the current challenges to American education. The educational program in Parma secondary schools is then briefly presented. Following this are general discussions of enrollment, site, design, and materials. In dis-

---

[4] *Educational Requirements for the New Senior High School*, Board of Education, Parma, Ohio, City School District, 1959, mimeographed.

cussing design and materials, the plan does not dictate to the architect, but rather indicates the general effect desired.

After these introductory sections, a listing of facilities is presented. This list is divided into the following general categories: administration, instruction and related student services, maintenance areas, and outside areas. Under each category, types of rooms and number of each are listed. The remainder of the report provides detailed descriptions of the facilities listed.

The discussion of the classrooms for art education is reported in full below:

> Three Art rooms should be provided in the new school. These rooms, if at all possible, should be located so that they will have north light. The size of the rooms should be somewhat larger than the standard classroom and should provide for a great deal of storage and workbench space. One of the Art rooms should be provided with an area for ceramics work, which will mean the installation of a minimum of 3 kilns and bins for the storage of clay and other materials used in ceramics. The orientation of the Art rooms to the rest of the building should be such that they are close to the auditorium and possibly one of the auditorium work rooms might double as a studio room for the Art Department. It would also be most helpful if the Art Department were located near the Vocational Department so that some of the heavy work could actually be done in the shops.
>
> The Architect should give considerable study to the design of the entry ways into the various Art rooms. It would appear that some attempt might be made to provide free vision from corridor or lobby locations into exhibit areas of the Art Department.[5]

Although this statement is short and simple, it obviously reflects educational planning. A later specification referring to equipment gives more insight into the activities that will make up the art program in this school. It should be noted that the authors of this statement do not pretend to be architects. They present certain needs and assume that the architect will meet them through his own professional skill.

Continuous planning. Once the educational specifications have been developed, architectural planning begins. It should not be assumed that architects will not be consulted during the preparation of educational specifications nor that educators will be ignored as the architects interpret these specifications. The two stages of planning are, however, quite distinct. Once drawings have been prepared, educators and architects need to discuss the ways in which the architectural plans meet the edu-

5 *Ibid.*, pp. 22–23.

cational demands. Here, again, the principal should play a key role as a constructive critic.

The principal's role.   Planning a new secondary school involves at least four stages: (1) clarification of the program and related activities that are to take place in the new building, (2) conversion of this information into a set of educational specifications, (3) conversion of the educational specifications into architectural plans, and (4) analysis of architectural plans to ascertain the degree to which they meet the educational specifications. The faculty of the school and others in the community should contribute in each of these steps. The development of the proposed program should include appropriate involvement of teachers, students, and lay citizens under the leadership of the principal. The principal should play a major role in translating program into educational specifications. Finally, the principal should be an active member of the group of educators who work with the architects as architectural plans are developed and analyzed. If a new plant is to meet the needs of an educational program, the principal should be in the forefront in the planning operation. Although many matters of finance and contracts may be decided in central administrative offices, educational planning will be a major responsibility of the secondary school principal.

Utilizing the school plant

An effectively planned school plant should facilitate a planned educational program. Using the plant for educational purposes, however, requires careful direction, or much of its effectiveness can be lost. In addition, many secondary school principals will find themselves operating in outmoded or poorly planned buildings. In these cases, effective utilization is a greater problem than in an educationally sound building.

Utilization includes several factors. First, there is the quantitative problem of assuring that each room of the building is used somewhere near its capacity. Although there may be times when a principal has more room than he needs, it is his function to ensure that some spaces are not overcrowded while others sit idle. Coupled with this quantitative problem is the question of the educational effectiveness of the use of school plant facilities. Here, again, the principal must ensure that space is well used and that space assignments reflect careful considerations of the best educational use of each available space.

Quantitative aspects.   In a consideration of utilization in terms of quantitative aspects, two types of measures are needed. The first is the

extent to which rooms and other spaces are used; the second, the extent
to which working stations (seats, laboratory spaces, table spaces, and so
forth) in each room are used. Utilization is normally calculated as a percentage. For example, if a school operates on a six-period day for five
days a week, maximum utilization of any room for the regular school
program would be thirty periods per week. If a room were used four
periods a day for three days a week and five periods a day the remaining
days, that room would be used 22 periods per week and its room utilization would be about 73 per cent. If this same room had thirty pupil
stations, its total capacity during the thirty-period week would be nine
hundred pupils. If the average class size during the twenty-two periods
the room is in use is twenty-five, the room is actually accommodating
five hundred and fifty pupils. Accordingly, its pupil station utilization is
about 61 per cent.

It is apparent to any person with secondary school teaching experience that these percentage figures need careful interpretation. The first
question revolves about a definition of a desirable degree of utilization.
Certainly, 100 per cent utilization is neither possible nor desirable. Secondly, utilization should mean much more than use in the formal teaching situation. For example, when a teacher spends one period per day
in his room preparing materials, conferring with students, or working
with small groups of students on special problems, the percentage of
utilization of that room will be less than it might be. However, the
lower percentage figure probably reflects a higher quality of use than
might be the case if the teacher did not have this period to use his room.

In addition, utilization figures do not usually account for use of
rooms outside of regular school hours. Nor do such figures reflect maintenance time, which, particularly in the case of certain special rooms, may
be quite necessary and time-consuming.

The quantitative aspects of space utilization are closely related to
other administrative problems. For example, although space might permit small sections of certain advanced courses, the budget might not
permit the employment of sufficient teachers to allow this. Undoubtedly,
scheduling problems sometimes create larger or smaller sections of certain classes than might be desirable or than might lead to greater space
utilization.

In short, the principal is responsible for seeing that the space assigned to him for the school program is utilized quantitatively to a degree
that is defensible. Just because a room may be labeled "Sewing" and
because sewing is taught only two periods a day does not mean that that
room should sit idle while classes that might use that space meet in

broom closets. Teachers sometimes develop an ownership complex toward their assigned spaces. The principal should ensure that such a complex does not lead to a waste of space. On the other hand, the principal himself should not develop a utilization complex in which he loses sight of the value of unassigned space. Although 100 per cent utilization is not a desirable goal, 100 per cent educational efficiency in the use of available space is both desirable and defensible.

Qualitative aspects. This last statement leads directly to a consideration of the qualitative aspects of utilization. Here several things need to be considered. In the first place, certain special rooms are designed to serve specialized needs. Such spaces as those for industrial arts, fine arts, business machines, or music are specially arranged and equipped to meet the needs of specific subject-matter areas. Ordinarily, careful consideration is given to program and enrollments when such rooms are planned. The secondary school principal should, however, periodically review the use of such rooms to insure that they are being used in terms of their planned purposes. For example, in one school in which considerable space was assigned and equipped for chemistry and physics laboratory use, the chemistry and physics teachers believed more in demonstrations than they did in student laboratory work. This meant that the laboratory space was little used, in spite of a serious space shortage in the high school. The alternatives were to convert the space to other uses or to convert the teachers to other methods. By astute administrative leadership, the latter alternative was followed successfully.

In addition to the effective use of special rooms, the principal must be concerned with what are usually called the academic classrooms. Teacher use of space for consultation, for working with small groups, or for study can be most effective. However, some principals in crowded schools have assigned such space usage only to have teachers spend their free periods in the cafeteria kitchen, in the faculty lounge, or elsewhere. An assessment of the effectiveness of the use of rooms is a responsibility of the principal.

Another qualitative aspect of utilization concerns the assignment of rooms to teachers. Too often, certain rooms considered desirable because of size or location are assigned in terms of a teacher's seniority rather than in terms of the teacher's job. For example, a teacher with twenty-five years of service, who teaches mathematics extremely well in what might be called a traditional manner, works in a room with fixed desks. He finds this very satisfactory, but would like to move to a larger, sunnier room, which happens to have tables and chairs. To accomplish this move, a young modernist is given the fixed-desk room. In this case, the fixtures do not match the teaching methods, and neither the teachers nor the rooms are used effectively. Actual educational needs rather than length of service should determine room assignment.

This discussion could be expanded to include consideration of cafeteria, gymnasium, office, or school nurse space. Space for storage or for business machines is equally subject to analysis in terms of the quality of utilization. School facilities should be designed to serve educational or other school purposes, and the principal needs to evaluate regularly the degree to which such facilities are effectively used to meet the purposes. If the effectiveness of use is low, either a change in the facility or a change in the methods of use is indicated. Decisions as to change required and action to create such a change are elements of the leadership role of the secondary school principal.

Equipping the school plant

Equipment is that class of material items that are of a permanent, non-expendable nature, as opposed to the other major class of material items —supplies. Lengthy and involved definitions are developed for accounting purposes to differentiate between equipment and supplies.[6] The selection and utilization of equipment—chairs, desks, bookcases, globes, library books, typewriters, laboratory furniture, or drawing tables—involves the same problems and considerations as have been mentioned with relation to the school plant. Actually, in a formal definition, equipment is a part of the school plant.

This means that the principal and his staff need to consider educational specifications for equipment in order to determine the educational purposes it is to serve and to determine the amount of equipment of any given kind necessary to serve the enrollment expected in the courses in which the equipment will be used. In addition, the principal should assign equipment in terms of the purposes it is designed to meet and should make periodic reviews of the extent of utilization of equipment in terms of amount of use and of quality of use.

Technological advances in education in the 1960's have been both rapid and great. Various kinds of programmed learning devices, listening centers or laboratories, television, and other equipment have been

[6] See, for example, United States Office of Education, *Financial Accounting for Local and State School Systems*, State Educational Records and Reports Series, Handbook II, Bulletin No. 4 (Washington, D.C.: Government Printing Office, 1957), Chapter 2.

developed for utilization in secondary education. Under the impetus of developments such as the National Defense Education Act, studies of the Educational Facilities Laboratory, and studies made by subject-matter specialists in mathematics, physics, and biology, much new equipment has been developed for school use.

The principal's task in selecting equipment, then, has grown to include a knowledge both of the needs of the school and of the great variety of equipment available to meet those needs. Several publications for school administrators devote major attention to the presentation of brief reviews of new school equipment. The principal should follow one or more of these publications regularly to enable him to assist teachers as they attempt to secure equipment to meet effectively the instructional needs of the school program.

It is a rare school indeed that has all the equipment it needs. The principal and his staff need, then, to develop procedures for anticipating equipment needs and for assigning priorities to various needs. If, as often happens, the principal is told by his superintendent that he has $5,000 for all equipment for a given year and the principal has requests for $10,000 worth of equipment, what does he do? The success of what he does depends to a large extent upon the degree to which he has established a long-range plan for purchasing new equipment and replacing old equipment. The faculty needs to be involved in this planning, and a teacher should know when his turn can be expected. Certainly, emergency situations that cause some deviations from a long-range equipping plan will arise but the plan is still necessary. Without such a plan, the principal must often make decisions on the spur of the moment, when he is subject to pressure and his actions to suspicion.

If, for example, the commercial education group in the high school seems to other teachers to be always getting new equipment while 1927 maps hang in the social science rooms, the principal will face major problems. If, however, the faculty understands that the needs of the commercial area are to be met this year but that social science equipment is the "number one" priority for the next year, and if the faculty is aware of the reasoning behind this decision, the problem will be minimized. This is not to say that the social science teachers will be happy about the decision, but they will understand it and will not be suspicious and resentful.

If it is a rare school that has all the equipment it needs, it is an almost equally rare school that does not have unused, antiquated equipment hidden in various corners and closets. This equipment is usually using needed space and often has a cash value that can be used in purchasing new equipment. The principal needs to assure himself that equipment is being used. If it is not, he should either determine ways that it can be used or recommend that it be disposed of in the most profitable manner.

In summary, equipment should be purchased and used to meet educational or other school-related purposes. The utilization of equipment should be reviewed regularly by the principal in terms of the amount and quality of use. The principal and his staff should develop a long-range plan for replacing old equipment and for purchasing new equipment so that priorities can be assigned each year for making the best use of whatever equipment funds are available.

Maintenance and operation of the school plant

Maintenance refers to those "cyclic but intermittent services intended to keep the plant near its original state of preservation; in other words, repairs and replacements," while operation refers to "the normal routine daily services required to keep the school open and usable for its intended purposes."[7] In the former category are included such things as painting, roof repairs, repairs to desks, and the like. In the latter category are such activities as keeping the building warm or cool, daily sweeping or mopping, care of the grounds, and the like. Although such differences have some importance in financial accounting, they are of little concern to the principal. His concerns are that the school be ready for use each day and that sufficient care be taken of the plant so that it does not deteriorate as a useful school facility.

Responsibilities for maintenance and operation. A secondary school will normally have one or more custodians assigned to it. These men will assume major responsibility for the operation of the plant and, in addition, may assume certain maintenance responsibilities. However, no team of custodians can keep a school building fit for use all by themselves. Much of the responsibility for the maintenance and operation of a school must be borne by those who use the school. If custodians must devote a major portion of their time to picking up after careless students and teachers or to repairing damage caused by carelessness or maliciousness, the regular maintenance and operation program will suffer.

There are several ways that this problem can be attacked. First, waste paper and other miscellaneous trash tend to accumulate in a school

---

[7] Henry H. Linn (ed.), *School Business Administration* (New York: The Ronald Press Company, 1956), p. 381.

building, and ample containers for such material should be provided. Secondly, an attractive building is generally treated with more respect than is a shabby building. This means that every possible step should be taken to brighten up the school. Halls should be attractively painted and decorated. The building should be as light as possible. Attractive pictures might well replace the usual reproduction of "Washington Crossing the Delaware." In short, a pleasant building calls for respect. Thirdly, and perhaps most important, is the general matter of morale. If the principal's staff personnel and pupil personnel procedures lead to a healthy school spirit, to a high morale, maintenance and operation problems decrease along with many other problems.

School custodians. Regardless of the general responsibilities related to maintenance and operation of the school plant, the school custodians will have specific duties in these fields. The principal should make certain that the custodians have a definite work schedule and that they know the duties they are to perform. The principal should protect the custodians from having too many people giving them directions. Too often, each teacher in a building feels that he has authority to request service directly from the custodians. This can lead only to trouble. The custodian's work schedule becomes impossible to maintain; custodians become frustrated and the quality of their work may suffer; and antagonisms develop between teachers and custodians, teachers and teachers, and custodians and custodians. The custodians should be directly responsible to the building principal or to some one designated by the principal.

The development of work schedules for custodians should be under the direction of the principal. Such schedules will need to conform to district policy, but custodians should feel that they are directly related to a school building rather than having a rather general relationship to the school system. The same principles that apply to the development of assignments for teachers apply to the development of schedules for custodians. Hours of work, overtime arrangements, and general work assignments should be included in the schedule.

Sometimes school custodians are called upon to make equipment repairs that should be done by specialists. The principal would do well to see that school district policy clarifies the type of repair work that custodians are to perform. Certainly, the average custodian should be able to make simple repairs, such as replacing washers in valves, replacing glass, or replacing window shades. However, the average custodian should not be expected to be a plumber, electrician, heating engineer, carpenter, painter, and interior decorator. In many instances, makeshift repairs by unqualified people lead to major repair expenses. Principals, teachers, and custodians should be aware of their limitations in maintenance work, and clear policy should guide the principal as he faces repair problems in his school.

Maintenance schedules. The principal should assist the superintendent in the development of maintenance schedules. Too many school administrators do not concern themselves with maintenance until something falls apart. There should be regular schedules for painting, inspection of equipment, and other preventive maintenance measures. Teachers whose work involves the use of equipment should be encouraged to follow regular preventive maintenance schedules. The principal needs to know when equipment will be available for inspection and upkeep. Summer periods and vacation periods during the school year should be used for maintenance purposes. A school plant should be useful for fifty years or more, but such a period of usefulness cannot be realized without wise maintenance procedures.

Records and reports

In administering the school plant, the principal will find it desirable to make use of certain records and reports. The following list is indicative of the kinds of written materials that should be available for or made available by the principal as plant problems are met:

Scale drawing of each floor of the school plant, indicating room numbers and type.

Inventory of equipment, including current assignment status by room number.

Enrollment data by room and subject for each period of the day.

Custodians' work schedule.

Maintenance schedule.

School board policy relating to community use of school facilities and other school plant matters.

Calendar of use of school facilities by both school and nonschool groups outside of regular school hours or, for example, in the case of an auditorium, during school hours.

File of instruction manuals relating to various pieces of equipment in the building. This file should include guarantees unless these are filed with the central administration.

List of equipment serving agencies authorized by central administration to make necessary inspections or repairs of the equipment in the building.

In making judgments concerning the adequacy of existing plant and equipment, the principal will need reactions from staff members using these facilities. Because of wide differences in types of space and of equipment, a single form would probably not be acceptable for gathering such reactions. The principal should solicit regularly the opinions of his staff regarding ways in which plant and equipment are helping or hindering the program of the school. These opinions should be organized so that interpretation is possible. Then these organized opinions can become the basis for planning for future expenditures and for future space and equipment assignments.

SCHOOL FINANCE

In school finance, the role of the principal is that of director of a large-scale internal financial operation. The principal has at least three major responsibilities in this field. First, he has definite responsibilities in the preparation and administration of the school district budget. Second, he must be knowledgeable about the general area of school finance so that he can assist the citizens of his school community in understanding this field. Finally, he is responsible for the management of the financial accounts within his school—the activities accounts, the athletic accounts, and the like.

The school district budget

A school budget should be an educational plan expressed in dollars and cents. It should reflect an education program—teachers, books, laboratory equipment, and all the other aspects of such a program. This means that budget-making must be something more than dividing a pool of money in accordance with some mathematical formula. It means, as DeYoung stated years ago, that a budget should be balanced educationally as well as balanced technically.[8]

The principal's role. If the budget is to reflect a program, it is apparent that school principals will play important roles in budget-making. In Chapter 5 we discussed the instructional leadership role of the principal. The instructional plans developed in a school under the leadership of the principal will lead to the development of school budget

[8] Chris A. DeYoung, *Budgeting in Public Schools* (Garden City, N.Y.: Doubleday & Company, Inc., 1936), pp. 14–15.

plans. A superintendent should involve his principals early and regularly as budgets are prepared.

The principal is faced with several key questions as the budget is prepared. Usually close to 80 per cent of a school budget is for personal services of one kind or another. Around 70 per cent of the total budget is for teachers' salaries. In terms of educational planning, then, the principal will have to bring to budget sessions answers to questions such as the following:

How many teachers are needed because of:
  Enrollment trends?
  Class size trends?
  Curriculum changes?
  Addition of services?
What kinds of new teachers are needed:
  Experienced teachers?
  Beginning teachers?
  Holders of advanced degrees?
What special personnel are needed:
  Guidance workers?
  Health personnel?
  Psychologists?

These are educational questions, but they also involve budget questions. Similar questions can readily be envisioned concerning instructional supplies, noncertified personnel, special services, and other areas.

Specific procedures. Because budget-making is a primary responsibility of the superintendent of schools, it is difficult to suggest to principals exact budget-making procedures that they should follow in the absence of knowledge of the plans of the superintendent. Assuming, however, that a superintendent does involve his principals in budget-making, several concrete ideas can be presented. If the budget year runs from July 1 through June 30—the most common pattern—the final budget is usually adopted early in June. Preparation of the budget for a specific year should begin around October. Principals should work with their teachers and other staff members at that time to develop educational plans and to determine educational needs. By late January, the principal should be able to provide the superintendent with a concrete educational plan for his school for the ensuing year. The superintendent and his principals will then need to consider costs, priorities, and alternatives. In some cases, the principal may be asked to discuss alternatives with his faculty. When the budget is discussed with the board of education, principals should be present to describe the educational planning underlying the budget figures. In this way, a sound, educationally balanced budget can be developed and adopted in June.

This description should make it clear that budget-making needs to be based on long-range plans. Program considerations do not begin anew each year. Program planning and, thus, budget-making are continuous undertakings that require intelligent involvement of principals by superintendents and of faculty and staff by principals.

Administration of the budget.   The details of administering the school district budget are important central administration responsibilities. These details include accounting, reporting, and auditing procedures that lead to effective budgetary control. Undoubtedly, the administration of the budget will require that principals follow certain procedures, particularly with reference to the purchase of supplies and equipment and to the use of services that are not provided by personnel under contract with the district, such as repair services and consultants. Here, again, procedures vary from district to district. In general, a school will receive certain allocations for the year for specific purposes. The principal will probably requisition the expenditures of these allocations to the central administrative office and will be responsible for checking and reporting the receipt of purchased articles from the vendors. The storage and distribution of supplies within the school will also be under the direction of the principal.

Probably the key responsibility of the principal in the administration of the school district budget is to understand and to follow the procedures developed for this purpose. School district money is public money, and its use must be accounted for accurately. This means that the principal should accept his share of the responsibility for assuring that school district financial operations are conducted in an efficient and businesslike manner.

General finance

Every educational administrator should be a community educational leader. Among other things, this means that he should understand certain facts about the public school system in his state and district so that he can provide accurate and meaningful information to the citizens of his school community. School finance, a topic of interest to all taxpayers, is a topic that lends itself to inaccuracies and misinformation. Although a secondary school principal need not be a scholar of school finance, he should know enough about the school finance program to speak intelligently about it. Finance programs vary greatly from state to state. All that we can do here is to suggest finance areas with which principals should be familiar and to encourage principals to become aware of the facts in these areas. The following questions indicate the finance areas that should be covered:

1. What is the total school district operating budget for the current year?

2. What portion of this budget is supported by local, county, state, and federal funds?

3. What tax sources provide school funds from each of these levels of government?

4. What expenditures is the district making for capital outlay purposes for the current year?

5. What is (are) the source(s) of capital outlay funds for the district?

6. What are the expenditures per pupil for the operation of the school for the current year?

7. What factors have led to increased school costs, if any, in recent years?

8. What kinds of educational activities must be carried on or educational standards met in order for the district to receive its full share of county, state, or federal funds?

9. What is the meaning and purpose of a salary schedule and what are the provisions of the schedule in this district?

10. What specific increased expenditures, if any, have led to improved quality of education in this district?

In addition to knowing the facts needed to answer these questions, principals should have some familiarity with school finance terms. It is amazing, for example, to find taxpayers who do not understand the meaning of assessed valuation of property, millage, or bond issue. It is equally surprising to find school principals who know nothing of the foundation program principle, equalization, or the differences between current operation expenses and capital outlay expenses. Every school principal should have on or near his desk a good basic textbook in school finance and should have in his mind a number of basic financial facts and understandings. The principal should also take steps to pass some of this financial "know-how" on to his staff. Teachers should understand basic school finance and should at least be aware of the sources of the funds that pay their salaries.

BUSINESS MANAGEMENT

Business management encompasses those jobs that relate to the efficient and effective handling of money and materials within the school. This task area is an important part of the principal's job and one that needs to be performed with care.

Internal accounting

As any secondary school principal knows, free public secondary education involves a great deal of money management within the school. Student clubs, class groups, athletics, musical programs, Future Farmers of America, Junior Red Cross, each of these groups and many more spend and receive money. The responsibility for these internal funds or nonappropriated monies almost always rests squarely with the principal. This means that the principal needs to be responsible for the development of a system that provices for the following:

1. Preparing budgets.

2. Recording receipts.

3. Crediting receipts to the proper fund.

4. Banking receipts.

5. Authorizing expenditures.

6. Receiving invoices or statements.

7. Making payments for expenditures.

8. Billing expenditures to the proper fund.

9. Issuing regular financial reports.

10. Providing for periodic outside audits.

Although the size of a school and the number of activities within a school influence the exact nature of this system, no school in which internal funds are handled can afford to deal with such funds without a regular system embodying these ten elements. The principal who operates an internal accounting system in his head, without any records to provide a basis of checking for accuracy, is treading on dangerous ground.

Several general factors need to be considered before the specifics of the internal accounting system are discussed. First, those groups within a school that are to be permitted to receive and to expend funds should be defined. The fewer such groups, the better. For example, one school has close to one hundred such separate entities, including the Class of 19XX (Boys), the Class of 19XX (Girls), the Class of 19XX (General), the Class of 19XX (Senior Trip Account), the Class of 19XX (Senior Gift Fund), and the Class of 19XX (Special Fund). This, of course, is a ridiculous extreme. Fund accounts should be established with some sense of order and with the provision that the responsible persons in each group with a fund account will keep the necessary records to eliminate the establishment of subfunds at the school level. Thus, the Class of 19XX should have a fund and the officers and advisers of the class should keep track of any subfunds in their own books. Groups that can logically be combined should be; those that need to be separate for good reasons should be kept separate.

A second general consideration relates to the use of students in operating the internal accounting system. Students can play important roles in this activity, but they should be so supervised that the burden of financial responsibility is on a faculty member. Large sums of money are often involved in internal accounts. It is neither fair nor professionally sound to place the burden of responsibility for these monies upon a student, regardless of how capable that student may be. Students can accept responsibility for preparing and living within a budget, for keeping financial records, and for issuing receipts. However, these activities should be done under the direction of a teacher or administrator with responsibility. Certainly, there is no excuse for sending a student from the school to a downtown bank carrying a sack of money because the money is student body receipts. Nor can shortages or inaccuracies be excused with the statement, "We let the students handle their funds; it's such a good learning activity!" Student participation in internal accounting procedures needs to be intelligently planned so that this participation is a good learning experience undertaken with responsible adult supervision.

All of those charged with responsibility for managing financial accounts should be bonded. The cost of bonds should be charged to the internal accounts.

A third important point concerns the mixing of student body or internal funds with school district tax funds. If at all possible, it is advantageous to keep these two kinds of funds in separate banks. Otherwise, bank employees can easily become confused and charge student body fund checks to school district accounts or vice versa. If these two kinds of funds must be deposited in one bank, the check blanks used for each account should be distinctive and the fact that the two funds are separate and not mutually interchangeable should be clearly established with the officials and employees of the bank.

One final general point should be raised. Although policy will differ from district to district, some clear understanding of valid uses of internal funds should be developed. A secondary school often has three sources of funds. First are the regular, school district funds, primarily from tax sources. Second are the internal funds under discussion in this section. Finally, various outside groups, such as parent-teacher associations or booster clubs, often raise and expend funds for school purposes. Policies should be developed at the district level to define the types of expenditures appropriate for each class of funds. Some of these policy statements will be dictated by state law. In some states, for example, equipment for interscholastic athletics cannot be purchased with tax funds. In general, internal and outside group funds should not be expended for purposes that clearly fall within general school district obligations. Thus, although student body funds may have to be used to purchase athletic equipment, such funds should not be used to purchase equipment for the regular school physical education program. This latter use of student body funds leads to the support of the school program by a few rather than by the citizens of the total district. By the same token, expenditures for special purposes clearly beyond the scope of school district purposes (i.e., a dance or a banquet for athletes) should be made from funds of the student body or of outside groups.

General accounting

In a system for internal accounting, at least one and possibly two ledgers should be maintained. In a situation that is not overly complex, a general ledger in which both receipts and expenditures are posted is sufficient. Such a ledger is illustrated in Figure 1. In a complex situation, a receipts journal is maintained and total receipts rather than individual items are posted to the general ledger. Figure 2 illustrates the use of a receipts journal.

Sample entries in Figure 1 illustrate how the general ledger provides a picture of the over-all condition of the student body account as well as of each fund within it. Totals for each fund can be used to check general totals. The bank account will be carried in the name of the general account and bank statements can be checked against the over-all columns. Many variations of this form are available. Some provide for the calculation of a balance at each entry, that is, receipts minus expenditures. Others provide a "purpose" column following the "to or

STUDENT BODY ACCOUNTS,

Date	To or From Whom	Check or Receipt No.	Amount	
			Received	Expended
	Balance Carried Forward		$9,320.00	$5,000.31
4/2/65	Acme Athletic Supply	321		52.31
4/2/65	Mr. Jones (Senior Play)	1052	105.00	
4/2/65	John Jones (Insurance)	1053	2.50	
4/2/65	Smith Jewelry	322		96.49
	Totals			

FIGURE 1. GENERAL LEDGER, ITEMIZED RECEIPTS AND EXPENDITURES

from whom" column. Additional pages provide enough columns for the number of funds existing in the total internal accounting system.

If a receipts journal is used, the general ledger for any one day would carry one single receipts entry. The total from the journal for the day would be entered in the column to the left of the dark line (Figure 1) and the appropriate subtotals would be entered under each fund account. In our example (Figure 2) there are seven receipt items for February 3, 1965, but only the totals are carried to the general ledger. In a school where there is a large number of receipts each day, the use of the receipts journal leads to a general ledger that is more easily read than if this general ledger contains all details of both receipts and expenditures.

In addition to these central records, each group with a fund should maintain its own record of receipts and expenditures. This will provide

TOWNSHiP HIGH SCHOOL

Fund, Athletics		Fund, Dramatics		Fund, Class of 19XX	
Received	Expended	Received	Expended	Received	Expended
$4,321.12	$2,015.89	$339.62	$161.05	$875.28	$536.15
	52.31				
		105.00			
2.50					
					96.49

an additional check upon the accuracy of accounting and will assist organizations in living within their budgets.

Fund budgets. In considering budgets for school groups, the principal often faces a nettlesome policy question. Should each group be asked to live within the income it can raise or should all income be pooled and allocated in terms of budget requests? Should athletics, for example, which often has a large income (and, coaches will be quick to point out, large expenditures), be asked to help support a student poetry club? Or, if the poetry club wants to spend money, should it find ways to raise money?

As a general policy, it is wise to pool income into a general fund and allocate money to each group in terms of a budget request. If a group requests funds and suggests no source of income, the allocating body can investigate whether this lack of income is due to legitimate reasons or to lethargy. The allocation should include consideration of this finding. The allocating body should be a student body group, such as a student council, that operates with the advice and consent of the principal. For the most part, this policy leads to a situation in which the expenditures of each group closely approximate income.

An additional problem arises with regard to class funds. Often, a senior class has raised and saved money during its three or four years in the school and uses this money for a trip, a gift to the school, or some similar purpose. The pooling of income does not lend itself to this practice of carrying a fund balance from year to year. This problem should be considered and a solution to it made a part of the policy related to budgeting. A common practice is to permit class groups to keep their funds out of the general fund pool, to live within their income, and to carry balances from year to year.

Regardless of the exact nature of the policy relating to budgets, each group with a fund account should be required to submit a budget for the year. If possible, these budgets should be submitted in the spring so that the financial operations can begin on a businesslike basis at the start of the new school year. If this is not feasible, budget preparation and approval should be the first order of business for each group at the opening of the school year. Approved budgets should be filed and periodic reports made to each group by the central accounting agency concerning the relationship between the projected and actual financial operation for the year.

Receipts.   Each receipt of money should be recorded at least in duplicate. Serially-numbered receipt forms should be used. Several companies make small receipt machines that make it possible to issue and file receipts in an orderly manner with a minimum of expense. Each receipt should contain the date, name of person or organization from whom money is received, purpose of payment, fund to be credited, and signature of person receiving payment. One copy of the receipt should be given to the person making payment and one kept on file centrally. In some schools, a third copy of the receipt is given to the treasurer of the organization to be credited with the payment received.

If an organization is sponsoring an event for which payments are to be received, some arrangement should be made for the orderly receipt and acknowledgement of such payments. For many events, serially-numbered tickets of admission will serve this purpose. A school can

RECEIPTS JOURNAL, URBAN SENIOR HIGH SCHOOL

Date	From Whom Received	Purpose	Receipt Number	Amount Received	Fund, General Amount	Fund, Athletic Amount	Fund, Photo Club Amount
2/3/65	Sadie Smith	Class photo	3012	$ 1.50			$1.50
2/3/65	John Jones	,,	3013	1.50			1.50
,,	William Williams	,,	3014	1.50			1.50
,,	Fred Fredericks	USHS activity card	3015	2.30	$2.30		
,,	Sally Jenkins	Basketball tickets	3016	3.50		$ 3.50	
,,	Bruce Watkins	Class photo	3017	1.50			1.50
,,	William McCord	Class photo	3018	1.50			1.50
	Daily Totals			$13.30	$2.30	$ 3.50	$7.50
2/4/65	Ida Lacey	Basketball Tickets	3019	15.00		15.00	

FIGURE 2. RECEIPTS JOURNAL

purchase serially-numbered tickets in quantity in various colors quite inexpensively. The central treasurer can then issue tickets to any group needing them, and the numbers can be used to check receipts. If this is not possible, receipt books of some kind should be used by the group to account for its income. All receipts received by a group should be turned in daily to the central accounting office and a receipt issued to acknowledge such payments.

The copies of the receipts kept by the central accounting office are used to credit the various funds in the receipts journal or in the general ledger. Individual receipt forms should be saved for at least a year and receipt numbers should be posted in the journal or ledger to facilitate checking if necessary.

Depositing funds. Secondary school internal account receipts often involve fairly large sums of money. The safest place for such money is a bank. Arrangements should be made for the daily deposit of the internal account funds of a school in a bank, keeping out only enough money to make change. Money received should be tallied with receipts issued each day and should then be deposited.

One problem that arises often in these days of night football and basketball games is safeguarding the large receipts from such activities. In almost every community it is possible to make arrangements with police officers to stand by while receipts are counted and checked and to accompany a school official to a bank to deposit receipts in a night depository. No other alternative is as satisfactory as this. Receipts may occasionally have to be placed in a safe, but if this is done, an adequate vault should be installed and the money deposited in a bank as soon as possible.

Expenditures. No expenditures should be made in cash for any purposes. Each group with a fund account should be supplied with purchase orders and with vouchers. Figures 3 and 4 illustrate common forms for these uses. All purchases by any representative of a student group should be made only with a signed purchase order. When goods have been received, a voucher should be sent to the central accounting office, and the authorized person will issue a check. Vouchers will be used for posting expenditures to the general ledger and should be saved for at least one year to facilitate checking individual payments.

It should be noted that the forms shown here provide for both faculty and student signatures. Checks to be drawn upon student body funds might also require these two types of signatures. Here, again, this is a matter of policy. In general, students should play a role in approving

```
┌─────────────────────────────────────────────────┐
│                                                 │
│            HILLY VALLEY HIGH SCHOOL             │
│                  Purchase Order                 │
│                                                 │
│   No._____  Date_____    │
│                                                 │
│   Deliver to _____   │
│              _____   │
│                                                 │
│   Representing _____   │
│                      (Fund account)            │
│  ─────────────────────────────────────────────  │
│   Quantity        Description          Cost     │
│                                                 │
│                                                 │
│                                                 │
│                                                 │
│                                                 │
│                                                 │
│                                                 │
│                                                 │
│  ─────────────────────────────────────────────  │
│   Approved by: _____   │
│                    (Authorized student)         │
│                                                 │
│                _____   │
│                    (Faculty adviser)            │
│                                                 │
└─────────────────────────────────────────────────┘
```

FIGURE 3. PURCHASE ORDER FORM

purchases for student body groups and in approving and making payments from student body funds. Each organization should designate one or two students who are authorized to sign purchase orders and vouchers. Such forms should also require the signature of a faculty adviser. Checks should require the signatures of both a student and a faculty person. Such a procedure provides a healthy atmosphere of student participation and responsibility and also avoids any appearance of unbridled faculty or administration control of student body funds. Regardless of what the procedure is, however, it should be absolutely clear who is to sign what so that business procedures are orderly.

Financial reports. Regular reports of the status of internal funds should be made to the student body, to the superintendent, and to the board

```
┌─────────────────────────────────────────────┐
│                                             │
│         HILLY VALLEY HIGH SCHOOL            │
│                  Voucher                    │
│                                             │
│   No. _____     Date _____      │
│   Pay to   _____    │
│            _____    │
│            _____    │
│                                             │
│   Amount $_____                        │
│   From fund _____ │
│   Purpose: Purchase order _____  │
│        Invoice _____(Attached)   │
│                                             │
│            _____    │
│            _____    │
│            _____    │
│                                             │
│            _____   │
│                 (Describe purpose briefly)  │
├─────────────────────────────────────────────┤
│  The goods or services mentioned above      │
│  were received and payment is approved.     │
│                                             │
│   _____        _____    │
│  (Authorized student)    (Faculty adviser)  │
├─────────────────────────────────────────────┤
│                    PAID                     │
│   Date _____    Check No. _____  │
│                                             │
│            _____   │
│                 (Authorized signature)      │
│                                             │
└─────────────────────────────────────────────┘
```

FIGURE 4. VOUCHER FORM

of education. Most schools issue monthly reports. These reports should include the information illustrated in Figure 5. The information concerning the check between the report and the bank statement is not essential, but it provides clear evidence of accuracy. In many schools, a report such as this is sent to each treasurer of a student group, each faculty adviser, the superintendent, each board member, and is posted on bulletin boards for the student body. The information for such a monthly report is readily available from the general ledger.

Audits. In some states, internal accounts are audited by state examiners at the same time as school district accounts are audited. In other states, state auditors do not examine internal accounts. No matter who does the audit, internal accounts should be checked by an outside auditor once a year. This yearly audit is necessary because the students working on these accounts will probably change yearly and new personnel should not assume charge of accounts that have not received an outside audit. Most auditors will check for clarity and accuracy and will also make suggestions related to the efficiency of the accounting procedures. Such suggestions should be encouraged and changes should be

HOPEVILLE HIGH SCHOOL

Monthly Statement, Internal Accounts

_____   _____
(month)   (year)

Fund	Balance Carried Forward	Receipts	Expenditures	Balance

Total

(1) Total balance checked with bank statement as of _____
                                                               (date)
(2) Checks not cashed as of that date $_____
(3) Bank statement balance equals $_____plus $_____
                                  (Total balance)   (2, above)

The above represents a true and accurate statement of the financial condition of the internal accounts of Hopeville High School.

Date _____

_____   _____
(Authorized student)   (Faculty adviser)

FIGURE 5. MONTHLY FINANCIAL STATEMENT FORM

made if improvements are likely to result. A careful, yearly audit provides a sense of security and often results in improved procedures, which may save time and lead to increased accuracy with decreased effort.

EQUIPMENT AND SUPPLY MANAGEMENT

In addition to the business management responsibilities already mentioned, the principal has certain tasks related to the administration of the school district budget and to the care and distribution of district supplies and equipment. Here, again, district policies govern many of his procedures. But regardless of these policies, he will undoubtedly need to develop procedures for requisitioning supplies and for maintaining inventory records.

Supply management

Supplies are delivered to a school in accordance with the budget requests. Certain of these materials, such as laboratory supplies, can be delivered to and stored in teaching areas. Other materials need to be stored in central spaces for distribution during the year. The principal needs to know what supplies are expected for the year, what supplies have been received, where supplies are stored, and to whom supplies have been issued. A simple form, such as is shown in Figure 6, will assist in this task. In a large school, records such as this need to be kept by personnel in a supply room; in a smaller school, such records can be maintained in the principal's office.

Procedures need to be established so that supplies are not "grabbed" off the shelf by any and all teachers or students. Although the form shown in Figure 6 provides a running inventory of supplies, it does not indicate whether, for example, Miss Jones had asked for typewriting paper when the budget was prepared or whether she suddenly decided she needed some in September. In some schools, a companion file to the running inventory, which shows teacher requests for supplies and the degree to which such requests have been met, is maintained. An example of this type of form is shown in Figure 7. The left-hand side of this form can be completed by the teacher during the budget preparation period and the approved figures entered when the budget is completed. The use of this form is not meant to lead to complete inflexibility. Alterations in assignment of supplies should be possible, but the form will provide a guide, which is much better than haphazard controls over supplies.

WHITNEY COUNTY PUBLIC SCHOOLS

Supply Control

School ___Adam Junior High___   School year ___1965–66___

Paper, typing, white 8½ × 11   ream
_____(Item)_____   (unit)

Number units budgeted for year   100

Date	Units Received	Units Disbursed	To Whom	Balance on Hand
7/15/65	60		Supply office	60
9/3/65		5	Miss Jones	55
9/3/65		5	Mr. Smith	50
9/10/65	40		Supply office	90

FIGURE 6. SUPPLY CONTROL FORM

One final point should be mentioned in discussing supplies. Almost every principal is faced occasionally with the problem caused by the teacher who decides that he needs some special material, goes to a store and purchases it, and has the bill sent to the school. No procedure or process will completely eliminate this problem. However, several things might help. First, teachers should know that this procedure is not correct and that such special purchases can be requested through district channels. Second, merchants should be aware of district procedures and should know that purchases made without correct purchase orders are not legal. Finally, persistent violators of the correct procedures should pay for their purchases. A school district cannot long operate if each employee of the district considers himself a purchasing agent of the district.

WHITNEY COUNTY PUBLIC SCHOOLS

Supply Control

School ___Adam Junior High___   School year ___1965–66___

___Jones, Mary Ellen___   Subjects___English II, III, IV___
(Teacher's name)

Supplies requested		Units Approved	Units Delivered
Units	Description		
10 ream	White typing paper, 8½ × 11	8	8, 6
1 gross	Pencils, 2 H	1	1
2 boxes	B.B. Chalk, white	2	1, 2

FIGURE 7. TEACHER SUPPLY CONTROL FORM

Inventory

A principal is generally responsible for the care of equipment in the school he administers. This means that he should know how many desks are in the building, what kinds of industrial arts equipment are in the building, and so on. In other words, he should have an accurate and up-to-date inventory.

A useful inventory indicates both the quantity of equipment within a building and its location. The most difficult part of an inventory is its original establishment. Once good records are available, the maintenance of the inventory becomes somewhat routine. Very large schools with machine accounting systems often use machine inventory procedures. With these procedures, a separate card is maintained for each item of equipment and processing these cards can indicate either total quantities or location of equipment. In smaller schools, two forms may be used, such as those illustrated in Figures 8 and 9.

The form in Figure 8 has been completed. The last entry illustrates one method of indicating the movement of equipment within a building. The use of negative numbers in the "quantity received" column is a method of recording the movement of equipment out of the building. The use of an adding machine will quickly show the total quantity of any item in the building. The form shown in Figure 9 is useful for determining the exact equipment within a single room. It can also be used to check the location columns in an item inventory card. A common procedure in the use of a room inventory form is to provide the teachers with copies of the previous year's inventory for their rooms to assist them in checking for the current year. Room inventories should be taken yearly and the room figures checked with the item cards.

WHITNEY COUNTY PUBLIC SCHOOLS

Inventory Card

School   Adam Junior High

Desk, Teacher's, Single Pedestal, Wood
(Item)

each
(Unit)

Date Received	Quantity Received	Unit Cost	Received From	Location
8/15/55	15	$72.50	manufacturer	Rooms, 1, 2, 3, 4, 5, 15, 17, 18, 19, 21, 22, 23, 24, 27, 30
9/1/59	−2	−	traded in	Rooms 4, 22
9/1/59	2	$87.65	manufacturer	Rooms 4, 22
8/11/60	−4	−	sent to high school	Rooms 1, 15, 18, 19
8/11/60	−	−	Rooms 27, 30	Rooms 1, 15

FIGURE 8. INVENTORY CARD

WHITNEY COUNTY PUBLIC SCHOOLS

Inventory Card

School _____   Room _____

Date_____

Quantity	Description of item

FIGURE 9. INVENTORY CARD FOR ROOMS

SCHOOL OFFICE MANAGEMENT

The secondary school principal must number among his tasks the responsibility for the management of the school office. This office is the contact point between the school and the public. The impression that people receive from this office is often the impression they have of the entire school. Thus, it is not only important to the operation of the school that the office be well managed, but it is an important phase of the public relations program of the school and of the school district.

The secondary school principal, however, must avoid making himself an office manager. He is an educational leader. Office management is only one part—and a small part—of his job. Too often, the principal allows himself to become enmeshed in office trivia—answering the phone, sorting mail, manning an information counter, writing receipts, recording absences, and the like. Although this may result in an efficient office, it can lead to a most inefficient use of the principal's time. All of these office tasks must be provided for, but the principal is not meeting his challenge if he provides for these tasks by doing them himself.

A principal of a secondary school should have at least one full-time adult clerical assistant. In addition, students can be used as office assistants, provided that they are not placed in positions where confidential matters relating to fellow students are available to them or where they devote an undue portion of their time to this work.

Well-trained students can answer the telephone, sort mail, maintain certain files, and greet visitors. They can assist in distributing material from the office to classrooms. These student office assistants should be responsible to the chief clerical worker in the office and should not be expected to take orders from a number of people. The chief clerical worker is responsible to the principal and should not be expected to serve as a private secretary to each member of the faculty. The organization of the office and the assignment of office work should be delegated to the chief clerical assistant. The principal should hold periodic conferences with his clerical assistant to evaluate progress in office management.

In evaluating the work of the school office, the principal must be provided with an account of the kinds of activities being done there. In some cases, school office personnel will be performing services that might better be assigned elsewhere. In others, additional duties might be undertaken by office personnel. In the last analysis, the principal should do the following:

1. Be aware of the office work necessary for the efficient operation of the school.

2. Staff the school office with sufficient personnel—student and adult—to make it possible for the necessary office work to be done.

3. Delegate the management of the office to a responsible clerical assistant.

4. Periodically evaluate the effectiveness of the school office.

Much of the school office work can be made routine. Whenever possible, forms should be developed to facilitate the work of the school. Not only do forms make work go faster; they also eliminate errors that occur from the random recording of information. A number of firms print standard school office forms that can be purchased in quantity inexpensively. Often such a purchase results in long-term savings of time and of energy.

MISCELLANEOUS MANAGEMENT CONCERNS

It is difficult to predict the exact nature of the management concerns that will face any given principal. In some schools, he will have responsibilities for the management of a school cafeteria; in others, he will have duties related to the transportation system; in still others, he may oversee the operation of a student store. In each of these and in many other areas, the principal will undoubtedly delegate the direct management of the service to another employee.

The principal's task will be to understand the purpose of the service, to staff the service, to select a manager to whom direct operational management can be delegated, to develop in cooperation with the manager a system of records that will permit control of the operation, to submit necessary reports concerning the operation to appropriate people within or without the school system, and to make periodic evaluations of the service, which will lead to suggestions for improvements.

If, for example, the principal has responsibilities for the management of all or part of a school transportation program, he will work with a head driver, a director of transportation, or some other staff member with operational management responsibility. It will be necessary to develop records relating to the students transported, to the miles of travel, to the maintenance of equipment, to fuel usage, and the like. Forms for requesting the use of buses for field trips or athletic events will be needed. Reports will be submitted to the superintendent and possibly to state department of education officials and others.

Without attempting to provide details for each of these management concerns, let us merely repeat that the principal, in any management task, will need to devise a system that permits him to plan, to control, and to evaluate the operation. This system will vary from district to district and from school to school. The test of the system is not that it be similar to what some expert has called an ideal system, but that it meet the needs of the principal as he fulfills his role in the management tasks in a given school situation.

In short, the administration of noninstructional personnel is not a task requiring techniques or principles different from those used in dealing with instructional personnel. Indeed, probably the major factor needed by the principal is an attitude or point of view that leads him to accept the fact that no basic difference in personnel administration principles exists regardless of the roles assigned to the personnel.

CONCLUSION

The management functions of the principal are necessary, important, and legitimate. The performance of these functions is, however, well adapted to system and to routine. The principal who does not develop system and routine for meeting these management problems will find either that the problems are poorly met or that the meeting of the problems requires an undue expenditure of his time and effort.

No attempt has been made here to present systems which can be adopted *in toto* by any school. Such systems do not exist. Our attempt has been to point out the management problems likely to arise in a secondary school and to describe some ways in which these problems might be met. A crucial phase of the principal's management task, however, is to study the problems as they exist in his school and to proceed, utilizing all possible advice, to develop plans for dealing with these problems. It is the ability to meet this kind of a challenge that is characteristic of the successful secondary school principal.

SUGGESTED ACTIVITIES

1. Prepare a statement of educational specifications for a given subject-matter area in a school with which you are familiar. Assume that these specifications are to assist an architect in developing plans for a new school with a projected life of fifty years.

2. Prepare a paper defending the affirmative or negative side of this statement: One hundred per cent utilization of secondary school facilities is neither possible nor desirable.

3. Prepare a short paper that could be used as a guide for a presentation of the school finance program in your state to a group of parents.

4. Describe the questions you as a secondary school principal would ask your teaching staff as you prepared an educational plan to underlie your budget requests for the next school year.

5. Prepare a policy statement to guide the development and administration of an accounting procedure for student body accounts. Include consideration of the number and kinds of funds to be established, the role of students in the plan, and a system of internal checks and balances.

6. Develop the outline of a handbook for use by students who are to serve as clerical assistants in a secondary school office.

7. Prepare a brief talk that you as a secondary school principal could use in welcoming new noninstructional staff members to your school.

SELECTED READINGS

Association of School Business Officials of the United States and Canada, *A Manual of Accounting Principles and Procedures for Student Activity Funds.* Bulletin No. 17. Evanston, Ill.: The Association, 1957.

Benson, Charles S., *Perspectives on the Economics of Education.* Boston: Houghton Mifflin Company, 1963.

Corbally, John E., Jr., *School Finance.* Boston: Allyn and Bacon, Inc., 1962.

Herrick, John H., *et al., From School Program to School Plant.* New York: Holt, Rinehart & Winston, Inc., 1956.

Hill, Frederick W., and James W. Colmey, *School Business Administration in the Smaller Community.* Minneapolis: T. S. Denison & Co., Inc., 1964.

Linn, Henry H. (ed.), *School Business Administration.* New York: The Ronald Press Company, 1956.

United States Office of Education, *Financial Accounting for Local and State School Systems.* State Educational Records and Reports Series. Handbook II, Bulletin No. 4. Washington, D.C.: Government Printing Office, 1957.

Yeager, William A., *Administration of the Noninstructional Personnel and Services.* New York: Harper & Row, Publishers, 1959.

10

COMMUNITY
RELATIONS

THE BOUNDARIES OF THE SECONDARY SCHOOL ARE THE boundaries of the community it serves. It is not an island set apart; it is a social institution intimately related to the individuals, the families, and the other social institutions in the area with which it is identified. When we think of school-community relations or, as it is often called, public relations for the secondary school, the dimensions of our concern for understanding, communication, acceptance, and goodwill are broad and involved. Relations with the community cannot be avoided. The community will inform itself and formulate and register opinions about the secondary school in spite of any effort by the school to condition such relationships. But such community relations, left more or less to chance, may or may not be of a positive, enlightened nature. In fact, case after case could be pointed out where school-community relations left to chance have resulted in opinions based on the lack of information, misinformation, gossip, and rumor. It is the school administrator's prerogative to organize and develop a school-community relations program that will nurture community enlightenment and understanding.

The contents of this section included a definition of school-community relations, an analysis of their importance, the principal's role in public relations, ideas for working with the staff on school-community relations, concepts on working with internal and external people related to the school, and some suggestions for evaluation of the school-community relations program.

SCHOOL-COMMUNITY RELATIONS DEFINED

"This high school needs a better program of school-community relations." How often we hear some such statement, and in many instances the pronouncement is sound. Every secondary school needs to improve its relationship with the community it serves. But more often than not the critic has in mind some flamboyant publicity program that will make the school known above all other high schools in the area. This, in the minds of many, is good school-community relations—good public relations. Really, it is merely publicity.

Actually, the publicity-centered concept of school-community relations has possibilities for negative results when weighed against the basic understandings desirable to both the school and the patrons. Publicity as such is not undesirable; on the contrary, it can be a most useful tool in public relations. Basic to the concept of school-community relations is what the school is, what it does, how it does it, and what it needs to do the job. It is the conduct of the school that comes first and, based on it, communication and publicity about the school come second. In other words, all the publicity in the world will not make a good school; it is the quality of the school that is the paramount requisite for any discerning community appreciation or understanding. Concerns about the quality of the educational program, the guidance program, the success of graduates in college, the costs of education, and the effectiveness of instruction are not easily glossed over. Publicity about some favorable aspects of the school is most desirable, but it cannot be counted upon as a substitute for broader understandings.

Briefly, then, school-community relations is the harmony of understanding that exists between the school and the publics it serves. This composite of singulars and plurals is intentional. The conduct of the school relates itself to many publics in the community, including students, parents, nonparents, teachers, merchants, farmers, tradesmen, and others. Good community relations anticipates a two-way understanding—the school must understand the community and the community must understand the school.

The student constitutes the principal's first public with whom he must develop fruitful relations. What is good for the student and his education is a concern of the entire community. The school that studies the community and its youth and plans with the community for its youth has established a proper foundation for an effective program of school-community relations. The process of working together, the co-operation of school and community, opens and maintains channels of communication for a two-way flow of information, and information is the basis of all understanding.

Internal and external publics

The secondary school in its community relations program must be concerned with publics both within the school and outside the school. The students constitute an internal public. The teaching staff is an important internal public, the custodial force, the cafeteria workers, the bus drivers, all groups directly connected with the operation of the school may be considered internal publics for school-community relations purposes. All of these have outside contacts in which they may play a positive or a negative role as far as communication and understanding about the school is concerned.

Every community has many external publics with sincere interest in education. Nearly every worthwhile community group has some plank in its platform that relates it to education; patriotic societies, veterans' groups, service clubs, women's clubs, church groups, and civic groups are good examples. The well-formulated community relations program of the school will relate itself to these organizations to tie into their educational interests and concerns and capitalize on ready-made interests and contacts. Among the external publics are community agencies dedicated to youth service. The secondary school must work closely with such agencies without taking over their work, on one hand, and being exploited to accomplish the agencies' purposes, on the other hand.

The parent-teachers association, the parent advisory council, and, to a large extent, the booster clubs and the music parents organizations, are both internal and external publics. These groups are identified with both the school and the outside community. Many members in these groups are also members of other external groups. As such, they provide effective entree to many external publics not as closely related to the school. These "in-between" publics have become the bulwark of the school-community relations programs in many high schools. Such groups have been major strengths in interpreting school needs, bond issues, curriculum changes, activities programs, and school projects, while at the same time lending support and providing media and means for obtaining patrons' reactions and ideas on what is wanted in the school program in the process.

THE IMPORTANCE OF SCHOOL-COMMUNITY RELATIONS

Schools generally have lagged badly in developing sound programs of public relations. Invariably, when school administrators are asked to list their most pressing current problems, public relations lands near the top, along with finance and improvement of instruction. In reality, all three are closely related. Finance and quality of instruction are linked to the level of understanding and the values seen in education by the citizens. Although shortcomings in public relations efforts seems to have been generally admitted and recognized, far too few schools have attempted to do anything constructive about it. In some instances it has been lack of "know-how," in others, lack of leadership on the part of the administrator, and yet in other instances, a tendency to rationalize that the public does not want to be bothered about education.

Engineering consent

We live in an age when many people are attempting to engineer consent. Everywhere one turns he is confronted with the highest power advertising yet devised—urges and appeals to use, to buy, to discriminate, to enjoy, to be happy, to live better. Competition is truly keen. Industry and business have found that it pays to inform the people, to develop understandings, and to get into harmony with the buying publics. Competition employs every known means of influence—status appeal, comfort, taste, beauty, and a multitude of "hidden persuaders." Every media of communication is exploited. In an average day, almost everyone is exposed to several experiences that call his attention in one way or another to some product. Education is not a commercial enterprise and cannot employ the same methods as industry and business. The point remains, however, that we in education face serious competition for John Q. Citizen's time, attention, understanding, and values. It may profit us to learn some lessons from our competition. Schools need to learn the basic lesson in human relations, namely, that it is well to make friends even when one does not need them if they are to be available when one does need them.

Necessity for cooperation

The execution of a sound school-community relations program is not a one-man job. It cannot be left to a school's director of public relations alone. Granted that such a program needs leadership and that the key person in that leadership role is the principal, still, he cannot do the job by himself. Cooperation is required. The greatest task of the principal is in the area of encouraging and stimulating cooperation and wide involvement in a school-community relations program. There are many areas in which this cooperation should obtain with parents, students, teachers, other schools, community organizations, and other publics in the environment of the school. Over and over again the teamwork aspects of public relations must be emphasized—it is an all-important element in a successful program of this nature.

Good school-community relations are not founded on a bag of tricks. There are no known gimmicks that alone spell success in the development of harmonious understandings and goodwill. This is not to say that tricks and ideas should not be used. To be effective such must be in the context of a well-defined program. In other words, there is no such thing as a single "cure-all" that will lift the public relations program by the bootstraps to a high level of effectiveness. Were this true many schoolmen would have seized upon it long ago. Only an orderly, well-conceived, and comprehensive program of school-community relations, one that integrates the tricks and the gimmicks with planned intelligent purposes, objectives, and formulated goals of a comprehensive program of lifting levels of understanding, winning support, and earning goodwill, can succeed.

The warning against the tricks and gimmicks approach to a school-community relations program is not meant to discourage for a moment the use of many excellent materials available. The "Gold Mine" series from NSPRA, now in six volumes, Trends, Classroom Newsletter, Teachers Letters, and similar materials available through the National Education Association and other sources are most commendable.

Continuous effort

Efforts in school-community relations are never-ending. Kindred lists four reasons for school-community relations programs: interpretation, correction, information, and promotion.[1] These are continuous reasons, since schools have a constant turnover of those directly connected with it—students and parents.

The orientation of students and parents for the first year of high school is an annual event on the public relations calendar. Each crop of graduates sees another group taking its place next year. Each year finds new people in the community. Census tallies show that varying percentages of students move in and out of the school district and in and out of attendance units within the district.

There are two kinds of mobility; mobility through the program, and mobility of people in and out of the community. Still another mobility factor, which is becoming of increasing concern to many secondary school administrators, is that of serving several communities in new secondary school complexes. In other words, the secondary school becomes a community of communities and draws students from several neighboring natural communities. This has come about particularly in areas where small schools have been abandoned and new school districts established. Here we have mobility across natural community lines, and this social phenomenon must be considered in the new school public relations efforts.

The reasons for a continuous program of public relations cited thus far are rather obvious. Another reason, however, may be less apparent —the changing climate of opinion locally and nationally regarding education. The publication of a book, the work of a zealot with an idea of how education should be accomplished, or the scientific achievements of other nations can and does influence the thinking of many people with respect to the kind and quality of instruction desired in the secondary school. It is not enough for the principal to shake off indictments of secondary education by the simple statement, "It may be true in some high schools, but not in ours." This feeling must be shared by the constituents and this can be accomplished only through a continuous effort of keeping the people informed as to what the school is, what it does, how it does it, and what it needs to do it.

THE PRINCIPAL'S ROLE

The chief responsibility for a program of school-community relations rests with the principal. This is one of his most important task areas. The

---

[1] Leslie Kindred, *School Public Relations* (Englewood Cliffs, N.J.: Prentice-Hall, Inc., 1957).

attitude of the principal toward his responsibilities for school-community relations is a matter of primary significance. Does he actually see public relations as a part of his job? Is he willing to work at improving school-community relations, or does he see this task as one to be handled in the main by the central office or by specialized staff personnel? Does he take an active part, or is this just another chore he delegates to someone else? The principal must assume the attitude that interpreting his school to the public, developing sound working relations with the community, and promoting understanding is a professional responsibility he cannot abdicate. Upon him, and him alone, rests the primary responsibility of initiating and maintaining a sound program of public relations.

Although attitude is very important and serves as a springboard for motivation and initiative, the principal must also possess a sound knowledge of what constitutes an effective school-community relations program. He must be a student of public relations, avail himself of opportunities to study the subject, know how to appraise a program feature, be willing to test ideas, experiment, use his imagination, make good use of consultative help, elicit and make use of assistance available on the staff and in the community, organize and channel efforts for developing wide understandings, and possess a sense of timing. Competition, precept, and example in modern society through every possible media leaves the educator no choice but to become alert, knowledgeable, and competent in the arts of influence and persuasion. It is difficult to imagine a cause more worthwhile than the sound education of the future citizens and consumers of the nation.

The modern school administrator must possess and develop skills and competencies in public relations techniques. It is often said of better principals, "He knows his community." What does this statement mean? Usually it describes an individual's competence in understanding the social forces, the power structure, the social groupings, interactions, loyalties, institutions, and the peculiarities of the community. This skill of "knowing the community" does not come about by chance. Men who are successful in this regard work at it constantly. They are social scientists in the true sense of the word. Their approach is systematic, organized, objective, and thorough.

Another characteristic of the principal successful in his public relations effort is that of being able to communicate. "His grapevine really works," "He gets ideas across to the people of his district," "The people in his community are informed about their schools." Again, this is not mere accident. Communication techniques must be studied and skills developed to produce effective results. "Know your schools" must be more than a slogan or a theme for an open-house event. People "know" only as they are informed and according to the kind of information they receive.

Again, one hears, "He certainly has good involvement of people in his operations," "He knows how to use people effectively," "He gets everybody in on the act," or "That community has wonderful cooperation between the citizens and the schools." Without doubt, an analysis of such situations would show that the principal is skilled in group dynamics, knows how to channel group effort, helps people to gain satisfactions from working with and for the schools, and gives credit for accomplishments.

Key responsibility

The principal has a key role in any public relations program. It is one of his primary responsibilities. His attitude toward school-community relations, his knowledge of what constitutes good school-community relations, and his skills in public relations techniques are minimum essential expectancies and requisites for the leader of today's schools. Some suggestions and ideas as to the implementation of desirable attitudes, knowledges, and skills in community relations efforts are related in the balance of this chapter.

Over the desk of every secondary school principal might well be inscribed these words, "Dedicated to Community Service." In a very real sense, he, his office, and the school he heads is dedicated to community service. As a recognized community leader in the area, the principal will identify himself with service clubs, youth organizations, churches, civic groups, and such other positive efforts in his environs as his time will permit. He gives freely of his time and talents not just because he is a public servant but because he has a deep conviction that he has an obligation to set an example for others. In turn, he has the right to expect reasonable willingness on the part of staff members and citizens in the community to contribute time and effort for school enterprises.

In most communities, the secondary school is called upon occasionally to contribute to some aspect of social and civic service. Schools have an enviable record in service projects such as civil disaster programs, safety programs, beautification and clean-up projects, school forests, and many other worthwhile enterprises. Such efforts, in addition to having instructional value, have helped to bring the school and the community into closer harmony with each other on a basis over and beyond academics and instructional services. Such programs are another way of telling the people what the school is, what it does, and how it does it. They also demonstrate the fact that the secondary school as a social institution has a community consciousness and a willingness to participate in community services.

Community service can be defended not alone on its public relations value but on its merits as a means of early development in youth the sense of responsibility for community responsibility and service. The secondary school students of today will be the citizens in charge of the community in a very short time.

Relations with central office

School-community relations is not only the concern of Central High School but of the entire school system. Articulation and coordination of the system's program of public relations is most important. There is a good example of the administrative team-work discussed in Chapter 4. In most instances the system will have some general policies with regard to school-community relations, use of facilities by the public, purchasing, news releases, release of records, giving out lists of students and staff, graduation procedures, and a host of similar items having a direct bearing on relations with its publics.

Since the high school principal is responsible for his unit in the system he has an obligation to see that his school keeps in line and coordinated with all of the other schools and the general district policies. He has an obligation to provide leadership in the formulation and creation of policy, but once the policy is adopted his responsibility becomes strictly administrative. He will not want to embarrass himself, his school or the system by operating outside of the agreed upon policy structure. The desired harmony of understanding between the schools and the public is equally pertinent and desirable between the internal units of the system.

WORKING WITH STAFF

Explorations of the processes involved in school-community relations have consistently revealed that the classroom teacher is one of the most fundamental links in the entire process. Generally speaking, people do not react to the brick-and-mortar aspects of the school; they react to people identified with the institution—teachers, students, coaches, administrators, clerks. Although admittedly an oversimplification, the statement, "The teacher is the school," takes on considerable significance in the family discussion around the dinner table where Jane is complimenting or condemning her science teacher. The echoed phrase, "It starts in the classroom," is an apt description of the genesis of school public relations. Although the importance of the classroom teacher has been widely recognized, there have been very few significant studies of the public relations activities of teachers. The popularity of teachers, once thought to be some kind of a gauge for public relations value, has seemingly been devalued when graduates, in naming their best teachers in high school, select them on bases other than their popularity. On the basis of what we know about the teacher's impact on school-community relations, it seems safe to conjecture that teacher effectiveness in building harmonious understandings between the school and the community is a composite of many things—popularity, good teaching, fairness, empathy, understanding, discipline, communication, and other things—but primarily effective teaching.

Teachers make impressions upon the public whether they realize it or not. They cannot avoid it. Normal classroom activities have public relations implications. In addition, there are the activities sponsored by the teacher specifically pointed to improving school-community relations. The nature, extent, and effectiveness of the public relations activities of the teacher will depend very largely upon his concept of the purposes of the public relations program, and the support, assistance, and coordination given him in his efforts by the administration. It is well recognized that some teachers seemingly have more of a flair for good public relations activities than others on the staff, and these talents should be used in the over-all program. However, it is most unfortunate when, as in some situations, one or two staff members apparently carry the load in public relations activities. Improving public relations is a task requiring teamwork.

Stimulation and motivation

It may be trite to suggest that teachers are people, but it is an inescapable fact that they respond to stimulation and motivation. They desire recognition, response, safety and security, and the other human wants sought by everyone. The relation of these facts to an effective utilization of an internal public in the program of school-community relations is evident, but many times is overlooked by the administration.

There are many ways of recognizing the contributions to the school-community relations effort of the school made by a teacher, clerk, custodian or other staff member. In a recent edition of Central High News, a house organ which came to our attention, a well written article on the contributions of one of the custodians serves to illustrate our point. A bulletin from Central High School contained an account of a high school science teacher's involvement of local scientists from a research laboratory in science instruction. Perceptive school-community relations committees detect and initiate feature stories for the local press, radio and TV outlets involving staff and student personnel.

Regardless of the mechanisms, of which there are many, the principle involved here is that stimulation and motivation of staff personnel in school-community relations efforts should be earnestly and vigorously supported and implemented. It is good for staff morale as well as for public relations.

Teachers' views on public relations

One of the few studies of teachers' views on public relations was conducted by the National Education Association, in which 5,000 teachers were sent questionnaires in urban communities of 2,500 or more population.[2] The survey included elementary and secondary teachers. Over 3,000 completed questionnaires were returned. The study revealed that most teachers think of public relations as a means to stimulate the interest and participation of laymen in the school program. A small per cent of the respondents thought the purpose should be to "sell" the educational program.

Better than three-quarters of the respondents believed that their principals kept them adequately informed about school policies, school board decisions, and possible trouble spots.

Teachers generally felt that visits to pupils' homes is a constructive public relations technique, but relatively few of the teachers polled made use of such visits as part of their programs. Fewer than ten per cent of the schools had an organized program to encourage home visits. Of those reporting, almost twice as many elementary schools had a program of home visiting as high schools. Sixty-eight per cent of the high schools responding indicated that home visits were left to the guidance counselors or other special personnel; the same was true for 40 per cent of the elementary schools represented in the survey. More than half of the

[2] Research Division, National Education Association, *The Classroom Teacher and Public Relations* (Washington, D.C.: The Association, 1959).

teachers responding had not visited in any home in the district for any
purpose during the previous school year. Teachers in the larger cities
reported making the fewest home visits and contacts. Less than 10 per
cent of the respondents had visited more than half of the homes of their
pupils.

The study revealed that from the teacher's point of view the sending of newsletters and notes to parents still falls considerably below the
degree to which it is considered a useful public relations technique. This
is somewhat surprising in view of the findings of surveys made in some
cities as to parent and teacher appraisal of the school newsletter.[3] A
study recently completed in the Metropolitan School District of Washington Township, Indianapolis, involving returns from more than
8,000 citizens, showed that Metro News, a regular printed school newsletter, received the highest rating among the media for communicating
information about the schools. These studies appear to indicate that
citizens and teachers give a high priority to newsletters both as to acceptance and to effectiveness. The acceptance of the school newsletter,
as in the case of any media, is undoubtedly related to the factors of
quality, format, and content of the communications.

The NEA study further revealed that some kind of parent-teacher
organization was as yet one of the best media for involving parents in
school affairs. With reference to class contacts with the community, the
study revealed that teachers look upon it as a good public relations technique, but less than half of those polled in the study made any use of it.

The teachers' views and studies cited above suggest a careful recon-
sideration of home visitation and home-school contacts, parent-teacher
activities, school newsletters, and class contacts with the community as
school-community relations techniques. The class contact with the community appears to offer several possibilities: (1) class visits to projects
and establishments in the community; (2) visits to classes by representatives of the community enterprises; and (3) cooperative class-
community activities.

Teacher participation in community activities

In the eyes of many parents and citizens in the community teachers are
rather special people. They are the people to whom a major portion of

---

[3] Informal interviews and surveys made by the authors of newsletter acceptance
and values in Akron and Columbus, Ohio, and in Shorewood, Wisconsin.

the nurturing of the community's youth has been entrusted. Regardless of the isolated instances and the occasional unpleasant experiences of a few teachers, generally speaking, teachers command a definite degree of prestige. When a teacher participates in a community activity, it is noticed and invariably appreciated.

The results of research on whether people in the community feel that teachers are one of them indicate mixed reactions. Studies made in some metropolitan areas indicate that citizens are not concerned whether or not the teacher is identified with the community, and that many teachers in these situations do not live in the community where they teach. Surveys made in the less metropolitan situations indicate that the citizens desire teachers to identify with the community.

Teacher identification with the community has definite plus values for school-community relations. It is a means of person-to-person contact and communication. It helps to reduce the social distance between the school and the community. If someone knows and communicates with a high school teacher he is likely to feel closer to and a bit more knowledgeable regarding the institution represented by the teacher.

Several studies have indicated a positive relationship between teacher participation in community affairs and an effective public relations program. That is, in selected communities where the school-community relations were considered good by several measures, there was a high incidence of teacher participation in community groups and affairs. In one high school the staff public relations committee made a survey of staff participation in local affairs and utilized these teachers as communicators of information and materials prepared by the committee for general dissemination.

Checks made on teacher participation in community organizations show the following priority: church activities, social and recreational clubs, church related clubs, fraternal and lodge groups, service clubs, and civic welfare organizations.[4] It would be most unwise for the principal to attempt to dictate the kind and nature of staff participation in community affairs or organizations, but he should encourage rather than stifle such participation, recognizing the liaison values of these school and community contacts. Where teachers take on special responsibilities in connection with outside organizations it should be taken into consideration as a part of the school's community service load and obligation.

[4] Informal survey made by members of a class in School Community Relations at Ohio State University 1958. See also: NEA *Research Bulletin* Vol. 37, No. 2, p. 40, April 1959.

Nonschool public relations activities

Almost anything the school or its personnel does can be given a public relations twist. There are times when the school and school personnel are called upon to do things that are sheer exploitation for personal gain or the advantage of special interest groups. For instance, some people reason that since school property is purchased from public funds there is no good reason why they should not be allowed the private use of it now and then, even at the expense of depriving the school of its use for the time being. It is doubtful that public relations is served in allowing the private use of a projector when it is needed in the classroom. In quite another vein, it is doubtful that public relations is served by permitting someone to advertise in the school at the expense of others or to exploit the students in other ways for special gain or advantage. If the schools would permit it, they would be the finest captive audience for advertising and propaganda imaginable.

High schools are asked to do many things in the name of goodwill and public relations. The principal must carefully weigh such requests to determine their true relationship to the educational program and the community service values of the enterprise. The intent may be good in asking the school to run a post-season football game for some charity, to foster a poster contest or an essay contest of some sort, but does this truly serve the educational or the public relations interests of the school? This is clearly an area in which the principal must demonstrate good judgment and educational statesmanship as well as finesse.

WORKING WITH SCHOOL PATRONS

School patrons rank as the number-two public with which the principal must be concerned. They are second only to the students who are the direct consumers of the experiences offered by the school. The strong concern for the welfare of youth is one that is mutually shared by parents and the school. After all, parents have a vested interest in that their own children stand to gain or lose. The vested interest is twofold: through the student and the kind of an education he receives, and through the financing of the educational program and the economics of providing educational opportunities. These form the best bases imaginable for interest and grass-roots contacts between the school and community. Yet, the history of school-parent relationships often reveals the lack of intelligent utilization, on the part of the school, of an existing foundation upon which to build real partnership efforts. Indeed, in some quarters the relation of the school to parents is looked upon as an anathema, the source of gripes, trouble, and interference with the school's operation. Many teachers and administrators continue to overlook the importance of parent cooperation. In fact, in some instances, school personnel insist upon the recognition of their own infallibility as professional experts. Of course, such attitudes and behaviors have alienated parents, created chasms of antagonism, and laid the foundation for suspicion and doubt.

On the brighter side, a rapidly increasing number of schools are putting forth an all-out effort to establish and nurture a school-parent partnership. The parent teachers association, once considered by many as an organization more or less limited to the elementary school, is showing substantial growth on the secondary school level. Much credit is due here to the parents and educators for recognizing that the program emphasis on the secondary school level must be geared to the needs of secondary education and youth welfare. A good example of a successful high school PTA program adjustment to needs may be observed at Madison West High School, Madison, Wisconsin. A unique feature of this long-successful organization in a large school is the student council representation in the membership of West High PTA. Here, students, teachers, and parents work together for common goals and objectives.

School-parent organizations

The PTA is the most universal parent-school organization, backed by a national organization with a membership of several million teachers and parents. This organization has several definite advantages to be considered by the school seeking to enhance its school-parent relationships: (1) It has a well-defined organizational pattern on the local, state, and national levels. (2) Its policies are defined and provide a framework of operation that keeps the organization from wandering into spheres outside its established limits. (3) It provides means for cooperative efforts between schools working toward the same objectives. (4) It provides opportunities for leadership training for the officers and committee chairmen in local organizations. (5) It has recognized strength and influence in promoting positive action for the welfare and education of youth. (6) Its operation is national in scope backed by a substantial membership in every part of the country.

Some school-parent groups, restive with the limitations imposed by the tenets of the PTA, have organized what have come to be known as

PTO—Parent-Teacher Organization. In many situations, these organizations are quite effective and satisfactory, but some well-intentioned organizations of this kind, lacking the defined policies and guidelines of a more established association, have assumed prerogatives in areas of administration and school operation that embarrass the board of education, the principal, and the teachers. When any school-parent group becomes a threat to any segment of those working for the education and welfare of the students, it has lost its opportunity to be truly effective.

Parent advisory groups

Aside from the PTA, PTO, booster club, band mothers, music parents, and similar structured organizations found in high schools, another means for working with parents appears to be gaining favor—the parent advisory council. The function of this organization is to advise the principal and the school staff. In one successful operation of this nature, a six-year high school with about 1,600 students, the advisory council consists of four sets of parents from grades seven through twelve, elected by each grade parent group at the beginning of the school year. In this instance, the principal and the deans invite the parents of each grade level for separate meetings as soon as school commences in the fall. These meetings serve to communicate with parents relative to school expectations, the social program of the school, guidance, and the many special problems at each grade level. Questions are invited and matters of interest are discussed informally. Parent committees are established to assist staff and students with affairs such as the open-house, concerts, exhibits, and similar events. Every effort is made to establish a spirit of cooperation and channels of communication. Upon occasion, study groups are organized around problems of concern to the parents and the school.

In the instance described here, the principal meets with the advisory council four times during the school year. Each meeting has a prepared agenda. Topics for discussion usually come from the principal but may also originate with members of the council. Both the principal and the parents claim the meetings to be fruitful sources of interchanging ideas and promoting understandings. The council understands that it is not a second board of education, and that its function is that of sharing ideas and giving assistance to the staff in meeting the operational problems of the school. On some matters of general school interest, such as the prom and Halloween, the parent advisory council join with the student council and the staff in the planning process.

Open houses, exhibits, concerts, demonstrations

Affairs held in the high school to which parents and the public are invited serve several purposes and objectives. One of these is the public relations function. Through the media of the concert, demonstration, exhibition, and similar events, the public is brought into close touch with the actual achievements of some phases of the instructional program. Students are motivated to do their best for a public showing and incidentally become active partners with others in the school in efforts to build better school-community relations. Although the exploitation of students purely for the purposes of providing program and entertainment for the public is rightfully frowned upon, the potentials of properly conceived special events involving students and the public for building understandings and appreciations should not be overlooked.

One of the most effective programs in this regard was an assembly program put on by the assembly training class, a special class for the gifted in English and dramatics, in which the problems of guidance and instruction were dramatically presented to the student body. The student council and the school leaders thought parents and the public should be invited to see it. As a result, the group was asked to put on a "command performance" to which the public was invited. Every person in that auditorium left with a much fuller understanding and appreciation of the instructional and guidance program in the high school.

Public events in the high school should have instruction and information-giving goals as chief purposes. We need to use our imaginations as to how these events can better communicate ideas about the school, what it is, what it does, and how it attempts to do it. Too many times, opportunities to tell a story about the scholars are lost when they might well have been highlighted in a special event.

Bulletins, letters, report cards

A good school-community relations program takes advantage of every opportunity and media of communication to keep the public informed. Principals with imagination are making increasing use of ready-made channels of communication, such as the report card message. Here, several times each year, an opportunity is presented to send some graphic message into the home about the school. It may be on some program feature, homework, school need, new course offering, or other information that will improve parent understanding.

A personalized form letter is very effective. We recall a letter written by the principal to the parents of juniors and seniors regarding prom activities, and another describing changes in the schedule to accommodate students desiring to take a more diversified program of studies. The letter should be well-written, short and to the point. Letter-writing is an art the principal can well afford to develop. Teachers, too, should be encouraged to use the written note or letter. Next to face-to-face contact or the voice contact via the telephone, the written message is a most effective way of communication.

The potential of the school newspaper as a medium of communication to parents should not be underestimated. Studies have indicated that the high school newspaper takes on considerable importance in the homes of students, particularly if the name of the student appears in print. The well-conceived school-community relations program will make good use of all student publications. Feature stories, pictures, guest editorials, and special articles provide excellent media for telling the school's story. Some preplanning will assure programmed releases at regular intervals throughout the school year.

The yearbook is another student publication that should not be overlooked for public relations values. Although it has a limited audience and restricted possibilities for copy, the book represents the school. Better no yearbook at all than one for which everyone is apologetic.

The newsletter

The newsletter, according to Burke, is a publication of two to twelve pages, produced by liquid duplicator, mimeograph, multilith, photo offset, or ordinary printing.[5] It may be issued on some regular basis— monthly, at report card issuance, quarterly, and the like, or it may be issued irregularly as the need arises. For example, after considerable study, one high school recently found it advisable to change from a six-period day to an eight-period day, in order to provide for more flexibility in meeting instructional needs.[6] The school had been operating on a six-period day for more than twenty years. This was a change that needed to be explained to patrons. A neat, four-fold, mimeographed letter, describing the change and its implications for improved instructional opportunities for students, was prepared by the principal and sent to every home.

[5] Virginia M. Burke, *Newsletter Writing and Publishing* (New York: Bureau of Publications, Teachers College, Columbia University, 1958).
[6] Shorewood High School, Shorewood, Wisconsin.

Some schools have adopted a plan of sending home a newsletter with each report card, in which various aspects of the school program are outlined for parent consumption. The newsletter differs from ordinary printed material sent home with the report card in that it is personalized, bearing the name of the principal and directed to the parents.

Other schools have adopted a standard letterhead format for all newsletters. Modern duplicating techniques allow a wide range of possibilities in layout and form. The message can be arranged in single or multiple columns and spaced effectively and attractively. Even the general newsletter can be personalized with a message from the principal set apart from other content in the publication. The tone of the publication should be warm and outgoing, informal, professional, and positive.

Conferences with parents

Many excellent opportunities for cementing good relations between the school and the community come through conferences with parents. In these face-to-face relationships, many understandings can be made clear that could not be accomplished by any other means. In such situations, the principal or the teacher must first be a good listener—let the parent tell his story. Parents should be made to feel that they are invited rather than thwarted in seeking conferences on school matters. An effort should be made to try to see the situations from the parents' points of view and to help the parent to see the situation from the school's point of view. Many a troublesome situation that otherwise might grow into disproportionate significance and act as a barrier to a harmony of understanding can be talked out in a conference.

Another type of parent conference—the student-parent-teacher conference as a supplement to reports on student achievement—is rapidly gaining favor in secondary schools. In addition to the regular report cards, the homeroom teacher holds a scheduled conference once each semester with the student and parent relative to the academic and school citizenship progress of the student. The homeroom teacher gathers the general information about the student—grades in courses, special achievements, problems, general school citizenship, study habits, and the like—which is shared and discussed at the conference. Here the home, the school, and the student are brought together for a more harmonious and cooperative relationship with respect to the student's achievement and general welfare.

WORKING WITH THE GENERAL PUBLIC

There are many publics in the community that have little or no relationship to the schools. Yet these publics are counted upon to support the school function by way of taxes, building programs, referendums, and the like. Many of these publics have only limited ways of learning about the schools. A good program of public relations will take this into account, and through the use of the press, the radio, and general bulletins delivered to each residence provide all citizens with essential information about the schools. This cannot be accomplished by the secondary school alone, but the principal has a responsibility to work with the general public relations program for the school system in a manner that will make sure that the secondary school is included.

Space does not permit a full discussion of all the mechanics available or the techniques for working with all of the publics in the community. It seems reasonable, however, that the secondary school in the community should take a significant responsibility in the general program of school-community relations by assisting in opinion polls, interpreting education to the people, and generally demonstrating some of the values of good schools. Secondary school students are young adults. As such, they can do much to demonstrate good community citizenship in and out of school.

WORKING WITH STUDENTS

Students are the basis of the secondary school and, as such, should assume definite responsibilities in the school-community relations program. Students are also a very important public to be considered in school-community relations. Assuming that this priority has been recognized and that in many ways the students represent the school in the community, it seems appropriate to consider the nature and amount of leadership that should be given to student participation in public relations activities, and what students may do to assist in the program.

Student activities and community relations

Every student activity has public relations implications. Somewhere in the inservice training program for teachers this fact should be stressed. The principal must continually alert his staff to be aware of the impact of student affairs on the reputation of the school. Student loyalty to the school should be fostered and encouraged, but when this loyalty is carried to a point where students splash paint on the entrance of the rival school prior to the big game some leadership should be exerted. When students on trips behave in a manner that brings discredit to the school; when students disregard the rights of others in parking about the school and litter the yards and streets; when students cause trouble for merchants or become nuisances in hangouts, these student activities take on a negative value as far as school-community relations are concerned.

Experience indicates that leadership that works through and with students helping them to see their role in developing favorable relationships is most fruitful. For instance, the faculty sponsor working with the student council can do much to give leadership to the development of positive attitudes on the part of the student body toward fostering a favorable reputation for the school. The principal can do much with some words of encouragement and recognition of exemplary behavior on the part of students and school groups. Students should feel that they are a part of the team in promoting goodwill for their school and they should take pride in upholding the good name of the institution of which they are an integral part. We know a coach who insists that the members of his team dress up and, as he puts it, "Look like men, not slouches, when we go on trips representing this school." This coach does not countenance malicious souvenir-gathering or other behavior that might undermine the reputation of his school. In all probability, the students under his guidance acquire an attitude very favorable to good public relations. As we have intimated here, it is a host of little things that students do or do not do that count in their participation in an over-all program of public relations. Schools are branded by the behaviors of their students.

Student community service

Student activities of various kinds, the things observed by the public about the school, have been mentioned briefly and the relation of such to school-community relations cited. However, there is one area in working with students in public relations that should not go unnoticed—community service. Many excellent community service projects have received their primary impetus from work carried on by secondary school students. It is not only the service projects that are carried on by students alone but the opportunities they provide for working with other elements in the community on service efforts that makes such activities worthwhile from a public relations point of view. Each time the school identifies itself through the students in some positive manner with elements of the community, opportunities unfold for creating goodwill and understanding.

EVALUATION

It is often helpful to check the high school's school-community relations program against accepted criteria and practices. The following are some general points that may prove to be of value in such an assessment.

1. *Have a definite organized program.* The high school school-community relations program should be planned and well organized.

2. *Take the initiative.* A good offense is often the best defense. It is easier to shape opinions than to change them once established.

3. *Use authorities.* Use opinion leaders. In carefully scheduled and well worded statements the principal, teachers and others in authority ought to be used as spokesmen for the schools and education.

4. *Be honest.* The school-community relations program must be honest with respect to the school's strengths and shortcomings.

5. *Use continuity and repetition.* The program should be continuous, have continuity and allow for repetition of important messages worthy of being repeated. Your publics are constantly changing.

6. *Make use of all available media.* Unless the message is repeated through a variety of media it may be lost to many people.

7. *Stress achievement.* Point with pride to the achievements of students, the staff and the school.

8. *Avoid complacency and self-satisfaction.* Always assume that anything can be improved upon.

9. *Maximize involvement.* Enlist the services and interests of as many as possible in the public relations program.

10. *Personalize.* People are more interested in people than in objects, records, and the like.

11. *Use good timing.* There is a right time and a wrong time to send letters, broadcast, release news, and the like.

12. *Stress appraisal.* Continuous appraisals should be made of every aspect of the school-community relations program. Check now, don't wait until much of the reaction and information is lost.

A checklist

A very fine checklist on school-community relations has been developed by the American Association of School Administrators.[7] The authors have adapted it to fit the concerns of the secondary school as follows:

Do you . . .

_____ See public relations as a two-way process—as a cooperative search for mutual understanding and effective teamwork between community and school?

_____ Try to establish favorable attitudes as well as opinions, and take into account the influence of both emotions and intelligence?

_____ Keep in mind that there are many publics to be served?

_____ Know and serve the interests of various publics in the community?

_____ Check the honesty and accuracy of interpretations of the information which goes out about the high school?

_____ Emphasize the positive approach in public relations?

_____ Present your ideas in simple, understandable, and accurate form?

_____ Have a friendly school in which the public regularly finds cordial welcome?

_____ Maintain working conditions and relationships that attract and hold competent school employees?

_____ Take into account the factors of mobility in student and parent populations in the public relations program?

_____ Provide adequate leadership to student efforts in school-community relations efforts?

_____ Encourage and work effectively with parents and parent groups in your school?

_____ Keep the public well informed through bulletins, newsletters, and reports?

_____ Help students to understand and contribute positively to community-school relations?

_____ Manage the business office of the high school in a way that commands respect and good will?

_____ Counterattack with factual data and evidence when your high school is unjustly attacked?

[7] *ABC's of School Public Relations* (Washington, D.C.: American Association of School Administrators, 1959).

_____ Work closely with parents—P.T.A., advisory groups, parent conferences?

_____ Call to the attention of the central administration weaknesses in management that are known to have damaged or hindered school-community relations?

_____ Encourage employees to take an active part in community affairs?

_____ Stress the importance of every member of the staff in the public relations activities of the school?

_____ Have an effective training program of inservice training in school-community relations for all school employees?

_____ Have a policy of honesty, courtesy, and forthrightness in dealing with employees, the press, and the public?

_____ Believe that people can and will help to plan and support good schools when they understand the essential needs?

_____ Practice democracy in the exercise of your leadership functions?

_____ Interpret education as an investment in people?

_____ Look upon school buildings and sites as expressions of educational functions and purposes?

_____ Listen to complaints carefully, investigate the facts objectively, and seek to use them constructively?

_____ Assist in planning new buildings and manage the school plant in such a manner as to create public confidence and goodwill?

_____ Organize and plan routines to avoid misunderstandings, confusions, delays?

_____ Make effective use of available technical assistance from staff members, laymen in the community, and special consultants?

_____ Engage regularly in inservice activities to improve your skills in public relations?

_____ Merit community recognition because of your professional competence?

_____ Participate actively yourself as a member of key local, state, and national organizations in your field of professional interest?

_____ Recognize the public relations values of professional educational organizations?

_____ Systematically appraise your public relations efforts and effectiveness?

_____ Weigh your actions as to the positive or negative effects on public relations?

_____ Try to determine what might be newsworthy about your operations activities?

_____ Avoid playing any favorites in purchasing or other business transactions?

_____ Work for general high morale in your department and your department's relation to other departments or segments within the school system?

_____ Try to be sensitive about the public relations effect of your actions and activities?

_____ See public relations as a definite part of your responsibilities?

_____ Try to be a good listener?

_____ Recognize good human relations as a bulwark of morale?

_____ Try to explain things that might be difficult to understand?

_____ Have patience with those disturbed or disgruntled about something?

CONCLUSION

Community relations, school-community relations, and public relations have been used interchangeably throughout this chapter to indicate the harmony of understanding that exists between the high school and the publics it serves. There must be communication and an interchange of ideas and information in a manner that will develop understandings as to what the school is, what it does, how it does it, and what it needs to do the job.

The school deals with various publics, internal and external—students, staff, parents, nonparents, civic groups, service groups, and other community publics. The chief responsibility for organizing and nurturing the school-community relations program lies with the principal. He must have the proper attitude toward public relations, knowledge of what constitutes an effective program, skills in public relations techniques, and a scholarly ability to know and analyze the community he serves. The principal sets the tone for the entire effort of the school in public relations.

Since the public identifies the teacher with the school, he is a very important contributor to school-community relations. Teachers become a part of the community and have opportunities for many face-to-face contacts through which they can interpret education and the local secondary school contributions. Students, likewise, play an important role in the public relations efforts. Leadership should be provided to assist students in developing a good reputation for the school and in establishing goodwill.

Good communication—two-way communication—is essential in the development of understandings. Conferences, bulletins, newsletters, PTA organizations, the use of mass media, and other techniques are good practices utilized by many schools.

Finally, good school-community relations are important, particularly in view of the competition schools face with reference to engineering consent, broadening understandings, and creating goodwill. Full cooperation and wide involvement are essential. School-community relations is not a bag of tricks or gimmicks; it is a program of continuous effort, intelligent planning, teamwork, and shared responsibility with wide involvement of everyone concerned.

SUGGESTED ACTIVITIES

1. List and discuss the criteria by which you would judge a good school-community relations program.

2. Write a news story about a current educational event.

3. As a principal, write a letter to parents announcing a significant curriculum change in the secondary school program.

4. Cite illustrations of how students may assist in fostering goodwill and improved school-community relations.

5. Discuss the problems of working with parents in efforts to improve goodwill and better understandings about the schools and education.

6. Discuss the relative merits and values of open houses, demonstrations, exhibits, and other public school events for public relations.

7. Make a list of the publics that must be served by a secondary school of your acquaintance.

SELECTED READINGS

Austin, David B., Will French, and J. Dan Hull, *American High School Administration*. New York: Holt, Rinehart & Winston, Inc., 1962. Part 6.

Burke, Virginia M., *Newsletter Writing and Publishing*. New York: Bureau of Publications, Teachers College, Columbia University, 1958.

Campbell, Roald F., and John A. Ramseyer, *Dynamics of School Community Relationships*. Boston: Allyn and Bacon, Inc., 1955.

Dapper, Gloria, *Public Relations for Educators*. New York: The Macmillan Co., 1964.

Ehlers, Henry, and Gordon C. Lee, *Crucial Issues in Education*. New York: Holt, Rinehart & Winston, Inc., 1964.

Kindred, Leslie W., *School Public Relations*. Englewood Cliffs, N.J.: Prentice-Hall, Inc., 1957.

McCloskey, Gordon, *Education and Public Understanding*. New York: Harper & Row, Publishers, 1959.

National School Public Relations Association, *Feel Their Pulse*. Washington, D.C.: National Education Association, 1956.

——, *Let's Go to Press*. Washington, D.C.: National Education Association, 1954.

——, *School Photojournalism*. Washington, D.C.: National Education Association, 1958.

——, *Print It Right*. Washington, D.C.: National Education Association, 1953.

——, *Gold Mine Series*, Vols. 1–6. Washington, D.C.: National Education Association, 1957–64.

National Society for the Study of Education, *Social Forces Influencing Education*, 60th Yearbook. Chicago: University of Chicago Press, 1961.

III

THE PERSON

PART THREE PROVIDES AN EXAMINATION OF THE AD-
ministrator as a person. A major purpose of this book is to help the
reader examine himself as a potential administrator. These two chapters
describe much of the research on the competencies required in administration and the process by which the individual can measure his
own administrative potential. These separate areas are discussed in
Chapters 11 and 12.

11

REQUIRED
COMPETENCIES

WE HAVE EXPLORED THE JOB OF THE SECONDARY
school principal both in terms of general leadership and in terms of the
specific tasks of the secondary school administrator. It is now time to
consider the kind of person who is most likely to achieve success as a
secondary school principal. It is impossible to describe a model person
who will be a successful principal and to say that unless an individual
fits this model perfectly, he cannot be a successful principal. It is, however, possible to describe the competencies that research and common
sense reveal should be possessed by a secondary school principal. Such
a description will help to clarify the nature of the job. Then, Chapter
12 will discuss the ways in which an individual can measure his personal
potential for the principalship in terms of these competencies. These
discussions will help one consider his fitness for administration, and will
lend further insight into the administrative process.

THE MEANING OF COMPETENCIES

There have been a number of attempts to relate personal abilities and attributes to potential success in some field of work. These personal abilities and attributes have been classified under various kinds of headings. This discussion uses the term "competency." In order to clarify the meaning of this term, it is necessary to start with the simpler term "trait," and show how the concept of competency has developed from the trait approach.

The trait approach

Early efforts to define leadership qualities relied heavily on the trait approach. For example, in 1929, Charters and Waples listed the twenty-five most important traits of teachers. They found such items as breadth of interest, good judgment, self-control, scholarship, self-confidence, and forcefulness to rank at the top.[1] The study made by Cowley also put such traits as self-confidence and conviction high on the list of the necessary personal equipment of leaders.[2] There have even been rumors that the tall man with a booming voice is predestined for administrative success, but Gibb's studies tend to discredit this report.[3]

The trait approach to defining leadership ability, then, involves bringing a set of measuring instruments to the man in isolation. If he registers sufficiently high scores in capacity, achievement, responsibility, sociability, and status, he is rated as a potentially successful administrator.[4] If his scores are not high in these areas, his chances of success are rated poor. This approach has certain apparent deficiencies, which have led to the development of what we call the competency approach.

Competencies

The principal must not merely possess traits, but he must be able to use his traits as a leader in a variety of situations. The leadership behavior

[1] W. W. Charters and Douglas Waples, *The Commonwealth Teacher-Training Study* (Chicago: University of Chicago Press, 1929), p. 18.

[2] W. H. Cowley, "The Traits of Face-to-Face Leaders," *Journal of Abnormal and Social Psychology.* 26:310, 1931.

[3] Cecil A. Gibb, "Leadership," in Gardner Lindzey (ed.), *Handbook of Social Psychology*, Volume II (Reading, Mass.: Addison-Wesley Publishing Company, Inc., 1954), pp. 884–885.

[4] R. M. Stogdill, "Personal Factors Associated with Leadership," *Journal of Psychology* 25:64, January 1948.

expected of a secondary school principal is much different, for example, from the leadership behavior expected of the leader of a criminal gang. This obvious fact led to studies of administrative behavior in school situations; and from these studies were developed descriptions of traits in action, that is, competencies. Thus, although intelligence is an important trait of a leader, the use to which this intelligence is put in leadership situations is even more important. Although a good speaking voice is an important trait, what the voice says and when is even more important.

The competency approach does not abandon the trait approach nor does it imply a loss of faith in the importance of traits. What the competency approach does is to adapt the trait approach so that behavior is described and the behavior required in given situations pinpointed. A competency, then, is a factor that contributes to or is an integral part of effective administrative behavior. Competencies may include personal attributes, knowledge, understandings, or skills, but to be classified as a competency for a secondary school principal, each of these factors must be shown to be related to effective administrative behavior in a secondary school.

Administrative behavior and situational factors

One of the primary reasons for the development of the competency approach to defining leadership abilities was the recognition of the fact that effective leadership behavior is often strongly influenced by the situation in which the leader finds himself. Two people with similar traits, for example, might find themselves assigned as secondary school principals, one in a large city school and one in a small rural school. In spite of a similarity of traits, one principal might succeed and the other fail, not because of some undiscovered differences in traits but because of differences in the situations in which the two men found themselves. The competency approach, which is related to behavior much more directly than is the trait approach, provides a better means of considering these situational influences upon administrative effectiveness than does the trait approach.

A wide variety of people and things make up the situation that influences administrative behavior. The natures of the community and its many publics, the board of education and the superintendent, the teaching staff and the noninstructional staff, and the student body, all influence the effectiveness of various kinds of administrative behavior of the principal. By the same token, the size, location, topography, and climate of the school district; the legal structure for education in the state and locality; the financial resources of the state and school district; and the established school organization and program in the school district and in a given school, all are nonhuman situational factors that influence the effectiveness of administrative behavior. For example, regardless of the self-confidence, physical appearance, intelligence, or scholarship possessed by a man, his administrative behavior as a principal in a rural, conservative, fairly isolated school district must reflect understandings of his school and community or his chances of effectiveness are decreased.

Required competencies

Recognizing the shortcomings of the trait approach to defining leadership qualities and recognizing the influence of the situation upon the effectiveness of a principal, how can we develop a list of competencies for the secondary school principal? A number of studies in university centers throughout the nation were focused on this problem largely through the efforts of the Cooperative Project in Educational Administration. Although most of these studies were concerned with educational administration in general rather than with specific administrative positions, it is possible to relate conclusions drawn from these studies to the secondary school principal.[5]

In general, these studies dealt with three questions: What is the purpose of educational administration? What are desirable ways of meeting this purpose? What specific behaviors are necessary to perform in these desirable ways? We have already discussed concepts of the purpose of administration and of desirable administration in the secondary school. Admittedly, these discussions are based on value judgments. Nevertheless, it is from these concepts that competency statements are developed and it is in terms of this framework that specific competencies are required.

Development of competencies

Before describing the competencies required of an effective secondary school principal, it is important to indicate that principals can be developed. A man is not necessarily born with leadership qualities to be-

[5] For a summary of these studies, see Hollis A. Moore, Jr., *Studies in School Administration* (Washington, D.C.: American Association of School Administrators, 1957).

come a successful leader. The trait approach implies innate qualities that are, to a great extent, present or absent at birth. On the other hand, the competency approach stresses behavior and the use of abilities. Behavioral changes seem much more possible than do trait changes. It must be recognized, however, that certain people will have a head start toward leadership success because of congenital qualities. Others may have enough congenital deficiencies to make it extremely unlikely that they can become successful leaders. Most people are in the middle ground, where they can, with sufficient motivation, develop competencies for leadership.

PERSONAL ATTRIBUTES

Remembering that a competency is a factor that contributes to or is an integral part of effective administrative behavior, let us first look at those competencies related to personal attributes. Most of these competencies contribute to effective behavior, but the mere possession of a given personal attribute is not in and of itself a predictor of effectiveness. The absense of these attributes, however, will make effective behavior difficult to realize.

Physical characteristics

The secondary school principal's job is a physically demanding one. Long hours are the rule rather than the exception. It is apparent that effective administrative behavior requires that the principal possess reasonably good health and physical stamina.

In addition to health and energy, the principal also must consider his physical appearance. The leader with pronounced physical abnormalities is rare. So much of the principal's effectiveness depends upon successful person-to-person contacts that it is apparent that a normal physical appearance is helpful to the principal. Although there are obviously no weight, height, and "beauty" criteria that must be met by the successful principal, pronounced physical abnormalities will prove a definite handicap.

Mental attributes

There seems to be no question but that there is a definite and positive relationship between intelligence and leadership ability. Here, again, however, a qualification is needed. The mere possession of above-average intelligence does not guarantee administrative success. It is the possession of intelligence plus its wise use in administrative situations that mark administrative effectiveness.

Secondary school teachers are generally of more than average intelligence. A principal's fellow administrators will also be of above-average intelligence. A principal, then, without mental quickness and the acuity associated with good intelligence will be at a disadvantage as he works with these groups and with other community and professional leaders.

The problem in discussing intelligence is that little is known about the specific factors of intelligence. Such things as verbal facility, computational skill, memory, and spatial judgment are but a few of the components of intelligence. Insight, which is probably a factor of intelligence, is closely related to administrative effectiveness. However, knowledge of specific relationships between factors of intelligence and administrative skill or effectiveness is not now available. For the present, it must suffice to state that intelligence, whatever its components, is positively related to leadership.

An interesting point concerning intelligence has been revealed by a number of studies. Although specific quantitative data are not available, it seems that if a leader is a great deal more intelligent than are the members of the group he is to lead, his effectiveness is reduced. In other words, there may be upper limits of intelligence as well as lower limits for the effective administrator, depending upon the group with which he is to work.

Philip Smith developed a framework that he used to relate critical thinking and administrative effectiveness. He characterized the thinking of an effective administrator as follows:

Comprehensiveness:
Viewing particulars in relation to a large field.
Relating immediate problems to long-range goals.
Utilizing the power of generalization.
Maintaining tolerance for theoretical considerations.

Penetration:
Questioning what is taken for granted or is self-evident.
Seeking for and formulating fundamentals.
Utilizing a sensitivity for implication and relevance.
Basing expectations on an abductive-deductive process.

Flexibility:
Being free from psychological rigidity.
Evaluating ideas apart from their source.

Seeing issues as many-sided and developing alternate hypotheses, viewpoints, explanations, etc.

Maintaining a tolerance for tentativeness and suspended judgment.[6]

It is apparent that Smith's statement represents intelligence in action. Although intelligence is required to meet the demands of this statement, the demands are for a particular use of intellect rather than for a particular measured level of intellect. This is the basic difference between intelligence as a competency and intelligence as a trait.

Social personality attributes

We use the term "social personality" to refer to a person's reaction pattern to the social scene. The social personality is influenced by all of the attributes that have been and will be discussed in this chapter, but the social personality as a separate entity is revealed by an individual's reaction pattern.

The primary requirement in this area is balance. The extreme extrovert is not more advantageously endowed than is the extreme introvert; and both have less potential for administrative effectiveness than does the individual nearer the center of the introversion-extroversion scale. Both the very aggressive and the very meek are less likely to succeed than is the more balanced individual.

The leader is one who possesses originality and adaptability. These attributes are closely related to the element of flexibility. The secondary school principal may deal in succession with a gifted science teacher, a student of low academic ability and a high level of troublemaking, a community leader, and a troubled parent. Each of these individuals calls for a different approach. Stereotyped behavior on the part of the principal can be disastrous. He must adapt to situations, and this requires originality in thinking and in acting.

The principal also needs to possess initiative and ambition. Although unbridled personal ambition can lead an individual to become a dictator, a measure of personal ambition is a necessary attribute of a principal. This needs to be an ambition to contribute as well as an ambition to succeed. Unless a secondary school principal has a clearly developed concept of the success he wishes from life, the contribution he wishes to make to life, and the ways in which he wishes to reach

[6] Philip G. Smith, *Philosophic Mindedness in Educational Administration,* School Community Development Study Monograph Series, No. 5 (Columbus, Ohio: The Ohio State University Press, 1956), pp. 30–31.

these goals, his actions will probably be less effective than they could be. Then, of course, he needs to possess the initiative that leads him to do more than to talk about his ambitions.

Another important social personality attribute of the principal is his disposition. A principal needs to have a sense of humor and an even disposition. A disposition in which periods of intense moodiness or temper flare-ups are rare is a valuable asset to any leader. The principal's task involves working with people and an even disposition makes this much easier.

Although there is no extensive research in the field of the relationships between social personality and effective service as a principal, there is some evidence that confidence and self-assurance and gregariousness are helpful attributes—again, if not carried to extremes. In general, the best social personality pattern a principal can possess is one in which balance, an absence of extremes, is present. There are, of course, exceptions to this statement, but the preponderance of evidence, both from research and from common sense consideration of the problem, is that the effective principal tends to be a balanced person.

Character attributes

Character attributes are those elements of an individual's behavior about which a society tends to have definite value judgments. We do not say that it is "good" or "bad" to have a sense of humor, but we do have such feelings about, say, honesty. It is unlikely that a lengthy discussion of character attributes and effective administrative leadership is necessary. School personnel are expected by a community to be of good character. The principal of a school is often in the public eye, and character deficiencies will decrease his effectiveness markedly. This good character must be more than a façade. The principal needs an underlying set of values, a philosophy of life, which leads him to act with good character. Otherwise, his actions may lack consistency, and he may be faced with indecision or confusion with regard to moral or ethical problems.

EDUCATIONAL BACKGROUND

The secondary school principal will certainly possess a bachelor's degree and often will have earned one or more advanced degrees. The formal education necessary to earn these degrees should have led to the development of many skills and understandings that are necessary parts of the competency pattern of the principal. In addition, this educational experience should have provided a number of opportunities for the prospective principal to work with people in a variety of situations.

Undergraduate education

The formal education of the secondary school principal at the undergraduate level should provide him with knowledge about such things as the following:

1. Child growth and development—particularly at the adolescent stage.

2. Methods of teaching.

3. Curriculum development.

4. Group processes.

5. Teaching aids.

6. Counseling and guidance.

7. Educational tests and measurements.

8. The aims of education.

9. Community sociology.

10. Social values and beliefs in a democracy.

11. Human behavior.

12. Governmental structure in the United States.

13. Economic systems.

14. General legal structure in the United States.[7]

In addition, the prospective secondary school principal, in first preparing himself to be a secondary school teacher, will have gained mastery of at least one field of knowledge as a teaching area. Also, he should have a number of courses in education, so that he has the broad educational background that will enable him to perform the role of a community educational leader. Certainly, skill in the written and oral use of English is an important outcome of this educational program for the principal.

[7] Adapted from Southern States Cooperative Project in Educational Administration, *Better Teaching in School Administration* (Nashville, Tenn.: McQuiddy Printing Company, 1955), pp. 125–177.

It should be apparent that the principal should first become broadly educated and only then turn toward a specialty in educational administration. There is some evidence that a good academic standing indicates leadership potential. This is not necessarily so, but it confirms the point that applied intelligence and leadership potential are positively related.

Coupled with the learnings that the prospective principal gains in the college classroom are some important understandings that he should gain from college life. The principalship is a leadership position. One of the best ways to prepare for such a position is to engage in leadership activities. While an undergraduate, the prospective principal will have a number of opportunities to engage in student activities, as a participant and as a leader. Although research on this point is limited, the undergraduate records of successful secondary school principals reveal that these people tended to assume leadership in at least one student activity and often participated in a wide variety of such activities. Undergraduate learning, then, should not be restricted to "book learning."

Graduate education

It is at the graduate level that the prospective principal begins to learn the specialized skills of secondary school administration. Although we have stressed certain physical and personal attributes of a principal and have mentioned a broad, general educational background, the principal also needs to have at his command basic knowledge and skills directly related to his profession. While gaining this knowledge and skill in graduate education, the prospective principal should continue to broaden his educational background. One of the key tasks of the prospective principal as he pursues graduate education is to integrate his learning, to see applications of facts, and to understand the importance of critical thinking and investigation.

Graduate education should include field experience, so that the prospective administrator has opportunities to observe and to practice the application of theories and concepts. Many school districts are developing cadet principal programs in which young men and women are given the opportunity to serve as interns under the direction of able principals and in cooperation with university personnel.

The following statement, made with relation to general administration and graduate education, is a pertinent summary of this idea:

From his graduate education program, then, the student should be expected to develop competency in the technical aspects of school administration, in the use of sound problem-solving or research procedures in dealing with administrative concerns, and in the process of administration itself. In addition, competencies which have been developing prior to the graduate program should be reinforced and further developed through formal class work and through experience. Finally, the potential administrator needs to gain through his graduate program a conviction that he wants to be an educational administrator and that this desire is based on a well-founded analysis of his own strengths and weaknesses.[8]

EXPERIENCE BACKGROUND

It is perhaps an error to separate education and experience, but it is done here to stress the importance of learnings gained through experience as part of the background of a secondary school principal. Although experience can be educative, it is not necessarily so. The ability to learn from experience is one that the principal needs to develop and foster.

The secondary school principal will no doubt have spent at least a few years as a secondary school teacher. From this experience, he should gain a number of understandings about secondary school students, about the role of the school in a community, about the problems and possibilities in secondary school teaching, and about some of the administrative problems of a secondary school.

Because the principal works with a wide variety of people, it is valuable if his experience background includes some work experiences outside of the field of professional education. Even summer jobs while a high school or college student will give a person insight into the problems, hopes, and dreams of those who are the patrons of his school. A feeling for the dignity of all men regardless of their work or background and for the importance of all kinds of jobs is an important attribute of the effective principal. Work experience in jobs outside of professional education is one valuable way to gain this feeling.

Through various kinds of experiences, then, the prospective principal can gain understandings and skills both in the professional field of education and in the broader field of working with people, if he recognizes the opportunities for learning from experience and if he consciously works to take advantage of these opportunities.

[8] Roald F. Campbell, John E. Corbally, Jr., and John A. Ramseyer, *Introduction to Educational Administration*, Second Edition (Boston: Allyn and Bacon, Inc., 1962), p. 310.

There are, in addition, a few attributes that may not properly be classified as competencies but that do have some bearing on ability to perform effectively as a principal. Some of these are completely irrelevant to professional ability and, yet, they assume major importance. For example, experience in working with placement officers, boards of education, and superintendents indicates that a married man has a much greater chance to secure and to succeed in a principalship than does a single man. Why is this? Primarily it is a matter of tradition and community mores. Although we do not recommend that all readers of this volume who are single marry immediately, it does seem important to point out that the ability to be a successful head of a family seems to be a part of the competency pattern required to become the head of a school.

Another point worthy of mention is that an effective principal needs to be a person with wide interests. He is expected to be interested in education, in athletics, in almost every community issue, and in all young people's activities. Unless an individual person has or is capable of gaining wide interests, he will find himself increasingly uncomfortable in his service as a principal.

Finally, a principal who finds being a "joiner" repugnant to him will experience difficulty in his job. In most medium-sized or small communities, the secondary school is a major if not the major community enterprise, and the secondary school principal is expected to be a civic leader. This carries with it the responsibility to participate in community activities and to join various community groups. Not only does this require physical stamina, but it requires willingness and enthusiasm.

COMPETENCIES AND BEHAVIOR

Such are the important competencies required by a secondary school principal. Possession of these competencies should lead to effective administrative behavior. A major portion of this behavior is devoted to working with people—with individuals, with small groups, or with large and formal groups. In using his competencies to work with people, the principal should base his behavior on some basic understandings.

Working with individuals

In the first place, the behavior of the principal should reflect his respect for people and his belief in the preservation of each individual's self-respect. This is particularly true of his dealings with secondary school students—those young men and women who are not really children and are not yet adults. Adolescents are groping for independence and they defend their self-respect vigorously. The principal is a key figure in establishing a climate in which these young people can mature and develop with dignity and with grace. A principal who loses the confidence and respect of the students cannot be effective in promoting learning.

By the same token, the principal needs to help safeguard the confidence and self-respect of his staff. It is amazing how easily offhand remarks or slightly untactful comments can be magnified by a person into major attacks. As the administrator of an organization devoted to human growth and development, the principal should act so that every individual with whom he comes in contact is assisted in growing and developing. It is sometimes so easy to become engrossed in problems of groups that the problems of individuals are lost. This is an error the effective principal cannot afford to make.

One final point should be mentioned in discussing the principal's relations with individuals. Time and time again the principal will have to face student, teacher, or parent behavior that seems to him to be completely irrational. Psychologists point out that irrationality of behavior is primarily a matter of perception and that behavior always appears rational to the one behaving. If the principal tends to dismiss certain acts as irrational and does not attempt to assess the reasons behind these acts, his ability to deal with both the acts and the actor will be lessened. The irresponsible student or the highly-emotional parent act as they do for reasons that are not always readily apparent but that need to be discovered if improvements are to be realized.

Working with groups

The administrator also spends many hours working with groups of various sizes. Professional literature in recent years has been replete with discussions of group dynamics. The principal needs to approach such literature with some caution. Too often, descriptions of ideal group action ignore the fact that an organization has status administrative leaders with definite assigned responsibilities. The principal often must approach group tasks in terms of goals and time schedules assigned to him. He cannot abdicate his responsibilities and turn them over to the group. This is not a plea for dictatorial action, but rather a statement of the need for intelligent, responsible group leadership.

As the principal works with groups, be they students, teachers, parents, or others, his behavior should reflect his understanding of the following points:

1. The task of the group should be made clear.

2. A tentative timetable for action should be established.

3. Participation of each member of the group should be encouraged.

4. The principal's opinions and values should not be allowed to dominate or to stifle group thinking. If the group perceives that its only purpose is to "rubber stamp" the ideas of the principal, its willingness to work—now and in the future—will be diminished greatly.

5. The group should work on real problems rather than be drawn together for mere "groupiness."

6. Group recommendations should receive serious consideration and should lead to action. If group recommendations cannot be followed, this fact and the reasons behind it should be communicated openly and frankly to the group.

7. A principal should recognize that it is almost never true that every member of the teaching staff is interested in working on one given problem. Honest nonparticipation of members of a faculty in a group working on a single problem should be accepted as inevitable and should not lead to the exertion of pressure or the infliction of penalties upon those not interested in participating.

8. When it is apparent that a principal can delegate responsibility for group leadership to another without shirking his own responsibilities and when it seems likely that such delegation will produce superior results in attacking a specific problem, he should delegate the responsibility.

9. When the task of an action group is completed, the group should be dissolved. Nothing is more deadly than the continuation of a group after its task is completed, merely because no one quite knows how to terminate the meetings. Secondary schools are full of teacher committees meeting from force of habit rather than because of jobs to be done.

It is also important that the principal not lose sight of individuals as he works with groups. Often the ideas of individuals become submerged in the preparation of committee reports. The principal should be sensitive to these ideas and should provide the individuals with opportunities to present or develop their ideas.

The true test, then, of the competency of a secondary school principal comes as he combines his personal, educational, and experiential attributes into a pattern of administrative behavior as he works with people. More than one principal has observed, "This would be a fine job if it weren't for the students, teachers, superintendent, and parents!" But the principal works with people, and his ability to do so and to develop from this an outstanding educational program is the measure of his competency.

CONCLUSION

In concluding this discussion of the competencies of a secondary school principal, we refer to a statement developed to guide the planning of a university program for the preparation of educational administrators. Such a program is obviously dedicated to the development and refinement of competency patterns in prospective principals. This statement describes the required competencies as follows:

A. Personal Attributes

1. Possession in reasonable degree of appropriate personal attributes and of a disposition to improve them. These attributes should include such basic qualities as intelligence, adequate energy, courage of one's convictions, and a warmth toward people.

2. An ability to apply sound problem-solving procedures to school concerns and a disposition to use this ability. Intelligent action may not be suggested by the prevailing opinion of those concerned with the action. Much depends upon a consideration of the pertinent available facts in the formulation of this opinion. The administrator must be willing to act on the basis of judgments derived from studying the available facts.

3. An inclination to act in terms of conscious value judgments. Educational leadership should be built upon sound principles of action that have been derived from a study of the role of the school in society, how children grow and develop, and the learning process. An educational leader so motivated avoids opportunistic decision-making as much as is possible.

B. Educational Background

4. Understandings, attitudes, and skills resulting from an adequate general education. A general education should have provided the following: some knowledge of man, his history, and his behavior psychologically, socially, economically, politically, and morally; some power to do quantitative thinking; skill in oral and written expression; some appreciation for music, art, and literature; and a set of values consistent with the ideals of our culture which tend to give his behavior consistency.

5. An understanding of the role of the school in the social order. An understanding of the social order seems to be a prerequisite to comprehending the place and potential power of the school in a culture. Such understanding should be basic to determining the needs of the people of any school community, of ascertaining means to meet these needs, and of deciding the place of the school and of other community agencies in achieving such ends.

6. An understanding of the instructional program and skills in curriculum development. To understand the instructional program the administrator must have a foundation in human growth and development, in the characteristics and values of our culture, and in the principles and techniques of learning. He must be able to give leadership to teachers and to patrons in the development of the curriculum.

C. Working with People

7. An ability to cooperate with other people in planning, executing, and evaluating courses of action and a disposition to use this ability. Such a way of working must be based upon a fundamental conviction in its contribution to the achievement of the larger goal and upon a belief that cooperation produces better solutions to problems, results in more effective implementation of discussions, and promotes desirable growth on the part of the participants.

8. An ability to understand one's own motivations for action and how they affect his way of working with other people. To be an effective leader an administrator should have some conception of how other people see him and how this perception affects his relationship to them. The effect of the administrator upon others may depend greatly upon his own willingness to examine, evaluate, and rebuild his reasons for the way he works.

9. An ability to lead lay and professional people in considering the continuing improvement of the school and community; the ability to discover and promote such leadership in others; and a disposition to use these abilities. Leadership implies developing leaders. By such action on the part of the administrator, many people—lay and professional alike—become identified with a program and they learn the skills needed in responsible participation.

D. Professional Skills and Techniques

10. Understandings and skills in the task areas of educational administration. The competent administrator will operate in these specialized areas in ways which are consistent with the values implied by the other items in this statement.

11. Understandings and skills in the administrative process. The competent administrator will insure that the administrative process

remains the servant and does not become the master of the administrator.[9]

SUGGESTED ACTIVITIES

1. What seem to you to be the strengths and weaknesses of the trait approach to describing leadership qualities? Do you think that the competency approach is markedly different? Why or why not?

2. Describe the differences you think exist between the competencies required of a secondary school principal and those required of a secondary school teacher.

3. It is often claimed that almost all secondary school principals are former coaches. Assuming that this is true (it is not), can you explain it in terms of the competencies required of secondary school principals?

4. Many successful insurance salesmen and book salesmen are former secondary school principals. How would you account for this fact?

5. "Experience is the best teacher." Evaluate this well-known statement briefly.

SELECTED READINGS

Campbell, Roald F., John E. Corbally, Jr., and John A. Ramseyer, *Introduction to Educational Administration*, Second Edition. Boston: Allyn and Bacon, Inc., 1962. Chapters 10, 11, and 12.

Campbell, Roald F., and R. T. Gregg (eds.), *Administrative Behavior in Education*. New York: Harper & Row, Publishers, 1957. Chapters 7 and 9.

Chase, Francis S., and Egon G. Guba, "Administrative Roles and Behavior," *Review of Educational Research*. 25:281–298, 1956.

Clark, Dean O., *Critical Areas in the Administrative Behavior of High School Principals*. Columbus, Ohio: The Ohio State University, unpublished doctoral dissertation, 1956.

Gibb, Cecil A., "The Principles and Traits of Leadership," *Journal of Abnormal and Social Psychology*. 42:282, 1947.

---

[9] Adapted from Committee on Educational Administration, *Areas in Which Educational Administrators Need to Develop a Pattern of Competence* (Columbus, Ohio: Center for Educational Administration, Department of Education, The Ohio State University, 1958), pp. 3–11 (mimeographed).

Graff, Orin B., and Calvin M. Street, *Improving Competence in Educational Administration*. New York: Harper & Row, Publishers, 1956.

Stogdill, R. M., "Personal Factors Associated with Leadership: A Survey of the Literature," *Journal of Psychology*. 25:35–71, 1948.

Whyte, William F., *Leadership and Group Participation*. New York State School of Industrial and Labor Relations, Bulletin No. 24, Ithaca, New York: Cornell University, 1956.

12

THE MEASUREMENT
OF ADMINISTRATIVE
POTENTIAL

CHAPTER 11 DESCRIBES THE COMPETENCIES OR COM-
petency pattern the secondary school principal needs in order to be
effective in his work. From this general discussion, we now move to the
question of how an individual can assess his own potential to gain administrative competency and to become an effective secondary school
principal. This is both a necessary question to ask and a difficult question to answer. Before attempting to answer the question, let us first
consider some of the difficulties and dangers inherent in this process.

MEANING AND MEASUREMENT OF POTENTIAL

It is difficult to "measure" a prospective principal as he is today and then
to rate his "potential" as a principal. Ability is, in a sense, the present

state of a person's competencies. In an attempt to measure potential, then, present abilities must be measured and from these measurements inferences about the future drawn. This process gives rise to several problems.

In the first place, the measurement of present ability is a process that cannot be done with precise accuracy. The measurement of intelligence, for example, must proceed in the absence of a concrete definition of the factors of intelligence and with the recognition that each measurement device used for this purpose has certain inadequacies.

Secondly, competencies are behavioral competencies. It is difficult to measure with pencil-and-paper instruments the ability to engage in certain kinds of behaviors. In judgments about potential competence, the inferences must often be made in the face of a lack of complete information.

In the third place, potential and performance in a specific position are related, but not on a one-to-one basis. Potential indicates a capacity to perform, but there must also be a desire to perform and a favorable environment in which to perform if success is to result. Every secondary school teacher has known students who have great potential but who, for one reason or another, have never reached the heights possible for them. There is no guarantee, then, that potential will result in a quality performance.

In spite of the uncertainties present in both the definition of competency and the measurement of potential, efforts to do both are necessary and important. The attempt to measure an individual's potential for the secondary school principalship provides an opportunity for self-analysis and introspection that should help an individual know himself better and make a reasoned judgment concerning the wisdom of his choice of occupational goals. It is with these words of caution and support that we approach a discussion of the measurement of potential.

PERSONAL ATTRIBUTES

The extent to which a prospective secondary school principal possesses certain of the personal attributes that lead to competency is fairly easily measured. Potential in others of these attributes is only very slightly subject to measurement. Over-all, however, this competency area is the one most subject to measurement and to prediction of success or failure as a principal.

Physical attributes

The possession of general good health and adequate physical energy is a quality that should be known to an individual. There may be cases where a person thinks he has physical energy only because he has never tried to use too much of it. The prospective principal should have some evidence that he does possess physical energy and that he will be able to stand the physical demands of a principalship. This evidence can be gathered by participating in community groups, by continuing graduate studies, by taking an active role in professional organizations, all while performing successfully as a teacher. The rigors of such an existence are little different from those encountered by a principal. If such activities overtax an individual's physical energy, or if they lead to tension and personal anxiety, the principalship will undoubtedly create strains that will lessen the individual's effectiveness as a person as well as in the specific job he is attempting to perform.

A health record is generally well-known to the individual. The person with a history of illnesses or with a record of periodic absences from the job due to health problems has little likelihood of real success unless the health situation can be corrected. If this record is due to carelessness, the prospective principal should realize that he cannot afford not to take care of his health if he wishes to succeed. If medical care of one kind or another can correct the situation but has been delayed or avoided, such medical care should be received before the individual assumes a principal's job. A program of regular health check-ups is a particularly important habit for the school administrator.

The final physical attribute to be considered is personal appearance. Personal appearance plays a key role in influencing effectiveness in a leadership role. This is particularly true in working with secondary school students. Although the prospective principal cannot completely alter his physical appearance if such alteration seems necessary, he can take certain steps to overcome handicaps he may possess. Proper attire and diet, good personal grooming, and attention to social personality attributes can be instrumental in overcoming some physical handicaps. However, persons with severe handicaps in the area of personal appearance should face the fact that these handicaps may make success as a principal unlikely and may even make it difficult to secure a principal's position.

As the prospective principal considers his potential for administration, his analysis of his physical attributes should include consideration of the following:

Health—generally good.
Energy—more than average.
Appearance—normal and shown off to best advantage.

Mental attributes

The secondary school principal needs to possess better than average intelligence, but the possession of intelligence is valuable only if this intelligence is used effectively. In addition, recent studies show that there are various factors of intelligence and that a general intelligence test may not provide sufficient data about these factors to make an absolute judgment of intellectual potential. It is important, then, to consider both general intelligence and the specific factors of intelligence in a consideration of potential for secondary school administration.

General intelligence.   A study by Hopper and Bills revealed that the median intelligence quotient of a large sample of school administrators was 127 and that the range of scores in this group was from 109 to 133.[1] This gives some idea of the meaning of above-average intelligence as applied to school administrators. The prospective principal may have some idea of scores he has made on past intelligence tests. If not, any one of the following examinations provide good norms for adults:

Army General Classification Test: First Civilian Edition (AGCT).
   Science Research Associates, Inc., Chicago, Illinois.
California Short Form Test of Mental Maturity, Advanced Form. California Test Bureau, Los Angeles, California.
Ohio State University Psychological Examination (OSPE), Form 21.
   The Ohio State University Press, Columbus, Ohio.

Although there are always exceptions, the student who scores much below the range cited above on one of these tests has little chance for distinct success as a secondary school principal and is, as a matter of fact, probably experiencing some difficulty in being an outstanding secondary school teacher.

Factors of intelligence.   Several standardized tests show promise of having real predictive value in measuring administrative potential in terms of one or more factors of intelligence. Both the *Miller Analogies Test*[2] and the *Cooperative English C2*[3] tend to measure reasoning ability

----

[1] Robert L. Hopper and Robert E. Bills, "What's a Good Administrator Made of?" *School Executive,* 74:93, March 1955.

[2] *Miller Analogies Test* (New York: The Psychological Corporation).

[3] *Cooperative English Test, Form C2* (Princeton, N.J.: Educational Testing Service).

and insight, although the former test is essentially a high-level scholastic aptitude test and the latter emphasizes reading comprehension. The *Watson-Glaser Critical Thinking Appraisal*[4] is designed to measure ability to sort facts, to develop valid conclusions, to discover assumptions that underlie generalizations, to choose among relevant and irrelevant data, and to draw accurate inferences from related data. Studies at the University of Texas suggest that a candidate for work in the field of educational administration should score above 55 on the combined percentile scores for these three tests.[5]

Low scores on these tests may reveal a lack of practice in the use of certain factors of intelligence more than they reveal a lack in the factors themselves. Be that as it may, the prospective principal whose performance is poor on these tests should be aware that he has some work cut out for him if he is to be an effective administrator.

Indirect indicators. There are other indices of intelligence that the prospective administrator should consider. Academic records are related to some extent to intelligence. Certainly, a student knows—even though his grades may not accurately reflect this fact—whether a certain course of study was "easy" or "difficult" for his mental equipment.

In addition, a mature person is somewhat aware of his laziness or energy in approaching intellectual problems. The prospective principal who tends to seek out tough intellectual problems, who is challenged by problems that make him reach out into new learnings, or who enjoys reading thought-provoking essays as well as escape literature is undoubtedly more given to the exercise of his intelligence than is a person who avoids these activities.

In other words, although certain tests can provide excellent and fairly direct measurement of mental attributes, the prospective administrator must also be aware of the use he makes of his attributes.

As the student considers his potential as a principal in terms of his mental attributes, he should pay attention to the following:

Gross measurements of intelligence (IQ)—above average, preferably in 120's.

Measurements of factors of intelligence—strong in reasoning, insight, comprehension.

Evidence of use of intelligence—intellectually awake in everyday life.

[4] *Watson-Glaser Critical Thinking Appraisal* (New York: Harcourt, Brace & World, Inc.).

[5] Kenneth E. McIntyre, *An Experiment in Recruiting and Selecting Leaders for Education* (Austin, Texas: Southwest School Administration Center, 1956), pp. 29–35.

Social personality attributes

The measurement of social personality attributes is more inexact than in other personal attribute areas, and the exact requirements for the effective principal are not well known. Here we must deal almost entirely with common sense rather than with common sense backed by research evidence. Although a few studies have attempted to relate administrator effectiveness to certain personality inventory scores, the results are not sufficiently clear to permit the development of firm generalizations.

Thus, although it would be helpful in the selection and preparation of secondary school principals if we knew that a given profile with a given personality inventory indicated potential success, this is not the case. Each of us knows successful principals with greatly different personality attributes. It is both unlikely and undesirable that a common personality mold for principals will ever be developed. Nevertheless, there are certain indications that help assess potential for secondary school administration in terms of social personality attributes.

Standardized instruments. The use of a standardized instrument for measuring social personality attributes offers two advantages. In the first place, the results can be compared with results obtained in studies that have attempted to relate test scores to administrator effectiveness. Of even more importance is the fact that the use of these devices often reveals to a person some things about himself that he did not know. The self-diagnosis feature of these tests, then, is probably their most important feature.

One instrument which appears to provide insight into one's potential for administration is the *Guilford-Zimmerman Temperament Survey.*[6] This survey provides measurements dealing with a number of social personality areas. Experience has shown that those rated by other means to be high in administrator potential score consistently high in the areas of sociability, freedom from depression, masculinity, freedom from inferiority feelings, freedom from nervousness, objectivity, and cooperativeness. In all fairness to female readers, it should be noted that this study was conducted with male administrators and no evidence was produced to show that femininity was a disadvantage for the woman administrator.

[6] *Guilford-Zimmerman Temperament Survey* (Beverly Hills, Cal.: Sheridan Supply Company).

The *Allport-Vernon-Lindzey Study of Values* is an instrument that proposes a number of forced choice situations.[7] The patterns of an individual's choices tend to reveal certain value attributes. These attributes are placed on a profile revealing relative value feelings in the theoretical, political, economic, aesthetic, social, and religious areas. Although some trends seem apparent, it is safe to say only that this instrument is of particular help in giving a prospective administrator some insight into his own value system.

In an excellent discussion of leadership, Gibb reports several studies in which the *Bernreuter Scale* has been used to relate certain social personality atttributes to leadership behavior.[8] In general, these studies revealed that leaders tend to score higher than nonleaders in the areas of self-confidence, sociability, and dominance, and lower in the areas of introversion.[9]

Although a number of other excellent personality inventories exist, these have not been used in studies of administrative effectiveness. In general, however, regardless of the lack of research relating any of these tests to the principalship, it is apparent that the effective principal should understand himself and that the use of these inventories will aid in meeting this need.

Other approaches. In assessing potential for the principalship in terms of social personality attributes, it is necessary to do some introspective thinking independent of any standardized inventories or guides. Chapter 11 lists originality, adaptability, initiative, ambition, evenness of disposition, sense of humor, confidence, self-assurance, gregariousness, and general balance as social personality attributes that the effective secondary school principal should possess. For the most part, careful thought on the part of the individual prospective administrator will provide a valid assessment of the degree to which his behavior reflects each of these attributes.

For example, in the matter of originality, the prospective principal might well examine his own teaching practices to discover the answer to questions such as the following:

[7] *Allport-Vernon-Lindzey Study of Values,* Revised Edition (Boston: Houghton Mifflin Company, 1951).

[8] *Bernreuter Personality Inventory* (Stanford: Stanford University Press). (Distributed by C. H. Stoelting Company, Chicago, Ill.)

[9] Cecil A. Gibb, "Leadership," *Handbook of Social Psychology,* Volume II, edited by Gardner Lindzey (Reading, Mass.: Addison-Wesley Publishing Company, Inc., 1954), pp. 886–888.

Do I follow the same teaching methods from year to year or do I try to
develop new approaches from year to year and from class to class?

Have I developed some novel ways to deal with discipline problems,
with student learning problems, or with other teaching problems?

Am I willing to question traditional practices and to propose and to
experiment with what might be called "radical" ideas?

These, and other questions, will assist the prospective principal to
assess his behavior in terms of originality. The same kinds of questions
can be framed for each of the other attribute areas mentioned above.
Certainly, each individual is quite well aware of the reputation and
condition of his disposition. Some of us know that we have "terrible
tempers." As we assess our potential for administration, we need to look
at ourselves critically, to examine habitual ways of behaving, to pay some
attention to the impact that we have on other people, and to face up
honestly to the nature of our social personality.

In short, the prime requisite in assessing potential in terms of social
personality attributes is to take the time and to make the effort to do the
job. This job also requires the assistance of friends and acquaintances
who can talk frankly. For example, if the prospective principal thinks
that he has a good sense of humor, it would be valuable for him to
check this feeling with those who live or work in regular and close
contact with him. As the prospective secondary school principal assesses
his potential in terms of social personality attributes, he should examine
himself in at least the following areas:

Originality—an inclination and ability to develop and try out new approaches to problems.

Adaptability—an inclination and ability to face a variety of situations;
flexibility.

Initiative and ambition—wants to get things done; not willing to sit
back and "let things happen"; wants to play an active role.

Disposition—even; not a "limp rag," but also not given to tantrums.

Sense of humor—including the ability to laugh at one's self if necessary.

Self-confidence—faith in one's ability, but not egotism.

Sociability—likes and is liked by people.

General balance—an interesting personality, neither dull nor flamboyant.

Character attributes

A principal obviously needs to be a man or woman of good character.
This means that he must behave in terms of an acceptable and consistent
moral and ethical code. It is not enough for the prospective principal to
be able to say that he is "no worse than a lot of people."

The secondary school principal is closely related to the younger generation, a group groping for independence and sometimes consciously or unconsciously striving to shock their elders in an attempt to gain recognition. This means that the secondary school principal should not be a person whose moral and ethical code is unrealistic and impractical to deal with members of the current social scene.

There should be little need to spell out in detail how to assess character. However, if the prospective principal is not willing to have his character put in the spotlight where it will be viewed by teachers, students, parents, and others, he will not enjoy educational administration. Although every American has the right to live his life in privacy, that right must to some extent be subjugated to professional requirements if the person chooses to enter a given profession. The principalship is no exception, and an individual's code of behavior must meet high standards if he wishes to enter this field.

In addition to general character attributes, the prospective principal should be able to subscribe willingly to a code of ethics for his profession. The prospective principal who cannot subscribe to such a code wholeheartedly or who cannot understand the basis for such a code should seriously doubt his readiness for an administrative position. A recently-developed code of ethics for school administrators follows:

> The school administrator is in the forefront of the American public school system. As such, he shall reflect the highest type of ethical character, and serve as an outstanding example to his coworkers and associates in his personal and professional life. To this end, he subscribes to a rigid code of personal and professional standards. The following statements reflect the type of behavior demanded of the administrator.
>
> I. Community Relations.
>   1. He shall take appropriate steps to keep the community continuously and truthfully informed about the school. Information released to the community shall be clear, accurate, honest, and free from misleading or confusing statements.
>
>   2. In public life, the school administrator shall observe and respect the mores of the community.
>
>   3. Service to the community in the best interests of the public and the school system shall be the hallmark of all activities, personal and professional.
>
>   4. School funds, supplies, and data shall not be used in connection with partisan politics, advertising, or personal gain.
>
> II. Board of Education.
>   1. The school administrator shall not use his influence to promote or prevent the election of individual members of the Board of Education.

2. Contracts and agreements of employment made with the Board of Education shall be honored until fulfilled or released.

3. Abilities and qualifications of administrators and other employees shall not be misrepresented.

4. Matters pertaining to the welfare and operation of the school system will be discussed with members of the Board of Education as a whole.

III. Relations with Other Administrators.
1. Information pertinent to the school system or systems involved shall be honestly and accurately exchanged between administrators, and all such information shall be kept confidential as the situation demands. Such information should be cordially given.

2. The school administrator shall not seek positions not known to be vacant, nor shall he undermine the position of other administrators for personal or professional advancement.

3. He shall respect the normal channels of administration in his dealings with other members of his staff.

4. In seeking to secure a position or a promotion, the school administrator should use fair means at all times.
   a. He shall apply for positions only when they are known to be vacant.
   b. He shall not underbid a rival candidate on salary.
   c. He shall not misrepresent his qualifications.
   d. He shall not apply for another position for the sole purpose of forcing an increase in salary in his present position.
   e. He shall not make promises to do something against the best interests of pupils, the profession, or the public.

5. Gossip concerning other administrators or school systems shall not be indulged in by him.

IV. Teachers and Employees.
1. Contracts with teachers and other employees shall be honestly and clearly stated, and salaries shall be in line with existing schedules and practices.

2. Contracts with teachers and other employees shall be honored and shall be terminated only in terms of the conditions thereof.

3. Duties of employees shall be clearly understood at the time of initial employment.

4. Channels of communication shall be observed, and the school administrators shall not indulge in matters with teachers and other employees that lie in the province of other administrators.

5. The school administrator shall not interfere in disciplinary matters between teachers and pupils unless it is clearly evident that unfairness or violation of regulations is present.

6. Deficiencies of teachers and other employees shall be discussed only with the people concerned and in confidence.

7. The school administrator shall encourage his teachers and employees to maintain the same type of ethical character and professional attitudes that he demands of himself.

8. The school administrator shall not use his influence to force teachers to subscribe to things because of his position.

9. The school administrator assumes responsibility for the success of all employees, realizing that failure of an employee is at least partially an administrative failure: in selection, in supervision, or in assignment.
   a. He is alert to opportunities to further the advancement of each employee. He attempts to make vacancies known to present employees so that they may apply for preferred positions.
   b. He spares no effort to maintain and increase professional standards, he utilizes all professional placement agencies to obtain properly qualified teachers and administrators.
   c. He makes no offer of employment effective while the candidate is known to be under contract to another district unless that district has first notified him of its willingness to release the employee.
   d. He does not seek applicants for professional positions by advertising in newspapers or other publications of general circulation.
   e. He accepts no remuneration from commercial placement agencies whose candidates he interviews or employs.
   f. He makes sure that observed weaknesses are called to the attention of the employee and that assistance toward their correction is extended, but he does not jeopardize the educational welfare of children in order to avoid an unpleasant dismissal relationship.
   g. He reports no negative criticism of any employee to the board without having first discussed the criticism with the employee involved.

10. The school administrator is alert to inform the board about good performances and contributions of employees and does not accept the credit for service performed by others.

V. Relations with Pupils.
   1. Information relating to pupil abilities, deficiencies, or behavior shall be kept in strict confidence and shall not be released except to authorized personnel.

2. Disciplinary measures shall not be taken except by referral, and shall be in the best interests of the school and the community.

3. The administrator will deal justly with students regardless of their mental, physical, emotional, political, economical, racial, or religious characteristics.

VI. Agents and Salesmen.
1. Lists of pupils, teachers, and employees shall not be made available to agents or salesmen for advertising, canvassing, or personal profit.

2. Orders and contracts entered into shall be honored, and shall be made on the basis of need and value only.

3. No gift, remuneration, or discount based on giving preference of personal gain to any agent or salesman shall be accepted.

4. The school administrator shall not act as an agent or salesman for any item purchased by the school system or an employee thereof.

VIII. Professional.
1. The school administrator shall evidence interest in professional standing through membership in local, state, and national educational associations.

2. He shall constantly strive to better his professional standing through study and activity in professional organizations.

3. He shall rigidly adhere to the code of ethics adopted by his state.[10]

In summary, then, the prospective principal should subscribe to a high personal standard of conduct and to a sound professional code of ethics. He must be willing to let his actions stand in the light of community and professional appraisal. He should know the rationale that underlies both his personal and his professional conduct. Lastly, he should be willing to stand as a good example for the people whom he will serve.

EDUCATIONAL BACKGROUND

Many factors influence growth and development and thus help create potential as principals. Important among these factors is educational background. Although a given kind of background guarantees very little,

[10] "Directory of the Ohio Association of School Administrators, 1960," *Bulletin of the Ohio Association of School Administrators*, January 1960, pp. 5–8.

it should provide certain understandings, which influence potential, and certain clues to potential.

General academic background

Perhaps the most deflating experience that a student can undergo is to be examined with the *Graduate Record Examinations.*[11] Covering almost every field of learning, these examinations are an excellent diagnostic instrument. Although it would be unreasonable to expect that a prospective principal would receive high scores in every area, from fine arts to chemistry, the background of a principal should lead to knowledge in more than one field of specialization.

If the student has no knowledge in areas other than his one or two teaching fields, he will find it difficult to communicate with teachers whose fields cover a wide range. As the prospective principal analyzes his academic background and his potential, he should determine in how many areas he has at least a minimum level of knowledge. Although the history teacher-football coach cannot be expected to be an expert in art or in vocational agriculture, his potential as a principal will be enhanced if he has some familiarity with the contents of these fields. The greater the breadth of study, then, the greater the opportunities for effective administration by the secondary school principal.

One other general academic factor should be considered in any analysis of potential. This is the often-criticized, but ever-present evidence of academic achievement—the grade point. To begin with, the grade point serves as partial evidence to superintendents and boards of education as they select principals. Potential is reduced if the likelihood of securing a position is reduced. Even more important, however, is the fact that the academic record does reveal a great deal about ability to learn, motivations, and adaptability to academic situations. A generally poor academic record, then, should serve as a warning signal that administrative potential is subject to question. If reasons for this record are discovered that can be corrected or removed, this should be done. Otherwise, the choice of a career as a principal of a secondary school seems to lack wisdom.

Professional academic background

The secondary school principal needs to have at his command a great deal of professional knowledge, much of which is gained through univer-

[11] Princeton, N.J.: Educational Testing Service.

sity study. Earlier in this text we have described in some detail the general requirements of leadership and of the specific task areas in which the principal will work. Although all of the learnings necessary to success in meeting these requirements cannot be gained through academic work, an adequate academic background in these areas is essential. This means, then, that the academic background of the prospective principal should enable him to be a good teacher; and he should build upon this background to gain the learnings necessary to become a good principal.

This requires a careful assessment of professional knowledge. Chapter 11 lists fourteen knowledge areas that should be mastered by the prospective principal. This list can serve as an excellent device for measuring potential. How much, for example, do you know about adolescent growth and development, about the aims of education, or about curriculum development? To what extent are you up-to-date on research findings that relate to teaching and learning? Do you recall any psychology other than that some Russian did something with dogs, dog food, and bells?

One way to discover the extent of professional knowledge is to take the *National Teacher Examinations*,[12] or the *How I Teach Inventory*.[13] Each of these instruments provides evidence concerning the degree to which a teacher understands the basic concepts of teaching and learning.

Each of the task areas that we have described also can lead to assessment of potential. To what extent, for example, does your knowledge of sociology assist you in becoming a community leader for education? Although the prospective principal is not expected to have studied all that is necessary to be a principal, this kind of assessment can help the aspiring principal plan his future academic work so that gaps can be filled.

The prospective principal should realize that he has a great deal of control over his potential in terms of academic background. If gaps are revealed, he can take steps fairly easily to remedy this situation. In making this assessment, the following points should be considered:

Academic record—Good grades; Phi Beta Kappa not necessary, but at least a B average preferable.

General academic background—Some specialization, but also breadth.

Professional academic background—Secure grasp of the basic concepts and disciplines that underlie the teaching-learning situation; beginning knowledge about leadership and the principalship.

[12] Princeton, N.J.: Educational Testing Service.
[13] *Kelly-Perkins How I Teach Inventory* (Minneapolis, Minn.: Educational Test Bureau).

EXPERIENCE BACKGROUND

The prospective principal should have had a variety of school and non-school experiences. The local boy who goes to local schools and a local college and then starts teaching in the local high school has much less potential for leadership than does the person who has had a variety of experiences in a variety of situations. If one learns from experience—and this is not automatic—a wide variety of experiences should provide him with great potential to face various kinds of problems with originality and confidence.

The principal will work with a number of representatives of his community. If, for example, the principal has spent some time engaged in common labor, he may better understand those people who spend their lives in this type of work. If he has traveled fairly widely, he may better understand the problems of those who move to his community from much different localities.

There are, of course, no hard and fast rules governing the relationship between quantity of experiences and effectiveness of administration. As the prospective principal assesses his potential in terms of experience, however, he might well consider his range of experiences in all areas. A lack of experience can decrease his potential for effectiveness. It might indicate, then, that next summer instead of going to school, a trip or some work experience would be beneficial. He should consider the following areas of experience:

School experience—Have you:
    Taught in large and small schools?
    Taught children at various age levels?
    Taught children at different ability levels?
    Taught more than one subject?
    Taught in rural and urban schools?
    Worked with various cocurriculum activities?
    Experienced teaching success in varied situations?
Work experience—Have you:
    Worked at an unskilled job?
    Belonged to a union?
    Been a foreman or a supervisor?
    Experienced success in various jobs?
Travel—Have you:
    Traveled outside of your own region?
    Been in a foreign country?
    Studied the mores of different regions?
    Strayed from "beaten tourist paths"?

Although experience does not guarantee success, the principal cannot afford to be parochial or provincial as he fulfills a leadership role. If university training cannot provide all the knowledge, skills, and understandings that the principal needs, it is apparent that these must grow from experience. If experience is limited, efforts should be made to expand this background before assuming a principal's position.

MOTIVATION

Even though a young man or woman may appear to possess all the factors that would seem to lead to great success as a principal, these factors would be meaningless unless that person was strongly motivated to be a successful principal. Studies relating motivation and success are legion. Perhaps motivation is the key variable that causes two apparently equal people to achieve differing degrees of success. This means that in a consideration of potential, a consideration of motivations must loom large. It is safe to say that the person motivated toward a principalship for reasons of power or of money alone will have little chance of achieving effectiveness. As any secondary school teacher should know, the power of the principal is something that, in the last analysis, is delegated to him by his teaching staff. And certainly, the financial rewards of the principalship rarely lead to riches. Power and wealth, then, are unrealistic motivations toward the principalship.

We have mentioned earlier the possibilities that a leadership position presents. Such a position also presents problems and frustrations. If the prospective principal is motivated by a desire to make a contribution to secondary education and to use his talents as effectively as possible, there is every possibility that this will lead to a maximum realization of his potential. The principalship is not an escape from teaching nor an easy road to glory; it is hard work. Unless one is motivated to be a successful principal on a sound basis, his potential will not lead to effective administrative behavior.

BEHAVIOR

The competency approach to describing effective educational administrators involves descriptions of behavior, of traits or attributes in action. Although we have been discussing attributes here for the most part, the reader should remember that his future administrative effectiveness will be measured primarily in terms of behavior. For example, the mere possession of self-confidence is not in itself a measure of effectiveness. What is significant is the way in which this self-confidence shows itself in the behavior of the principal. The self-confident person generally has an easier time making decisions than does a person with little faith in himself. The self-confident person generally makes a better impression upon people he meets than does the person who lacks this confidence. The self-confident person is generally able to criticize his own behavior and to accept criticism from others. Thus, it is not self-confidence that is important; it is the ways in which self-confidence manifests itself in behavior.

The factors that affect potential can be roughly divided into three categories—attributes, skills and knowledges, and understandings. Each of these categories leads to effectiveness or ineffectiveness as the items within the categories are used in working with people. It seems important, then, for the prospective principal to review his potential for administration in terms of his effectiveness in working with people.

One of the best devices for checking ability to work with people was developed by workers at the National Training Laboratory at Bethel, Maine. This form provides forty-five statements to be used in self-diagnosis. Although there are no "right" or "wrong" reactions to these statements, the implication of each answer for one's behavior as a principal is quite clear. For each statement, the prospective principal should decide whether it is a very accurate description of him, is quite descriptive, is both true and untrue as description, is generally not a true description, or is a decidedly false description of him. After reacting to the statements and reviewing our descriptions of the role of the principal, the reader should gain valuable insight into his behavioral potential as an administrator. This form follows:

"Ideas About Myself" Inventory

1. I think I have a pretty clear understanding of how the people I work with see themselves and the job they are trying to do.

2. I am not the kind of person who can stand up to his superiors and disagree with them.

3. It is important for me to maintain my individuality within any group to which I belong.

4. My relations with other people never present much difficulty for me.

5. I enjoy following a good leader more than being a leader myself.

6. I will stand up for my own ideas even under a lot of pressure from others to change.

7. I often get so involved in doing a particular job that I don't pay much attention to the feelings and reactions of other people concerned.

8. My first reaction to a proposal that things be done differently is usually negative.

9. I try to have things thoroughly thought out before taking an active part in the group.

10. I am aware of most of the shortcomings in my social behavior.

11. I always try to achieve a position of power in a group.

12. I feel that I am more fully expressing my personality when I am working in a group than at any other time.

13. I am often tactless and hurt people's feelings without meaning to.

14. I often get so wound up in what I want to say that I do not really listen to what other people are saying.

15. I do not like to express my ideas unless I know they have the support of others.

16. I usually react positively to new people.

17. I am pretty good at taking initiative in a group to keep things moving along.

18. If I believe in something, I will work for it even when this requires opposing friends and associates.

19. I do not pay enough attention to the needs and feelings of individuals with whom I work.

20. I am better at arguing than at conciliating and compromising.

21. I am easily persuaded by others to see things their way.

22. I often detach myself psychologically from the group and just watch what is going on.

23. When someone is talking, I not only listen to what he says but also notice how people react to the things he says.

24. I find it very frustrating to have to work on an important project with other people instead of alone.

25. I get quite upset when people allow their personal feelings to affect the work they are doing.

26. I am quite fearful about going into new social situations.

27. I am happier when working on a project with others than I am when working on something of my own.

28. I can usually predict the reactions of people I know to new suggestions.

29. I enjoy sticking up for my own ideas.

30. I cannot stand up against others in support of unpopular ideas.

31. I am pretty good at finding ways of bringing together two people who seem to be disagreeing.

32. I think I have quite a lot of influence on other people.

33. I sometimes feel that a group or relationship in which I am involved gets so strong that it hampers my individuality and freedom.

34. I am often amazed at the variety of impressions different participants have of the same meeting.

35. It is relatively easy for me to persuade people to see things my way.

36. It does not matter to me whether other people agree with my opinions or not.

37. I get emotionally upset when a group member begins to introduce side issues into the group discussion.

38. I do not like to have the final responsibility for making decisions.

39. I would say I am more likely to dominate a group than to be dominated by it.

40. I am able to silence a group member tactfully when he attempts to introduce his personal feelings into the discussion.

41. I feel blocked and frustrated in my own school situation because of the difficulties resulting from the attitudes of certain people there.

42. I work better with individuals than I do with a group.

43. I feel very much on the spot when people discuss faults I know I have.

44. I take a lot of initiative in starting new activities or procedures.

45. I can make a greater contribution by working as part of a group than I can by working alone.[14]

Another vital factor influencing a person's ability to work with other people is his ability to communicate. Good written and spoken English are necessary, but, in addition, the principal needs to be able to get ideas to and from others. It is difficult to assess potential in the field of communication, particularly in the communication of ideas. However, we

[14] Gordon N. MacKenzie and Stephen M. Corey, *Instructional Leadership* (New York: Bureau of Publications, Teachers College, Columbia University, 1954), pp. 202–204.

have all tried from time to time to give directions to an individual and to groups, to pass on information, or to give assignments. By carefully reviewing the degree of success or failure in these acts of communication we can come to some judgments about our communication ability. Certainly if a prospective principal has experienced difficulty in getting students to understand assignments, this is an indication of a weakness that needs to be overcome before he can expect to perform effectively as a principal.

The best evidence of ability to work with people is success in working with people in the past. As a student, a teacher, and a person, the prospective principal has had ample opportunities to work with all kinds of people, individually and in groups. As one assesses his potential as a secondary school principal, he needs to review his record in working with people and to discover the extent to which his potential seems high or low in this all-important aspect of administration.

CONCLUSION: OVER-ALL VIEW OF POTENTIAL

The time has now come to put together the various appraisals of potential, to reach a judgment about the wisdom of one's choice to enter the principalship, and to plan for future growth. In the summary of Chapter 11 we presented an eleven-point outline of the competencies required of an educational administrator. This framework will serve well for a summary analysis of potential. The tests, questions, and self-diagnosis presented in this chapter can be used to arrive at a judgment of one's present state in each of these competencies. After arriving at a judgment of potential in each competency, the prospective principal can plan for improvement where it is necessary. If too much improvement is indicated or if the work required for improvement does not seem worth the effort, a career choice other than the principalship is wise. In any case, unless plans to improve potential are accompanied by action, there is little likelihood of improvement.

Following are two forms to assist in summarizing self-appraisal. The first deals with an analysis of professional knowledge and skill. The second is based upon the eleven-point competency pattern.

Professional knowledge and skill

In Chapters 5 through 9, we have described five task areas of the secondary school principal. It is in these areas that the principal must bring his professional knowledge and skill to bear. A form similar to the following should be developed for each of these task areas. The task area of school-community relationships is presented as an example. The specifics of the area as listed in the form are incomplete and should be added to as the prospective principal's understanding of the requirements of the task area broadens.

Progress in Gaining Professional Knowledge and Skill[15]

Task Area: School-Community Relations

Specifics:	Have Studied	Have Observed	Have Participated
Studying community characteristics			
Assessing community opinion			
Providing information			
Working with community leaders			

Pertinent reference material:

Plans for improving knowledge and skill in this area:

Areas of competence[16]

The following figure is self-explanatory. It can and should be used both to consolidate appraisal of potential and to establish a record of plans for improving this potential.

[15] Adapted from Roald F. Campbell, John E. Corbally, Jr., and John A. Ramseyer, *Introduction to Educational Administration*, Second Edition (Boston: Allyn and Bacon, Inc., 1962), p. 346.
[16] *Ibid.*, pp. 348–350.

For each area of competence place a check mark at the position on the scale that most nearly represents your judgment of your own competence. Your present competence should be considered in relation to the competence required of an effective educational administrator. The following scale can be used:

5—Superior
4—Somewhat above average
3—Average
2—Somewhat below average
1—Very low

Below the scale in the space provided, indicate plans for improving your competence. These plans might include teaching or other experience, university course work, and considerations of certification and advanced degree requirements.

A. Personal Attributes

1. Possession in reasonable degree of appropriate personal attributes and a disposition to improve them.

```
|           |           |           |           |           |
5           4           3           2           1
```

Plan: _____

_____

_____

2. An ability and a disposition to apply sound problem-solving procedures to school concerns.

```
|           |           |           |           |           |
5           4           3           2           1
```

Plan: _____

_____

_____

3. An inclination to act in terms of conscious value judgments.

```
|           |           |           |           |           |
5           4           3           2           1
```

Plan: _____

_____

_____

4. Understandings, attitudes, and skills resulting from an adequate general
   education.

```
  |             |             |             |             |
  5             4             3             2             1
```

Plan: _____

_____

5. An understanding of the role of the school in the social order.

```
  |             |             |             |             |
  5             4             3             2             1
```

Plan: _____

_____

6. An understanding of the instructional program and skills in curriculum
   development.

```
  |             |             |             |             |
  5             4             3             2             1
```

Plan: _____

_____

B. Working with People

7. A disposition and an ability to cooperate with other people in planning,
   executing, and evaluating courses of action.

```
  |             |             |             |             |
  5             4             3             2             1
```

Plan: _____

_____

8. An inclination and an ability to understand one's own motivations for
   action and how they affect his way of working with other people.

```
  |             |             |             |             |
  5             4             3             2             1
```

Plan: _____

_____

9. A disposition and an ability to lead lay and professional people in considering the continuing improvement of the school and community; the ability to discover and promote such leadership in others.

```
  |           |           |           |           |
  5           4           3           2           1
```

Plan: _____

_____

_____

C. Professional Skills and Techniques

10. An understanding of and skills in the technical aspects of school administration.

```
  |           |           |           |           |
  5           4           3           2           1
```

Plan: _____

_____

_____

11. An understanding of and skills in the administrative process.

```
  |           |           |           |           |
  5           4           3           2           1
```

Plan: _____

_____

_____

Simulated experience for over-all appraisal

While the final test of one's potential and competency comes only when this potential and competency is put to the test of an actual leadership position, major efforts have been devoted to the development of a simulated situation in which a potential administrator can be faced with as real an administrative challenge as is possible short of the real thing. Using the "in-basket" test method, a simulated experience known as the Whitman School situation has been developed under the leadership of the University Council for Educational Administration.[17] With

---

[17] The best analysis of the use and results of this technique is in John K. Hemphill, et al., Administrative Performance and Personality (New York: Bureau of Publications, Teachers College, Columbia University, 1962). Regular reports on the availability of the test materials are available from the University Council on Educational Administration, c/o The Ohio State University, Columbus, Ohio.

this test, the individual is assumed to be the principal of a school; he is provided background information about the school and the community through readings, film strips, films, and recordings; and he is faced with a series of decisions to make about materials found in the principal's in-basket. While there are no "right" decisions, an analysis of the decisions made provides insight into the probable effectiveness of the potential administrator and also serves as a diagnostic instrument.

SUGGESTED ACTIVITIES

This entire chapter is itself a series of suggested activities. It is hoped that each reader will conduct a self-appraisal as suggested by this chapter and will develop records of the appraisal and of plans for the future. Friends or colleagues can rate you independently of your own rating. By comparing results, you will gain much insight as you to some extent see yourself as others see you.

SELECTED READINGS

Campbell, Roald F., John E. Corbally, Jr., and John A. Ramseyer, *Introduction to Educational Administration*, Revised Edition. Boston: Allyn and Bacon, Inc., 1962. Chapter 12.

Crow, Lester D., and Alice Crow, *Understanding Our Behavior*. New York: Alfred A. Knopf, Inc., 1956.

Gibb, Cecil A., "Leadership," *Handbook of Social Psychology*, Volume II, edited by Gardner Lindzey. Reading, Mass.: Addison-Wesley Publishing Company, Inc., 1954.

McIntyre, Kenneth E., *An Experiment in Recruiting and Selecting Leaders for Education*. Austin, Texas: Southwest School Administration Center, 1956.

Thorndike, R. L., and E. Hagen, *Measurement and Evaluation in Psychology and Education*. New York: John Wiley & Sons, Inc., 1955.

IV

THE PROFESSION

PART FOUR IS DEVOTED TO A DISCUSSION OF SECOND-
ary school administration as a profession. Chapter 13 discusses the
professional opportunities. In this chapter the focus is on the kinds of
positions that exist for administrators, salary data, and the routes by
which these positions are secured. Chapter 14 describes the exciting
career challenges that await those who choose secondary school administration as their avenue of service. Chapter 15 describes the special
administrative challenges of the junior high school—a unique institution
within the general framework of secondary education.

13

THE PROFESSIONAL
OPPORTUNITIES

THOSE WHO SERIOUSLY CONTEMPLATE A CAREER IN
secondary school administration need certain "avenue" kinds of data.
What kinds of positions are available in the field? How many of them
are there? How are they secured? What qualifications must a person
have to be eligible for these positions? How much do they pay? What
job security exists? What opportunities do they hold for continued
professional growth? These, and other questions, should cross the mind
of any individual who aspires to a position in secondary school administration, for a knowledge of these things enables a person to plan his
career with greater precision. We believe that career planning will be
much more prevalent in the future than it has been in the past, because there will be far fewer opportunities for a person to become a
secondary school administrator by mere chance. The competition, of
course, will probably be much more severe, hence the need for more
thorough education and planning.

THE CURRENT SCENE

Kinds of positions available

As yet there is not the diversity of administrative positions in secondary schools that exists at the central administrative level in a school district. Secondary schools are growing in size, however, and more variation is beginning to appear. Basically, the administrative personnel are junior and senior high school principals. The trend is for these to be non-teaching positions. In the smaller schools, however, the principal may be required to teach at least part-time, although this situation is disappearing quite rapidly.

Most secondary schools with an enrollment of 500–1000 pupils now have an assistant or vice-principal, whose responsibilities may be defined in a number of different ways. In many instances, for example, he may oversee the attendance function, administer student extracurriculum activities, and have some responsibilities in the field of discipline. The assignment of duties is very flexible, and desirably so, for this flexibility permits the administrative organization to be designed on the basis of the individual's unique competencies and the particular needs that exist in a school during any given year.

Increasingly, in these larger schools, a second assistant or vice principal is being appointed, whose major responsibility is in the instructional area. This has been especially common where the principal functions as a generalist who has very limited time for the detailed, time-consuming responsibilities involved in planning, implementing, and evaluating today's complex curriculum. Time, though, is not the only dimension involved in this development. More and more, it is recognized that the secondary school curriculum requires the participation of a full-time administrator who has depth understandings of curriculum and leadership skills in those processes by which curriculum is developed.

In some secondary schools, this trend has been carried forth even further. Various areas have been grouped together, such as English-social studies and mathematics-science, and each area is headed by an assistant principal for instruction. This development has some promise, we believe, for it places a line administrator squarely into the curriculum mainstream. Ideally these administrators are employed because of demonstrated competence in curriculum, and they can be held accountable for marked accomplishments in this area. Being line administrators they also have authority to make certain decisions which staff administrators often cannot make. Thus their function in the staff appraisal process can be carried out much more openly and directly than might otherwise be the case.

Yet another organizational pattern of the larger secondary school is one which illustrates an attempt to decentralize, administratively, by grade level. Sometimes, when a junior and senior high school are housed in the same building, each will have its own administrative staff. A further modification is for each grade level to have its own administrators. Usually, when this happens, one principal, a generalist, heads the administrative staff, with grade level administrators serving on his cabinet. No one pattern of organization, of course, provides the magic touchstone, for an organization chart, *per se*, rarely solves problems. Best employed, organization is a flexible tool in the hands of those who know what is feasible, what are the goals to be accomplished, and what are the resources which can be brought to the task.

Less dependent on size and complexity than those administrative positions just highlighted are other types of assignments which should be mentioned briefly. These represent positions for those who are interested in specific rather than general administration, and in most cases they are not established on a full-time basis. Some of them, however, provide excellent opportunities for the person interested in eventual full-time administration to gain valuable experience. Chief among these positions are those of dean, department chairman, and director of student personnel services.

Another frequently occurring position is that of school treasurer. This is one of increasing importance, as more and more secondary schools are handling thousands of dollars annually in student activity, athletic, and cafeteria funds. Accounting for these funds in a safe, orderly fashion is a must, and increasingly the task should be entrusted to someone who has the time and skill to perform it competently. Asher's recent master's research is offered as documentation of this point and as an excellent resource for the administrator who wishes to become more knowledgeable about his fiscal operation.[1]

A position growing in importance is that of coordinator of extracurricular activities. Many secondary schools have a faculty manager of athletics. Another position of considerable promise for the future is that of administrative assistant. Often this person functions in this capacity only one or two periods a day, discharging responsibilities as-

---

[1] Clifford R. Asher, "A Comparison of Current Practices in Ohio High Schools with Accepted Accounting Principles and Procedures in School Activities Finance," unpublished master's thesis (Columbus, Ohio: The Ohio State University, 1960).

signed to him by the principal. This is an excellent way to free the principal for staff leadership functions, to discover administrative potential of a resident staff member, and to develop stand-by administration for those times when the principal is ill or needs to leave the building.

Number of positions, salary data, and security factors

Estimating the number of existing positions in secondary school administration is a complex undertaking. Differences in organizational patterns, administrative terminology, reporting responsibilities, and the constant shifting resulting from consolidation and reorganization, are but a few of the factors that help to create the difficulty. Campbell, Corbally, and Ramseyer, in their *Introduction to Educational Administration*, estimate that in 1962 there were about 9,000 secondary school principals in charge of schools with fifteen or more teachers.[2] Although precise determination of a number is virtually impossible, the figures may be helpful in indicating the variations in the national picture. The student of secondary school administration should contact the department of education and the state Association of Secondary School Principals in those areas in which he is interested in locating. This will yield data with sufficient accuracy for his own career planning. When such data are coupled with data received through conferences with university placement officers, a precise picture develops.

Remuneration data are likewise difficult to present in a short analysis, for the picture is complicated by the different sizes of school districts involved, their financial potentials, and differing lengths of periods of employment. Further, considerable time is needed to collect, assemble, and analyze data on a national scale. The National Education Association, Research Division, however, conducts an almost constant study of salaries, and those who wish specific information can frequently find it in the research bulletins prepared by that office.

An analysis of salary trends for secondary school administrators indicates that the differential schedule is becoming more and more prevalent, particularly in those districts containing several secondary schools. This plan attaches a numerical weighting to such items as responsibility, length of the working year, and number of teachers under the supervision of the principal. A factor is then determined; most commonly for junior

[2] Roald F. Campbell, John E. Corbally, Jr., and John A. Ramseyer, *Introduction to Educational Administration*, Second Edition (Boston: Allyn and Bacon, Inc., 1962), p. 393.

high school principals this is between 1.30 and 1.50; and for senior high school principals between 1.40 and 1.60. The administrator's salary is then determined by multiplying the maximum salary of a classroom teacher at the administrator's level of preparation and experience by the weighted figure established for the position. If, for example, the maximum teaching salary for the master's degree classification is $8,000, and the factor for the secondary school principal is 1.50, his salary would be $12,000.

In smaller school districts, the most common practice seems to be that of establishing administrative salaries independently of the classroom teacher schedules. Frequently, under these less structured conditions, then, administrators' salaries are set on an individual basis, as the result of personal bargaining between employer and employee, although prevailing regional circumstances often play a prevalent role in determining the general range of these salaries.

As salary data are analyzed on a national scale, figures pertaining to urban districts often are the first to be reported, since these districts are fewer in number but employ a substantial percentage of the country's teaching and administrative personnel. Table 5 shows salary medians for selected urban school districts.

It should be noted that salaries paid in these large urban districts tend to be somewhat larger than those obtainable in the smaller districts. Competitive conditions and increased recognition of the fact that administrative salaries need to be raised is narrowing this gap.

As far as job security is concerned, the secondary school administrator should recognize that he is classified as a teacher according to school legislation. As a teacher, then, he is protected by existing tenure laws. His assignment is subject to the discretion of the superintendent of schools and ultimately, of course, of the board of education. The tenure of a secondary school administrator results from his demonstrated competence. As an educational leader, this is the only type of security he could justify.

Research bulletins of the National Education Association and the United States Office of Education continue to show the decline in the number of operating school districts. Somewhat paradoxically, however, this will likely result in more, rather than fewer, secondary school administrative positions. The diminishing number of school districts means larger schools, particularly at the secondary level, which indicates that the number of nonteaching principals will increase. There is also a steadily increasing number of students in today's secondary schools because of our expanded population and percentage decreases in high school

TABLE 5. MAXIMUM SCHEDULED SALARIES FOR ADMINISTRATORS, 1963–64

	Median maximum salary for classroom teachers[1]	Supervising principals			Central-office administrators		
		Elementary	Junior high	Senior high	Supervisors	Directors	Superintendents[2]
Stratum 1—enrollment 100,000 or more							
Number of reporting systems	19	19	16	19	18	18	17
Median maximum scheduled salary	$9,000	$11,800	$12,415	$13,250	$11,612	$14,506	$25,000
Range: Low	6,876	9,120	9,120	9,290	9,400	11,250	16,000
High	10,630	14,735	16,460	18,885	17,910	23,645	48,500
Stratum 2—enrollment 50,000–99,999							
Number of reporting systems	46	41	33	39	33	32	32
Median maximum scheduled salary	$8,059	$11,075	$12,000	$12,525	$10,665	$13,228	$22,500
Range: Low	5,075	7,020	7,020	7,218	6,690	8,200	15,000
High	11,150	15,792	16,305	18,420	17,535	18,125	31,000
Stratum 3—enrollment 25,000–49,999							
Number of reporting systems	71	51	46	50	35	36	32
Median maximum scheduled salary	$8,200	$11,030	$11,661	$12,414	$11,360	$13,110	$20,000
Range: Low	5,049	6,900	8,500	8,928	7,750	9,800	14,500
High	11,775	15,455	15,653	17,241	15,374	17,241	25,700
Stratum 4—enrollment 12,000–24,999							
Number of reporting systems	242	154	139	151	91	92	137
Median maximum scheduled salary	$8,173	$10,500	$11,280	$12,255	$10,132	$12,550	$18,293
Range: Low	4,140	6,588	6,778	7,443	5,713	8,000	8,800
High	11,720	14,952	16,200	17,500	16,350	16,598	26,000

[1] Median maximum scheduled salary for highest level of preparation recognized in schedule.
[2] Salary paid in 1963–64; relatively few are paid on a formal schedule.
Source: "Maximum Scheduled Salaries for School Administrators, 1963–64" NEA Research Bulletin, Vol. 42, Number 1, February, 1964 (Washington, D.C.: National Education Association, 1964), p. 31.

drop-outs. These factors, coupled with the tendency of secondary schools to become very complex enterprises, seem to warrant the prediction of more administrative personnel.

Not only will there be an increased demand for the services of secondary school administrators in the next several years, but if reorganizations continue at the anticipated pace, there will be a premium placed on administrators with special kinds of skills. When a new secondary school is constructed subsequent to reorganization, it pulls a student body from several smaller schools. These students are characterized by considerable apprehension. Most likely they have had a diversity of experiences, many of them makeshift in nature, while the new school was in the process of being built. During the first year of operation of these new schools, then, the administrator needs to give serious attention to orientation and induction procedures in order to develop the sense of security from which productive learning so often results. Sanders, finding himself in this position of principal in such a new secondary school, undertook a study of the first year of operation.[3] His experience is worthy of analysis by those who anticipate being in comparable positions.

During the next few years more "team players" in administration will be needed. Larger secondary schools will need coordinated administrative effort, for the days of the one-man autonomous operation are numbered. The abilities to plan, to delegate, to evaluate, to work together in a pooling of complementary skills will be valued attributes in the anticipated scene.

MEANS OF SECURING POSITIONS

Qualifications

The most ostensible of the qualifications needed are those reflected in certification patterns. Certification, regulated in most places by the state department of education, is an effort to define the criteria for holding a position. It represents professional college or university preparation in specified areas of study and years of experience. Recently, the trends in certification patterns for the secondary school principalship have become broader than they previously were. Instead of requiring a master's degree in educational administration or a specified number of hours of

[3] Robert E. Sanders, "An Orientation Program for Students and Faculty Entering the New Licking Valley High School, Hanover, Ohio" (Columbus, Ohio: The Ohio State University, unpublished master's thesis, 1959).

work toward one, the tendency now is to make necessary a master's degree, with some work in each of the following areas: general or secondary educational administration; general or secondary supervision of instruction; general or secondary curriculum; guidance; social, philosophical, or psychological foundations; and research and/or evaluation.

In addition to the hours of work in these areas, the requirements call for a minimum of twenty-seven months of successful teaching experience, of which at least eighteen must be at the secondary level.[4] The exact requirements vary from state to state, however, and it is wise for the aspiring administrator to check them as early as possible in the process of his preparation.

Applicants for positions in secondary school administration will also find that local criteria are often established in addition to the state certification requirement. If a certified person holds an administrative position, this fact will often entitle a district to a specified allocation from the state foundation program. Additional criteria often guarantee something of much more fundamental importance; namely, that the person selected has the characteristics that are considered to be important for the successful filling of a particular position. Some placement officers report, for instance, that boards of education are requesting the names of applicants who have work beyond the master's degree, who have a demonstrated ability to work in instructional leadership, who have strong public relations skills, and the like. For those who look forward to a career in secondary school administration, therefore, it is wise to confer with placement officers at the college or university of their attendance regarding the emerging pattern of requests. As students round out their graduate programs, then, there are opportunities to fill some voids in their preparation, thus enhancing their chances of ultimate selection.

Teaching routes

Those who write speculatively about the science of administration often express the opinion that a person might be an excellent administrator in public education and yet never have had a day's classroom teaching experience. Further, it is also seemingly true that some excellent teachers, either rewarded for their good teaching or seeking additional rewards, usually of money or status, go into administration with miserable results

---

[4] These are an abstract of the requirements for the provisional high school principal's certificate in the state of Ohio, as of January 1, 1963.

both for themselves and for the schools they serve. Whatever the long-range implications of these factors may be, the current picture is that secondary school administrators pass first through the teaching ranks. For the professional rapport vital to the success of administration, as well as for some other reasons, it is probably well that this route exists.

Every teaching position has its administrative aspects. There is constant planning, delegating, coordinating, and appraising activity. With these component aspects of teaching, there is ample effort for the teacher to assess his own skills and satisfaction pattern in reference to these processes. If teaching brings satisfaction because it is a one-man effort, primarily, then this should be a clue that an administrative future would likely not be advisable. If, however, considerable satisfaction exists in having set the stage so that others can see relationships, comprehend problems, work individually and cooperatively toward their solution, then the evidence augurs well.

Further signs for the individual teacher to note are the following: Am I comfortable in positions of responsibility? Can I make needed decisions with dispatch, when they need to be made that way? Am I inclined to look for best evidence before deciding on a course of action? Do I enjoy working with adults at least as much as I like working with teenage youngsters? Do my interests in education go beyond my own subject-matter fields? Do I have a tolerance for frustration and ambiguity? Answers to these questions are vital to an individual considering a future in secondary school administration.

Given favorable responses to these and like questions, there is much that a teacher can do to gain administrative experience. Dozens of tasks that need leadership exist in every secondary school. Classes need advisors, dances need chaperones, extracurricular activities need guidance and coordination, committees need volunteer members and often volunteer chairmen, to mention but a few. The energetic teacher, interested in testing his administrative potential, often finds ample opportunity to do so by expressing interest in one or more of these activities to the principal. Many find opportunities in out-of-school functions as well, in church work, in service club activities, in civic ventures. Initiative and energy can supply the opportunities; a personal satisfaction pattern can supply the evidence.

Planned graduate program

When the first stirrings of interest occur, it is well to get a planned graduate program underway. The resourceful teacher will find ways to do this. Most universities offer work in the evenings and on Saturdays. Car pools reduce the expense of otherwise costly long trips if the university is some distance from the site of teaching. Some scholarship and assistantship money exists for the qualified individual who is assertive enough to pursue the trail.

Each beginning graduate student should start his program under the guidance of an advisor. This puts the program on a purposeful track from the outset. For the young teacher who will spend some years in the teaching field before venturing into administration, a master's degree in his teaching area often is most advisable. Elective hours, however, can be used to take introductory courses in administration. If enough electives exist, it is often possible to fulfill the certification requirements for administration and thus be ready for an opportunity when it ultimately arrives.

During the graduate program it is also advisable to revise credentials and to become acquainted with the placement officer. It is especially important to do this before leaving graduate school if one aspires to an administrative position. Thus, a personal touch is added to the otherwise rather cold set of data on a personnel record form.

Internal and external promotion routes

Often those who aspire to positions as secondary school administrators need to face the question of the most promising routes. Some relevant generalizations about the internal-external possibilities will, perhaps, aid those who have this problem.

Although there is no inflexible pattern, large city systems tend to select from within for all but their top-level administrative staff. This may be an unstructured process, but in many cases cadetship programs or other formal selection processes exist for this purpose. Because of the anticipated growth of this now relatively frequent practice, the administrative cadetship program is discussed in the following section. Medium-sized and smaller cities, as well as most smaller local school districts, usually go outside the system to select their secondary school administrators.

At first glance, it might appear that the advantages of internal promotion far outweigh the disadvantages. This is not necessarily true. In many cases a person must teach in a system for three to five years before he becomes eligible for serious consideration as a secondary school administrator. For the person who is young in the profession, this is no serious deterrent. For the older applicant, however, this route means a late start. Often, too, promotional routes are somewhat standardized in the larger systems. The first opportunity might be as assistant principal of one of the smaller junior high schools. Then, after a successful performance in this position, the next step would depend on what opportunities developed in the system. It might be a more responsible assistant principalship, at either the junior or senior high level, or it could be the principalship of a smaller junior high. Frequently it takes years for these opportunities to develop, because high mobility rates are not characteristic of secondary school administrators in city systems. However, there are some factors on the credit side as well. With the opportunity to begin as an assistant principal, administrative responsibility can be assumed gradually. Larger systems, too, are more apt to have written policies and procedures, which can act as guidelines. There are the obvious advantages of serving in a community that has become familiar through previous teaching experience. In itself, coming "up through the ranks" has advantages or disadvantages that are largely dependent on the person himself, in the final analysis. In a large city system, particularly where a well-established cadetship program exists, personal jealousies of unsuccessful applicants are rarely a problem. In the absence of a formal selection process, and where limited administrative positions in secondary schools exist, this factor can often exist. Serving as an administrator in a building in which one has formerly taught can have its hampering effects, but this is primarily a function of the individual's own adaptive mechanisms and other personal abilities. In many cases, if the environment is right, this kind of experience can be most rewarding and productive.

External promotion will likely continue to be the most prevalent route to secondary school administration, often because of the real or imagined harmful effects of inbreeding. Experience often enables an administrator to bring a fresh viewpoint to a school unhampered by resident biases and custom. Whereas there are unique problems in each secondary school, knowledge about which is needed to do a successful job of administration, there are also many problems that are reasonably uniform from school to school. These are the component task areas in scheduling, reporting, attendance, finance, and the like. Having competence in the performance of these jobs will permit the new administrator to devote his time to building an acquaintance with the unique aspects of the position.

To tap the potential of external promotion possibilities, the applicant should have several things in readiness. Perhaps the most important of these dimensions is a state-of-mind. There must be a willingness to move and to undergo what for many are very unpleasant tasks. Homes often must be sold, there is separation from friends, and certain responsibilities have to be adjusted. A disposition to change and a readiness to accept the challenge of the unknown must be part of the personality structure of the administrator who would keep mindful of his professional opportunities. Certification, where needed, should be accomplished and personnel folders completed in placement offices. And, of utmost importance, the candidate should be able to communicate well about himself and about the problems in secondary school administration that he is likely to be asked in an interviewing situation. It also is important to be able to state a value position in reference to problems without undue hesitation and equivocation.

The administrative cadetship

In the years following the end of World War II, the tremendous expansion of enrollments and building led to several new developments. Among them was the rapid growth of the administrative cadetship program. Largely designed to man the administrative positions anticipated in hundreds of planned elementary schools, the cadetship program offered to the city systems numerous other advantages as well. During interim periods, while new construction was underway or anticipated, those on cadetship programs were able to perform many specialized jobs at the central administrative level as well as to serve as a reinforcement pool for current administrators in times of illness or other special need. The program, too, grew because of an increasing realization of the vital importance of making the best possible administrative selections. A year, sometimes more or less, of guided experiences under the direction of skilled administrators provided a wealth of data about the cadet's potential for an administrative assignment.

Briefly, what are the components of the cadetship program? Most of the plans have a selection phase, the criteria for which are usually under constant revision. In most instances applicants must have from one to five years of successful classroom teaching experience in the system. Holding an administrative certificate or being in the process of securing one is likewise a criterion in most of these plans. In some instances the applicant must possess a master's degree. Age is a more flexible criterion, but the candidate must usually be from twenty-five to forty-five years of age.

Most cities with a cadetship plan have a fixed time limit by which external criteria must be met and applications presented for processing.

In larger districts, this deadline is an annual event. In places where the need is less constant, deadlines are established and announced when the program periodically is resumed. In many systems, after applications have been screened, a competitive examination is announced. Not all cities have this feature, but it is reasonably common. Sometimes the examination is developed by the employing system; in other cases consultants from outside the system are secured to conduct this phase of the process. In the latter instance, the consultants have developed their own examination batteries.[5] After this phase, successful applicants are then interviewed in an administrative conference. Sometimes the interview is conducted by the superintendent, but it is more likely by the assistant superintendent of staff personnel or general administration and by others on the administrative selection committee named for this purpose.

Those who come through this process successfully are released from their teaching assignments and they begin, in most cases, a year's planned program of orientation and service. Often they receive the same remuneration that they would receive as a teacher. Cadets frequently spend several weeks in central office operations, becoming familiar with the over-all operation of the systems. In many instances, they work under the direction of an assistant superintendent on such specialized jobs as collecting data for the establishment of attendance district boundaries, purchasing supplies, and other tasks of this nature. The next phase of the program is often assignment to a principal or assistant principal in the system. There the cadet gets an opportunity to work in the kind of school in which he is likely to be an administrator. Usually, once a week at least, the cadets assemble in the central office to discuss their progress with the administrator in charge of the program. One modification of this practice was that used in Columbus, Ohio. For a period of six months, in addition to the weekly conference in the central office, cadets from the area met in a two-hour seminar each week with one of the authors. In those sessions some of the broad aspects of administration were discussed and the personal dimensions of leadership analyzed. This seminar seemed to provide balance between the broad and specific aspects of the program.

A note of caution is in order concerning cadetship programs. A system can easily find that it has developed a mass production operation.

---

[5] W. R. Flesher and Marie Flesher have been active in this consultative process. For additional information, see their report, A Procedure for Evaluating Prospective School Administrators, Supervisors, and Other Special Personnel (Columbus, Ohio: Bureau of Educational Research and Service, The Ohio State University, 1959), mimeographed.

The real value of the cadetship program does not lie in turning out "replaceable parts"; rather, the experience should sharpen the leadership sensitivities of an already able group of potential administrators. A constant appraisal of the cadetship program by the sponsoring system will enable it to stay alive and fulfill its function.

Administrative internship

Although the idea is not new, there has recently been a reawakened interest in administrative internship. Internship provides a significant field-laboratory experience for the administrative aspirant. Such administrative organizations as the American Association of School Administrators and the National Association of Secondary School Principals have funded a certain number of these internships, to be tried on an experimental basis. Most internships have been established cooperatively between school districts and universities.

In general, the plan works as follows. Applicants of particular promise who currently are pursuing master's, specialist's, or doctoral programs in educational administration are screened in terms of their areas of specialization, their need for certain kinds of administrative experience, and their availability to spend time, usually one year, in an internship. The participating school district makes the final selection and employs the intern to perform specific administrative responsibilities. A compact is usually developed by the intern, the cooperating school district, and the intern's university adviser. During the course of the year there is frequent interaction between administrators of the school district, the intern, and his adviser. The intern usually gets, in addition to his salary or stipend, university credit toward his degree.

Until very recently the internship has been used almost exclusively at the superintendency or central office staff levels. It now is appearing in secondary schools, which we regard as a significant development. In essence, this places field administrators and university professors of educational administration in a working partner relationship. Each shares the responsibility of preparing future administrators in an environment which provides the best possible data about the aspirant's administrative potential. There are other practical ramifications of this preparation device. School districts may be experiencing some unique, short-term situations where additional administrative assistance is vitally needed. A new building may be under construction, which demands considerable amounts of administrative time, or large-scale curriculum development may be underway. Further, a school district may wish to test the feasibility of establishing a new, permanent administrative position. Whatever the situation may be, the internship device is proving to be very helpful in meeting the need. From the intern's point of view, the opportunity to be field-tested is of inestimable value. It provides evidence to him, under conditions of actual responsibility, how it "feels" to be an administrator, how he can apply that which he has learned about administration in an academic setting, and how he performs, as seen by his administrative colleagues in the field and by his university adviser.

So promising is this trend that some national and state associations of administrators are advocating that the internship year be counted as a year of experience toward fulfilling certification requirements. Because of the increased willingness of school districts to invest time and money in the internship, we feel that this will soon become an integral part of the preparation program for educational administrators.

OPPORTUNITIES FOR CONTINUED PROFESSIONAL GROWTH

So far, the material presented in this chapter has a preparatory ring to it. The externals involved in preparing for a career as a secondary school administrator have been emphasized. These aspects are vital. Important as it is to the aspirant to get an initial opportunity to become a secondary school administrator, it is however of infinitely more importance to the profession and to the administrator himself that he have opportunities for continued growth once he becomes an incumbent of that role. The teaching staff or the secondary school itself can be dynamic, in the main, only if the administrator is alert, perceptive, and mindful of his own professional growth. Let us review some of the opportunities for this kind of continued development.

Building autonomy

An accompaniment of the larger school district has been an increased realization of the diversity of the community it serves. Decentralization has been one organizational approach used in the attempt to enable the individual school to serve the needs of its attendance district better. Even districts of phenomenal size and complexity, such as Chicago, have found building autonomy valuable. Decentralization heightens the responsibility of the individual school. Often this means unique curriculum developments, special services, policies and operating procedures, all tooled especially for resident needs.

The principal is involved much more directly in staff selection, orientation, induction, and other professional development programs, because his school requires specialized personnel with unique competencies. He is called upon to be the district's interpreter of the characteristics and needs of the secondary school community. This kind of leadership often demands that he be a student of curriculum. Certainly, it requires that he understand sociological and economic phenomena. To operate in this fashion requires continued study and constant professional growth.

Growth through associational affiliation

Unfortunately, often the hardest work a secondary school administrator does of an associational nature is the annual drive to obtain 100 per cent staff affiliation. It is obvious that this effort alone does little to add to professional knowledge and skills. Regional and state organizations and the national organization, the National Association of Secondary School Principals, represent a rich resource for the alert administrator. At the national level, the available professional literature can keep the administrator abreast of the problems common to secondary school administrators at large and alert to challenging experiments that are reported by his colleagues. The national organization, too, offers the best single source for professional upgrading through policy development, refinement of ethical positions, and stimulation of research effort. In state associations of secondary school principals machinery is available for preparation data needed in legislative development, for cooperative activities with state departments of education, and for program development of annual conventions.

Although many will find profitable outlets for their energies at the national and state levels, it is in the regional association that the greatest numbers of secondary school administrators find opportunities for professional growth. The regional association can be particularly sensitive to the needs of its members. Meeting once each month or six weeks with those colleagues he knows well, the secondary school administrator can do a great deal personally to push these meetings beyond a social plane. In fact, many regional principals' associations already have a long and distinguished record of professional service. Many of them have initiated discussion group projects, focusing on those topics of very practical concern to the members. Study groups have gathered data for consideration at the meetings, and consultants have frequently been invited to bring their special competencies to the programs. Recent promising developments have been the structuring of these meetings as inservice workshops, at which perceptive looks have been taken, over time, at the human relations aspects of leadership.

Too often administrators confine their activities in various professional associations to a narrow base. Much is to be gained by broadening into related fields. It is very desirable for the secondary school administrator to affiliate with and work actively in such organizations as the Association for Supervision and Curriculum Development. To perform his responsibilities in curriculum leadership, the secondary school administrator must know, by involvement, what new understandings and skills are being developed by such associations.

This has taken on added significance with the development and phenomenal growth of national curriculum movements, especially in the sciences and mathematics. While it is not necessary for the secondary school administrator to know about these programs in depth, it is important for him to have broad understandings of them. Knowing this much, he is then better equipped to recognize the administrative implications involved, such as needed inservice preparation of staff to teach in the new programs, the relationship between the new content and external testing, and the cost of establishing new programs.

Plan of continuous professional development

Although professional development is a state of mind, it must get beyond this stage and take on structural aspects. The difference between the successful and unsuccessful administrator, often, is that the successful one has a somewhat systematic plan for his professional growth. Such plans usually have both internal and external phases to them.

The internal aspect refers to those activities he undertakes day-by-day on the job. They are based on his own keen interest in personal growth. A staff, once it works with an administrator for even a short period of time, knows whether he is interested in self-improvement. Through mutual respect and demonstrated warmth of personality, a rapport can be established that permits two-way evaluation. In an atmosphere of goodwill, a staff whose members have learned to trust one another can give and take. It is a false concept of status to consider oneself to be beyond the pale of evaluation. Where those right relationships have been established, many secondary school administrators ask the staff at intervals to check them on such items as, "Do I seem to appear too busy, and thus 'scare off' your wish to discuss a matter with me?" "Are activities planned sufficiently well in advance to permit the scheduling of your own affairs?" "Are communications from my office clear?" "Am I sufficiently alert to those things that will facilitate your teaching?" When such administrative appraisal is welcomed and constructive suggestions acted upon, doors are opened for a much more meaningful evaluation of teaching.

Other aspects of the secondary school principal's work are best appraised by his own administrative superiors, although such appraisal often comes only if the administrator seeks it. Appraisal is often facilitated if the administrator prepares a list of areas about which he is particularly concerned and with which he wants professional help. This list serves a double purpose. It lends structure to the appraisal conference with the superintendent or assistant superintendent, and it illustrates that more is wanted and needed than a reassuring pat on the back.

Often this appraisal can best be made if it is done along lines of previous goal-setting. As an administrator looks ahead to the next year's operation, certain things can be pegged for accomplishment. Benchmarks can be made to indicate progress along these lines, then, during the year. This type of planning greatly facilitates self-assessment.

There are external phases of a professional development plan, too. Preparation for a position in secondary school administration certainly does not terminate with the acquisition of certification or a master's degree. Following the leadership of the American Association of School Administrators, which in 1959 passed a constitutional amendment requiring those who apply for membership after 1964 to have completed two years of graduate study, principals' associations are beginning to move in the same direction. This is recognition that the complexity of administration will likely continue to increase and that advanced graduate study can equip those with a commitment for professional growth to perform better their administrative functions.

A desirable pattern, perhaps, for those who wish to develop a plan for personal growth is to undertake a master's program relatively early in their professional careers. This program should be broad-based, with the primary focus on the individual's teaching field if he has not yet entered administration. Elective hours might be used to pick up requirements for administrative certification. Shortly after becoming a secondary school administrator, then, it would be well to resume graduate study, this time taking depth courses in such administrative specialties as school law, finance, and business management. Reflecting the increasing demand for advanced graduate study, some universities have developed two-year programs in educational administration. In addition to depth courses, a promising development of these programs is a year's seminar in which the coordinated aspects of administration are analyzed in problem settings.

In increasing numbers, however, secondary school administrators are serving on ten-and-one-half or eleven months assignments. This, of course, makes extended summer participation in graduate programs very difficult. Study possibilities are not eliminated, however, for many one- and two-week workshops are given at convenient times for the partici- pants. In addition, many colleges and universities are developing one-day workshops throughout the school year. Pegged to a very specific topic of considerable interest, these experiences are a valuable way to do the forefront thinking demanded in a dynamic profession.

Opportunities in civic involvements

Quite characteristically, school-related activities with the parents of secondary school youngsters tend to cluster around specific rather than broad educational activities. The parent-teacher relationships that typify the elementary schools seem to wane. Frequently, the coaches come in contact with the parents of athletes, or the band director will meet with band parents' organizations. There are not too many occasions, however, when the secondary school administrator meets systematically with groups of parents or other patrons of the community. The resulting dis- tance is often detrimental to the public relations of the secondary schools and deprives the administrator of a source of professional growth.

Perhaps the size factor of many secondary schools has proved to be a deterrent to general meetings of parents and teachers. If this is the case, there are effective ways of working productively other than face-to- face meetings with the entire group. Some secondary schools, for exam- ple, have organized study councils comprising selected, representative parents and nonparents of the community, representatives of the teach- ing staff, and the administrator. With this smaller group, then, problems of special concern have been studied, data have been gathered and com- municated to the general public, and recommendations have been ar- rived at for the consideration of the board of education, the teaching staff, and the parents themselves.

Secondary school administrators must use their ingenuity to dis- cover ways of working productively with parents and nonparents in the community. Professional growth is likely to result, because these activi- ties make the administrator a more sensitive interpreter of the com- munity and its needs and a more skillful worker with adult groups.

Whereas the kind of involvement about which we have been writing is important, there are yet other kinds of involvements of particular importance. Civic planning ventures are becoming more and more prevalent. Communities are working together to take a careful look at their own problems and possible ways of solving them. The secondary schools need to be involved in that kind of planning, for clearly evident reasons. Often cooperative arrangements can be developed for use of recreational facilities. Opportunities, too, can be discovered for meaningful learning experiences for secondary school students. Most of all, however, the involvement of the administrator and other members of the staff demonstrate quite clearly that the secondary school personnel are interested in wider community affairs than those immediately concerned with the profession itself. Turning outward, then, is yet another way of continued professional growth.

CONCLUSION

Professional opportunities in secondary school administration exist particularly for the person who, in making a realistic assessment of his potential in this field, develops a positive program of preparation. As a teacher, he seeks assignments that can strengthen his administrative skills. As a graduate student, he plans a program with his adviser that is most meaningful in terms of his professional goals.

For the practicing administrator, opportunities exist for continued professional development by working as sensitively as possible in those areas where he has autonomy, by participating in the activities of his professional associations, by cooperating in civic affairs, and by maintaining sincere, open relationships with those who work with him to develop the type of evaluation that permits ongoing growth.

SUGGESTED ACTIVITIES

1. Consult the latest educational directory published by your state department of education. Check the different kinds of secondary school organizational patterns. How many administrative positions are there in these different classifications?

2. Assume that the secondary school administrators in a city system have been asked to conduct a study of the components that should be considered in developing a new administrative salary schedule. If you were a member of such a committee, what factors would you wish to investigate?

3. What community resources exist in the community where you live that seem particularly promising for secondary school administrators to tap? What kinds of cooperative involvements seem particularly promising?

4. Develop a plan for your own professional growth for the next three years. How did you determine what your strengths and weaknesses are in the process of developing this plan?

SELECTED READINGS

Campbell, Roald F., John E. Corbally, Jr., and John A. Ramseyer, *Introduction to Educational Administration*, Second Edition. Boston: Allyn and Bacon, Inc., 1962.

Chase, Francis S., and Harold A. Anderson, *The High School in a New Era*. Chicago: University of Chicago Press, 1958.

Conant, James B., *The American High School Today*. New York: McGraw-Hill, Inc., 1958.

Culbertson, Jack A., and Stephen P. Hencley (eds.), *Preparing Administrators: New Perspectives*. Columbus, Ohio: University Council for Educational Administration, 1962.

Midwest Administration Center, *Administrator's Notebook*. Chicago: University of Chicago, 1954–55.

National Education Association, *Research Bulletins*.

14

CAREER
CHALLENGES

FOR THE NIMBLE OF MIND, TOMORROW IS EXCITING
and challenging, primarily because today is seldom stultifying and hum-
drum. The student of secondary school administration who is enthusiastic can approach a future in this profession with full knowledge that
its problems will challenge his creative best. Secondary school administration is a career in itself; no longer is it merely a step toward the
superintendency. For those who sense the stimulation of working with
the educational problems of the teenage student, a position in secondary school administration can be a professional home.

CURRENT PROBLEMS

The secondary school administrator whose major satisfaction lies in
looking beyond the next hill for anticipated challenges, often stumbles

over the exciting ground through which he passes day-by-day. Lest the focus narrow solely to the future challenges, let us examine those that confront the profession currently.

Traditional commitments

Every profession, at any given point in time, has its value positions. In a profession, such as education, that is responsible to the people it serves, these value positions are seldom developed by the professionals alone. Rather, they represent the admixture of thinking that occurs over time in a society. In a society characterized by idealism and broad principles, the job of interpretation, implementation, evaluation, and continued growth is often a most difficult one. If the principle is a good one, it usually survives the vicissitudes of the years. To survive, though, it must be reworked and revitalized. This is particularly true when the principle seems to be in conflict with others likewise prized by the culture. Let us examine one or two of these values for their relevance to the current challenge confronting secondary school administrators.

To educate all of the children of all of the people is a prized value in our society, and universal compulsory attendance laws have been passed to provide concrete evidence of its acceptance. As long as this principle was an ideal on the banner of those who marched against vested privilege, it gained reasonably steady momentum. Now that we are close to realizing the ideal, we are recognizing, with increasing clarity, the impact of its implications. As has been the case with many of our freedoms, hard won, not all choose to accept the opportunity with its concomitant responsibilities. Society-at-large pays the price, either directly or indirectly, for each high school drop-out. The expansion of technical education at the secondary school level, seen by many as one effective deterrent to the drop-out problem, is a very costly venture. Combating the ravages of cultural deprivation, when the affected student is at the secondary level, requires the deployment of critically short resources. Thus, it costs vast amounts of money to realize the goal of universal secondary education, just as we have found that it is extremely expensive to fall short of it.

Those both inside and outside the profession recognize that we are on the horns of a dilemma with this problem. There are those who would take the position that a secondary school education is an opportunity which rightly belongs to those who are willing to exert sufficient energy to make it a profitable experience, and that the dullards, the maladjusted, the rebels, and the lazy, not willing or able to do so, should fall by the wayside. In the past most of them could fall into the reservoir of unskilled labor and be profitably employed. No longer is this the case, however, and the secondary schools are increasingly called upon to meet the challenge of this new turn of events. Their administrators must come up with creative, practical solutions.

That education is primarily a matter of local concern is another principle long valued in our society. Pressures from the national and state levels have been resisted with vigor. In many school districts the major source of funds is still the local tax dollar. Local boards of education, in countless ways, affect markedly the quality of education. There are, however, two developments that will affect this situation. The local property tax is working overtime in many communities, and administrators must spend increasing amounts of time in efforts to raise money from local sources for buildings and programs. Often, however, because of limited local resources, this maximum effort is not enough. The state, then, exercises its prerogative, a right not understood by many. Local control of education is delegated by the state; therefore, this power can be modified, increased, or withdrawn at its discretion. When this occurs, there is often upheaval.

Many administrators of secondary schools, particularly those who serve in small rural areas, must cope with the issues brought into play when pressures from the state for improvement run counter to the wishes of people in their localities. When this happens, on what grounds can stands be taken? Perceptive administrators will need sensitivity to understand and interpret the issues involved, since there is no magic size, financial, or communication formula guaranteed to work in any given situation.

Increasingly, the schools have become the battleground for those vitally interested in social change. Many secondary schools have experienced the dramatic impact of religious and integration problems. Following historic decisions of the Supreme Court, implementation issues have been fought, sometimes literally so, within these schools. In the absence of effective enforcement agencies, or where the Supreme Court decision ran counter to then-existing community beliefs, it has often been difficult for these schools to hew to the law of the land. In more difficult cases, ambiguities about enforcement, or about implications of these decisions, have beclouded the issues further. Caught in such a web, many administrators feel that they have been placed in untenable positions. Not to act, though, has been impossible.

Many more issues of this nature are with us today, and others are sure to come. To the administrator for whom problems are challenges, these will not be burrs in the saddle. Instead, they will be spurs to his imagination as he works resourcefully to provide optimum learning environments for secondary school youngsters.

Traditional organizational plans

Eight-four and 6-3-3 organizational plans are no longer the only alternatives. New plans, conceived in the exigencies of mounting and shifting school populations, have added to our understanding that organization is a servant of man and not his master. For instance, one school system housed first graders in a senior high school while a new elementary building was being constructed. The experiment worked so well that the high school principal was reluctant to see them leave at the end of the year.

Perceptive looks are being taken at the maturational patterns of children. There are those who feel that today's fourth and fifth graders are almost as mature, physically, socially, and emotionally, as yesterday's seventh graders. An accompanying factor is the tendency to teach subject matter, *per se*, at earlier grade levels than we have for the past twenty to thirty years. These circumstances, coupled with the necessity to get maximum utilization from existing buildings, have accounted for the development of organizational patterns which differ from those traditionally employed. Common among these have been K–3, 4–8, 9–12 and K–4, 5–8, 9–12. In a sense, this reactivates a modification of the middle school concept.

Imaginative plans will be needed, then, for many years to come, to organize existing and new facilities for increasing numbers of youngsters for whom mobility is a standard way of life. As a member of the administrative team, the secondary school principal will be called upon to make careful forecasts of needs in terms of personnel, space, and teaching materials. His thinking will make a contribution to the understanding of organizational flexibility.

Grouping for effective learning. Heterogeneity and homogeneity are again at the door of most secondary schools. Undue delay in making decisions, while a value position is being considered, is ludicrous and unwise. Here, questions seem best to be answered in terms of needs and other characteristics of the student body involved, the community in which the school is located, the society's present and future needs, the staff involved, and numbers of other factors. A knowledge of clear objectives, a consciousness of the values of research, and a willingness to try new approaches are needed. To refuse homogeneity because it is undemocratic represents a naive concept of democracy. To discard heterogeneity because it is an inefficient way to induce learning is pedagogical dogma. As with so many things, leadership by the secondary school administrator continues to be needed to find out what is the best method of learning.

Departmentalization

Since 1959, when the first edition of this book was written, we sense a further shift on the departmentalization question. At that time we indicated a swing away from the practice. Now it appears that the values of departmentalization are being reexamined. Several reasons probably account for this, but the central one, we believe, is the dramatic development of national curriculum movements. To keep abreast of them requires a knowledgeable specialist in the field, who has time to devote to the task. Further, it takes someone in an administrative or quasi-administrative position who can give leadership to the necessary implementation, such as continuing, inservice preparation of the staff.

Expanding enrollments

When the onrush is seen from afar, a sandbagging operation sometimes is appropriate, and it sometimes works. In education, though, the problem is to capture the potential. New sluiceways, expanded areas, and additional ways to harness the power are needed. Orientation and articulation activities are needed as never before, to facilitate the flow of productive learning. Knowing that new experiences call forth mistakes, fears, and inefficiency, secondary school administrators must have in readiness those programs that best will absorb the waves of elementary youngsters during the coming years. If this were solely a numerical problem it would be difficult enough to solve. In the majority of cases, however, these youngsters will be coming from self-contained classrooms to departmentalized ones, and this will add one more variable to the problem.

Optimum use of facilities. With increased enrollments, the administrator is called upon to make the best use of physical facilities. In some districts there will be double sessions, lengthened school days, and perhaps more use of the four-quarter system. These may be necessary, and conceivably may represent organizational flexibility with real educational values accruing. If they must be tried, they should be tried open-mindedly, experimentally. Schools often have not been in a competitive position in the past, and they perhaps have not been called upon to develop creative approaches. For years to come, however, the schools will be competing with other agencies for funds. Increased services, more efficient use of facilities, imaginative skills in communication, all can put education in a better competitive position.

Expansion, mobility, and the demand for better education will lead to continued school district reorganization, with hundreds of new secondary schools. In many of these districts the secondary school will be in a tactical position to exert a cohesive influence. If it is true that the high school is often a community image, the place in which new aspirations can be hammered out and articulated, the secondary school administrator is in an excellent position to exert real leadership. The need for establishing the reorganized school requires evidence, for there are often those in the community who do not accept the necessity for reorganization. Too, the administrator needs to demonstrate his own personal contribution, for before reorganization many smaller schools do not have a full-time administrator, and having one may be regarded as waste.

Mobility. Yet another challenge is found in the mobility factor itself. Traditionally, families that moved did so in the summertime. Now, and in the foreseeable future, this process will occur constantly. The problems of mobility cannot be solved by the individual school. Through professional organizations and state departments of education, uniformities that will facilitate the meaningful reporting of pupil data as the student moves from district to district can be developed. Guidance services can be strengthened at the local level to expedite the adjustment of these students and a diagnosis of their unique learning problems. There is an increasing amount of research concerning the problems produced by transient or migratory youngsters in the schools. This should be studied with care by the secondary school administrator and those teachers especially affected by the problem. Schools where mobility is a considerable factor should participate in the research program and report findings to the profession. The alert administrator can profit, too, by watching to see if the mobility takes any predictable course. In several cases, for instance, principals have found that a high percentage of incoming students migrated from one particular out-of-state locality. In one instance, school personnel visited that locality, talked with local school people, and worked out some agreements that eased problems considerably.

The curriculum

The history of secondary education reveals that the curriculum has been a long-standing battleground. Critics view the secondary school product in terms of their values, and he is judged good, bad, or indifferent accordingly. At the present time, the secondary schools are under watchful scrutiny. This is a healthy state of affairs, for evaluation is vital to the life of any organization. The secondary school administrator can work most productively in this period of stress on the curriculum by keeping a sense of calmness, as well as a sense of humor, in raising such questions as "What is the issue?" "What are our objectives?" "What is the evidence?" and by anticipating the problems.

At present there is considerable concern about the able student in the secondary school. Is he being challenged sufficiently? Are his talents being channeled in the right directions? There is spirited competition for the academically talented that places a value question squarely in the laps of the secondary schools. None but the naive imagines that the school only nurtures, not creates, interest in vocations. Just how actively the secondary schools are to serve as an agent of society in this respect has not been determined as yet, however. Little imagination is required to envision the possibility of so gearing our educational program that "needed" interest could be stimulated. The line between preparing the student for a vocation and allowing for a reasonable area of free choice often is a very thin one. This is a value question of considerable importance. Here, too, the secondary school administrator finds a challenge in working with the community, the staff, and the student on the issue.

Another curriculum issue is the role of general and specialized education in the secondary school. With the increasing cost and complexity of specialized education, many are suggesting that the schools concentrate on presenting general educational offerings. Technological change occurs so rapidly, these people argue, that the schools can never hope to stay abreast of it. Specialized training can, therefore, be taught most profitably by business and industry. This, then, would free the schools to concentrate on the development of core learnings. This question has fascinating ramifications and is of sufficient importance to stimulate the resourceful secondary school administrator for many years to come.

A modification of the concept of the comprehensive secondary school is the resurgence of the technical or vocational high school. These have been springing into existence within the past few years, established primarily on a regional basis where they serve students from several school districts. Often suburban districts, whose secondary schools long have been considered college preparatory in function, are showing interest in the cooperative development of these regional technical schools. These districts are sensing a shift in their student population, but it usually is not appreciable enough to justify the development of broad technical offerings in each of their secondary schools.

Sobering illustrations have been provided, within the past few years, by the rapid development and spread of national curriculum movements in science and mathematics. We have seen how resources, largely knowledgeable people and money, marshalled on a national scale, have produced a dramatic effect on subjects long traditionally taught. What has happened in science and mathematics is occurring in foreign languages, the social studies, and English. Subject matter, teaching methodology, and the accoutrements of teaching are all being substantially affected. The secondary school which ignores these developments finds that the price is high. Its students often do poorly in those external tests which reflect the new content, and frequently they experience difficulty when they confront college courses which presuppose familiarity with the material.

The curriculum, then, long the undisturbed giant of the secondary schools, is posing challenges to all who work with these schools and particularly so to its administrators who are charged with leadership responsibilities.

CONDITIONS ENHANCING CAREER CHOICE

There are strong reasons for the secondary school administrator to consider his position as a career choice. Let us consider some of the conditions that create this situation.

New role on the administrative team

The administration of larger school districts is infinitely more complex than it has previously been. The days are gone when administration was essentially a one-man job, the province of the superintendent. The teaching-principal, particularly at the secondary school level, is a vanishing phenomenon. The position of the principal has become a full-time position demanding leadership vital to the over-all operation of the

school district. Increasingly, secondary school principals are called upon
to play a key role in forecasting and developing budgets, in making and
administering policy, in assisting in the selection and orientation of new
personnel, and in exerting forceful leadership in the continuous development of curriculum. These roles, in addition to the ones traditionally
associated with the position, demand leadership from those who see a
career in the position.

Administrative councils are a growing phenomenon, and many
superintendents have been heard to remark that the secondary school
principal is a key man in the operation, for he can make or break the
school's reputation. In that council operation, then, the principal must
be the district's specialist in the problems of secondary school education,
at least on a broad base.

The secondary school in a larger setting

When school districts are reorganized, a wider, more changing community usually is represented by the school. In many of these communities growth is taking place at a phenomenal rate. Secondary schools that
served well the smaller, stabler community, if they face the implications
of their growth, now have many new needs. New elements move into
older communities and either bring new problems or new aspirations or
encounter difficulties in adapting to resident values in the community.
The school has an obligation to keep a finger at the pulse of these changing communities if a program is to be offered to facilitate cohesion
rather than disintegration. Secondary school administrators must provide impetus to the inquiry necessary to stay abreast of sociological
change.

Increased professional criteria

There is stimulation and challenge in belonging to a profession which
offers a long-term career opportunity and one which expects its members
to participate in growth activities. Both external and internal motivation
are necessary to most of us, if this growth is to be a continuous process.
Largely through the leadership of our professional associations, the
criteria for entering and continuing to practice the profession of secondary school administration are constantly being revised upward. Work
beyond the master's degree is now relatively common. The administra-

tive specialist's program, representing a planned year of graduate activity beyond the master's degree, is now offered on a national scale and is attracting increased numbers of secondary school administrators. In many states, certification requirements have been reworked and are now more stringent. Universities which offer graduate programs in educational administration increasingly are spending more and more time in screening activities. Thus those who enter and stay in the profession of secondary school administration are cognizant of their responsibility to continue learning.

Salary pattern

Increased leadership expectations have led to increased salaries for secondary school administrators. One of the most important reasons for this is a realization of the increased responsibility of the position. In addition, the position is increasingly established on a ten-and-one-half, eleven, or eleven-and-one-half months' basis. These are hopeful signs. The secondary school administrator must continue to be his own best emissary in the drive for increased professionalization of administrative salaries. This will happen as he resourcefully and diligently provides evidence of his personal contribution, as one who by his leadership evokes the best efforts possible from those with whom he has the responsibility to work.

New challenges in articulation

For some time to come, the secondary school will continue to represent society's last opportunity to provide formal educational opportunities for the majority of its young people. Articulation represents a still virtually new tool whose power we do not fully comprehend. Superficially, the word has been used as a synonym for orientation. There is something deeper in articulation, however, than orientation devices, although these are important. Articulation is concerned with the promotion of understanding about the objectives of an education to the level that it leads to a personal commitment to make the most of educational opportunities. This is idealistic, yet it exists in the consciousness of many, many secondary school students. Understanding of this phenomenon must be increased. Herein, too, there is challenge for the secondary school administrator—to help create an atmosphere in which maximum growth can take place for maximum numbers of youngsters.

NEW SKILLS NEEDED

Increased autonomy is frequently bewildering. The administration of a secondary school where policy essentially is established at a higher level requires skill, to be sure; to administer a school and to have at the same time major responsibilities in policy development, the recommendation of personnel for employment, and development and evaluation of the curriculum, demands top-flight leadership. The latter are but some of the implications of autonomy, and they are worthy of some sober reflection. With the increasing size and complexity of school districts, component schools in the districts will have both broad common purposes and unique specific ones if they are to serve well the needs of diverse attendance units. Principals in these schools will require sociological skills to uncover and understand these needs and to translate them into program. With the secondary school representing the largest of the attendance units in most of these districts, the challenge to its administrator does not need to be belabored.

Larger specialized staffs

As secondary schools continue to grow in size and complexity, the growth will be reflected in increased staff specialization. Whereas in many schools the administrator will continue to function as a generalist, a significant challenge in and of itself, in many other schools additional administrative staff, guidance personnel, remedial reading and other types of specialists will be added. These additional staff members will lengthen the service arm of the school. They can best accomplish their purposes if the way has been paved, organizationally, prior to the establishment of the new function, and if effective coordination follows. Many a principal has been delighted at the prospect of acquiring a specialist, only to find out that "something has gone wrong." Most frequently what has gone wrong is that inadequate preparation was made for the new service, its function was not clearly understood, and staff confusion and suspicion led to decreased effectiveness, rather than to the anticipated increased effectiveness. Increased organizational skills, therefore, will be needed by tomorrow's administrators. Lines of communication need to be clear; time needs to be found for coordinating, reporting, and evaluating sessions; purposes need to be clearly understood, and delegation needs to be sharply defined if optimum working relationships are to exist.

Skills of perspective

Unparalleled technological developments and swift-moving social and political currents make for the kinds of uncertainties that cause otherwise able people to look for quick solutions in their quests for some security. At such times, pressures mount for school curriculum panaceas. Transfer of training regains its respectability. Often there is a desire to re-establish the type of school that existed when life was more serene and stable, implying a direct cause-and-effect relationship, or there is an urging to forge ahead into the technological horizons and to reflect in the curriculum that which best will prepare students to meet current demands. At such times stable heads are required to bring into sharp focus what the role of the school should be in the social order. Here, too, is a challenge of considerable magnitude for secondary school administrators in the upcoming years.

Leadership in staff development programs

There is increased realization that educators grow in competence throughout their entire careers. This has taken a more systematic turn, recently, in the growth of staff development programs. There are at least two components of these programs. The first of these manifests itself in inservice activities that are designed to add to the professional understandings needed for increased competence in the field. Thus, there is challenge in selecting the right topics at the right time to be studied in the right ways. Research findings make it virtually axiomatic that staff members must see purpose in what they are doing in inservice activities for their involvement to be more than token involvement. Secondly, a staff development program should promote self-evaluation, an analysis of one's own effectiveness in the teaching-learning process. The desire to achieve professional competence is a strong one; but external evaluation, if superficial or mismanaged, can step on psychological toes and result in lowered morale and decreased effectiveness, thus defeating its own purposes. To give leadership to a staff development program calls forth the best skills the secondary school administrator can marshal. That leadership requires a clear understanding of the objectives of the secondary schools and of the structural requirements necessary to promote their fulfillment. In addition, excellent human relations skills are needed by the administrator, for the objectives can be reached only through the work of people, who, in education, will exert most of their effort as individuals.

Better communication

In any public office, the role incumbent does not have complete autonomy in defining what his job should be and how he should discharge his responsibilities. The secondary school administrator, for example, has those within the organization who hold different views about what the role of the principal should be. There are also many divergent opinions in the community about his role. In addition, he has his own ideas on the subject. It would appear that this could result in an untenable state of affairs and, indeed, it sometimes does. Although the administrator is often called upon to be many things to many people, the impossibility of keeping everybody happy when there are mutually exclusive demands is obvious. Also, keeping everybody happy, in this sense, is not synonymous with good leadership. When diverse expectations exist about the purposes of the school, the roles of teachers and students, and the way in which he should act as an administrator, the secondary school principal can find that good skill in communications is often his best ally. Communications, of course, has many ramifications; and the administrator needs to be a good student and practitioner of each of them. It is particularly important to be skilled in face-to-face communications, for it is by this means that conflicts are most easily resolved. Open channels of communication exist because of conscious effort, exerted over time, and not by invitation. A principal, for example, might announce in staff meeting that his "door is always open," and yet discover that few ever pass through it to discuss professional or personal concerns. This will happen only if he is approachable, if he demonstrates an ability to discuss problems open-mindedly, and if he sees that something is done about the problem once it is discussed. Thus, tremendous challenge exists in the area of communications for the secondary school administrator.

POST-SECONDARY SCHOOL EDUCATIONAL EXPERIENCES

In hundreds of communities, secondary schools are extending their services beyond the accustomed scope; and each extension contains its challenge for the administrator. The last period of the day is often a signal for preparations to be made for night school or for branch college classes. Graduation in May or June brings an end to one program and marks the beginning of another—the summer school program. Whether or not the secondary school principal serves as the administrator of these programs, they at least require planning and coordinating activities on his part. Since a continued expansion of these programs is likely, a brief analysis of their implications seems appropriate.

Specialized terminal education

Many jobs that exist in our specialized technological society require special preparation, although not preparation of sufficient scope or depth to justify a full college program. For example, many engineers today are required to do things that could be performed better by trained technicians. There is a renewed interest, therefore, in the establishment of terminal educational opportunities, under the control of local boards of education, that represent upward extensions of the regular secondary school program. Since in many cases these require the use of secondary school facilities, the secondary school administrator is called upon for cooperative activity, often at the very important level of helping to assess the need for the program.

University and college offerings

The tidal wave of students born during the post-World War II days is currently passing through our secondary schools and into colleges and universities. Critical shortages in higher education have produced some creative approaches toward solving the resultant problems. One of the most promising of these, we believe, has been the establishment of college and university branches. Representing cooperative development and operation between local school districts and institutions of higher learning, these branches now exist in many secondary schools. They offer freshman and sophomore level courses, largely liberal arts in nature, although some are pre-professional, and are taught by a staff drawn from many sources. Some are university personnel, who move to these new locations and devote full time to branch operation, some commute between the university and the branch site, and others are recruited from local school districts, industries, and professions.

Most of the branches operate during late afternoon and evening hours, which permits students a maximum opportunity to hold full- or part-time employment. This also makes possible the employing of instructors who are otherwise occupied during earlier hours. In most cases, the total cost of attending the branch is about 50 per cent of what it would be if the student followed the more conventional pattern of full-time residence on a college campus. With an opportunity to begin a college education close at hand, many more students than would otherwise be possible are testing their potential for such an education.

There is tremendous potential in further branch development. It seems realistic to speculate that more and more secondary schools will offer at least freshman level college courses and that these will be taught primarily by a staff from the local or surrounding school districts, who will divide their time between secondary school and college teaching. This will bring about better articulation between secondary schools and colleges. It will make available the opportunity of higher education to a larger number of students. It will permit a more efficient use of physical facilities. The personal experience of one of the authors, who recently spent a year in directing such a branch, led to the conclusion that here is a most promising development, whose possibilities we have just begun to tap.

Another promising line of cooperation is the increased amount of workshop activity offered by the college in the local school district, primarily for the professional development of the staff. These activities, of course, require administrative initiative and continued effort if they are to perform the service function for which they are designed.

Other offerings

Although night school offerings in adult education have had a long and respected history, in many communities this program is still in its infancy. Vocational, avocational, and other motivations account for the growth of this movement. Since, again, secondary school facilities and staff, in the main, will be called upon in this program, the administrator will be involved in making policies regarding the use of space and materials, helping to select staff, and many other ways.

Summer schools, too, seem to be on the increase. These enrich the existing program and make additional offerings available to students. They are a much more economical way to cope with the problem of academic failures. Lastly, they offer opportunities to staff members to add to their existing salaries by doing that for which they are best qualified. Again, though, the successful operation of such a program is dependent, in large measure, upon administrative effort. Increased supply and maintenance problems exist. Record-taking and other aspects of scheduling become more complex. Staffing problems must be handled tactfully. Increased service, again, requires the leadership that results when a challenge is sensed.

Untapped potentials

Many school districts use a continuous census to ascertain how many students will appear at certain predictable times. Very few, however, use a continuous census of graduates or drop-outs to facilitate educational planning. There is considerable promise for the growth of this practice, for those who have used it report excellent dividends. It is an additional finger on the pulse of the curriculum, providing clues on needed progress development and insights into how retention rates can be kept as high as possible.

Another promising device is the community survey. Valuable data can be secured from a carefully constructed questionnaire. Several have been developed as a result of interdisciplinary research involving sociologists and educational administrators. An example of these is the Bullock Questionnaire, which yields measures of a community philosophy of education and other such helpful data.[1]

The resourceful administrator, then, who is alert to the research potentials at his doorstep, can do a great deal to make the secondary school he serves reflect, in a very sensitive way, the needs and aspirations of the community.

ASSOCIATION INVOLVEMENT

Because of the many local demands on his time, the secondary school administrator can fall prey to provincialism. To keep the problems of the profession in broad focus, expanded associational involvement can be particularly rewarding.

Regional study groups

Regional principals associations have long existed, and many worthwhile projects have been undertaken by them. Often, however, a normative approach has been taken in reference to common problems and com-

---

[1] Robert P. Bullock, *School-Community Attitude Analysis for Educational Administrators*, School-Community Development Study Monograph Series No. 7 (Columbus, Ohio: The Ohio State University Press, 1959).

mon solutions to them. A more recent and very significant development has been the emphasis of these associations on the problems of leadership. Thus, administrators have confronted the problem of their own professional growth. For example, members of regional study groups have role-played the staff appraisal conference, analyzed their responsibilities in inservice programs, and in many other ways held their own positions up to careful scrutiny. There is considerable promise in these activities for they are the earmarks of a profession involved in upgrading itself.

State and national involvements

Valuable as regional associations may be, when professional advancement on a broader base is considered, state and national efforts are required. Inherent in the obligations a secondary school administrator assumes with his position should be the participation in the activities of his state organization and of the National Association of Secondary School Principals. Not only are the publications of these organizations a link with the problems and issues of his profession; more importantly, membership enables him to take an active part in making policy and in determining lines of development. These state and national organizations have programs of considerable variety. Particularly important are their professional relations, legislative, and research committees. Those who work in these activities come in contact with others who have comparable interests, and the work they stimulate is often of considerable importance.

One example of such cooperative activity is the Ohio Council for the Advancement of Educational Administration. Many organizations and institutions, including the Ohio Association of Secondary School Administrators, are members of this council. By mutual effort, then, and a pooling of resources, research is stimulated. Continued involvement in state and national professional organizations is clearly a most promising way for secondary school administrators to work toward goals vital to professional growth.

Increased contacts with colleges and universities

Colleges, universities, and secondary schools are shareholders of common stock, a serious concern that the able student continue his education. Playing the game of guessing how much is lost because this potential is left untapped leads to staggering, sobering conclusions. It is more profitable, however, to do something about it. Hopeful signs exist that something is now being done, and it is likely that cooperative activity will increase rapidly in the future. In many colleges and universities, for example, secondary school principals and others, such as counselors, are invited to campuses for conferences with former students. Information from these sessions is taken home, discussed with staff members, and put into the program to facilitate articulation between secondary school and college. Vertically organized associations in the subject-matter areas contain members from both secondary school and college staffs. Problems associated with continuous learning in these areas are discussed to the mutual profit of both groups. Advanced placement programs, which permit the capable student, as an individual, to profit from close attention to his unique abilities and needs, have also been developed between secondary schools and colleges.

These are but a few of the ways in which progress has been made with this problem. Much can be done in the future through continued cooperative effort of the secondary schools and institutions of higher learning. For example, the development of a standard transcript form would be of tremendous help to the secondary schools. Joint conferences of college and secondary school counseling staffs would permit a communications link that would benefit the work of both groups. Increased information to secondary schools about the availability of scholarships and about the mechanics involved in applying for them would also be beneficial. These and many more worthwhile projects can be accomplished if secondary school administrators keep alert to the problems of the able student and exert some vigorous leadership to bring needed projects to fruition.

RESEARCH OPPORTUNITIES

Perhaps the most exciting challenge of all awaiting those who choose a career in secondary school administration lies in the vast research possibilities. This is especially so if research is defined broadly as the trying and evaluating of new ways of solving problems. Confronted with issues of real magnitude, it is the applied spirit of inquiry that will enable us to meet them with imaginative solutions.

Those who function as secondary school administrators in the future will not necessarily be skilled researchers, for research is a discipline in itself. A sensitivity to research possibilities, a willingness to experiment, and an understanding of the ways in which research assistance can be secured is a far more realistic goal for which to strive. Experience has indicated that this pattern is desirable in many phases of administration, school law and finance for example.

There are some very practical ways in which research can be undertaken cooperatively. In most state departments of education, colleges, universities, and laboratory schools there are research specialists skilled in design, appraisal, and other methodological aspects of inquiry. One of their major requirements is an action laboratory, however, in which to conduct their work. The schools can be that laboratory, provided lines of cooperation can be established; and quite frankly, those lines can be established only if there is administrative initiative and willingness to experiment. In this way, a team approach to research can be established, with each unit making the kind of contribution that it best can bring to the effort.

The secondary school administrator, for example, after initial arrangements have been made for a cooperative research project, might be required to arrange for necessary space and other facilities needed in the experimentation, to schedule participating personnel so that they are available at certain places at certain times, and to handle many of the other coordinating jobs that arise when people work together. Staff members who have the interest and special abilities required in the research effort need to be selected. In general, the administrator can do much to create a research environment through his own enthusiasm, by encouraging staff members to try new approaches and to report progress to the others in staff meetings and in the professional periodicals. He can supply references and make them available through bulletins, discussions in staff meetings, and the school's professional library. He can assist by helping to procure needed equipment for trying instruction in new ways. He can aid in developing an understanding on the part of the community that better education can result from research effort. This understanding is often vital to build up the kind of effort required for meaningful experimentation.

The research opportunities in the secondary schools are legion for the inquisitive and resourceful. The following are but a few that seem particularly promising.

Group experimentation

Carefully controlled experimentation is needed to determine the effects of grouping for different kinds of learning experiences. There are, of course, many variables that exert their effect on the learning process. For meaningful research on the grouping questions, these variables have to be accounted for by carefully controlled research procedures, or the results obtained in group "experiments" have very limited value. Obviously, if variables are not controlled, we cannot determine what factor or combination of factors cause certain results of the learning experience. Until we know with greater precision what factors help to bring what results, grouping cannot be done with the accuracy demanded of real professional performance. Then, too, as we add to our understandings of the effects of grouping, we add to our knowledge of meaningful criteria to be used as a basis of selection. This will permit far more efficiency in the teaching-learning process.

Organizational studies

We have stated often in this book that organization is a tool to be used flexibly and creatively by the secondary school administrator. Surface factors, however, often seem to bar its frequent use. First, organizational patterns become traditional, and we ascribe values to them, *per se*, which we accept without question and which probably would be very difficult to prove. As an illustration, try to list the values which are inherent in the traditional 6-3-3 organizational plan and then document each of them as best you can. Part of the anticipated difficulty in this exercise can be explained by the lack of research about organization. In fact, it is a difficult area to research, because of the variability involved.

It seems probable that organization, *per se*, is not the crucial dimension it often is thought to be. An organizational plan may facilitate or impede the solution of a problem but only because it establishes a better or worse structure in which the resources which must be utilized can interact. The task of isolating each dimension which plays a part in the solution of a problem and attaching a weight to its importance is an extremely complex one. The difficulties of conducting tightly-constructed research on organization should not close the door on the subject, however, for we often learn more than we now know by meaningful experience.

The meaningful experience might begin as the secondary school administrator asks such questions as the following:

Have we tried anything different recently in regard to the way we organize for learning?

What kinds of learning problems do we have, and might we organize any
  differently to cope with them more successfully?
What can be said for and against the homeroom period, the large study
  hall?
Do we have a systematic way of handling our guidance services?
Are certain courses better adapted to handling large and small groups of
  students in terms of the values we hope to promote, and how do we
  know about this?

Secondary school administrators, as they ponder these and other
organizational problems, need not feel hamstrung by brick-and-mortar
limitations. The schools they administer might be as traditionally constructed as can be imagined, but organizational flexibility exists first as
a state of mind. When the administrator is convinced that some experimentation is worthwhile, he will find ways to try new approaches, no
matter how many physical barriers seem to exist.

Staffing research

How do we know what potential exists in a secondary school staff for
promoting an optimum environment for learning? This seemingly in-
nocent question has a host of implications behind it. Consider the way
in which staff assignment often is made in the secondary school. The
teacher's major and minor fields are noted, and an assignment, in the
larger schools, is made on the basis of whatever vacancies exist. The
teacher often stays where first assigned, frequently for many years. In
smaller schools, the teacher is often asked to serve in from four to six
areas, clustering about two broad headings, such as English and social
studies, but not necessarily so if shortages exist. How often are realign-
ments made on the basis of a reassessment of the new staff picture and
existing curriculum needs? How frequently are teachers approached
about their possible interest in shifting from their major to their minor
fields for a year, for whatever possible stimulation the change might
contain? These questions concern only the classroom teaching aspect of
the problem of potential. There are other questions that can be raised
that pertain to different ramifications of the problem of potential.
Which teachers are particularly capable in course selection guidance?
Who works, or could work, ably with the gifted, the dull normal, the
emotionally unstable child? Who is particularly adept at taking responsibility and evoking solid, critical thinking from others? These, and
similar questions, need to be answered by the secondary school ad-

ministrator if he is to use organizational skills to employ his staff imaginatively and productively.

Staffing research is particularly crucial for our large city school districts where culturally disadvantaged youths by the hundreds of thousands are creating problems of unprecedented magnitude. Conventional programs taught in slum schools by teachers who would prefer to be elsewhere have proved to be an unworkable formula. Imaginatively designed programs, it would seem, need to be developed and taught by staffs of educators who have especially keen perceptions in sociology, economics, and psychology, if the needs of these youths are to be met more meaningfully.

Trial-and-error answers to these questions are not sufficient. Research in staff personnel can provide sound answers if the necessary effort is made.

Value studies

What really are the basic needs of mature, productive, responsible people in our society today? What will they be tomorrow? What is the relationship of those needs to the basic values by which we need to live in a democratic society? What are the ways in which those values best can be inculcated in secondary school youngsters, so that they can see real purpose in acquiring them to enhance their current living and the living they will experience as adults? How can we keep alive the sense of excitement and adventure that characterizes the learning of young children?

The case cannot rest on adult values and deferred satisfactions. Further, youngsters themselves cannot call the learning tune in terms of their current recognized needs. An artfully developed mixture still needs to be found, and considerable research effort will have to be exerted in the search.

Communications studies

Secondary schools, with their increased size and complexity in the future, will have a correspondingly greater communications problem. Certainly the administrator will have far less opportunity than he now has for face-to-face relationships with students, staff members, and citizens in the school community. Lacking these opportunities, how can the channels be kept open, permitting a two-way flow? What are the most effective ways in which the many media can be used? When the written message is used, is there evidence that the message accomplished its purpose? What are the values of handbooks, the public address system, written policy? What ways are available to relate effectively to the parents, if there are 500 or 1,000 students in the secondary school? How can parents express their concerns to the school? How can the community and school speak together about purposes, effectiveness, aspirations?

Communications, then, with its almost infinite complexities, beckons the inquiring mind who would search for the better way.

CONCLUSION

Yes, challenges exist in abundance for the person who finds excitement in working with people and experiences the thrill of helping them find solutions to their problems. To the secondary school administrator who feels that the teenage youngster and those who work with him in the teaching-learning situation represent the most challenging and rewarding people with whom he can work, a career awaits that demands the best he can give.

SUGGESTED ACTIVITIES

1. Now that you have nearly completed reading this book, select a task area or problem which has interested you, but which we have tended to deal with rather broadly, and read about it, more specifically, as it is discussed in one of the other contemporary books on secondary school administration. A few of them are listed in the selected readings.

2. Following the guidelines given in this book, draw up a balance sheet which lists, for you, the advantages and disadvantages of a career in secondary school administration. Discuss these with your adviser and/or with an experienced secondary school administrator.

SELECTED READINGS

Anderson, Lester W., and Lauren A. VanDyke, *Secondary School Administration*. Boston: Houghton Mifflin Company, 1963.

Austin, David B., Will French, and J. Dan Hull, *American High School Administration*, Third Edition. New York: Holt, Rinehart & Winston, Inc., 1962.

Burrup, Percy E., *Modern High School Administration*. New York: Harper & Row, Publishers, 1962.

Douglass, Harl R., *Modern Administration of Secondary Schools*, Second Edition. Boston: Ginn & Company, 1963.

15

THE JUNIOR
HIGH SCHOOL

THIS CHAPTER IS NOT AN AFTERTHOUGHT, NOR A COM-
pendium on secondary school administration. Throughout the volume
the assumption is made that secondary education includes the junior
high school. However, even at the risk of some duplication, it is felt that
the uniqueness of the junior high school deserves some special recognition and treatment.

This section presents: (a) a brief overview of the development of
the junior high school, (b) basic concepts related to the junior high
school, (c) special problems and issues in junior high school education,
(d) characteristics of the junior high school in the 60's, (e) trends and
directions, (f) staffing problems peculiar to the junior high school, (g)
special administrative problems, and (h) some unique aspects of the
role of the principal in a junior high school setting.

DEVELOPMENT OF THE JUNIOR HIGH SCHOOL

The eight-grade elementary school is typically American, and little is known of the exact reasons for this form of organization. It developed in the early 1800's, when American educators were studying Prussian education. It can be conjectured that it was an attempt to combine the *grund-schule* (grades one through four) and the *mittel-schule* (grades five through eight). Most European school systems provide a break in the school organization, which comes around the child's tenth to twelfth birthday. In Denmark, the *Grundskole* ends with the fourth grade or age eleven; in France, the primary school for all takes the child through the fifth grade or through age eleven; in England, Johnny starts to school at five years of age and the junior school takes him through the first six grades and up to age eleven. Thus, there is a relationship between school organizational patterns and the age of the child, with the shift coming at approximately the onset of adolescence.

The early development of our elementary schools was not without variety. In the South, there were seven-year elementary schools; in New England, a nine-year elementary school; and in the rest of the country, an eight-year school.

Similarly, our secondary school pattern is typically American, beginning with the first four-year secondary school, the English High School, in Boston, in 1821. These schools were the genesis of what has come to be known conventionally as the 8-4 plan in American education.

Shortcomings of the 8-4 plan

The 8-4 plan had achieved general acceptance in this country by 1900, except in the South and a few communities in New England, but already critics had begun to point out the shortcomings of the plan. Undoubtedly, part of the criticism came about as the result of fundamental oversights by the original planners, as pointed out by Gruhn and Douglass.

First, there is no evidence that the eight-year elementary school and the four-year high school were influenced in their origin and early development by any recognition of the nature of the physical, social, and psychological development of children. Second, the elementary and the secondary schools began as two entirely separate institutions; furthermore, throughout much of their early history there was little or no attempt to bring about satisfactory articulation between them.[1]

Earliest criticisms came from representatives of colleges and universities, who were quickly joined by leaders in elementary and secondary education in investigations designed to improve the educational program below the college level. The period 1890 to 1910 provided a series of studies, conferences, and events that brought on the reorganization movement in upper elementary and secondary education, out of which developed the junior high school. Charles W. Eliot of Harvard University is credited with being among the first to call attention to some of the educators' concerns about the 8-4 plan by pointing out the fact that the plan made for late entrance into college—age 19 in 1885–1886. Eliot, in his lectures to educators, proposed to shorten the period of elementary and secondary education.

Committee of ten. In 1892, the National Education Association appointed a Committee of Ten on Secondary School Studies. President Eliot served as chairman of the high school and college teacher group, which studied each major subject taught, "the proper limits of its subject, the best methods of instruction, the most desirable allotment of time for the subject, and the best methods for testing the pupil's attainment therein."[2]

Although unintentionally, at least in the beginning, the Committee soon found itself looking at the organization of the entire school system. Among the Committee's recommendations were the following:

1. Some material from such subjects as English, arithmetic, natural history, and geography should be introduced as early as the primary grades.

2. Well-organized instruction in Latin should be introduced at least a year earlier than was the custom.

3. German and French should be offered as electives at the age of ten.

4. Systematic instruction in concrete or experimental geometry should begin at the age of ten.

5. Elementary subjects and elementary methods should be abandoned earlier.

6. The secondary school period should begin two years earlier, leaving six rather than eight years for elementary school.

[1] William T. Gruhn and Harl R. Douglass, *The Modern Junior High School* (New York: The Ronald Press Company, 1956), p. 6.
[2] National Education Association, *Report of the Committee of Ten on Secondary School Studies* (New York: American Book Company, 1894), pp. 3–7.

The Report of the Committee of Ten has not only been recognized as one of the great documents in the history of American education, but has had a profound influence on subsequent reforms and reorganizations of secondary education. Even though the proposals of the group were not immediately adopted, twenty years later they were reflected in the early programs of junior high schools.

Committee of fifteen. In 1893, before the report of the Committee of Ten was formalized, the Department of Superintendence of the National Education Association appointed a Committee of Fifteen to investigate the organization of school systems, the coordination of studies in the primary and secondary schools, and the training of teachers. The work of this committee was directly related to the reorganization of elementary and secondary education. Although the Committee of Fifteen opposed any change from the 8-4 plan, it laid strong emphasis on better articulation between the elementary and secondary schools and the earlier introduction of some subject matter to ease the transition between elementary and secondary school. It is interesting to note that these two recommendations pointed directly to the basic junior high school philosophy to come just a few years later.

Committee on college entrance. In 1895, another committee of the Departments of Secondary Education and Higher Education of the National Education Association considered the question of better understandings between the high schools and the universities with respect to entrance requirements. Again, as with the Committee of Ten, this group looked at education in its entirety and in its report, in 1899, recommended a six-year high school program—the 6-6 plan.

In contrast with previous committees, the Committee on College Entrance Requirements presented a definite plan. Also, it presented some definite reasons for introducing subject matter earlier. Among these were the following:

1. Introduction of subject matter should be related to child development.

2. The transition from elementary to high school should be more gradual.

3. The 6-6 plan would serve to encourage greater retention of pupils in the upper grades.[3]

[3] National Education Association, *Report of the Committee on College Entrance* (Washington, D.C.: The Association, 1899).

Arguments for the 6-6 plan

Other significant developments toward reorganization of secondary education came with the appointment of a standing committee on equal division of time between elementary and secondary education in 1905 by the Department of Secondary Education and the work of the National Education Association standing committee on Economy of Time in Education.

Significant among the reasons set forth by the latter committee favoring the 6-6 plan were:

1. Pupils could be taught by teachers especially trained in the various subject fields.

2. Departmentalized instruction would give seventh and eighth grade pupils contact with several teacher personalities.

3. The 6-6 plan would make laboratories available so that science could be introduced earlier.

4. Manual training shops would be made more readily available to upper-grade pupils.

5. Modern languages could be begun earlier.

6. The transition from elementary to secondary school would be less abrupt.

7. More pupils would likely go on into the ninth grade.

8. The equal divisions would make the schools more like the European schools.

9. The six-year secondary school would give the pupil more time to prepare for college.

10. The expansion of the high school program to six years would allow the introduction of some new courses.

11. The 6-6 plan would permit certain economies of time.

12. The 6-6 plan would allow for more flexibility.

13. The plan would more nearly meet the educational needs of youth in relation to their developmental patterns—socially, physically, emotionally, and academically.

14. Better provisions would be available for exploration experiences to meet individual needs and interests.

15. Better individualization of instruction would be made available.

16. Better articulation between elementary and secondary education would be made possible.

Early departures from the 8-4 plan

In the preceding pages we have seen the bases and gradual development of a rationale for reorganization of secondary education. Implementation of the ideas on reorganization moved slowly. In 1911, Bunker reported that a survey of 669 cities revealed that only 24 had introduced any departure from the traditional 8-4 plan.[4]

Richmond, Indiana, is credited with placing the seventh and eighth grades in a separate building in 1896, not merely as a housing convenience but with some program modification as well. Among other cities to break early with the traditional 8-4 plan were Ithaca, New York; Lawrence, Kansas; and Saginaw, Michigan.

First junior high schools

1909 seems to have been the magic year in the history of the junior high school. On July 6 of that year the Board of Education in Columbus, Ohio, and later in the year the Board of Education in Berkeley, California, took action to establish the 6-3-3 pattern of organization for the 1909–1910 school year. Berkeley called the new unit an "Introductory High School." Thus, after two decades of expressed concern about reorganization, the junior high school came into being.

These two school systems pointed the way for many school systems to follow, first, by implementing the educational concepts and philosophies implied in the stated needs for reorganization of secondary education, and secondly, by officially recognizing the organizational change and the name for the new intermediate school. In both instances, the change in organization combined special housing and adjusted programs as the reasons for modification of the old organizational pattern.

Growth of the new school organization

Encouraged by the pioneers in reorganization and capitalizing on their experiences, the junior high school movement caught on, with many small systems going to the 6-6 plan and larger systems to the 6-3-3 plan. By 1952, it was estimated that about 75 per cent of the students

[4] Frank F. Bunker, *Reorganization of the Public School System*, United States Office of Education, Bulletin No. 8 (Washington, D.C.: Government Printing Office, 1916), p. 101.

attending high schools in this country were in some form of a reorganized high school (see Table 6). Of the reorganized patterns, the 6-3-3 appears most frequently, then the 6-6, and then a much smaller number of other combinations.

TABLE 6. PER CENT OF SECONDARY SCHOOL ENROLLMENTS IN VARIOUS TYPES OF SCHOOL ORGANIZATION PLANS, 1920–1952

Year	Regular (four years)	Junior High (three years) and Senior High (three years)	Junior-Senior High (six years)	Total
1920	83.4%	2.8%	13.8%	100%
1930	50.9	30.3	18.8	100
1938	43.5	32.1	24.4	100
1946	38.5	35.4	26.1	100
1952	25.2	39.7	35.1	100

Source: United States Office of Education, *Junior High School Facts—A Graphic Analysis* (Washington, D.C.: Government Printing Office, 1955).

Since 1952, the separate junior high schools increased in number by half and in enrollment by a fourth.[5] The junior high school, which represented 35.1 per cent of all secondary schools in 1952, in 1959 represented 42 per cent for a total of more than 10,000 schools, enrolling 32 per cent of the nation's secondary school students.[6]

Thus, in a period of a little over a half-century the junior high school has taken deep roots in American education. Even the small per cent of systems still operating under the 8-4 plan, in various manners and ways, recognize the junior high school period in youth development and make educational overtures expressly directed toward meeting the problems of this age group.

The functions and purposes of the junior high school that seem to have weathered the criticisms and tests of time include exploration, guidance, differentiation, integration, socialization, articulation, and provision of a climate of learning and experiences for the early adolescent learner. Even those who claim that there is little justification

[5] Grace S. Wright and Edith S. Greer, *The Junior High School*, U.S. Department of Health, Education and Welfare, Bulletin 1963, No. 32 (Washington, D.C.: Government Printing Office, 1963) (OE–20046), p. 3.

[6] Edmund A. Ford and Virgil R. Walker, *Public Secondary Schools*, No. 1— Statistics of Education in the United States, 1958–59 Series (Washington, D.C.: Government Printing Office, 1961) (OE–20032–59), pp. 8–10.

for the junior high school functionally and psychologically admit that the problem of developing a satisfactory curriculum for early adolescence remains. Any school organization should encompass the general functions and purposes ascribed to the junior high school as a matter of good education. However, if there is a uniqueness about education at the early adolescent level, which there apparently is, it lies in the provision of an administratively convenient organization in and through which the curriculum problems can be brought into sharp focus and dealt with in a manner that best meets the needs of youth.

The arguments for and against the various forms of reorganization of secondary education are left to the reader. The plans of widest acceptance appear to be the 6-6, the 6-3-3, and the 6-2-4 plans. Such factors as local conditions, size of school population, housing requirements, economics, staffing problems, specialized community need, and the educational philosophy of the locale seem to us to be the chief determinants of the organization pattern for secondary schools. All things being equal, the principles underlying six years of elementary and six years of secondary education appear to have gained general acceptance. However, local conditions, particularly in large cities, often favor the subdivision of secondary education resulting in the 6-3-3 plan. Regardless of plan or organization, the significant phases of child development and the educational provisions attendant thereto, particularly coordination and articulation, must be provided for in an effective program of instruction.

Since a thorough knowledge of the development and evolution of the junior high school is imperative to a comprehensive understanding of secondary school administration, and since space limitations preclude a full treatment of the subject here, the reader is urged to explore the writings of Van Til, Vars, Lounsbury, and others.[7]

BASIC CONCEPTS

Preceding chapters in this volume make insistent demands for quality in secondary education. Quality has been defined as excellence in the school program, characterized by a curriculum that makes possible, and teaching and guidance that make real, the promise of educational opportunity for each pupil. The junior high school or the beginning phases of secondary

[7] William Van Til, Gordon F. Vars, and John H. Lounsbury, *Modern Education for the Junior High School Years* (Indianapolis: The Bobbs-Merrill Company, Inc., 1961), Chapters 1 and 2.

education take on tremendous importance in setting the pace and providing a climate that will nurture high quality educational experiences throughout the secondary school program.

Considerations leading to a recognized need for reorganization of secondary education eventually led to the development of basic concepts for the junior high school. The traditional 8-4 plan proved to be inadequate in several details, and some other plan or organization was obviously necessary to provide more effective and efficient educational experiences and instruction on the early adolescent level. It must be assumed, then, that some basic concepts, agreed upon and implemented in educational practice, undergird the provisions for junior high schools. We shall examine a few of the most important concepts here, recognizing that there are other general educational concepts applicable to the over-all tasks of providing effective instruction to youth at all levels and under all organizational patterns.

Flexibility

A basic concept in the realistic junior high school organization is that it provides a flexibility for the educational program not normally found in the traditional 8-4 organization. The developing of a satisfactory curriculum, providing for individual differences, guidance, and exploration, along with meeting the needs of early adolescence, integration, and articulation, demand a degree of flexibility not usually found in the traditional elementary or high school.

Flexibility poses some interesting problems in practice. Too many junior high schools are merely downward extensions of the senior high school or, in other instances, upward extensions of the elementary school. Either case defeats the flexibility necessary for a good junior high school program. In other instances, the junior high school imitates the senior high school to such an extent that it loses sight of its original purposes and objectives. Likewise, in some schools operating on the 6-6 plan, the junior high school is totally dominated by the operational patterns geared to the senior or upper grades of the high school. These pitfalls must be avoided and the junior high recognized for its uniqueness if flexibility is to be sustained and implemented.

The ungraded school is receiving increasing attention, use and study as a means of recognizing that the model for learning is more like a ramp than a set of steps. The ungraded organization provides better opportunities for flexible pacing and dealing with individual differences among students. Mindful of the concern for flexibility, some authorities point to the need for re-examination of policies regarding the length of time students remain in junior high.[8]

There is convincing evidence that education in the future will be different. Many interesting efforts and developments form the bases for change. Earlier introduction of foreign language instruction, new concepts of use of time, new uses of technological aids to teaching, the uses of instructional resources including teachers, increased emphasis on science and mathematics instruction, and a new look at instruction in the humanities are but a few of the innovations that appear to have lasting value and that require flexibility in thought and deed.

Continuity

Scenarists have a penchant for continuity; the scenes must hang together to make an unbroken, coherent whole. Each scene must have internal and external continuity, coherence within the scene itself and coherence of the scene with what came before and what comes after. In education, we are striving for much the same thing. An educational organization should provide as nearly as possible a smooth ramp of experiences, geared to the needs of youth and the goals and purposes of education at all age levels. Any sharp breaks create problems of transition, time lags, problems in articulation and coordination, and the like, that result in conditions which are out of synchronization with the imperative needs of youth at various stages of development, and establish hurdles which impede progress and stand in the way of quality education.

The junior high school, as an organizational innovation, properly conceived, was originated to improve continuity both in the educational program and in its relatedness to the growth and development patterns of youth. It is a means of providing, through organizational structure, opportunities, experiences and programs that will assist youth in making a satisfactory adjustment to adolescence and to developmental objectives with a maximum of effectiveness and a minimum of frustration. It is necessary, then, to consider the junior high school program with relation to what comes before it and what comes after it.

[8] Jean D. Grambs, Clarence G. Noyce, Franklin Patterson, and John C. Robertson, *The Junior High School We Need* (Washington, D.C.: Association for Supervision and Curriculum Development, National Education Association, 1961), pp. 22–23.

Internal continuity in a junior high school program is quite another matter. Many schools, unhappy with structuring students into curriculum patterns, have through guidance assisted students to develop programs with a high degree of individuality in terms of a variety of goals and interests. This is an ideal situation, except that more than usual care must be taken to provide continuity internally in the junior high school program and externally with what the student may want and what is available to him in the senior high school curriculum. What does the student do who comes to the tenth grade French II with three years of previous instruction in the subject and possesses competence and readiness for French III? Some of these innovations must assume some flexibility on the senior high school level to be fully successful. For example, in the Pascack Valley Regional High School, Hillsdale, New Jersey, secondary education is not divided into course patterns such as academic, business, or general curriculum. Instead, each student is expected to develop a program of studies that relates to his abilities, interests, and life work plans.

Continuity for its own sake may easily be a deterrent to the best program for the individual student. Schedules, timetables, loads, patterns, and the like, found in some schools, tend to build hurdles rather than provide for fluid program building. Students are occasionally "blocked out" of courses in their well-planned sequences simply because they cannot get them into their schedules; the excuse being, "Your course request just does not fit our planned and necessary continuum of subject offerings." Some of this is bound to happen in even the best-run high schools, but much more imagination might be exercised in this regard than has been demonstrated heretofore.

Peer culture intensification

As far back as biblical times man has recognized the concept of change and the "turning point" that comes at adolescence. Psychologists and physiologists have supplied us with evidence of the nature of this change. Sociologists have described the cultural changes that take place at the junior high age. This growth process is continuous, but there are certain modal points, differences in maturation rates between boys and girls, and other important factors that are readily recognizable.

A basic concept in any consideration of the junior high school is the recognition of the intensification of peer culture at adolescence. The appreciation and understanding of its many manifestations are enhanced by the several resumés of the imperative needs of youth, including Havighurst's original statement of the Developmental Tasks of Adolescence. These are as follows:

1. Achieving new and more mature relations with age mates.

2. Achieving a masculine or feminine social role.

3. Accepting one's physique and using the body effectively.

4. Achieving emotional independence of parents and other adults.

5. Achieving assurance of economic independence.

6. Selecting and preparing for an occupation.

7. Preparing for marriage and family life.

8. Developing intellectual skills and concepts necessary for civic competence.

9. Acquiring a set of values and an ethical system as a guide to living.[9]

Three major concepts have been highlighted here that have special relevance to the administration of the junior high school: flexibility, continuity, and intensification of peer culture. Obviously, there are other basic concepts that apply to the junior high school; major functions of the junior high school described earlier are actually symbols of basic concepts. The purpose of this brief treatment of concepts has been to emphasize the unique aspects of the junior high school, its functions, its importance in meeting the needs of youth at a particular age level, its relationship to what comes before and after, and some of its implications for the over-all secondary educational program.

PROBLEMS AND ISSUES

One approach to the consideration of the problems and issues in junior high school education is through a review of the principles upon which the school was originated. Briefly, something had to be done to remedy the "drop-out" situation in the seventh and eighth grades. Children needed more assistance in making the transition between elementary and high school (*articulation*). A better planned program of instruction appeared necessary to assist the child in obtaining more meaning out of subject matter and in utilizing these learnings in the development of his own personality (*integration*). The child needed more experiences that would be helpful to him in the selection of a possible vocational

[9] Robert J. Havighurst, *Human Development and Education* (New York: David McKay Co., Inc., 1953), pp. 2 and 111.

pursuit (*guidance*). Students at the critical early stages of adolescence needed experience and assistance in making adjustments to social situations and in establishing value patterns and ethics (*socialization*). Lastly, a suitable program was needed to provide for the individual differences among students.

These principles, translated into performance, became the conventional functions of the junior high school, the elements to be implemented through curriculum and instruction. The holding power of the school, an early concern of the junior high school movement, has in the main been erased by compulsory education laws. The day is long past, too, when the junior high school is considered to be the terminal educational experience for a large segment of youth.

The evidence that there are problems and issues regarding the junior high school is most convincing. More than two hundred doctoral dissertations have been produced in the past decade on some facet of the topic, a greater number of master's theses, surveys, self-studies, guides, evaluation instruments, research studies and the like—all dealing with concerns related to the junior high school.[10] An analytical review of the foregoing appears to indicate the following major areas of problems and issues:

1. ORGANIZATION. Which grades and age levels should be included in the junior high school complex? Should the sixth grade be included in the future junior high school? What does the ungraded plan have to offer the junior high school organization? How can time blocks, grouping, electives, core subjects and the like be more effectively related to organization?

2. ARTICULATION. What is the impact of curricular changes in both the elementary and senior high school upon the junior high program? How does the junior high school adjust to students with previous foreign language instruction, advanced mathematics and science and the like? How is competence acquired in various subjects in the junior high school effectively related to senior high school offerings? How can articulation be improved at both ends of the continuum?

3. CURRICULUM. In the light of modern developments above and below, what shall be included in the junior high school curriculum? How can innovation and change be effected? What changes should be made? How does the junior high school cope with the pressures and influences that relate to program and curriculum?

[10] See the contents of the bulletin "Junior High School Development, Practices. and Research," NASSP Bulletin, Vol. 46, No. 271, February 1962.

4. *CO-CURRICULAR ACTIVITIES.* What should be included in an acceptable program of co-curricular activities in the junior high school? What kinds of athletic, music, interest, social and similar activities should be sponsored? What activities truly meet the needs of the junior high age group?

5. *INSTRUCTION AND TEACHING.* What is unique about the teaching and learning situation in the junior high school? What methods have proven to be most effective? How do we meet the multi-complexity of demands made upon junior high school instruction? How do we relate to the spectrum of instructional needs represented in the age and developmental range included in the junior high school student body? How can we make the optimum use of the new technology in teaching, machines, labs, ETV and the like? How shall we make more effective use of programmed learning, independent study, small and large group instruction and clinical approaches to learning?

6. *GUIDANCE.* What is the role of guidance in the junior high school? Who works at and with guidance, and how? What guidance techniques and efforts have demonstrated effective results? What improvements seem to be needed?

7. *STAFFING.* What is adequate teacher preparation for teaching in the junior high school? Is this preparation generally available? What are some of the unique aspects of teaching requirements in the junior high? What can be done to help teachers to have a satisfying professional experience on the junior high staff?

8. *FACILITIES.* What are adequate facilities for the operation of a junior high program? Are adequate library and laboratory facilities being provided? How realistic is it to turn the "old high school plant" into a junior high school? How can the imaginative needs of an efficient facility for a modern junior high program be communicated and supported? Is the site adequate?

9. *ADMINISTRATION.* How shall we obtain and hold able career administrative leaders in junior high schools? What, if any, are the unique expectations of the principalship in the junior high school? From where shall we recruit the leadership for the junior high school? What special competencies should be sought? How obtained?

10. *EVALUATION.* How do we evaluate the effectiveness of the junior high school program? What are the measures of quality and excellence to be employed in evaluation? What means and instruments are available?

Certainly there are other problems and issues, both general and specific, that are being faced by junior high schools, not the least of which are sometimes generated by the schools themselves. Some of these are constricting pressures from within. As indicated by Patterson, some of the exploratory aspects and general education programs of the junior high schools are being challenged.[11] "Intensification" is being promoted. Early sorting of the academically able is being fostered. Parents of early junior high age students express concern about preparation for college, the success of their children in coping with scholarship tests, entrance board examinations and other hurdles ahead, and what the junior high school is doing about these things.

Justifiably but not always efficaciously, many junior high schools have attempted to do something about "excellence" and "quality" in education. In doing so they have emulated many of the best aspects of the senior high school program. It must be admitted that in many instances the influence of the senior high school is being increasingly felt in the development of junior high programs, particularly in school systems characterized by alert, forward-looking secondary education programs.

 ## Conant's findings

Conant's widely read treatise on the junior high school reflects his perception of some of the major issues and problems. He found great diversity in organization, at least five patterns or combinations of grades, and no consensus among educators as to the place of the ninth grade.[12] He found program to be a crucial problem regardless of organization. He found a need for an unusual combination of qualifications and competencies necessary in the teaching force, and he pointed out the special need for administrative services and leadership.

Likewise, his recommendations reflect what he believes to be the solutions to some of the problems and issues in the junior high school:

1. Required subjects for all pupils in grades 7 and 8.

2. New developments in mathematics and foreign languages.

3. Emphasis on basic skills.

4. Appropriate extra-class activities.

5. Block-time and departmentalization.

[11] Franklin Patterson, "The Adolescent Citizen and the Junior High School," NASSP Bulletin, May 1962, Vol. 46, No. 274, p. 72.

[12] James B. Conant, Education in the Junior High School Years (Princeton: Educational Testing Service, 1960), pp. 1–45.

6. Flexibility in schedule.

7. Challenges for all pupils.

8. Guidance and testing.

9. Homework, marking and promotions.

10. Program in grade 9.

11. Special facilities.

12. Coordination of subject-matter instruction.

13. Size and teacher load.

14. Leadership role of the principal.

In his detailed explanation of the above recommendations the issue or problem involved is made explicit. The implications of these suggestions make them deserving of careful consideration.

ASCD projections

Subsequent to the Conant study a Commission of the ASCD made a status assessment of the junior high school and speculated as to the junior high school we need for the future.[13] The Commission recognized the problems and issues confronting the present junior high school and classified it as essentially a *hybrid* in school organization.

While the problems and issues are acknowledged, the thrust of change, updating, recognition of new educational concepts, and the impact of innovation are clearly indicated in the report. In addition a yardstick of minimum adequacy was described for the junior high school of the early 60's. These include:

1. Moderate size—500–800 students.

2. Well stocked library with a professional librarian-teacher in charge.

3. Ample guidance services.

4. Block-of-time instruction each year so that one teacher will be identified with a group of students for a substantial period.

5. Flexibility in scheduling.

6. Teachers especially prepared for junior high teaching and devoted to this age group.

7. Ample teacher assistance—leadership, supervisory and clerical.

8. Modern instructional programs.

[13] Grambs, Noyce, Patterson, and Robertson, *op. cit.*, p. 37.

9. Adequate physical education programs.

10. Ample laboratory and workshop facilities.

11. Established and reasonable teacher load.

How many junior high schools would receive a rating of excellent in all categories mentioned above? And these are considered *minimum* adequacy. It seems fair to speculate that a majority of existing junior high schools face problems and issues in one or more of the yardstick measures.

CHARACTERISTICS OF JUNIOR HIGH SCHOOLS IN THE EARLY 60'S

Any analysis of the characteristics of the junior high schools of the early 60's must admit at the outset that the spectrum of quality and excellence is both broad and diversified. However, from the reports and studies cited previously and the status study reported by the U.S. Department of Health, Education and Welfare, there appear to be some commonalities worth noting:[14]

The usual organization included grades 7-8-9.
Most operated 175-day school year or more.
Six hours or longer constituted the school day.
A majority employed some forms of homogeneous grouping.
Planned block-time classes were employed in less than half of the junior high schools.
A majority had a fifteen-minute activity or homeroom period.
Study halls and study rooms were common.
Many small junior high schools had no central library or librarian.
Most schools had required subjects in grades 7 and 8, including language arts, social studies, mathematics, science and physical education; in grade 9, language arts, mathematics, science, social studies and physical education.
Standardized achievement tests were used extensively.
Uniform standards for promoting pupils were common practice.
Student achievement reports to parents were mainly in the form of letter grades.
The most common elective subjects were foreign languages, business education, agriculture and vocational education.
Extra-class activities were elective in the majority of schools.
The majority of schools sent progress reports to parents six times a year.
On the average, teachers spent three-fourths of their time teaching in the classroom and the rest on out-of-class activities.

[14] Wright and Greer, *op. cit.*

LOOKING AHEAD

Changes and innovations occur slowly in education, but they do occur. Every evidence points to an acceleration of change in the future based upon research findings, increased knowledge about the learning process, the use of automation and technological media in instruction, improved means of dissemination, an awakened interest in experimentation, and increasing demands for excellence and quality in education.

The junior high school must continue to improve upon its commitment to the development of democratic and personal values necessary to worthy citizenship in a free society. Increasing reliance will be placed upon experimental evidence in curricular developments and programs. More rather than less time will be devoted to education—longer days and more days per year. The junior high school will continue to mature and identify its unique role and contribution in the educational system and organization. Separate grades, as such, will take on increasingly less importance. Increasing interest will be given to the inclusion of the sixth grade age group in junior high school and perhaps relating the ninth grade age group to the senior high school. Instructional procedures will be vastly altered through the use of new media, ETV, teaching machines, programmed learning and the like. Creativity will receive more emphasis, as will aesthetics. More effective guidance will be made available. Accelerated maturity of youth, along many lines, will be recognized and provisions made for pupils to achieve satisfying productive self-actualization.

Curricular and organizational impacts

The exact impact of change and innovation ahead for the junior high school is difficult to predict with any accuracy, but it is certain that curriculum and organization will be effected. Increased pupil participation in planning learning experiences will be encouraged. Pupils will be encouraged to work with teachers, parents and others in establishing goals and purposes as well as planning meaningful experiences and activities to accomplish the desired ends.

Greater interrelation and coordination will be encouraged between various subjects—fusion of subjects, organization of subjects into broad fields, integration of subjects, core courses and the like. Accomplishments of this nature will demand greater flexibility in scheduling and the use of time. Modules and multiple periods will be necessary. Provisions will be mandatory for large group instruction, small group instruction and independent study. Viewing stations, listening labs and self-instruction apparatus will be utilized in new and imaginative ways.

The flexibility and freedom described here impose certain responsibilities and necessary determinants. Goals, purposes and desired ends must be kept in clear perspective. Means will have to be provided for measurement and assessment. Is the skill mastered? Has behavioral change been realized? Are the learnings consonant with the life situations and problems of the learner? Have the learner's values been changed? Does he become a better citizen? What happens to the pupil's attitudes and appreciations? Has he become a more intelligent consumer? Is there evidence that the pupil has become a better contributor to home and community life? Is the pupil receiving a better general education? Has each one been challenged to reach his or her full potential?

Trends

Admittedly, any effort to determine trends in secondary education and particularly with respect to the junior high school is somewhat speculatory. Many of the program features discussed here have become regularized in many junior high schools; all of them are being tried in some schools. It can be said with certainty that there is a positive trend away from the junior high school program being considered terminal in nature. Instead, encouraging progress is being made in junior high schools to assume a truly unique posture in our educational systems attuned to the particular needs of an age group and the educational needs of an era struggling to make a satisfactory adjustment to cybernetics and automation, a revolution in weaponry that makes all-out war intolerable in human society, and an age of evolving new nations in many parts of the world.

Temptations to copy the senior high school persist along with the tendency toward conventionality in form, program and structure; but a trend appears to be well established for the junior high school to be more innovative, more ready to try new ideas and to change, and to be increasingly conscious of the need for critical self-assessment.

STAFFING THE JUNIOR HIGH SCHOOL

To accomplish its purposes and objectives, the junior high school requires a staff of exceedingly high potential. Beginning with the principal, the personnel must have a thorough understanding and appreciation of the school's program, purposes, objectives and philosophy. Student-centered instruction takes on a very special meaning in the years of transition from childhood to young adulthood. The teacher must not only understand this but feel comfortable in working with it in the learning situation.

Practitioners have often commented that they get their best junior high school teachers out of an elementary teaching experience in the self-contained classroom rather than from the high school. Why? Perhaps it is because the high school teacher, on the average, is apt to be more inclined to subject specialization and accustomed to a more mature and sophisticated student. He is less experienced with the "block of time," "core," or "multiple period," which is usually a part of the junior high program. In addition, he has developed certain expectations of students somewhat beyond the junior high school level, and he has not developed or experienced the inclusive guidance approach so necessary in the junior high school. It would be an obvious error to generalize that high school teachers do not make good junior high school instructors. On the contrary, many of them do very well in the seventh, eighth, and ninth grades. The point is that the junior high school teacher has to have a combination of the finest attributes we have generally accorded to excellent elementary instructors along with those of the subject specialist senior high school teachers.

If curriculum change and improvement of instruction are to occur at all, they must take place in the classroom. Small classes, cooperatively conceived curriculum guides, excellent instructional equipment, and well-organized daily schedules are indeed helpful. However, an unimaginative teacher wedded to formal lecture-study-recitation routines, with the best of instructional aids, equipment and conditions, has very limited possibilities for making any contribution to change and improvement of instruction. Such teachers merely use the modern conveniences to accomplish the same job more easily. It is the attitude of the teacher toward the tasks of instruction, the interest in boys and girls, the willingness to experiment, the disposition to evaluate constantly, the desire to contribute special talents and abilities, the desire to be a constructive member of the instructional team, and the wish to improve constantly that count in the school's efforts to change and improve the curriculum and instruction.

Role of the teacher

Obviously, the role of the teacher in the modern junior high school is tremendously important. But how does the teacher assume this role?

Where does the teacher start to become the effective staff member? Let us assume that the teacher has the proper attitudes, good training, the courage to try new things, imagination, and the desire to be effective as an instructor of youth.

One answer would be, "Begin with boys and girls, the members of your class." Authorities agree that teachers must begin with child study. The teacher must learn all he can about the individuals in her group— their likes and dislikes, differences and similarities, their interests, their frustrations, their amusements, their home lives, their aspirations, and any other information that will help him to understand them better.

There are at least three good reasons for beginning with the study of children: to gain rapport; to understand their individual needs, differences, and potentials; and to acquire a basis for empathy. The teacher who has gained rapport with a group, who has come to understand each child with some degree of thoroughness, and who can imagine himself in the child's situation, has come a long way in establishing himself as a guide and teacher. A primary role of the junior high teacher, then, is that he be a student of human nature and development, particularly of the adolescent.

Role specialization.   There is developing gradually an increased use of specialized talent on the junior high school staff. Special service staff personnel are required for guidance, home visitations, psychological assistance, health services, activity coordination and other program requirements in the modern junior high school.

Opportunities for specialized talent in many phases of the instructional program are equally obvious. Increased use of the new instructional aids, such as closed-circuit television, call for personnel trained in mass presentation. Study laboratories call for people skilled in the techniques and use of recording, taping, viewing, listening, self-testing and other devices that will eventually become a part of every good school. Needs for skilled and inspiring teachers of art, music, dramatics and other special interest and activity areas will also call for staff role specialization.

Motivator.   We are constantly learning more and more about learning. The chances are good that we will continue to discover new things about the process of perceiving more intensively and extensively.[15] The heart of education is learning, and the teacher's role is to stimulate, to encourage, and to make that learning possible.

[15] Association for Supervision and Curriculum Development, *Learning More About Learning* (Washington, D.C.: National Education Association, 1959).

The most important essential for learning is motivation. As a motivator, the teacher must assume the role of marshaling and arranging conditions for effective learning. Tyler lists the following nine conditions under which effective learning takes place:

1. Motivation.
2. Dissatisfaction on the part of the learner with previous ways of reacting.
3. Guidance of learner's efforts.
4. Adequate and appropriate instructional materials.
5. Time.
6. Satisfying experiences.
7. Practice and drill.
8. Establishing new objectives, goals, and purposes.
9. Evaluation—judging one's own performance.
10. Employing the findings of evaluation for improving succeeding performances.[16]

Resource manager. Teachers are managers of all resources that bear on learning. The teacher's job is not only a matter of acquiring resources but of effectively managing the resources at hand. The imaginative teacher enlists the assistance of the students in providing resources and does not overlook the many community resources for enriching instruction. The role of management includes three kinds of resources: human, material, and time, each of utmost importance to effective learning.

Guidance role. Every teacher has a certain responsibility for guidance. This is particularly true at the junior high school level, where students are exploring widely in preparation for many vital decisions. Guidance is not something that can be relegated to the last ten minutes of the day, to scheduled sessions with the guidance counselor, or to the homeroom period. Every teacher contact should provide information and data that students can use in making strategic choices.

It is not necessary for every teacher to attain the excellence of a guidance counselor, but all teachers should be so guidance-oriented as to work effectively with guidance specialists in the over-all guidance program for junior high school youth.

[16] Ralph W. Tyler, "Conditions for Effective Learning," *NEA Journal,* August 1959, p. 47.

Teamworker. The nature of the junior high school experience, being partly that of the self-contained classroom and partly that of differentiated departmentalization, places a unique responsibility upon teachers for teamwork, staffings, committee work, conferences, team teaching, and other aspects of staff cooperation.

Junior high school teachers must work with and contribute to the professional understandings of teachers in the elementary and the senior high school divisions. This teamwork is, of course, a mutually shared responsibility of teachers on all levels. However, the junior high school teacher is in a pivotal position as regards articulation, guidance and differentiation functions, all so closely related to the adjustment requirements of the early adolescent.

Other considerations

The role of the teacher has been briefly touched upon here with particular reference to the unique functions of the junior high school. Being a student of child development, a motivator of learning, a guide and counselor, a manager of resources, and a skilled professional teamworker are aspects of the teacher's role that are valued at all levels of instruction, but they are particularly pertinent to the junior high school staff member.

Perhaps there is no such thing as a typical junior high school staff, but observations indicate some commonalities, such as approximately even distribution of men and women on the staff, a high per cent of experienced, mature teachers, a majority or near majority of married staff members with children of their own, teachers with four or more years of professional training, and teachers with a high interest in professional and community affairs and organizations.

Plato defined teachers as torchbearers—"Those having torches will pass them on to others." Others have called teachers artists, conscious of their purposes, aware of the conditions with which they work, able with creative ingenuity to work in many ways to stimulate students and guide them on to their destinies.

There are many good indications that we are on the threshold of increasing teacher prestige and are developing new concepts of the significance of the teacher's role in education. Better preparation, greater professionalism and increasing numbers of competent teachers are making tremendous contributions to better understandings about the status, expectations and functions of professional workers in education. For a more complete discussion of the role expectancies of teachers held by students, parents, peers, the community and the school itself we suggest a careful review of the Fourteenth Yearbook of the John Dewey Society, particularly Chapter 6.[17]

ADMINISTRATION

If one were to compare the modern junior high school curriculum with that of the early junior high school programs, the surface similarities would probably be somewhat surprising; yet beneath the surface many changes have taken place. Early efforts of program development held quite closely to the traditional subject-matter areas, to the content found in the 8-4 plan. Some educators feel that the changes that have been made are mainly in administrative organization, with relatively little change in curriculum requirement. Emphasis has been placed on the mechanics of providing better articulation, differentiation and recognition of the needs of the junior high school age group. In the process of implementing these functions, changes evolved in the kinds of experiences thought to be most appropriate for accomplishing the desired ends. Where the early programs were almost devoid of student activity experiences, modern junior high school programs require them. The evolving concerns about human relations, group processes and thought processes have brought about further changes in the curriculum. The "core curriculum," the "block of time," "problem identification and solution," "research activities," and the "multiple-period" concepts as means of improving the junior high school curriculum have been developed. Clearly, most of what has been related above has genuine implications for administration.

ROLE OF THE PRINCIPAL

Few, if any, opportunities in school administration offer greater challenges to leadership than does the junior high school principalship. The principal is the leader in all of the school's internal and external relationships, activities, functions and responsibilities. He relates himself to the management of learning through staff leadership, community relations, teamwork with peers and central office staff, relations with

[17] Lindley J. Stiles, *The Role of the Teacher in Modern American Society,* Fourteenth Yearbook of The John Dewey Society (New York: Harper & Row, Publishers, 1957).

students and parents, and the climate of opinion he helps to create and foster in his school. He is a teacher of teachers and a manager of all resources that have a bearing on instruction and learning.

Commonalities in competence for all high school principals are generally recognized. However, the uniqueness of some competencies for junior high school principals has been substantiated by observation and research. Rose found that high school principals and superintendents believe there are a number of competencies with which junior high school principals should be especially endowed.[18] The ten most statistically significant findings are:

a. Knowledge of child growth and development.

b. Background of successful experience as an elementary teacher.

c. Background of successful experience as a junior high school teacher.

d. Background of successful experience as an elementary school administrator.

e. Background of successful experience as a junior high school administrator.

f. Knowledge of development and function of elementary schools.

g. Knowledge of development and function of junior high schools.

h. Understanding of current issues, problems, and practices of core curriculum.

i. Knowledge and understanding of sound elementary school curriculum practices.

j. Knowledge and understanding of effective block-time teaching techniques.

Opportunities for creativity

A large number of junior high schools in all sections of the country are engaged in creating modern programs. Teacher-pupil relations and contacts are being studied. Scheduling is being examined in attempts to provide more time for the student with a single teacher. New ventures in meeting student needs are being tried. Subject-matter barriers are being broken down through adventures with common learnings, core curriculum, units, problem approaches, laboratory techniques and other imagi-

[18] Howard C. Rose, "A Study of the Competencies Needed for Junior High School Principals (1961)," *The Bulletin of the National Association of Secondary-School Principals*, Vol. 46, No. 271, February 1962, p. 405.

native devices and concepts. Research is being carried on with local, county, state and regional administrative units cooperating in the effort. Colleges and universities are contributing to the creative effort through experimentation, research, consultative services and training programs. New ventures in guidance, provisions for the gifted, extended class-rooms, uses of community resources, school-community relations, class and nonclass activities, and space utilization are to be found in many schools. Truly, there are abundant opportunities in the junior high school for the administrator with vision, courage, imagination and the will to do vanguard thinking and exploring.

This creativity is needed and welcomed. Everyone, even the arch critic of education, favors improvement. Teachers want to do their jobs more effectively and with greater efficiency. Creative improvements in education, however, are not the result of accident or chance. Attitudes have to be changed, understandings developed, new philosophies formu-lated, new skills perfected, trial runs executed, evaluations made and new patterns of action established. All these require administrative leadership, a challenge and opportunity for the junior high school principal.

Helping teachers gain new understandings

Every good administrator knows that in order to effect change he must begin with attitudes. Let us imagine that the principal feels that the conventional basis of grouping of students in elective activities (levels of achievement) is inadequate and that more attention should be given to the much neglected factor of intensity of purpose. How should he proceed? Surely, he could put through an executive order that, begin-ning next Monday, grouping for elective student activities will be based on two factors, levels of achievement and intensity of purpose. This is the poorest way to effect sound change. A wise principal wants his staff to assess the situation with regard to grouping and to arrive at under-standings that will cause teachers to want to include intensity of purpose as a factor in grouping. He is convinced of the value of the idea, and his convictions are supported by his readings of material such as the ASCD report.[19]

Discussion, study and group action on the problem is what the principal wants to achieve. These things precede changes in attitude,

[19] Kimball Wiles and Franklin Patterson, *The High School We Need* (Wash-ington, D.C.: National Education Association, 1959).

changes in philosophy and new approaches to situations. The principal must arrange and provide leadership for group discussion and thinking about this or any other problem related to new staff understandings. He also must be prepared to meet the usual roadblocks to progress—tradition, the aversion to the possibility of more work and the normal reluctance to try anything new. Three fundamental steps are necessary in the process: (1) By a variety of means he must make the problem clear to the group; (2) Through discussion, appraisal and evaluation of the situation, he must show the group that there is a good solution to the problem; and (3) He must demonstrate clearly that good will result to the staff members and to students if the derived solution to the problem is implemented in practice.

Helping teachers implement new understandings

Too often, the principal's role weakens at the implementation level. His teachers have assumed new attitudes and are ready to make changes, only to find that problems of mechanics, scheduling difficulties and the like impede the desirable actions. Here is where the principal has a role in helping teachers to attain new skills, to make adjustments and to "put the show on the road." His first task is to clear the way for change and provide the necessary resources to implement the change agreed upon. Then skills must be given attention, developed, shared, demonstrated and refined.

Big change is sometimes difficult to achieve all at once. Often small beginnings must be made with one section, one class or one activity. These become models to be studied, appraised and evaluated. Then another effort is made, sometimes with minor modifications. Perhaps more trials and new models must be studied until satisfactory implementation is finally attained. All of this calls for leadership from the principal.

Helping new and experienced teachers

Junior high school principals constantly face the task of working with new and experienced members of their staff. A special phase of working with the new teachers is orientation to the school, its philosophy, goals, practices and operations. The principal should have a systematized and organized program of orientation for his new staff members. He cannot do this alone, but must enlist the services of other staff members in the process. One very helpful practice is the inclusion of "freshmen" teachers from last year on a staff committee dealing with orientation. These people have first-hand knowledge of some of the problems they faced as new teachers in the system a year ago and can be most helpful in programming experiences that will aid new staff members in making a satisfactory adjustment to the school.

Orientation is usually thought of as the teachers' initiation to the school system, but new teachers also need inservice education. In fact, the inservice education program should be a natural outgrowth of the orientation experience. Too many times teachers are introduced to their new jobs and then are more or less forgotten and neglected. Naturally, they want to become identified with inservice education efforts such as staff committees, study groups, special project groups and the like, but new teachers often have peculiar problems related to their inexperience in the situation. Many of them have special interests and talents that should be discovered and exploited for the good of the school. Some may have special abilities that they seek to develop further. The alert principal will be mindful of these things and arrange for special attention to inservice education for new staff personnel.

Inservice education for experienced staff members is another aspect of the principal's role and responsibility. The principal must know his staff. Only by thorough acquaintance with various members of his staff can the principal hope to appreciate individual and common concerns, needs, interests and capabilities. Problems and points of dissatisfaction need to be discovered. Problem areas are often a good place to start with inservice education. When these are satisfactorily handled, projects of a wider and more involved nature can be undertaken. Professional study can be initiated. A professional library can be accumulated and added to with new materials about areas of immediate concern and study. Consultative services can be obtained to assist in study efforts, and resource persons obtained to share ideas with groups of faculty members.

Interpreting and communicating

The principal must be an interpreter and communicator. The school leader must continually interpret the operation of the school and the processes employed in terms of their relations to what goes on in the classroom. He must be able to do this for staff, parents, the public and the students. Likewise, the operation of the junior high school must be interpreted to the elementary schools from which it draws its students and the high school to which it sends them. This aspect of the junior high school principalship is unique. All such communication and interpretation is not necessarily done by the principal himself, but he is responsible for seeing that it takes place. For instance, joint meetings of sixth grade teachers with junior high school staff members can assist the latter to obtain more detailed information about incoming students and explain the junior high school program to the teachers preparing students for the experience. Meetings with parents of sixth graders can clear up problems of articulation and assist parents in understanding the transition. This is often done with parents of ninth graders as the student passes on into senior high school. In other words, the principal should use every means at his command to provide channels for communication and arrangements for lifting levels of understanding.

The public relations aspects of the role of the junior high school principal are somewhat unique also. If the school faces a particular problem with the growth and development of early adolescents, then so do the homes from which they come and the communities in which they live. The principal will want to work in close cooperation with the PTA, youth agencies and all other forces in the community dealing with the junior high school age group. Through these media he may be able to communicate the needs and aspirations of the school and correlate them more closely with other efforts of a similar nature. Occasions should be arranged where pupils, parents and teachers can get together to share, clarify, plan, evaluate and study activities and possibilities for better cooperation.

Organizing and coordinating

Organization can either enhance or impede the success of an operation. Organizational and coordinating abilities are legitimate expectations in the junior high school principal. In fact, this level often demands a certain expertness in these skills not always demanded in other levels of the school system. The very nature of the junior high school program raises particular problems with regard to organization and coordination. There is self-contained and departmental instruction going on at the same time in the same school. The principal must see that the philosophy of the school finds expression in the schedule, that in-class and out-of-class experiences are scheduled and that reasonable coordination exists to avoid unnecessary conflicts and interruptions. Some of the factors that must be taken into consideration are: building facilities, number of teachers in relation to rooms, nature of program offerings, variations in programs by grade levels, time allotments for various experiences and activities of various rooms for small and large group activities, number of periods to be included in the school day, student mobility and traffic during class changes, and many other factors that may have a relationship to the local situation. In many situations, before- and after-school activities are conditioned by school bus schedules. With the growth of larger administrative units it is likely that this factor will take on increasing importance.

Scheduling students under a traditional program presents some difficulties in avoiding conflicts, figuring loads, providing for differentiation and making the best use of staff time; but organizing blocks of time, multiple periods and staggered daily programs throughout the week, as called for in the modern junior high school program, demands ingenuity, imagination and coordination. The National Association of Secondary School Principals has suggested dividing the junior high school day into three parts: personal interests, common learnings, and health and physical fitness.[20] In a six-period day, two periods would be used for personal interests, three periods for common learnings, and one period for health and physical fitness.

The seventh grade, with its partially self-contained classroom program, and the ninth grade, where specialization sets in to coordinate with the senior high school, present special problems. Eighth grade programming is usually a variation of the seventh grade, having more in common with this grade than with the ninth. Then, there is the matter of time requirements for various subjects at different grade levels. There are some constants, to be sure, such as time for gymnasium periods, and perhaps one or two other subject areas, depending on the local situation, but beyond these the per cent of time for various subjects at differing grade levels is directly related to the nature of the instructional program. Where the modified core is employed a block of time is designated for what otherwise might be used for English, social studies, science, and guidance, or some modification of this combination. This means that departmentalization has to be broken down for many of the subject areas, with corresponding problems in scheduling and coordination. Barriers between subject areas must be lowered and the learnings fused, integrated and correlated without loss of values contributed by each subject.

Staff utilization presents its own problems in organization and coordination on the junior high school level. Often the principal is faced with having to use a teacher in a dual capacity: core program or a block of time for seventh and eighth grades, and specialized subject

20 *NASSP Bulletin*, Vol. 46, No. 271, February 1962.

teaching on the ninth grade level. These, along with the normal compli-
cations of staffing a school, call for the highest order of competence
on the part of the principal and his staff in effective planning and
organizing.

The uniqueness of the role of the principal in the junior high school
lies in the nature of the enterprise for which he assumes the leadership.
He must possess the characteristics and competencies ascribed to a good
principal in any school situation. However, the very complexity of the
junior high school organization gives rise to unusual opportunities and
challenges for creativity and imaginative administration.

CONCLUSION

This chapter calls attention to an important phase of secondary school
administration. No effort is made here to provide an exhaustive treatment of the junior high school. We have merely attempted to highlight
some of the particular problems of the junior high school division of
secondary education.

The reorganization movement in secondary education led to the
founding of the junior high school. At present, there are several plans
of organization for the reorganized secondary education program. These
vary according to purposes, objectives and functions but all plans endeavor to implement the basic concepts that characterize the ideal
junior high school.

A clear relationship is seen between the major problems of curriculum and instruction and those concerning leadership and administration.
The staffing problem, including careful definitions of the roles of the
teacher and the principal, is of paramount importance. The junior high
program, as described, is the product of evolution and it continues to
evolve. Several trends have been examined. All of this, when related to
the major concerns of secondary school administration, points to the
uniqueness of the principal's role at the junior high school level.

SUGGESTED ACTIVITIES

1. Trace the development of the reorganization movement in secondary
   education with particular reference to the emergence of the junior
   high school.

2. Compare the reasons postulated for reorganization originally with
   today's situation in education. Are all the reasons still valid? Why or
   why not?

3. Defend the functions of the junior high school. Are they realistic?

4. Discuss the merits of the various plans of organization: 8-4, 6-6, 6-3-3, 6-2-4, 7-5.

5. Write an essay on the unique needs of the junior high school student.

6. List the problems that you see arising between the junior high school and the elementary schools? The high school?

7. In what ways are the problems of administration different in the junior high school from those found in other divisions of the school system?

8. Describe what you believe to be a model organization for a junior high school. What grades would you include? Discuss the theory upon which your model is based.

SELECTED READINGS

ASCD, *Learning More About Learning*. Washington, D.C.: National Education Association, 1959.

Brimm, R. P., *The Junior High School*. Washington, D.C.: Center for Applied Research in Education, Inc., 1963.

Conant, James B., *Education in the Junior High School Years*. Princeton, N.J.: Educational Testing Service, 1960.

Ford, Edmund A., and Virgil R. Walker, *Public Secondary Schools*. No. 1, Statistics of Education in the U.S., 1958–59 Series. Washington, D.C.: Government Printing Office, 1961.

Grambs, Jean D., Clarence G. Noyce, Franklin Patterson, and John C. Robertson, *The Junior High School We Need*. Washington, D.C.: ASCD, National Education Association, 1961.

Gruhn, William T., and Harl R. Douglass, *The Modern Junior High School*. New York: David McKay Co., Inc., 1953.

Havighurst, Robert J., *Human Development and Education*. New York: David McKay Co., Inc., 1953.

Stiles, Lindley, *The Role of the Teacher in Modern American Society*, Fourteenth Yearbook of the John Dewey Society. New York: Harper & Row, Publishers, 1959.

Van Til, William, Gordon F. Vars, and John H. Lounsbury, *Modern Education for the Junior High School Years*. Indianapolis: The Bobbs-Merrill Company, Inc., 1961.

Wiles, Kimball, and Franklin Patterson, *The High School We Need.* Washington, D.C.: National Education Association, 1959.

Wright, Grace S., and Edith S. Greer, *The Junior High School.* United States Department of Health, Education and Welfare, Bulletin No. 32. Washington, D.C.: Government Printing Office, 1963.

―――, *Evaluative Criteria for Junior High Schools.* Washington, D.C.: National Study of Secondary Schools Evaluation, 1963.

―――, *Junior High School Development, Practices and Research.* National Association of Secondary School Principals Bulletin, Vol. 46, No. 271, February 1962.

INDEX

399

Teachers (cont.)
  demands on, 35
  guidance and the, 387
  inservice education and, 181–82
  junior high school
    principal and, 391–93
    role of in, 385–89
  motivation and, 386–87
  recruitment, 175–79
  retention of, 179–80
  supply, 173–74, 177 tab. 4
  welfare, 182–83
  See also Personnel
Teamwork
  administrative
    characteristics of, 71–72
    communications in, 70–71, 77
    delegation implications in, 69–70, 78
    House plan, 74–75
    leadership integrity and, 78–79
    objectives in, 68–69, 77
    pitfalls in, 76–78
    size and, 76
    team and, 72–76
    See also Teams

Teams, administrative
  central, 73
  secondary school, 73–76
  size, 76
Training and Experience Standards for Principals of Secondary Schools (Eikenberry, D. H.), 158N
Traits of Face-to-Face Leaders (Crowley), 276N
Trump, J. Lloyd, 173
Tyler, Ralph W., 387

Unit system, 31
Urwick, L., 53

Van Til, William, 373
Vars, Gordon F., 373

Waples, Douglas, 276
Watson-Glaser Critical Thinking Appraisal, 297
White House Conference on Education, Committee for, 32
Whitlock, James W., 112, 201
Woodring, Paul, 131
Wynn, Richard, 166